THE LAST CRUSADE

I saw prevailing throughout the Christian world a license in making war of which even barbarous nations would have been ashamed; recourse being had to arms for slight reasons or no reason; and when arms were once taken up, all reverence for divine or human law was thrown away, just as if men were thenceforth authorized to commit all crimes without restraint.

HUGO GROTIUS, *The Rights of War and Peace*

THE LAST CRUSADE

THE CHURCH OF ENGLAND IN THE FIRST WORLD WAR

Albert Marrin

DUKE UNIVERSITY PRESS   Durham North Carolina   1974

© 1974, Duke University Press
L.C.C. card no. 72–97471
I.S.B.N. 0–8223–0298–5

PRINTED IN THE UNITED STATES
OF AMERICA BY HERITAGE PRINTERS

For Yvette . . . who also fought

PREFACE

On August 4, 1914, Kaiser William II concluded his speech from the throne with a phrase which, with slight modification, might have commended itself to the leaders of any of the warring states: "From this day on, I recognize no parties but only Germans." The Great War, which cost him and other of his fellow monarchs their thrones, and in one case life itself, was the supreme instance of the power of nationalism to overwhelm everything binding men in different nations together. Neither a common intellectual heritage, nor the mutual interests of the workers of the world, proved a barrier to violence when the integrity and life of the nation was at stake. By the same token, the clergy of all the major denominations of the West threw their support, material no less than moral, behind the war efforts of their respective countries, while Catholic, Protestant, and Jewish laymen slew their coreligionists with as little compunction as atheists slew their fellow nonbelievers.

The aim of this study is to examine how just one religious body, the Church of England, responded to the world crisis of 1914–1918. Although a study of how all the religious bodies in England reacted would doubtlessly be of value to the historian, it was rejected as impractical at an early stage. Aside from the fact that there exists nothing of a scholarly nature that can be turned to account here, in doing research in the publications of the various denominations I was confronted by a phenomenon familiar to the photographer. In superimposing a number of photographic negatives, he causes a print to emerge showing the most general characteristics the subjects have in common—eyes, ears, feet—but which robs them of their individuality. Likewise with churches. Every church has a history, a temper, a "feel" peculiar to itself; and while the various bodies shared certain attitudes regarding the war, the interdenominational approach tends to gloss over and minimize the unique factors shaping their outlook. Except for a few references where they shed light on the Anglican experience, therefore, the other churches of the United Kingdom, as well as those of its allies and enemies, have been passed over.

There is, I think, ample justification for treating the Church of England separately. When the war began, it still exerted a significant, if steadily diminishing, influence on the society it served. Sociologically, it was recognized as representing the dominant classes in society. In the educational sphere, it had its own school system; its clergy were headmasters in practically all of the great public schools and held some of the most renowned professorships in the universities. In politics, though the bishops no longer served as political agents, a prime minister still had to weigh the consequences of provoking organized Anglican opinion. Even after the passage of the Parliament Act of 1911, the House of Lords was a body to be reckoned with; and twenty-six bishops sat in the Lords. The statements and activities of the two archbishops, the convocations of Canterbury and York, and the organizations of Anglican laypeople were newsworthy items, reported in newspapers read throughout the nation and the civilized world.

Despite its importance, however, historians of wartime England have overlooked it in their studies; to be sure, general historians seem to operate on the assumption that nothing of much importance happened in the church after the Newmanite secession or *Essays and Reviews* at the outside. The student has at his disposal innumerable accounts of military operations and biographies of the frequently incompetent men who directed them. The presses of Europe and America continue to turn out monographs on everything from munitions production to liquor consumption, from poetry to propaganda. Yet, upon examining the literature, one rarely finds more than a passing reference (and that derogatory) to the activities of the oldest pillar of the "Establishment." Similarly, church historians have overlooked the war and its influence on ecclesiastical developments. The major criterion in selecting material for inclusion here has been, therefore, the extent to which it sheds light on the position of the clergy in English life and their perception of the issues and conduct of the war itself.

Anyone investigating the sources for the activities of the church at this time is confronted by a unique situation—unique because he faces at once extreme poverty and an embarrassment of riches. Although a state church, a "department of the state" Sir Andrew Lusk called it, its response to the war has left scarcely a trace in the governmental records. The bishops' share in the *Parliamentary Debates* is minute; in the relatively few times bishops spoke about the war in the

Lords, they were wont to express themselves as individuals on a narrow range of topics—reprisals, conscientious objectors, and bawdy houses in France. The Parliamentary Papers are also largely barren, save for the reports of the ecclesiastical commissioners, which deal in general terms with the church's financial and real property holdings; the commissioners' archives are unrewarding regarding the development of the Anglican attitude toward the war. Finally, cabinet and departmental papers, recently made available under the fifty year rule, indicate that clergymen simply did not move in these exalted circles.

As to ecclesiastical sources, they, too, have their limitations. The annual church congresses, which usually heard lively and informative discussions of a broad range of topics of Anglican interest, were discontinued during the war, resuming only in 1919. Save for a resolution now and then on reprisals and meeting the spiritual needs of servicemen, the proceedings of the convocations followed their well-charted channels, being confined mostly to matters of church administration and matters of a specifically religious nature. As to manuscript sources, they are unfortunately less full and less available than in other areas of English history; and while I culled some valuable titbits from the papers of Archbishop Randall Davidson, it will be several years before the papers of two important personages, Cosmo Gordon Lang and William Temple, are opened to scholars. Whereas the archives of the Chaplain's Department at Bagshot Park, Surrey, and in the War Office, where are housed the papers of the chaplain-general, Bishop Taylor Smith, are a rich source for a monograph on the chaplains, they were disappointing with regard to the attitude of the church and the churches toward the war.

I have, consequently, had to rely heavily on printed sources. But here, too, there are several kinds of material of uneven value. The provincial press proved useful for certain people, at certain times, and on certain issues. Diocesan and parish publications on the whole confirmed the charge levelled by Dick Sheppard at the first church congress after the war: they do not "bite," being dull and packed with local small talk. The gold must be sought elsewhere, in the sermons and pamphlets, thousands of which were published separately, in collections, and in the ecclesiastical press. They are extremely important, because they provide a running commentary on how clergymen, in their capacity as public men and shapers of public opinion, felt about the war at a given time. We are, lastly, particularly fortunate in the ecclesiastical press. Although centered in London, the six major weekly newspapers represented every shade of opinion and party affiliation, had a wide geographic distribution, reviewed every book of Anglican interest, and reported in detail every major event and controversy of Anglican concern. The more specialized periodical press, also London-based, appealed to the more intellectual reader: if socialistically inclined, he might choose the radical *Church Socialist* or the moderate *Commonwealth*; theologically, the liberal *Church Quarterly Review* was always informative, the *Modern Churchman* always challenging.

The survival of much of this appallingly ephemeral material has been a matter of luck—a fact brought home to me on learning that of the four thousand sermons preached in 1912 for the Royal Society for the Prevention of Cruelty to Animals, evidently not one has survived in print. The ravages of time, the poor quality of newsprint —the bane of the historian since its introduction in the nineteenth century—and the neglect of overworked librarians have ensured the eventual loss of a good deal of valuable, and as yet largely unexploited, material pertinent to the social history of the period.

Concerning methodology, I am well aware of the pitfalls in selecting a number of examples, however large, to demonstrate some social phenomenon or attitude, as further investigation may uncover an equally large number to prove the contrary. Ideally, the solution would have been a parish-by-parish or diocese-by-diocese analysis of attitudes over the entire country. But as a practical matter, given the material that is available, such an undertaking is neither possible nor, perhaps, desirable in a single lifetime. Moreover, the nature of the issues and the nationwide reputation of some of the figures concerned, seemed to indicate the desirability of delineating general trends rather than concentrating on what may have been purely local manifestations.

The nature of the historian's craft is such that he is forever indebted to others. I owe much to scholars and institutions on both sides of the Atlantic. Professor Herman Ausubel of Columbia University and R. K. Webb, now managing editor of *The American Historical Review*, made freely available to me their experience and insights into modern English history. I am especially grateful to Dr. John M. Krumm, bishop of the Diocese of Southern Ohio, whose generosity with his time and deep love and knowledge of all things Anglican, prevented many a hapless step—whatever hapless steps I have taken, I have taken on my own. The common sense and good humor of Professor Maurice Wohlgelernter of Baruch College, The City University of New York, always managed somehow to resuscitate the spirit and stimulate the mind. I should also like to thank His Grace, the archbishop of Canterbury, for permission to quote from the Davidson papers, and to Mr. E. G. W. Bill and his staff at Lambeth Palace Library for helping me navigate through them.

The facility with which much of the research for this study was carried out is due in large measure to the patience and cooperation of the staffs of the following libraries: the Saint Mark's Library of the General Theological Seminary, New York; Columbia University Libraries; the New York Public Library; the Library of Union Theological Seminary; the photographic services of the Hoover Library on War, Revolution, and Peace at Stanford University; the British Museum; and the Library of the Society for the Promotion of Christian Knowledge, London.

Touro College generously provided some of the financial support that made publication of this volume possible.

CONTENTS

ABBREVIATIONS

The following abbreviations have been used throughout the notes and for articles listed in the bibliography.

Bell	G. K. A. Bell, *Randall Davidson, Archbishop of Canterbury* (Oxford, 1952)
Chadwick	Owen Chadwick, *The Victorian Church* (2v. 1966–1970)
Chron. Conv. Cant.	*Chronicle of the Convocation of Canterbury*
CH	*Challenge*
C.W.P.	*Christian World Pulpit*
Ch. Cong. Rpt.	*Church Congress Report*
C.F.N.	*Church Family Newspaper*
C.Q.R.	*Church Quarterly Review*
C.S.	*Church Socialist*
C.T.	*Church Times*
CWTH	*The Commonwealth*
Davidson MSS.	The Papers of Archbishop Randall Davidson, Lambeth Palace Library, London
G.	*Guardian*
M.C.	*The Modern Churchman*
R.	*Record*
S.F.T.	*Sermons for the Times* (a series of about one hundred sermons by religious leaders, mostly Anglican, published by Griffiths in the early days of the war)

THE LAST CRUSADE

I. CHURCH, STATE, AND SOCIETY

CHURCH AND STATE

It is always hazardous, if not indeed presumptuous, for the historian to present a few isolated statements as embodying the thought of an entire generation. Yet, if the statements be those of men who were prominent in the thought and activities of a particular sector of national life, a single one may capture dramatically something of the mood prevailing in their time. This is true of the Church of England in the fifty-odd years before the First World War, or, as it was known to contemporaries, the Great War. Speaking at Oxford in 1861, Disraeli noted, somewhat overoptimistically, that its future lay in the great towns, that "it will be in the great towns that the greatest triumphs of the Church will be achieved"; for, he reckoned, the larger the population and the higher its education, "the more will [it] require a refined worship, a learned theology, an independent priesthood...."[1] Disraeli, his native optimism buoyed by the new churches springing up everywhere—1,727 new structures were built and 7,144 old ones restored between 1840 and 1876[2]—and by the number of people worshipping in them, saw the road ahead open, with a world still to be conquered by the Church of England. Eleven years later, the Rev. William Stubbs, then the foremost historian of medieval England and a future bishop of Oxford, registered a shift in emphasis indicative of a less confident mood. In an address before the Leeds Church Congress, he compared the church to "a great army intent at once upon defence and conquest."[3] The realities of the society he could see emerging more clearly in this bustling factory town than in his own Oxford, a society in the throes of industrialization, had brought the church to a time of decision. The question was, could it defend its present position, the heritage of centuries, and at the same time formulate the plans and create the structures necessary for moving forward in God's work? It could, and to a certain extent it did. As Charles Gore, bishop of Birmingham (1905–1911) and in time also bishop of Oxford (1911–1919), noted in his sermon opening the 1906 church congress in Barrow-in-Furness, in the previous three decades the church had won impressive victories: the liberty of Biblical criticism vindicated, the battle for the liberty of Catholic ceremonial practically won, and the idea of a free and self-governing church astir in the land. He went on, however, to sound a note of disappointment; a note which, in those quiet moments, stolen from busy days, others in his audience must have heard in their heart of hearts. "And yet," he said, "—and yet it all hangs fire. 'We have been with child, we have been in pain, we have, as it were, brought forth wind; we have not wrought any difference in the earth; neither have the inhabitants of the world fallen.' "[4] No, they had not fallen, nor would they. If anything, it was the Church of England that was faltering. *It* was powerless over the big things of the world; *it* was not master in its own house, or of its own destiny.

Not that the church lacked imposing arguments to sustain its claim to a prominent place in national life. Its credentials were the oldest, and to Anglican minds the best, possessed by any body in Protestant Christendom. Its being coterminus with a majority of the nation was a powerful argument; as late as the 1960's two-thirds of the population of England and Wales identified themselves as Anglicans, with about another 10 percent each for the Church of Scotland, the free churches, and the Roman Catholic church. Another powerful argument was the fact that the coronation service is a religious service whereby the archbishop of Canterbury crowns the monarch, who by law must be an Anglican and pledge to "maintain and preserve inviolably the settlement of the Church of England and the doctrine, worship, discipline, and government thereof as by law established in England."

Over and above these considerations, the Anglican claim rests on a concept of the relationship of the church and the world carried forward from the Christian Roman Empire and retaining its vitality into the early twentieth century. Whether one describes it in the words of Richard Hooker, the great Elizabethan divine who wrote in his *Laws of Ecclesiastical Polity* (VIII, i, 7), "With us, one society is both Church and Commonwealth," or uses with the poet T. S. Eliot the term *The Idea of a Christian Society*, the title of an essay of 1939, the principle is the same: a certain mutuality must exist between the institutions responsible for the spiritual and the temporal aspects of human existence.

To enable man to realize his God-given potentialities, the church (the Divine Community) and the world (all social institutions outside the church) ought to be, according to this theory, complementary, interdependent, even interpenetrating. As an expression of the Divine will, the state, the primary social institution, has been instituted as a bridle on human nature, sin-warped and self-loving, and to secure the most efficient arrangement of the life of the community. Yet the efficiency with which it carries out its tasks, though important, is not, nor should it ever be, the sole criterion in evaluating the state. Outstanding personalities in English theology, literature, and politics —Hooker, Coleridge, Dr. Arnold of Rugby, Gladstone, Eliot—have maintained that the state must be more than a mechanism for keeping order, gathering the taxes, and cleaning the streets.[5] Since the human will is in-and-of itself an insufficient guide to right action, it must needs be informed by a higher wisdom. The church, as the custodian, teacher, and interpreter of the religious truths from which the moral principles underlying the social order are derived, is the agency divinely appointed for this task. As Mandell Creighton, the historian of the medieval church and bishop of London (1897–1901), observed in his primary charge, the object of the church "is to keep alive, and educate into increasing sensitiveness, that sense of righteousness which alone exalteth a nation. . . . [The church] must always be the guardian, the protector, the educator and the exponent of the national conscience."[6] Without this education, the state would degenerate into a power-crazed monster accountable to nothing outside itself. Here, then, in the belief that each is a vital instrument of social control, is the primary justification for the union of church and state in England.

On the basis of this justification other propositions, deduced logically or derived from historical experience, have become incorporated into the theory. The Church of England is more than a state church. It is a national church; for the state is, in a manner of speaking, merely the "arms and legs" of the nation. Each nation, that is, each people having certain habits, associations, and an outlook on the world conditioned by common experience, develops during the course of its existence institutions congenial to its collective personality. "It has," Cosmo Gordon Lang, archbishop of York (1909–1928) and Canterbury (1928–1942), told the House of Lords in phrases that could easily have been lifted from the writings of Edmund Burke, "an organic unity and spirit of its own, and that character and spirit are built up by traditions and associations running far back into the past. Its life is expressed not only by the policies and pursuits of the present, but also by a sort of subconscious continuity which endures and profoundly affects the character of each generation of citizens who enter within it."[7] The church, as England's oldest institution, predating even the monarchy itself, gathers up and expresses in its every fiber the characteristics of the English people; it is the nation on its spiritual side.[8]

As a national religious institution, its comprehensiveness was another characteristic offered in defence of the Establishment. Because its basic formularies, the Thirty-Nine Articles and the Prayer Book, originally resulted from compromises intended to allow as many Protestants and Catholics as possible to accept the Elizabethan settlement, representatives of nearly every possible type of Christianity have been able to find accommodation within its confines. In ceremony, liturgy, and theology it has something for everyone. One might, in fact, without exaggeration describe the Church of England as a conglomerate of several denominations held together in a state of tension, sometimes dynamic and creative, at other times marred by party spirit, petulance and animosity, but never uninteresting.[9] The comprehensive character of Anglicanism has been reinforced by the "parson's freehold," a form of tenure unique in ecclesiastical history. The incumbent's "living," so-called, is regarded in law as a form of private property from which he is irremovable for anything short of heresy, larceny, lunacy, or sodomy. Even dereliction of duty does not necessarily constitute cause for removal. All the authorities could do, as Bishop E. W. Benson found with the vicar at Truro who never set foot in his church or officiated at a religious service, was plead with him to mend his ways.[10] Such cases aside, fixity of tenure has tended to foster in the Anglican clergyman a freedom of expression and independence of mind that have made him the marvel and the envy of other Christians.

When comparing it with the rival forms of Christianity prevailing in England, Anglicans were confirmed in their high regard for their church. In the picturesque language of one seventeenth century divine, the Church of England trod the middle ground, avoiding "the meretricious gaudiness of the Church of Rome, and the squalid sluttery of fanatik conventicles."[11] Neither the Protestant sects nor the Roman Catholic church could, in their estimation, hold a candle to its comprehensiveness, intellectual freedom, and ability to adapt to external forces and enlist these in training national character.

To Anglicans, these forms embodied defects arising from the overdevelopment of one side of the personality at the expense of everything else. The terms "dissenter" and "nonconformist" implied more than a refusal to submit to law, serious as this was. The sects embodied the spirit of individualism in so extreme a form as to be schismatic, destructive of national unity, and, in the long run, productive of the secularization they pretended to detest. With the remorseless perfectionism of the autodidact, the sectarian becomes so attached to his "one truth" as to be incapable of associating with those of a different mind. As with water spilled on a table top, sectarianism, once clear of the confines of the Established church, must flow simultaneously in every direction. Individuals compete for the supremacy of their private versions of the truth within the sect, causing it to break up into new bodies. These continue to feud within themselves and with one another, until succumbing finally to secular control. As the Rev. George Ridding, headmaster of Winchester and the first bishop of Southwell (1884–1904), affirmed, secular control "[is] essential to endowed bodies, when minister and congregation are subject to purse or proprietor, and preachers are displaced for their virtues if they will not prophesy smooth things."[12] The so-called "free churches" were nothing of the kind; they were exclusive clubs, where nobody might belong unless prepared to conform in the smallest, most picayune, matters. The Roman Catholic church, it should be added, suffered from a different, though equally dangerous, set of defects. Extra-national in organization and outlook, it was a papal despotism run by Italian priests with the objective of stamping out independent thought, dominating the state wherever possible, and unchurching every other body in Christendom.[13] Only the Church of England possessed *all* the qualifications for ministering to Englishmen.

Unfortunately, establishment in practice meant something quite different from establishment in principle. The relationship of church and state was far from being one of reciprocity. Neither establishment in law nor an assured representation in the national legislature —the church is represented in the House of Lords by the two archbishops, the bishops of London, Durham, and Winchester, and twenty-one diocesan bishops in order of seniority—conferred power over its internal affairs. The church had no legislative body of its own. The convocations, composed of the bishops and clergy of the provinces of Canterbury and York, together with the Houses of Laymen attached to them; the Representative Church Council, consisting of both convocations and their Houses of Laymen meeting in joint session; and the nonofficial annual church congresses bore impressive titles, but they were strictly advisory bodies or forums for airing matters of common interest. Well might one wit exclaim: "It is absurd to say Convocation is the voice of the Church; it is hardly the squeak of the Church";[14] for neither it nor the other bodies could turn their words, entombed by the million in thick annual volumes, into deeds.

The power to take decisive action resided with the crown and Parliament. Although the crown has from time immemorial been influential in church affairs, going so far as to "nominate" (with papal approval) the great ecclesiastics of the realm, as long as there remained a church *in* England rather than a Church *of* England, it carried no weight in doctrinal matters. The royal supremacy became absolute only with the enactments of the Reformation Parliament and its successors. By the Act of Supremacy of 1534 the king was declared "the supreme head in earth of the Church of England" and given full power "from time to time to visit, repress, redress, reform, order, correct, restrain and amend all such errors, heresies, abuses, offences, contempts and enormities whatsoever they be . . . ." By various Acts of Uniformity, beginning in 1549, the crown undertook to prescribe its liturgy and public worship. The Thirty-Nine Articles, made obligatory for clergymen by statute in 1571, are the formal statement of the church's doctrine, Article XXXVII making the royal supremacy a matter of religious faith. With the Civil War and the Glorious Revolution in the seventeenth century, the royal supremacy was transformed into a parliamentary supremacy.

Apart from regulating the internal life of the church and determining its doctrine, the supremacy of the secular over the religious extends into another sensitive area, the appointment of the bishops. Save for the fact that the prime minister initiates the process, the method of appointing a bishop today follows exactly that prescribed in 1534 by 25 Henry VIII, cap. 20. As a travesty on the electoral process, it rivals any "people's democracy" of recent times. Upon the recommendation of the prime minister, the crown sends to the cathedral chapter of the vacant see a *congé d' élire*, or license under the Great Seal to elect a new bishop; this is followed by a second letter containing the name of the person to be elected. After appropriate "discussion," a vote is taken and the bishop-elect duly consecrated by his fellows. Once consecrated, he takes an oath to the crown, acknowledging it as "the only Supreme Governor" in matters temporal and spiritual, and affirms that no foreign potentate has any jurisdiction within the realm. Failure to elect or consecrate a royal nominee involves (however inconceivable it is that these should be applied in the twentieth century) all "the dangers, pains, and penalties of the Statute of the Provision and Praemunire": outlawry and forfeiture of lands and possessions.

The church succumbed to the state in the judicial sphere as thoroughly as elsewhere, losing its ancient right to adjudicate its own cases. By the Statute for the Submission of the Clergy, 25 Henry VIII, cap. 19, appeals to Rome as the final jurisdiction in ecclesiastical cases were prohibited and the power to hear them vested in a Court of Delegates. When this court was abolished in 1832, a special Judicial Committee of the Privy Council was designated as the court of last resort. Notwithstanding the fact that the archbishops and bishops are in their capacity as privy councillors members of the Judicial Committee, it remains essentially a lay court; moreover, since the laymen need not be Anglicans, and since it may rule in cases involving doctrine, the law actually places non-Anglicans in a position to legislate by interpretation for the Church of England. This has often proved more a blessing than a curse, because state control has served to keep party conflict within manageable bounds, thereby safeguarding comprehensiveness and avoiding mass expulsions and schism. The Judicial Committee's most controversial ruling, the overriding in 1851 of Bishop Phillpotts' refusal to institute

G. C. Gorham for refusing to subscribe to the High Church view of baptismal regeneration, enabled the Evangelicals to remain in the church; similarly, it prevented valuable elements from being forced out by supporting the Broad Churchmen embroiled in the controversy over *Essays and Reviews* (1861) and through its decisions regarding High Church ceremonial.

Such benefits might or might not be adequate compensation in the eyes of the ardent churchman concerned with the total picture of the fate of the Establishment at the hands of the state. When the legislature had been an entirely Anglican assembly, Parliament took an active and benevolent interest in church affairs. Those days are gone. Economic and social changes originating in the eighteenth century and developments in the wake of the French Revolution and Napoleonic Wars released forces that challenged existing arrangements. Segments of the population, hitherto excluded from the "political nation" for religious and other reasons, became restive, demanding that the basis of the constitution be broadened. Whereas a certain amount of liberalization, such as Catholic Emancipation, had been forthcoming in the early nineteenth century, it was not until the three Reform Acts enlarged the electorate, and until non-Anglicans, indeed occasional atheists, were admitted to Parliament that deep inroads were made in the church's prerogatives.

Year after year, its jurisdiction over areas traditionally its exclusive preserve was whittled away by the advancing secular state. The ecclesiastical courts were divested of their functions. In 1857 testamentary and matrimonial matters were transferred to state-created courts; their "police court" powers over the laity in cases of defamation and sexual offences were abolished; and brawling in church and churchyard became a civil offence. The church courts retained jurisdiction only where clerical discipline and the care of consecrated buildings were involved. Parliament, moreover, moved against the church's monopolies and the legislation protecting its disciplinary powers over laymen: the civil penalties of excommunication were abolished in 1819, the Test and Corporation Acts repealed in 1829, church rates abolished in 1868, the Episcopal church disestablished in Ireland in 1869 and in Wales in 1914, University Tests removed in 1871, the Nonconformist marriage acts repealed in 1836, and the use of rites other than those of the Church of England permitted in burials in churchyards after 1880.[15] By 1914 the church was well on its way to being disestablished in fact if not in name, a condition prompting Bishop Gore to remark acidly: "We are finding ourselves disestablished almost everywhere except in the lunatic asylums. As far as I know that is almost the only department of public life in which the Established Church is allowed to minister without competitors."[16]

The condition of the church might, in fact, be enough to send a sensitive man to an asylum. The church had entered the twentieth century with a vast backlog of items in its organization, rules, and manuals of worship crying for modernization. The Prayer Book itself, unchanged since the seventeenth century, required alterations in light of vexatious ritual controversies. Yet the church was impotent, "paralysed" said the 1917 *Report of the Archbishop's Committee on Church and State,* to do what it thought necessary to carrying out its mission. The dilemma, it seems, stemmed less from parliamentary ill-will (certainly present in a body composed of so many who resented the church's endowments and claims) than from its preoccupation elsewhere. The 1874 debates on the Public Worship Regulation Bill were the last time the bulk of a parliamentary session was given over to ecclesiastical business. The press of secular business became so heavy as the nineteenth century advanced that church measures could rarely receive a hearing. Between 1880 and 1913, 216 church-related bills, some of them dealing with important matters, were introduced into the Commons: 33 were passed, 182 dropped, and 1 rejected. Of the bills dropped or rejected, 162 were never discussed at all![17] The church was caught between the Scylla of a Parliament unable to allocate time to matters crucial to its life, and the Charybdis of its unwillingness to let it handle its affairs alone. So things would remain until, by the Enabling Act of 1919, Parliament took the first halting step toward granting it a measure of autonomy.

Given the gulf between their conception of the place of an established church in a Christian nation and its true situation, church people understandably felt constrained. At a time when surveys showed religion to be losing its hold on the populace at home, and when the World Missionary Conference of 1910 proclaimed the goal of "the evangelization of the world in this generation," they were thwarted by an antiquated system perpetuated by unresponsive constitutional forms. It is hardly surprising that a few individuals, among them peppery old William Connor Magee, appointed archbishop of York in the last year of his life (1891), entertained drastic measures to win self-government. "I am beginning almost to long, I have been for a long time looking, for Disestablishment," Magee informed a correspondent in 1876, adding, "It may very nearly drown us; but it will kill the fleas."[18] That one so highly placed had come to believe that the church must sever its connection with the state in order to serve society the better was itself significant; that so few of his colleagues in 1876, or for that matter in 1914, were willing to go so far is a testimonial not to their spinelessness, but to the discipline and conditioning of the clergy as a professional and social group.

THE CLERGY

According to the nineteenth century saying, the function of the National Church was to place a civilizing influence in the form of an educated gentleman in every parish in the kingdom. Patronizing, to be sure; but nonetheless an accurate statement of a truth self-evident to the Englishman of the governing classes. Visitors from abroad were immediately struck by the clergy's relationship to the dominant order in society. Karl Marx emptied the vials of his wrath upon the ruling oligarchy and its "twin sister" the church.[19] Hippolyte Taine, the right-wing historian of the French Revolution, wrote in his *Notes on England*: "Thus by their ideas, their conduct, their education, their manners, sometimes by their fortunes and birth, they can mingle with the local aristocracy. . . . The clergyman at table along side the landlord is the director of morals, along side the political leader, both of them allied together are visibly the superiors of those they lead, being accepted by them as such, and are generally worthy of being so accepted."[20] Ignatius von Döllinger, a leading Roman Catholic figure in Germany, reported in 1862: "There is no church that is so completely and thoroughly as the Anglican the product of the wants and wishes, the modes of thought and cast of character, not of a certain nationality, but of a fragment of a nation, namely, the rich, fashionable, cultivated classes. It is the religion of deportment, of quality, of clerical reserve."[21] Becoming a member of the Church of England symbolized a family's ascent on the social ladder; for, as another saying had it, "carriage and pair do not pass the church door for more than two generations"; when they stopped, the family had "arrived."

If the claim of Sir Francis Galton, the founder of eugenics and no friend of the church, that the clergy are the best sires from the eugenic standpoint is open to question,[22] there is no doubt that, measured in terms of the enrichment of national life, they have contributed a share disproportionate to that of any other professional group. In preparing an article on "The Children of the Clergy," the Rev. J. E. C. Welldon, successively headmaster of Harrow (where he formed a life-friendship with the young Winston Churchill), bishop of Calcutta, and dean of Manchester, combed *The Dictionary of National Biography* to find those who had achieved "eminence" or "prominence" since the Reformation. He found 1,270 clergy children who qualified for these designations, compared to 510 for lawyers' and 350 for doctors' sons. A fragmentary list of the "whelps of the parsonage" reads like a summary of English achievement during four centuries; in art, Joshua Reynolds and Christopher Wren; in the military, Eyre Coote, John Inglis (the defender of Lucknow), Abraham Roberts (father of Lord Roberts of Kandahar), and, after Welldon's survey, General Sir John Frederick Maurice (son of Frederick Denison Maurice) and Field Marshal Montgomery; in literature, Ben Jonson, Hallam, Marvel, J. A. Froude, Jane Austen, the Brontës, Mrs. Gaskell, Goldsmith, Kingsley, Coleridge, Leigh Hunt, and Matthew Arnold. The church has also given five lord chancellors, one viceroy of India (Curzon), and at least one empire builder (Cecil Rhodes).[23]

A partial explanation of their record lies in the fact that the clergy were drawn primarily from those elements in society best able to provide their offspring with the wherewithal, economic and otherwise, for success. Three characteristics stand out in the origins and recruitment of the pre–1914 clergy: the pattern of "self-recruitment," connections with the landed gentry and the peerage, and, together with the learned professions, with what has been termed "the intellectual aristocracy." By the term "self-recruitment" is meant the phenomenon whereby children follow in their parents' profession. The extent to which this occurred among the clergy is difficult to express statistically, as are nearly all aspects of the sociology of Victorian religion. The best estimate has 55 percent of the graduate sons of the clergy becoming clergymen themselves in the period 1872–1902; probably another 30 percent of the clergy were the sons of doctors, lawyers, and teachers. These figures are particularly revealing, indicating that in no other profession has fatherly influence been so great. In medicine, law, and teaching only 30 percent, in business 25 percent, in Parliament 14 percent, and in the military 14 percent of the sons continued in their fathers' footsteps.[24]

Within the ranks of the clergy another pattern emerges. The most prized forms of preferment—archbishoprics, bishoprics, deaneries, cathedral stalls, and archdeaconries—commonly went to those related by birth or marriage to the peerage or the well-to-do landed families. The figures for the Bench are the most complete, the same proportions probably obtaining for the other dignitaries as well. Aristocratic influence was proverbial in the period 1780–1830. Of the 63 men elevated during these years, 11 were the sons and 3 the grandsons of peers; the remainder included relatives of members of Parliament and of a chief justice, plus tutors in royal and noble households, having as their pupils young Pitts, Grenvilles, Peels, and Addingtons. For the period 1860–1960, 138 out of 183 diocesan bishops surveyed, or 75.4 percent, had landed or peerage connections; in 1900, when most of the bishops active during the Great War had already been on the Bench for several years, the figure was 29 out of 31, or 93.5 percent.[25]

The clergy were also connected with another, emerging, aristocracy, that of the intellect. As Noel Annan has shown,[26] from the beginning of the nineteenth century, members of a certain type of family, evangelical, financially independent, and intellectually gifted, began to intermarry and produce offspring who entered the learned professions when they grew to adulthood, eventually taking over many of the key positions in the universities, the public schools, and the civil service. Several of these families combined academic pursuits with careers in the church. Wilberforces, Vaughans, and Butlers, to name some of the more prominent, formed dynasties of scholars and parsons. The Inge-Churton connection produced in three generations thirteen archdeacons, Hebraists, college fellows, and colonial bishops. Its brightest light was William Ralph Inge, a classical

scholar, authority on Christian mysticism, popular columnist, and
dean (the "Gloomy Dean") of St. Paul's from 1911 to 1934.[27]

Aristocrats by birth and aristocrats of the intellect met early and
shared common experiences. In the period 1871–1902 the vast majority of candidates for Holy Orders were university men, with 60
percent coming from Oxford and Cambridge; in the longer period
1781–1945, every bishop save two was a university man, with Trinity
College, Cambridge, Christ Church and New College, Oxford, accounting for fully a quarter of the total.[28] Another, perhaps in the
long run more important experience came earlier, during the forma-
tive years in the public schools. Originally founded to educate poor
boys for the church, in the fifteenth and sixteenth centuries these institutions began to admit fee-paying boarders to meet expenses in-
adequately covered by endowments. As their reputation for excellence spread, the wealthy began sending their sons, until by the
nineteenth century they had almost completely ousted the poor "day
boys." The sons of the clergy made up a large proportion of the
boarders. An impression of how numerous they were may be gathered
from the experiences of J. E. C. Welldon. When he entered Eton in
the late 'sixties, nearly half of his schoolfellows came from clerical
homes; indeed, the sides in the annual cricket or football match were
nicknamed "Christians" and "Heathens," the Christians being the
sons of the clergy, the Heathens the sons of laymen.[29]

There are unfortunately no figures to indicate how many late Victorian and Edwardian public-school boys, Christian or Heathen,
took Orders; Crockford's Clerical Directory is useless in this connection, omitting reference to preuniversity training. The sociologist
A. M. P. Coxon is probably correct in saying, "almost certainly, the
majority [or ordinands] were from public schools, although this cannot be demonstrated specifically."[30] Figures from a later period may
at least indicate an order of magnitude: in the 1960's the public
schools, accounting for 7 percent of all male pupils at school, provided nearly 30 percent of all ordinands.[31]

There was (and continues to be) a close relationship between the
church, the public schools, and the governing classes. In the period
1868–1955, 91 cabinet ministers of aristocratic and 99 of middle-
class background were public-school educated or had studied under

private tutors; of these 190 ministers, 102 had attended Eton and Harrow.[32] During approximately the same period, 1860–1960, of 242 bishops, all but 20 were "old boys"; 93 came from the elite schools,[33] Eton leading with 25 bishops. Nor were the headmasters of these schools, invariably clergymen until Marlborough appointed Frank Fletcher in 1903, expected to stay at their posts long enough to collect their superannuation allowances. A headmastership was practically an assured steppingstone to a deanery or a bishopric; so much so, that in the last century six headmasters—Thomas Longley, A. C. Tait, Frederick and William Temple, E. W. Benson, and Geoffrey Fisher—have gone on to Canterbury. Here, in the public schools, the future leaders in church and state, whatever their origins, met, made life-long friendships, and had imparted to them a uniformity of outlook and manner. Welldon, again, is an apt illustration of the bonds of association that could be forged at a public school. Among his friends at Eton who later achieved a degree of eminence we find: E. C. Selwyn, headmaster of Uppingham; A. H. Cooks, headmaster of Aldenham School; H. E. Ryle, bishop of Exeter and Winchester; Lord Curzon; Viscount Middleton; A. C. Cole, governor of the Bank of England; and the Lyttelton brothers, Edward and Alfred.[34]

It is worth noting parenthetically that, in terms of the antecedents of their ministers, the Nonconformist bodies—Presbyterians, Congregationalists, Wesleyans, Unitarians, Quakers—on the whole stood lower in the social scale. Drawn from the sons of professional men, civil servants, wholesale traders, retailers, and, in the case of the Baptists, from the working-classes, their Anglican counterparts might refuse to credit them as being full-fledged clergymen. "They are to me as laymen," said one Anglican, "while I am a specially ordained priest; they may be better as laymen than I am, but in my eyes they are not ordained clergymen." Their patronizing attitudes were keenly felt by the Nonconformists. A Baptist minister complained to one of Charles Booth's interviewers that "the Church of England clergy look down on the Nonconformists; at most they tolerate us."[35] The Roman Catholics were regarded with even more disdain. Although a small number of their leaders were well-connected—Cardinal Vaughan and his brother, Bernard, and Cardinal Manning immediately come to mind—the rank-and-file priest was of humble origin;

the fact that he often sported an Irish brogue must have added to the belief that he was "no gentleman."

For the largest portion of Victoria's reign, the church experienced little difficulty in filling its ranks. Contemporaries assumed, correctly, that the young graduate who felt disinclined to study for the bar or take a commission in the armed forces, would take Orders and a wife instead, settling down for the rest of his life in a cozy family living in the country. Some years, of course, saw more recruits than others, and some observers worried more than others. But when the Bath and Plymouth church congresses of 1873 and 1876 took up the question of increasing the number of ordinands, the debates were poorly attended, the matter being thought unworthy of extended discussion. The ordination figures rose throughout the century; and if they failed to rise as quickly as the authorities would have liked, at least the thrust continued in an upward direction. Then, in the mid-'eighties, they levelled off, beginning a decline destined to continue until the 1960's, when they returned to the level of 75 years earlier.

The following table marks the milestones: [36]

1872	582	1892	737
1877	697	1895	720
1880	679	1898	638
1883	781	1901	569
1886	814	1904	569
1889	777	1907	587

These figures reveal only part of the picture, nor that the worst part by any means. Their true significance, as indicated by a special commission of the 1908 Lambeth conference, can only be fully appreciated when considered in relation to the annual increase in population. Late nineteenth and early twentieth century England was inundated, in the phrase then current, by a "devastating torrent of children." As with so many institutions—local government, public health, education—the church found its resources taxed beyond their capabilities. With 260,000 more souls to be cared for every year, and reckoning 2,600 people per minister, the commission concluded that the Church needed one hundred *more* clergy every year just to keep up with the population. In actuality it had to make do

with a *declining* number. Had the standard of 1886 (the best year
of the century) been maintained, 17,808 new deacons would have
been ordained in 1886–1907; only 14,784 were, giving a deficit of
3,024 in twenty-two years. This deficit, when added to the increase
needed to keep up with the population, gave the true deficit: 5,024.[37]
Moreover, given the normal attrition through deaths and retirements,
this deficit eventually showed up in a decline in the total complement
of clergymen. From a high of 23,670 in 1901, it declined by about
one thousand in each of the succeeding five censuses; the average age
of clergymen advanced accordingly, from 44 years in 1851 to 49 in
1901.[38] Anyone could see that, unless these trends were reversed
drastically and soon, the church's ability to fulfill its responsibilities
would be damaged beyond repair.

The reasons for the decline were debated back and forth. Some,
among them the Rev. A. E. Hillard, the headmaster of St. Paul's
School, thought "theological unrest," the unsettlement of belief due
to the findings of modern science and the higher criticism, responsible for dissuading university men from careers in the church. The
Rev. H. A. James, the headmaster of Rugby, agreed, but thought
doubts began earlier, in the sixth form at the public school, when
the boys began to read "the more thoughtful magazines," periodicals
laden with criticism of the miraculous elements in Christianity.[39]
Others, especially those engaged in training and examining ordination candidates, considered the intellectual problem "quite trifling."
True, it was fairly common for a young man, confronted with questions raised by men reading science, to have doubts during his first
year or so after public school, but he usually found his legs after
several terms at the university.[40] "We have no evidence," concluded
the 1900 report of the committee of the Lower House of the Convocation of Canterbury appointed to look into the matter, "to show that
religious doubts affect boys so far as to keep them back frequently
from Orders. . . ."[41]

The root causes of the decline must be sought elsewhere, in the
dislocation of the classic recruiting pattern, which in turn reflected
changes influencing society as a whole. Mandell Creighton exaggerated wildly when he informed the Convocation of Canterbury that
"the wealth of the country has entirely passed from the landed classes
to the industrial classes."[42] He was correct, however, inasmuch as

he recognized that the balance had tipped against the classes hitherto assumed to be the natural leaders of society. In the forty years
since Disraeli's Oxford speech, England had emerged as a mature
industrial nation, with an Empire covering one-seventh of the earth's
surface and comprising one-quarter of the human race. Exactly what
this entailed in economic terms must be studied elsewhere. Of importance for our purpose is the phenomenon, illustrated repeatedly by
societies in the mid-twentieth century undergoing rapid industrialization, whereby a profound economic change never occurs without
sending tremors through the entire social fabric.

The Church of England, wed to the old order in innumerable ways,
was buffeted by forces beyond its control. The years 1860 to 1900
witnessed a proliferation in the professions unlike anything in history.[43] Within a comparatively short time, teaching, commerce, and
the Empire became professions worthy of a gentleman's son. The
Home, Colonial, and Indian Civil Services were particularly attractive, albeit highly competitive, fields. It became essential for young
men contemplating these fields to arrive at a career decision between
the ages of sixteen and eighteen, so as to begin preparing in the subjects in which they would eventually be examined. These pressures,
testified Frederick Temple, who knew his boys, plus the fact that the
decision to seek Orders requires a level of maturity rarely found in
eighteen-year-olds (Anglicans deplored the Roman Catholic practice of placing boys destined for the ministry in seminaries when
barely into their teens), accelerated the decline of vocations among
public-school boys.[44] Chances were, moreover, that *their* sons would
never seek ecclesiastical careers. If, as we shall see, urbanization
contributed to the estrangement of the masses from religion, it had a
similar effect upon the classes staffing the church. Boys raised in an
urban suburb, where they had no contact with anyone outside their
own class except stewards and shopkeepers, lacked that sense of
noblesse oblige which the sons of the squire and the parson, accustomed to know and take an interest in everyone in the village, acquired from childhood.[45]

Associated with these general causes, from the mid-'seventies to
the outbreak of the Great War the church and the classes upon which
it relied were caught in an economic squeeze. More than half the
parochial clergy of England and Wales depended upon tithe, wholly

or in part;[46] and tithe depended on agricultural prices. By the Tithe Commutation Act of 1836, a money payment varying with the seven year average of the prices of wheat, barley, and oats had been substituted for the ancient tithe in kind. The tithe rent-charge, as it is called, continued with brief interruptions to rise with grain prices from 1836 onward, reaching its highest point of £112 15s 6¾d in 1875. From then on, as the virgin plains of the United States, Canada, and Russia were opened by the railroad, and as improved ship design and steam engines reduced the costs of ocean carriage, the prices of English grains fell precipitously. The tithe rent-charge fell accordingly, reaching its lowest point of £66 10s 9¼d in 1901.[47] Yet, because the cost of living (as measured by Sauerbeck's "index number" representing the average of the wholesale price of fifty commodities in common use) declined along with the rent-charge, clergymen managed to hold their own, albeit with some belt-tightening.[48] In the closing years of the century, however, with the opening of the Rand, Klondike, and Yukon gold fields, world commodity prices rose, leaving clerical incomes far behind. Summarizing the plight of the parochial clergy, Athelstan Riley, a director of the Clergy Sustention Fund, said: "the clergy are attached to the upper ranks of society, and are compelled to maintain their families and educate their children accordingly. In country districts, especially during the present century, they have become a kind of ecclesiastical squirearchy: the prosperous times have receded, and they are left high and dry in big parsonages and amidst biting cares."[49]

The professional and middle classes, next to the landed classes and the clergy themselves the main source of ordinands, were also affected, although less from the agricultural depression than from the rise in prices. Inflation left them with limited options: either they curtailed their standard of living, rising since the mid-nineteenth century, or they succumbed to the "gospel of comfort," even if that meant restricting procreation. They succumbed. Demographical studies indicate that, whereas birth rates remained high among the poor—35.6 per thousand in the nine poorest districts of London— whose knowledge and access to contraceptive devices was still limited, they fell markedly in middle- and upper-class districts—29 and 18.6 per thousand respectively.[50] "The decline in the birth rate," concluded a study by the public health expert Arthur Newsholme, "is not due to increased poverty. It is associated with a general rising in the standard of comfort, and is an expression of the determination of the people to secure this greater comfort. It is not caused by greater stress in modern life, but is a consequence of the greater desire for luxury. . . ."[51]

Mothers, denounced at the time as offenders against English gentility as well as Christian morality, advised their daughters about "prevention"; advertisers used the mails to send their lists of contraceptives to the homes of newlyweds; one might purchase rubber sheaths, largely of German manufacture, from vending machines in garages.[52] However they got them, or whether they resorted to infanticide or self-induced abortion instead,[53] the church eventually had to feel the impact. The middle-class family had fewer children, but these enjoyed a better education, usually for the professions; there was less money for the Sunday collection, but enough to provide the luxuries they had come to regard as necessities. There are even statistics, admittedly fragmentary, that indicate there were more clerical bachelors about in 1905 than a generation earlier, and that those who eventually married did so later and sired fewer children. According to a survey of clients of the Clergy Relief Corporation, the average clerical family had 5.4 children in 1885, 4.3 in 1905, and 3.5 in 1919.[54]

From the 'eighties onward, we hear of parents actually discouraging their sons from seeking ordination, as well they might, if they were interested in material rewards. With the cost of higher education keeping pace with the general trend in prices,[55] the church lost its former attractiveness, becoming a "bad investment" in terms of return on expenditure. There had been a time, Randall Davidson, bishop of Winchester (1895–1903) and archbishop of Canterbury (1903–1928) recalled in 1901, when "the profession of Holy Orders was one which, looked at from the lower point of view . . . parents might take, was a creditable one, and a sufficiently profitable one to enable their son to live fairly comfortable all his life; but those days are over. Now a boy who wants to go into the ministry will have to meet objections on the part of his parents . . . ."[56]

Assuming he could obtain parental consent and scrape together the requisite sums, the young man of average ability and moderate means had to think carefully before taking Orders. He was at a disadvantage from the very beginning. Of all the professions, the service of God held the least promise of ever attaining a decent standard of living. The offices of the church were filled by methods that would have warmed the heart of an eighteenth century patronage broker. There was no agency, governed by regular procedures, objective, and immune from influence, empowered to assign clergymen in accordance with the needs of the Anglican community as a whole. An incumbent might obtain his position in several ways. In the early years of the century, as now, the advowson, or the right of presentation to a benefice, was treated in law as a type of property to be transferred as the owner chose. Usually, if the "living" was in the gift of the crown, a bishop, a university, or a college, it went to the most "deserving" candidate. The church system, as the curate of St. James,' Fulham, aptly described it, was ensconced behind an "adamantine rampart of privilege," access to its good things being well-nigh impossible "to an unbeneficed priest without an influential friend to rise at the court of patronage at the proper moment, or a dignified relationship" to speak on his behalf.[57] Having a full purse was also helpful, as it is in most things. If the advowson was in private hands, it could be given to a relative, sold at auction (until 1898, when forbidden by a benefices act), or advertised for sale in the ecclesiastical press. As the value of livings declined, so did their prices, enabling a clergyman with £1,000 or £1,500 to buy the right of appointment and then appoint himself to the living.[58]

Income varied from office to office and from place to place. As a rule, the bishops received high salaries. The archbishops of Canterbury and York earned £15,000 (£10,000 more than the prime minister) and £10,000 respectively, while the bishops of London, Durham, and Winchester received £10,000, £7,000, and £6,500. Deans and canons fared equally well, considering their salaries and the work required to earn them. For example, when Bishop John Percival of Hereford offered the New Testament scholar B. H. Streeter a canonry with a stipend of £500, he accepted with the understanding that he need not remain in attendance for more than three months of the year; the remaining time was his own.[59]

The overwhelming majority of parish priests had to subsist on considerably less than £500. At a time when experts in church finance calculated that no clergyman should have to live on less than £300 a year, of the 12,990 livings in England and Wales, 3,275 were worth under £200, with another 5,860 at between £250 and £300.[60] These salaries might have sufficed when clergymen could supplement them from private means; but this became increasingly more difficult as the economic crisis deepened. The clergy of other denominations might derive some comfort from knowing that whatever they lacked in social standing was made up in hard cash. The United Methodists, Presbyterian Church of England, Congregational, and Baptist churches paid a *minimum* of £200, in addition to providing valuable side-benefits in the form of houses and paying the taxes and rates for their clergy.[61] Anglican stipends, moreover, lagged behind the earnings of other men of similar background. At the turn of the century, it was assumed that any man educated at a public school, with a university degree, and possessed of average ability could expect from £500 to £1,000 at the outset in almost any profession he chose.[62] Yet advocates of reform cited case after case to illustrate the depths of poverty to which clergymen sank. In 1896, W. S. de Winton, a member of the Canterbury House of Laymen, told of clergymen's daughters answering local newspaper advertisements for domestic servants. A typical letter contained these phrases: "My father can no longer afford to keep us at home"; "I have had no education, as my father could not afford it, and so can only hope to get a place as a servant."[63] Charged with administering a kind of outdoor relief for clerical paupers, the Clergy Relief Corporation was deluged with pathetic pleas, among them the following: "May I respectfully apply for a grant of clothing for my wife and self? I had hoped to wait until I get a bonus, but neither of us is able to go out decently. I would not apply if I could help it, but I am driven to do so. I am bound in this hot weather to wear my overcoat in Sunday School to cover my rags. I have no doubts."[64]

To compound the miseries of the poor clergy, they were frequently the victims of an obsolete parochial system and the resultant maldistribution of church resources. Developed during the Middle Ages, when the predominantly rural population grew slowly and was subject to sudden contraction due to plague and famine, the parochial system failed on the whole to grow and move with the population. The census of 1851 reported that the population was distributed fairly evenly between country and town; fifty years later, 72 percent of the population lived in urban sanitary districts (a misnomer, as they were often the most unsanitary districts) and 25 percent in rural districts.[65]

The clergy, despite a vast program of church building and the division of parishes in the nineteenth century, were not to be found where the bulk of the people lived. Taking as a standard of measurement two to three thousand souls, considered a manageable parish by contemporaries, more than half the incumbents should have been busier, as 55 percent of the parishes had populations of less than one thousand.[66] Underemployment and underutilization of manpower reached scandalous proportions in rural districts. In six Yorkshire parishes, to take an extreme case, the population ranged as low as 68 and as high as 388, with an average of 260.[67] Well might the country clergyman be described as a "spiritually-minded vegetable"; under such circumstances he would have had scant opportunity to test his skills and hone his mind on a variety of tasks. A similar situation prevailed on the diocesan level. Certain dioceses had more clergy than they needed relative to their population, others were understaffed. Take Canterbury and Southwark; with 309 and 312 livings respectively, their populations were 652,000 and 2,235,000! The figures for other dioceses are as outlandish: Lindon had 578 incumbents for 562,000 people, but London had 592 for 3,800,000; Oxford had 642 for 691,000, but Newcastle had 181 for 700,000.[68]

If the country parson ministered to smaller flocks than his forbears, his colleague in the town was overworked. Urban parishes expanded rapidly after mid-century. Towns such as Little Ilford, to cite some dramatic examples from the London area, grew from 200 in 1851 to 15,000 in 1899; Hackney grew from 34,527 in 1831 to 195,173 in 1881.[69] Other parishes, always large, grew still larger. That Robert Dolling, the controversial slum priest and ritualist, was able to obtain a semblance of Christian order in All Saints, Portsmouth, with its 27,000 poor parishioners and a shifting population of soldiers, sailors, prostitutes, and criminals was a feat not devoid of the miraculous.[70] In any case, the resources of many weaker men were taxed to the point where they suffered permanently debilitating mental and physical breakdowns.[71]

At least these men had parishes of their own, such as they were. The curate, the paid assistant of the incumbent, was in a more precarious position. A literary convention of the time made a butt of the curate: he was like "Blazer" Bumpstead of St. Ursula's, Stucco Square, in G. W. E. Russel's *Londoner's Log Book*, a tennis court hero lionized by the fashionable ladies of the parish; or the archetype of the effeminate "pale young curate of Asses'-Milk-cum-Water" in W. S. Gilbert's "Bab Ballad"; or simply a doddering incompetent. In real life, the curate without independent means or highly placed connections was an ecclesiastical proletarian whose average yearly income ranged between £123 and £130.[72] Some were in pitiful condition, as the curate who earned 15 shillings a week for himself, his wife, and six children to live (if that is the word) on. Mandell Creighton, who reported this case, affirmed "cases of this kind are constantly occurring."[73]

Because he was only a hired helper, the curate had no voice in the councils and assemblies of the church. Because he lacked fixity of tenure, he was subject to the laws of the market. If times were bad, or the living poorly endowed, the incumbent could dispense with his services, sending him out like any other "hand" to join the unemployed. Unlike the workers, however, he had no trade union to look after his interests. If so imprudent as to marry without the promise of immediate preferment (thirteen years was the normal waiting period from curacy to incumbency),[74] by the time he was forty he might find himself trapped in a dead-end position, his strength ebbing, and he, educated in a gentleman's calling, unable to educate his sons, properly marry-off his daughters, or provide for his old age—the pensions scheme sponsored by the ecclesiastical commissioners excluded unbeneficed clergymen.[75] In a country that boasted of being the workshop of the world, he might leave his widow and orphans with nothing more substantial than a claim to a pittance from the Poor Clergy Relief Corporation. No wonder some gave way under the strain. Father Dolling, who took them in when few others would, noted that good men became drunkards because they found it intolerable "through the bitterness of poverty, to have to live like gentlemen, when they had not enough income to keep body and soul together. . . ."[76]

Why, when bishops earned thousands of pounds and lived in sprawling palaces (the archbishop of Canterbury has two), were the poor clergy, incumbents and curates alike, willing to put up with their miserable conditions? Why was there no "revolt from below"?

Fear was certainly a factor. Lacking the workers' experience in uniting and agitating in a common cause, they believed that to criticize
the system publicly meant becoming a marked man without a chance
of advancement. Beyond this, however, they could not imagine
themselves emulating the workers, even if that meant the possibility
of improving their lot. As labor unions find when trying to organize
teachers and other white collar workers, self-esteem and public image often weigh heavier than economic betterment. The clergy regarded themselves as belonging to an aristocracy of intellect and
virtue, if not of wealth and position. They were gentlemen, holding
on to their gentility all the harder for their poverty. They shared the
gentleman's natural reticence to air his domestic arrangements to
public discussion. "They are reluctant to speak," said the Rev. Clement F. Rogers, lecturer in pastoral theology at King's College, London, "they do not wish to make complaints, they do not care to bare
the sores of the Church, they each have a horror of appearing a man
with a grievance."[77]

If clinging to an outmoded concept of gentility restrained the poor
clergy from protesting openly, it harmed the church by inhibiting its
use of a vast pool of potential manpower. With fewer recruits coming
from the traditional sources, logic would have dictated measures to
facilitate entrance to the ministry of those from lower social strata.
These measures were not forthcoming. Despite the warnings of a few
farsighted individuals that the idea of gentlemanly status as a necessary qualification for Holy Orders must be abandoned lest the church
suffer graver setbacks in the future, there persisted a real fear of
lowering the quality of the ministry through opening it to the same
sort of Bible-wielding zealot they imagined dominated Nonconformity. As late as 1900, the Committee of the Convocation of Canterbury on the Supply and Training of Candidates for Holy Orders
reiterated the old idea of the clergyman as gentleman, noting in its
report the need for clergy who were intellectually equipped, spiritually
disciplined, and of "suitable social status."[78]

By the end of the first decade of the new century, the church had
begun to draw from a wider social range, although hardly enough
to alter its complexion; this would happen only after 1919, and then
only partially. The proportion of candidates from the public schools,
Oxford and Cambridge decreased, while the proportion from the

grammar schools, Durham and Dublin increased, as did the number of nongraduates trained at theological colleges.[79] These institutions, however, though taking men generally older and lower down in the social scale than attended the ancient universities, remained essentially middle-class institutions.[80]

Anglicans, accustomed to a clergy who could afford their own training, made little effort to recruit among the laboring classes, providing little in the way of scholarships for those desiring clerical training. Woefully understaffed and underfinanced, the three main agencies for this purpose—the Ordination Candidates Fund, the House of the Sacred Mission at Kelham, and the Community of the Resurrection, Mirfield, Yorkshire—were usually able to accept only a quarter of their qualified applicants.[81] Sometimes the only route to the priesthood for a poor Anglican boy meant forsaking his church and its doctrine for the Unitarians, the Baptists, or the Methodists, who would assume the full cost of his education. Small wonder that the frustration of one critic, Father Paul Bertie Bull, a cofounder with Gore of the Community of the Resurrection, boiled over into a denunciation of the "so-called National Church" for having invented "a class priesthood with a money qualification."[82]

CHURCH AND PEOPLE

Failure to tap men of humble origin for the ministry was part of the church's overall failure, springing from multiple causes, to reach the masses and persuade them of the relevance of its teaching to their lives. Until the censuses of church attendance taken toward the end of the Victorian era proved the contrary, all denominations were confident that Christianity was advancing, albeit haltingly and unevenly, among the people. Insofar as progress in a quality so intangible as religious devotion is amenable to quantification, the only statistics available to them gave cause for encouragement. In conjunction with the decennial census of 1851, Horace Mann, the assistant commissioner for the census, conducted the only nationwide enquiry into church and chapel attendances. Mann's figures, much-criticized at the time and subsequently,[83] nevertheless showed that slightly under 40 percent of the population had attended some form of religious service on census Sunday; not the 58 percent he thought ought to have been in church, but certainly (as Disraeli implied ten years later at Oxford) a solid base to build upon. The most significant feature of the Mann figures was that fully half of the total attendances were in Anglican churches. Thirty years later, however, at a time when officials were voicing concern about clerical recruitment, private investigations of several large towns gave genuine cause for alarm. In Sheffield, Nottingham, Liverpool, Hull, Bristol, Southampton, Portsmouth, and Bath, Anglican services accounted for 37 percent of the attendances, a decline of 13 percent from the Mann figures.[84] Finally, statistical studies done later in the London area dispelled any lingering illusions. They revealed that between a religious census conducted in 1886 by Sir William Robertson Nicoll's *British Weekly*, and 1902–1903, when the *Daily News* issued the results of Richard Mudie-Smith's survey, all denominations suffered a setback. But none suffered as much as the Church of England. Whereas the Nonconformists lost approximately 6,000, a negligible amount, attendance figures for the Church of England fell from 535,000 to 396,000. Put another way, in 1902–1903 the church in London was drawing three worshippers in place of the four it had drawn seventeen years earlier, this during a period when the population of the metropolis had increased by a half million.[85] A similar pattern, associated with the decline of the village, prevailed in the countryside, although here we must rely on the impressions of contemporaries instead of statistical evidence.[86] Whether in town or country, Charles Booth's verdict was irrefutable: "the great mass of the people remain apart from all forms of religious communion, apparently untouched by the Gospel. . . ."[87]

If this mass be separated into its component elements, it will be seen that, sociologically speaking, the Established Church was losing ground unevenly. To the extent that London, the only city for which detailed district by district studies were published, may be deemed representative of urban England, church attendance was a function of position in society. The middle classes were the bulwark of religiosity. All denominations thrived wherever they predominated, although Nonconformity surpassed the Established Church in north and south London. No sooner did the metropolis, ever expanding and hungry for space, devour a new suburb, than houses of worship were built and filled; indeed, it was said that only studied nastiness on the part of the minister could discourage worshippers.[88] Churchgoing in Hampstead and Islington and Stoke Newington represented a convention of society, something people "did" automatically and without question. And as so often happens with responses that have become automatic, they tend to lose their significance with repetition. Observers remarked that the religion of the suburbs revealed an undercurrent of hollowness, conventionality, and want of spirituality. Bishop Gore thought the middle classes were in as much (maybe more) need of Divine mercy as the heathen. He was once walking with William Temple to a railway station, discoursing on faith and works to pass the time. To drive home a point, he stopped, pointed to the platform crowded with respectable citizens in business attire, and said: "You see those people; they'll have to be saved by works if they are saved at all. I am sure they haven't got any faith. Look at them!"[89]

At least they were willing to throw a sop to respectability; they were surrounded socially by a religious wasteland. The zeal of the upper classes, concentrated in the districts of west London, notably Kensington and Chelsea, had cooled since the mid-nineteenth century. Attendance had declined in almost every church in the district, sometimes catastrophically, as in St. Philip's, Earl's Court (from 1,752 in 1886 to 800 in 1903) and St. Mary's, Boltons (from 1,457 to 417 during the same period).[90] "Religion has never been a serious concern among the wealthy," the Liberal M.P. and journalist C. F. G. Masterman remarked in what is probably the best short essay on the religious life of London. "They play with it as they play with life."[91]

The religion of the workingman may be summarized for the time being thus: save for the Roman Catholics, mostly Irish, and small bodies of sectarians—Primitive Methodists, Baptists, and Salvationists—and save for the Anglican missions where pathetic souls gathered to be preached at as a prerequisite to their handout of food and coals, he was oblivious to the consolations of religion.

Two causal chains may be distinguished at this point: one deriving from the nature of late nineteenth century society and affecting organized religion as a whole, the other involving factors unique to the Church of England. As to the first, estrangement from religion was another consequence of the economic revolution transforming society. Sensitive observers, clergy and laymen alike, discerned a subtle, but nonetheless pervasive and penetrating, change in national psychology. Industrialization had created new wealth, raised standards of consumer expectation, and imparted to life an unspiritual, materialistic quality. Gladstone had discerned the change in 1890, warning that "the seen is gaining slowly on the unseen." By 1906, the Rev. Samuel Barnett, a keen social reformer and the first warden of Toynbee Hall, had become convinced that the seen had in fact triumphed: "this generation has within its reach delights for the senses which may well seem enough for satisfaction, and working men naturally imagine that nothing can be better than to have a share in those delights. They go after things that are seen, and have neither the time nor the will to go after the things which are unseen."[92] The decline in the number of religious books published is probably another little indicator of advancing worldliness: in 1870 religious books accounted for the largest number of new titles, fiction being fifth on the list; in 1886, fiction was first, but religion remained well ahead of the rest; by 1899, religious books had slipped far behind.[93]

The adage that religion is caught rather than taught presupposes a communal life sufficiently stable and continuous to permit the "virus" to be transmitted and to become established. In preindustrial England, rural England, churchgoing had been part of the routine of life, with only the likes of the village recluse and drunkard cutting Divine worship. The milestones of the individual's journey through this world—baptism, confirmation, marriage—were solemnized in church, while the dead, the link with the past, slumbered in the churchyard. This pattern of local and religious association was disrupted by large-scale urbanization, a social trauma whose consequences have still to be unfolded completely. Countryfolk, seeking better employment opportunities or fleeing agricultural depression, swarmed into the industrial towns, sped there over gleaming railroad tracks. By 1870, nine out of every ten town-dwelling families had taken up residence during the previous three generations.

A new "city race," to use C. F. G. Masterman's phrase,[94] evolved. Immersed in a man-made environment, memory of the other life in the country, even to the extent of being able to identify the commonest wildflowers,[95] was eradicated, frequently within a single generation. The social pressure to conform in religious matters disappeared as quickly. No longer under the watchful eye of squire and parson, living among people whose sole idea of neighborliness consisted of minding their own business, and distracted by the inexpensive and abundant amusements, country-bred habits of worship decayed. Significantly, those who had been churchwardens in the country might not feel obliged to attend church in the town.[96]

Churchgoing was at variance with the urban life-style. Sunday, for the minister of religion *the* "business day" of the week, became a day of rest and relaxation for professional and business people. The "English Sunday," described by Taine as a combination of clanging church bells, deserted streets, and boredom so unrelieved as to cause one to meditate suicide, gradually succumbed to the "week-end habit." Those who could, aped the Prince of Wales's Sunday luncheon parties at Marlborough House. Railway travelling (in Great Britain 1,400 regular passenger trains, in addition to any number of special excursion trains, were run on Sunday),[97] boating, golfing, and motoring became fashionable. The workingman emulated his betters. Thousands, of course, could not have attended church even had they desired, as railwaymen, tram drivers, busmen, and other service workers might receive one Sunday off in three or four.[98] But the "typical" worker's Sunday, according to Winnington-Ingram, who before becoming bishop of London had been active in mission work in the East End, passed as follows: rising at eleven or twelve, he had a leisurely breakfast, wandered down to the public house for a "wet" until it closed at three, spent a few hours gambling and pigeon-flying with his cronies, then home for the meal of the week, a pot of beer, his newspaper, and early to bed for work the next morning.[99] Marx was ludicrously wide of the mark in denouncing religion as the opiate of the people. Every parson who had dealings with the workers, every bishop of an urban diocese knew better. "Religion," as one worker told Archbishop Lang, "touches us fellows no nearer than the moon."[100]

Opinions differed on the role of anti-Christian propaganda in undermining belief. A profusion of "ethical" and secularist societies, spearheaded by the Rationalist Press Association, which boasted the historian G. M. Trevelyan on its executive board and the unfrocked Franciscan friar Joseph McCabe in its lecture halls, utilized reading circles and discussion groups to wean the educated from orthodoxy.[101] Others pursued a less sophisticated prize, the mass reading public created by the spread of public education. Half-educated, with an indiscriminating reverence for whatever passed for "science," this public could take up Robert Blatchford's *Clarion* and find knotty theological problems interestingly presented in elementary terms, all with an anti-Christian bias; the church had nothing whatever to send into the field against it.

Secularism drew the bulk of its working-class support from the East End, where, supposedly, you could hear its tenets expounded in every workshop and find its lecturers on every street corner.[102] The parks of London doubled as "open-air universities" where anti-Christian speakers of every description gathered on Sunday to air their views and badger the less numerous and less articulate spokesmen of the Christian Evidence Society. The orators of the Rationalist Society were notorious for their bad manners, barbed comments, and perverse insinuations regarding the circumstances surrounding the "virgin" birth. If Christ were really God, jibed one obnoxious character, then His words on the Cross—"My God! My God! Why hast Thou forsaken me?"—had to mean that "God was calling upon Himself to explain to Himself why He had forsaken Himself."[103]

For all their efforts, secularism gained little support outside of the East End; it scarcely penetrated the rural areas and the industrial North, where working-class dissent was stronger than the Church of England. It was certainly a nuisance Christian apologists could have done without. But secularism was nowhere near the menace it had been in the 'eighties, when, during the campaign to have the atheist Charles Bradlaugh seated in Parliament, it became momentarily identified with the political interests of the workingman.[104] Bradlaugh notwithstanding, the workingman was rarely an atheist or agnostic, harboring instead a vague belief in God and affection for His Son as "a down-right good fellow."[105] He had simply become indifferent to the claims of the Christian religion. As for the desperately poor, they were the victims of that numbing apathy everywhere characteristic of their condition, an apathy that frustrated with impartiality the efforts of socialist and Christian missionaries. "The fact is," a poor woman confessed, "me and me 'usben don't take no interest in anythink."[106]

Why, given the tendencies operating to the detriment of religion as a whole, was the Church of England affected most adversely? Why might one sense in the denizens of Whitechapel and Stepney and a hundred other places a certain inarticulate suspicion and resentment toward the Anglican clergyman? Some of it was linked to the fact that the gentlemanly qualities cultivated and valued as his chief assets militated against his effectiveness with his social inferiors. The positivist Frederic Harrison commented upon this in the 'seventies. The Anglican priest, he said, "looks on the 'poor' from without: usually kindly, often paternally, sometimes intelligently; but always from above, as the squire looks on them, as the magistrate looks on them, as the Board look on paupers. And the Official Church may perhaps be called the Church of the Poor, much as the Board are officially the Guardians of the Poor."[107]

There existed, to use an overburdened expression, a barrier to communications between the clergyman and his flock. His origins, class conventions, and educational experiences enclosed him in an invisible shell, isolating him from the very people he hoped to serve. His notions of respectability and the proper relationship between the sexes might easily be taken for priggishness, and himself for an undercover moral policeman. His politeness might be taken for "fancy manners," and himself denounced for putting on "airs." He carried himself differently, dressed differently, and differed physically from his flock: at a time when the height of the working-class male was stunted from childhood malnutrition—in 1900 the army recognized this fact in fixing the minimum height for recruits at five feet—he must have been taller. When he spoke, it was with a different intonation (easily mimicked) and with a professional vocabulary which, however suited to educated audiences, struck commonfolk as an affectation. They "tried," he "strived"; they "lived," he "dwelled"; they thought something "bad," he thought it "evil."[108] In their eyes, there was truth enough in the saying that the Baptists had all the water, the Methodists all the fire, and the Anglicans all the starch!

Not all Anglicans were "starchy," however. Those who won the workingman's affections were as rare in quality as they were in number. A Robert Dolling at All Saints, Portsmouth, or a Charles Lowder at St. Peter's, London Docks, attracted large congregations. Possessing diverse social views, and representing different schools of churchmanship, men of their stamp had one characteristic in com-

mon: a sympathy with the underdog combined with the innate ability
to reach out as human beings to their fellow human beings.

Contrary to the sensibilities of a democratizing age, indeed contrary to the doctrine of the Incarnation, which obliterated all conventional and arbitrary distinctions between men, the Anglican system
inadvertently accentuated the workingman's inferiority. The church
buildings, frequently Gothic-style structures, were cold and impersonal in their magnificence. The workers, clad plainly or in thread-
bare garments, voiced their shame, occasionally with tears in their
eyes, at the prospect of appearing in these surroundings before their
elegantly dressed superiors.[109] Attendance might also be costly, relatively speaking. Pew rents, cherished by incumbents as supplements
to inadequate endowments and defended by fastidious parishioners
because the poor stank, segregated the house of God along class lines.
As late as 1917 the going rate for pews in the center of London
churches was 5s 3d a quarter, 2s 2d in other parts.[110] Even the parson's wife, if she was a well-meaning but patronizing Lady Bounti-
ful, gave offence by rebuking those she helped for keeping dirty homes
and by otherwise meddling in their affairs.[111] Finally, the forms of
religious expression, in olden days wrung from the people's heart in
response to terror and suffering, seemed inadequate and lifeless in
terms of modern needs. The following is the way one observer, the
Rev. J. A. Castle, a young army chaplain, saw the situation in 1917.
It is a strong indictment, doubtlessly too strong because it reflects
the frustration borne of the war; but it contains the essence of what
critics meant when they scored the church for its inability to adjust
to modernity.

[The church] has been and still is content to be an ecclesiastical corporation which is out of touch with real life. It is . . . moss-bound and mori-
bund. We have divorced religion from life. We are lying and preaching
an accursed dualism. We tread the ecclesiastical ground with unfailing
regularity, we go through services, we perform religious functions and
exercises, we observe days and weeks, and times and seasons, we are ob-
sessed and stake our all upon doctrinalism and externalism, and nobody
cares, and nobody listens, and nobody pays any heed or is in the least interested, save, perhaps, fast dwindling congregations. In reality we are
walking in a stagnant pool of ecclesiastical formalism masquerading under
the name of religion. Our thoughts are locked up in forms, we are hide-
bound by traditions, we wrangle and dispute about nice points of theology

and doctrine and expend precious energy in fruitless discussions on the shape of a vestment or whether we shall have six candles or two or none at all. And this is our Church. This is our religion. This is our pathetic little water-tight compartment in which we hug ourselves and rejoice in our superiority in comparison with the great world outside. It is this spirit of smug, narrow self-complacency, this utterly futile tinkering with the forms and ceremonies and ordinances of an archaic ecclesiasticism, which is largely responsible for the alienation of the masses, and which has produced the spirit of torpor and coma within the Church itself which is threatening to suffocate it to death.[112]

These shortcomings, serious and wasting over the long stretch, were seldom sufficient to provoke open hostility. The church's role in politics and issues touching the workingman directly was another matter. A good deal of hostility stemmed from memories of past abuses sedulously kept alive for partisan reasons and by the indiscretions of leading church figures. Working-class, socialist, and secularist critics on the one hand, Nonconformist advocates of disestablishment and disendowment on the other, belabored it as an agency of the governing classes. It was a political church, they said; it was, in that masterpiece of political phrase-making, "the Conservative Party at prayer," having in its wealth and prerogatives "a good thing to conserve."

On the surface, these charges had an element of plausibility. Anglicans have indeed voted Conservative (about one in every two, according to a recent study),[113] and the governments they have helped elect have had a distinctly upper-class and Anglican complexion. No Dissenter has ever become prime minister in a Conservative government. Yet this hardly proves that "the Church" was an instrument of the governing classes. Nor does it prove that the bishops were appointed to sway the electors in the Tory interest and, in the words of Mr. Asquith, a man of high culture given to occasional demagoguery, to use their position in the House of Lords as a means of "obstructing and retarding the expressed wishes of the chosen representatives of the people . . . ."[114]

In the eighteenth and early nineteenth centuries, Liberals and Conservatives had used ecclesiastical patronage to secure political advantage. From Palmerston onward, however, the church became steadily depoliticized. Since Queen Victoria disliked purely political appointments, and since the various reform acts and the coming of the secret ballot in 1872 lessened their value as political levers, politics ceased to count in the choice of bishops.[115] In the opinion of Randall Davidson, as dean of Windsor the queen's closest advisor on ecclesiastical appointments, almost everyone on the Bench in the early twentieth century was without outward party affiliation.[116] The appointment of John Percival to Hereford in 1895 (by none other than Mr. Asquith) was the glaring exception, because, in his biographer's words, he "took an active and even vehement part in general politics," invariably in the Liberal interest. [117] Percival aside, the behavior of the bishops in the House of Lords was exceptionally apolitical. A survey of the division lists reveals that rarely in the last century have more than a dozen bishops voted even on major issues.[118] When they have voted, they have disregarded party lines. As Davidson pointed out to the Lords in 1909, they usually sided with the Tories in issues affecting religious life and the welfare of the church, notably education, and with the Liberals on issues of social reform. [119] The solid phalanx of reactionary bishops is a myth. On the Parliament Bill of 1911, an issue critical for the Tories, thirteen out of the fifteen bishops present voted, on Davidson's advice, with the Liberals.[120] Yet, despite assertions and evidence to the contrary, the charge of political hackery stuck to the church like a burr, sowing suspicion among those it would bring into communion with itself.

The most important cause by far of working-class animosity stemmed from the feeling that the church was unsympathetic toward its aspirations for an equitable social order. For in spite of industrialism's having provided a higher standard of living for the majority of Englishmen, a considerable portion of the population enjoyed its benefits only marginally if at all. Poverty was widespread. Urban poverty, more concentrated and therefore more visible than poverty in the countryside, was shocking; the bishop of Zululand thought it worse than the monstrosities of pagan Africa.[121] Charles Booth's survey of London, carried out between 1887 and 1892, revealed that 30.7 percent of its people were below the "poverty line," i.e. below the minimum standard for a healthy existence.[122] These figures take on added significance when seen in human terms: as late as 1902, 34 persons between the ages of 24 and 50 died of "simple" starvation in London alone, and His Majesty's Inspectors of Schools put the number of underfed children in London at 122,000.[123] A few shillings could still buy the use of a little girl's body for a couple of hours.

Articulate critics agreed that the church betrayed Christianity by permitting such poverty and exploitation. If it expected to make headway, if indeed it wanted to be worthy of its Divine charge, it would have to do a lot more than cast an occasional vote in the House of Lords. It would have to undergo a corporate change of heart. No more (in Ruskin's phrase) dining with the rich and preaching patience to the poor. When people were suffering *now*, no more pious hopes of the sort expressed by Archbishop Davidson himself, that, "given a little more time, say a couple of generations," extreme poverty "might be practically abolished."[124] It would have to become an impatient church, an activistic church preaching what the Americans called the "Social Gospel." If the evangelical revival of the eighteenth century rediscovered the worth of the individual soul and its personal responsibility, then, said Mudie-Smith, "the revival of the twentieth century we shall owe to the discovery of the worth of the entire man and the responsibilities of the community. Our forefathers were content with a Heaven after death; we demand a Heaven here. They regarded themselves as pilgrims with no continuing city, 'mere desert-land sojourners'; we are determined that this Metropolis shall become the City of God."[125]

By the end of the nineteenth century, the ideal of a Kingdom of God on Earth, usually embodied in some form of socialistic commonwealth, had established itself in nearly every denomination. Within the Anglican community, Christian Socialist societies, the spiritual descendants of the unsuccessful movement begun in the 'fifties by Frederick Denison Maurice, Charles Kingsley, and J. M. F. Ludlow, revived in the 'seventies.[126] Their approach regardless of their programmatic differences, represented a fundamental departure from the accepted method of the churches. For instead of contenting themselves with relieving suffering (and making converts) through a network of missions and other philanthropic enterprises, they proposed, in the name of God, to change the system that made suffering inevitable.

Three organizations, displaying all the fissiparous tendencies denounced in sectarianism, accounted for the bulk of Christian Socialist strength. The Guild of St. Matthew, founded in 1877 by the Rev. Stewart Headlam, then curate of St. Matthew's, Bethnal Green, professed a kind of "sacramental socialism" resting on the belief that Baptism, the Mass, and the Incarnation confirmed every person's worth and right to a decent life.[127] Never large (it had 400 members at its peak), and rent by internal bickering, Headlam dissolved it in 1909. The second organization, the Christian Social Union, grew at the expense of the Guild. It was moderate, seeking through tactics of propaganda and permeation to educate the Church of England to its social responsibilities and to aid the workers materially by circulating "white lists" of employers who treated their employees according to Christian standards. Under the direction of three of England's foremost theologians—Bishop Gore; Henry Scott Holland, canon of St. Paul's and Regius Professor of Divinity at Oxford; and Bishop Brooke Foss Westcott of Durham (1890–1901)—the C.S.U. developed into the most influential organization of Anglican socialists. By 1910, its peak year, it had 6,000 members, laymen and clergy; 16 out of the 53 episcopal appointments made between its founding in 1889 and 1913 were members.[128] The last organization of importance, the Church Socialist League, was founded in 1906 by dissidents who denounced the C.S.U. as, in Conrad Noel's words, a "mild and watery society"—too intellectual, too respectable, and too gradualist to get to the heart of things.[129] The movement had enough philosophers; it needed crusaders: "Socialism gives new life to the Catholic faith. It is worth while being a Christian. The soldiers of Christ . . . are summoned by Socialism to take part in a Holy War."[130] Although the C.S.L. never had more than 1,200 members, and although none of them became bishops, some had or were to have national reputations: James Adderley; F. L. Donaldson, vicar of St. Mark's, Leicester; Percy Dearmer, editor of *The English Hymnal*; and the young Hewlett Johnson, the future "Red Dean" of Canterbury and holder of the Stalin Peace Prize.

The high water mark of Christian Socialist influence in the pre-war years was reached during the Pan-Anglican Congress of 1908, praised at the time for its "splendid socialism" and as a "socialist field day." An entire morning was devoted to the question of "The Church and Human Society." Speaker after speaker damned capitalism and the values it inculcated. To the question "Does Christianity point towards a Socialist Society, and, if so, ought the Church to be in alliance with the Labour Party?" hardly a negative voice was raised. William Temple, then a newly ordained deacon and fellow of Queen's College, asserted that "the Christian is called to assent to great steps in the direction of collectivism."[131]

The plaudits and statements of principle notwithstanding, men as articulate and as influential as themselves assailed their principles. Mandell Creighton dismissed their doctrine in a devastating epigram: "Socialism will only be possible when we are all perfect, and then it will not be needed."[132] Dean Inge, who possessed a pen as sharp as his intellect, denounced socialism as contrary to the spirit of Christianity, a religion concerned above all with the inner life of man and the fate of his eternal soul. It was absurd and degrading, he argued, for ministers of the Word to be tumbling over one another in their rush to become court chaplain to King Demos and the Labour Party.[133] The dean was supported in this view by the *Church Times*, the largest and most influential of the five Anglican weekly newspapers. In an attack indicative of the animosity with which Christian Socialists had to contend, it warned the Pan-Anglican Congress that the workers' "greed, their self-indulgence, their dislike of obedience, call for stern rebuke. By administering such reproof in the spirit of love much more than by adulation or by pulpit-babblings about the tyranny of capital will the Church be furthering the 'welfare' of the poor."[134]

The *Church Times* needn't have worried, because the socialists failed to persuade the mass of their fellow Anglicans of the necessity of overhauling society. At best, they were a moderately effective advance guard, pathfinders for an army that had other interests and was engaged elsewhere.[135] In terms of gaining acceptance for their brand of socialism (let alone their brand of Christianity) by the Labour party and the trade unions, they made even less of an impression. Whereas many of the early labor leaders and politicians claimed a religious sanction for their socialism, only one maintained a connection with the Established Church. George Lansbury, Labour M.P. and vice-president of the Church Socialist League, was unique in that he remained a staunch Anglican. Contact with the workingman himself was kept to a minimum by all the socialist groups. Only the Christian Social Union attempted to found a working-class subsidiary. In 1897 it founded the Christian Fellowship League with Bishop Gore as president and Dearmer and Adderley on the committee; it disappeared unnoticed and unmourned by the workingman the following year.[136]

No undertaking, from social work to socialism, substantially improved the church's image or ended the estrangement of the workingman. Successes were credited to individual churchmen, not to the church as an institution. Bishop Westcott's arbitration of the strike of 1892 was remembered with gratitude in the coal fields; but it was remembered as his personal triumph. Even the Methodists, who predominated in the mining villages, regarded him as "Brooke our bishop."[137] Anyhow, Westcott's efforts, or the efforts of Bishop James Fraser on behalf of the agricultural laborers in the 'seventies, were generally not those the workingman recalled when he thought about the church; definitely not when he thought about the bishops. As a group, they were either "sky-pilots" lacking contact with the real world, or hard-bitten men, his natural enemies. Two incidents helped fix the latter image and perpetuate the enmity toward the church. Each incident was, ironically, the result of an indiscretion rather than malice. During the hard-fought London Dock Strike of 1889, a committee consisting of the Lord Mayor, Cardinal Manning, Bishop Frederick Temple of London, and three laymen was set up to bring the parties together. When the negotiations broke down, Temple, thinking he could no longer be useful in London, went on holiday to Wales; Manning stayed behind to work out the final compromise. Ben Tillett, the sharp-tongued dockers' leader, had nothing but "contempt" for "the square-jawed, hard-featured Temple," who *would have sacrificed the whole of the dockers to win for his church"*— Temple had, it is true, said "my heart is with the dockers, but my head is with the Directors."[138] From then on, as we shall see, Tillett bore a grudge against the church. Randall Davidson, about whom the second incident revolves, had not been primate long when he, too, acquired a reputation for callousness. In June, 1905, F. L. Donaldson, believing that "Christianity is the religion of which Socialism is the practice," led a highly publicized march of 450 unemployed men from Leicester to London, a distance of 300 miles. When Davidson, who had an instinctive dislike of "sensationalism," was asked to see a deputation, he refused in a manner ill-calculated to serve the church well. George Lansbury felt the affront keenly, remarking that "his answer was that he was in full sympathy, but it was no use seeing him, as he really had not the time to study the question, and so make up his mind what should be done."[139] It must be added in fairness that it was Davidson who intervened and helped mobilize Christian opinion in favor of settling the General Strike of 1926.

That neither the Christian Socialists nor the enlightened segment of the episcopate spoke for the church as a whole is, lastly, confirmed by the fact that, throughout this period, the church press fought the workingman along every inch of his road to a better life. It opposed the minimum wage in the South Wales coal strike of 1899; opposed reducing the work-week from 54 to 48 hours in the engineering industry; and opposed the eight-hours bill for miners.[140] It did, however, support the Taff Vale judgment holding unions liable for losses incurred by employers during strikes and the Osborne Judgment against using union funds for political purposes.[141] The *Guardian*, the highly respected organ of moderate High Churchmanship, was dissatisfied with the Trades Dispute Bill of 1906, because it guaranteed the right to picket peacefully; for if this were legalized, "no employer would ever again be victorious in a strike."[142] The Asquith government's old age pensions scheme was denounced as extravagant.[143] Given these and many other examples of insensitivity,[144] by 1914 it was amply clear that the Church of England had yet to prove itself the church of England's working people.

DOCTRINAL FERMENT AND STRIFE

Whereas everyone agreed that the reevangelization of England should be the primary task, it was impossible to obtain agreement on precisely what constituted the essentials of Christian belief. In theology, as in other branches of knowledge, the quarter-century before 1914 was a period of unsettlement. Theological unsettlement arose from two sources: natural science and the application of historical and textual analysis to the Holy Scriptures. Each threatened traditional beliefs; each stimulated the search for a new apologetic; and each heightened the factional strife within the Church of England.

Natural science in the form of Darwin's theory of evolution proved to be the least threatening to orthodoxy. When first advanced, of

course, it was viewed as a blow to the inerrancy of Scripture and subversive of the moral order. "Society must fall to pieces if Darwinism
be true," warned the *Family Herald* for May 20, 1871. But society
remained intact; to be sure, by 1871 the general theory of biological
evolution had gained respectability, if not total acceptance, among
the educated Anglican public.[145] Only one segment of this public
offered substantial resistance. To the Evangelicals or Low Churchmen, yielding on the age of the earth or the instantaneous creation of
all species meant weakening the authority of the Bible everywhere;
so they clung tenaciously to the doctrine of verbal inspiration.

The theory of evolution could be used to support as well as to undermine faith; for it provided an insight into God's revelation of
Himself in nature. According to the Rev. J. M. Wilson, a renowned
mathematician, Biblical critic, and headmaster of Clifton, evolution
was consistent with the basic tenets of Christianity: the Incarnation,
the Atonement, and the Christian doctrine of sin. The idea of evolution, he claimed in a paper on "The Bearing of the Theory of Evolution on Christian Doctrine," should give cause for pride instead of
scorn. "We are what we are, whatever our origin may have been. I
can imagine no sublimer conception of the nature and the dignity of
man, than that which sees all nature as the self-manifestation of God
rising into self-consciousness in man."[146] That Wilson's message was
not without influence is evidenced by the fact that an earlier sermon
had persuaded the barrister Cosmo Gordon Lang that one could be
intellectually honest and still be a Christian.[147]

More serious than Darwinism was the threat posed by the scientific
approach to the proof-texts of the faith themselves. At the worst,
Darwinism might challenge a tiny portion of Scripture, Genesis,
treated as an allegory in certain quarters long before the nineteenth
century; as early as the 1490's, Dean Colet of St. Paul's and his followers referred to its first chapter as "a poetic fiction."[148] Biblical
criticism, on the other hand, cut more deeply. Emanating from the
German universities, chiefly from Tübingen in the 'forties and after,
the critics ranged over the entire Bible. Through linguistic analysis
and the comparison of texts, the practitioners of the "lower" criticism
sought to establish the correct text of the Bible. The "higher" critics
went further, examining its substance and intent. Their results were
sometimes disquieting to orthodox Christians, as when Julius Well-

hausen revealed in his *History of Israel*, published in 1878 and available in English in 1885, that a substantial portion of the Pentateuch was not written until much later than the events they describe. Other critics, among them Wilhelm Wrede of Breslau, contended that the authors of Matthew and Luke wrote at different times, at different places, and in response to differing circumstances; to be sure, both had leaned heavily upon Mark's Gospel, itself containing interpolations originating elsewhere than with Jesus Himself.

Biblical criticism, high or low, was initially received in England with suspicion. To some of the pious, especially Low Churchmen and the Nonconformist bodies, whose theological position rested more on Scripture than that of the High Churchmen and Roman Catholics, with their strong attachments to tradition and authority, the conclusions of the critics were shocking, seeming to cast doubt upon the entire Bible as revealed and infallible truth. Despite initial resistance, however, from the 'eighties to the end of the century, criticism, first of the Old then of the New Testament, was gradually accepted by the English churches. The year 1889 marked a turning point for the Anglican church. In that year Charles Gore, then Principal of Pusey House, Oxford, edited a volume of essays by a group of Anglican theologians, including his friends Henry Scott Holland and Edward Stuart Talbot, the first warden of Keble College and subsequently bishop of Rochester and Winchester. The most controversial essay in *Lux Mundi* was Gore's own, on "The Holy Spirit and Inspiration." Accepting the verdict of the critics that Christ had mistakenly attributed Psalm 110 to David, he concluded that there were limits to His earthly knowledge. In the ensuing debate, Gore was denounced for having betrayed honest, truth-seeking Christians by questioning their Bible. His mentor, H. P. Liddon, canon of St. Paul's and reputed the greatest preacher of his generation, was deeply wounded and died the next year. Yet, despite the pain he caused, Gore rendered the church an invaluable service by establishing the rights of critical scholarship, thereby easing the transition to the modern age.[149]

Where Gore had passed, others were bound to follow. Before long, critics were ranging beyond the borders of *Lux Mundi*; so far, indeed, that when the theologian and historian John Neville Figgis surveyed the scene in 1910, he sighed "for the halcyon days when the Old

Testament was the main trouble and *Lux Mundi* was thought a dangerous book."[150]

Figgis's concern stemmed from a challenge to the dominant liberal Protestant interpretation of Christianity. Nineteenth century theologians, their work capped by Adolf von Harnack's 1900 lectures published as *What is Christianity?*, interpreted Jesus as the forerunner of their own liberalism. For them, the essence of Christianity was not its dogmatic theology, the product of "Hellenization"—the permeation of Christian thought by Platonic philosophy in the second century—but an undogmatic religion of love, peace, and humanitarianism. Jesus, like themselves, had been a social reformer, if not actually a socialist. "It is certain," wrote von Harnack, "that Jesus never and nowhere wished to keep up poverty and misery, but, on the contrary, he combated them."[151] This view of His nature might give rise to the most simplistic utterances, as when clergymen preached on "The Democratic Jesus and His Democratic Creed," and "the Divine Democrat of Nazareth" who founded His church "and set a handful of working men to preside over her interests."[152] Bishop Winnington-Ingram went further, presenting Father and Son as superheroes of the sort portrayed in the schoolboy adventure stories. God was "that winning Person with the understanding human character, and unfailing tact and wisdom; that Lover of children; that Friend of the young"; Jesus Christ was "that strong, that winning personality."[153]

Albert Schweitzer, scholar, medical missionary, and humanitarian, began the counterattack with a blow from which liberal theology has never fully recovered. Reexamining the liberal position in his 1906 *Von Reimarus zu Wrede* (published in translation in 1910 as *The Quest for the Historical Jesus*), he dismissed the Jesus of the liberal theologians and the critics as a caricature, "a figure designed by rationalism, endowed with life by liberalism, and clothed by modern theology in an historical garb."[154] It was a mistake, he contended, to view Jesus as the supreme moral teacher who set forth laws for achieving the good life on earth. He could only be understood in eschatological terms; for if He taught anything at all, it was that He was the Messiah and that the Kingdom was nigh.

Although dealing specifically with the German liberal theologians, the implications of Schweitzer's work were immediately apparent to

Englishmen. For decades after the Cambridge Church Congress of 1910, nicknamed the "Schweitzer Congress," New Testament study in England was concerned with the eschatological problem.[155] With good reason; for beside presenting Jesus as a prophet who had, in effect, deluded Himself into believing He was the Messiah, Schweitzer had unwittingly struck at the heart of Christian ethics. If his eschatological interpretation was correct, if Jesus had taught an *Interimsethik*, an intermediate morality meant to be practiced by a chosen few, and by these only during the short interval before the Last Days, how could it be made to serve as a guide for all men throughout historical time?[156] Pursuing the argument further, it might be asked what warrant Christians had to argue from the nature of their faith the imperative of social reform, not to mention the reorganization of society along socialistic lines.

While Schweitzer was attacking theological liberalism, others struck out in another direction. The modernists, as they were called, aimed at preventing the estrangement from Christianity of educated men by restating and bringing the basic articles of the faith into harmony with modern thought. Said J. H. F. Peile, archdeacon of Warwick, in the Bampton Lectures of 1907:

The hope and purpose of Liberal Theology have been, and are more than ever today, to make Christianity a possible religion for the intelligent man of the world. It makes its appeal to common sense by submitting the dogmatic and historical tenets of the Churches without reserve to the tests of critical investigation; and ultimately by presenting Christianity not as a creed but as a life, and faith not as the result of an intellectual surrender which is felt to be repugnant to sincerity, but of the normal intellectual processes which apply in the sphere of practice and secular knowledge.[157]

The leaders of the modernist movement in England were men of the caliber of Dr. William Sanday, Lady Margaret Professor of Divinity in Oxford, and B. H. Streeter, fellow of Queen's College, Oxford. Seeing themselves as the saviors of Christianity, it was their self-appointed task to strengthen the foundations of religious knowledge by purging them of obsolete philosophy and unauthenticated tradition. Everything had to be submitted to the tests of science and Biblical criticism; indeed, in 1927 Dr. Barnes, bishop of Birmingham and a trained scientist, suggested that experiments be conducted to prove the impossibility of distinguishing a consecrated from an unconsecrated Host. If science denies the possibility of miracles, so must faith. If the Virgin Birth seems a biological impossibility, strike it from the Creeds. Streeter wrote in a controversial essay on "The Divinity of Christ," his contribution to *Foundations* (1912), that it was unnecessary for the Christian to accept the Gospel account of the Empty Tomb.

Christian ethics must, in the wake of Schweitzer, be set on a base solid enough to stand independent of their namesake. Hastings Rashdall, canon of Carlisle and author of the standard history of the medieval universities, carried this idea to an extreme conclusion. In *Conscience and Christ* (1916), later in *Ideas and Ideals* (1928), he asserted that the validity of the Christian ethic depended not upon its having been taught by Christ Himself, by Him exclusively, or, for that matter, upon His having lived at all. The ultimate seat of authority in religion was to be found neither in Scripture nor in the Creeds nor in the formularies of the church, but in the individual's conscience. "If conscience tells us that the words of Christ are true, they would be true even if those words were wholly the creation of the Church, and none of them uttered by the historical Jesus."[158]

Of all the "foes" of Christianity, modernism was obviously the most dangerous. Whereas scientists and critics, popularizers and atheists, had chipped away at its outworks, the modernists betrayed the bastion from within. The inevitable reaction came first in the Roman Catholic church, where the movement was crushed between 1907 and 1910. Its ideas were condemned in the decree *Lamentabili* issued by the Inquisition and in the encyclical *Pascendi* by Pius X; its leaders, the Abbé Loisy and the Jesuit George Tyrrell were excommunicated; and an antimodernist oath imposed on all clerics.[159]

Given the traditions and the historical constitution of the Church of England, it was impossible to move against deviant tendencies in this fashion. The archbishop of Canterbury is not an Anglican pope; he commands nothing remotely resembling the Roman Curia and the Holy Office. The various ecclesiastical factions and parties abuse each other publicly and with gusto; yet excommunications and trials for heresy are rare; they are expensive, embarrassing, and risk schism and secular intervention. Nor do they always achieve their purpose, witness the decisions of the Judicial Committee of the Privy Council in the Gorham Case, *Essays and Reviews*, and the excommunication of Bishop Colenso of Natal (1865). If modernism was to be opposed effectively, the initiative would have to come from outside the official apparatus of the church.

The initiative for the crusade against modernism came primarily from the Anglo-Catholics, a proud, vocal, and frequently intemperate party. The descendants of those who had remained in the Church after the Newmanite secession, their society, The English Church Union, and the *Church Times*, its newspaper, were widely suspected of wishing to introduce the whole body of Roman Catholic doctrine and practice (everything, that is, except the papal infallibility) into the Church of England. Popular misconceptions about Anglo-Catholicism verged on the bizarre, as when one clergyman, on asking a cabbie to drive him to the offices of the Union, was asked: "Beg pardon, sir, but is it true what they say, as how that society wants to give all Protestants over to the Pope, that he may burn them at Smithfield?"[160]

All the tactics learned in a half-century of rough and tumble party dispute were now employed against this new challenge to orthodoxy. Their response to the appointment of Streeter as canon of Hereford amply illustrates the extent of their hatred. When the appointment became known, Frank Weston, a renowned missionary and bishop of Zanzibar, proceeded to "excommunicate" the bishop who had appointed him—i.e. to have no communion with him in spiritual things —and all those who accepted his action.[161] The war itself failed to silence them. The *Church Times*, which had a circulation larger than all the other Anglican newspapers put together, implied that the bishop and clergy of Hereford were pro-German in their sympathies:

The Chapter of Hereford is now a carefully packed society. The Cathedral is a little Modernist *enclave* within the Catholic Church of England. It is perfectly alien, and frankly hostile to Catholic tradition. For the time being we are compelled to acquiesce in this insulation of a part of the Church, and to regard it as a semi-pagan settlement, worked on principles which might have been made in Germany. The Bishop [John Percival] and his colleagues are determined to enforce upon the diocese their own particular 'kultur', but they will not succeed any more than their kultured models.[162]

This was no mean charge; by 1915 the word "*kultur*" had taken on sinister overtones.

A veritable witch hunt, organized by both Anglo-Catholics and

Evangelicals, was instituted to root out modernist clergymen. From every corner of England came petitions begging the Convocation of Canterbury to "banish and drive away all erroneous and strange doctrine." Some petitions were small, containing a few dozen or a few hundred signatures; others, such as the one gathered by the evangelical Dean Henry Wace of Canterbury contained over 45,000 signatures.[163]

As in so many other causes, Bishop Gore took the lead against modernism. *Lux Mundi* notwithstanding, he was a conservative in theology. Willing to welcome criticism and pursue it to the utmost, he stopped short at the Creeds.[164] When one of his clergy, the Rev. C. E. Beeby, the vicar of a parish outside Birmingham, published an article against the idea of miracles in general and against the Virgin Birth in particular, Gore publicly announced that he considered him unfit to be a teacher in the Church of England and invited him as an honest man to resign, which he did.[165] In the spring of 1914, the substance of his resolution condemning the new ideas was carried in Convocation. Dissatisfied, he then embarked upon a pamphlet war with *The Basis of Anglican Fellowship* (1914), a pamphlet which, from the standpoint of the modernists, undermined rather than promoted Anglican fellowship. Dr. Sanday, H. M. Gwatkin, Dixie Professor of Ecclesiastical History at Cambridge, and Professor A. C. Headlam of King's College, London, rose to the challenge, adding their contributions to the war of words.[166] *The Church Quarterly Review*, a scholarly journal with a liberal viewpoint theologically, received Gore's pamphlet with indignation; *The Modern Churchman*, the chief organ of Anglican modernism, denounced him in an article entitled "An Anglican Pope."[167]

While the struggle against modernism was disturbing the church in England, another storm was gathering in the quiet backwaters of East Africa; a storm that was to cause all of the church's material ills, ideological difficulties, and party rivalries to coalesce into one of the most serious controversies of the early twentieth century. In September, 1913, Frank Weston informed the primate that two of his colleagues were guilty of "the grievous faults of propagating heresy and committing schism."[168] The bishops in question, Willis of Uganda and Peel of Mombasa, anxious to combat "sheep stealing" among the Protestant missionary bodies in British East Africa, had convened at the village of Kikuyu a conference at which it was de-cided to allow members of the different denominations to take com-munion in the churches of societies other than their own.

A shortage of missionaries, precarious finances, and the dissemi-nation by Moslem propagandists of tracts proclaiming the superiority of Islam over Christianity, created a situation wherein tempers al-ready shortened by theological debate erupted with violence. Al-though the general public probably never completely understood, or cared to understand, about the doctrine of the Apostolic Succession as it applied to East Africa, week after week the press was filled with learned articles, letters, and editorials supporting or denouncing the stand of the Kikuyu bishops. For a time, there was a danger that some of the Church's most gifted intellectuals—Gore, Rashdall, and Her-bert Hensley Henson, dean of Durham and a future bishop of Here-ford and Durham—would renounce their Orders if the Kikuyu decision went against their respective parties; Archbishop Davidson made known his intention of resigning unless the parties came to their senses pretty soon.[169]

To break the deadlock, Davidson submitted the entire Kikuyu issue to a consultative committee of eleven bishops, which held its first meeting at Lambeth Palace, his London residence, from July 27th to 31st. But by this time Kikuyu[170] and every other problem plaguing this deeply troubled church had become overshadowed by still greater tragedies. The first day of the bishops' conference found Englishmen glaring at one another across hostile lines, finger on the trigger; on the second day, Austria declared war on Serbia; several hours after the conference adjourned on the 31st, Germany declared war on Russia, and the great peace of the nineteenth century came to an end.

II. THE COMING OF THE GREAT WAR

THF CHURCH AND THE DOMESTIC CRISIS

For the Church of England, as for Englishmen in general, the year 1914 may be divided into two roughly equal parts. Both parts were marked by crises so deep as to menace the survival of the nation itself. Yet, such are the imponderables and sudden changes influencing life in this aeon, that the predictions, optimistic as well as pessimistic, made in the first part of the year proved to be correct in the second part; correct, albeit for the wrong reasons. The year had begun with bright prospects for continuing peace among the nations and with the dismal prospect of continuing civil strife and the possibility of civil war. It ended with England united as never before, but fighting for her life in a war unparalleled in human experience.

The domestic crises represented the simultaneous coming to a head of problems originating in the nineteenth century and earlier, and desperately needing solution by 1914. Although each of the crises followed its own course, having little to do with the Church of England directly, each touched it in some way, threatening to pull it down in the general chaos. These crises, moreover, together with the internal problems unsettling the church, diverted clerical attention and absorbed clerical energies, with far-reaching consequences when the supreme crisis came later in the year.

The mood of the New Year was in marked contrast to the festivities that ushered out the old year, regarded by society columnists as the most lavish (or garish, depending on the viewpoint) within memory. The early months of 1914 found Englishmen troubled by forebodings of impending disaster. In January, the *Church Times* noted that the year had opened with a cloudy horizon. Equally apprehensive, the *Guardian* observed that "on the whole, the fourteenth year of a century would seem more or less under the influence of Mars."[1] Neither paper, of course, had the slightest premonition of the war that would begin in the summer. What they feared was the immediate danger of civil war in Ireland.

Ever since Mr. Asquith's government, armed with the powers of the Parliament Act of 1911 to override the Lords' veto, had introduced its Home Rule Bill in April, 1912, the rhetoric of violence had mounted in an ever-increasing spiral. Fired by hundreds of sermons, and led by Sir Edward Carson, a former solicitor-general for England and a demagogue of superlative ability, thousands of Unionists signed at Belfast (September 28, 1912) a document whose title must have had an ominous sound to anyone familiar with the history of England in the seventeenth century. "Ulster's Solemn League and Covenant" was a call to rebellion, pledging its signatories to refuse to accept a Home Rule parliament in Ireland. In the following July, another mammoth meeting of Ulstermen adopted a resolution to resist Home Rule by force of arms if necessary. By Christmas, their military preparations had matured to the point where the Society for Promoting Christian Knowledge (S.P.C.K.) thought it advisable to issue special collects imploring the Almighty to spare the nation the calamity of civil war.[2]

Believing its continued prosperity and ultimately its existence to be linked to the independence of Ulster, the Episcopal church in Ireland, never entirely reconciled to its disestablishment and disendowment in 1869, dug in its heels for a fight. It had long been taken as a truism that, once the seven northern counties were united politically with the rest of the country, the Protestant minority would face instant pauperization and persecution by the priest-ridden Roman Catholic majority in the south. It would be 1642 all over again, only this time without a Cromwell to defend Protestant interests.

The Home Rule Bill had barely been introduced, when the General Synod of the Church of Ireland, supported in due course by its Presbyterian and Methodist counterparts, declared its unalterable opposition to Parliament's violation of Ulster's ancient rights. The Irish episcopate stood solidly behind the Orange cause, the bishops of Down, Clogher, and Derry having signed the Solemn League and Covenant.[3] Archbishop Crozier abandoned any pretense to impartiality, sending his blessing to Carson, who received it while standing under massed Orange banners. C. T. P. Grierson, dean of Belfast, consecrated the colors of Volunteer units and encouraged them to show determination and steadfastness in maintaining their principles. In an unusual interpretation of the requirements of Christian love, he proclaimed: "The law of love demands that we should use force to protect that which God has committed to our keeping for the welfare of the community. If the proposed legislation would result in bringing economic ruin to our land, if our liberties would be contracted, if freedom of thought would be imperilled, if the free exercise of our common Protestantism would be endangered, then we hold that the law of love demands that we should resist unto the death."[4]

Ulstermen needed little encouragement to vent their hatred of Home Rule in terms of a virulent anti-Catholicism. To the old Orangist battle hymns, "The Boyne Water," "Derry's Walls," and "The Sash my Father Wore," they added "Dolly's Brae," a libellous tune commemorating a clash in 1849 of armed Orangemen and Catholics on Lord Roden's estate. Shouted rather than sung, one verse, concerning two Roman Catholic priests, should be sufficient to give its flavor:

> Priest Mooney and Priest Murphy went through the rebel
>   lines,
> Distributing the wafer God among the Philistines;
> Priest Mooney cursed the Orangemen with candle, book and
>   bell,
> While the rebel crowd did cry aloud, 'We'll drive them
>   all to hell.'[5]

The irate Catholics, determined to have the last word, retaliated in kind: "Up a long ladder and down a short rope, to hell with King Billy and up with the Pope."

Not content to aid Ulster with prayers, blessings, and words of encouragement, clergymen of the Church of Ireland put their public school rifle corps training to practical use, teaching local contingents of Volunteers the rudiments of military drill. Remote country rectories were designated for use as army headquarters and staging areas in case it became necessary to enforce an "alternative" on the day Home Rule became law.[6]

The Irish crisis was one of those occasions when the divisions of the Anglican church into High, Low, and Broad parties lost their significance. There was never any doubt that, if Home Rule became a serious issue, churchmen would feel bound to side with Ulster, as they had done in 1886 and 1893, when practically the entire Bench was present in the Lords to vote down Mr. Gladstone's measure.

None of these groupings, or the newspapers promoting their respective points of view, favored subjecting Ulster to a parliament sitting in Dublin. The Evangelicals, ever on guard against the triple-headed monster of Rationalism, Ritualism, and Romanism, denounced the advocates of Home Rule with a vehemence commonly reserved for their Anglican adversaries. From the introduction of the Home Rule Bill until the outbreak of war two years later, the chief organs of Evangelical opinion, the *Record*, an influential newspaper with a wide readership during its heyday in the nineteenth century, the *Church Intelligencer*, and the Protestant Truth Society appealed to ingrained fears of "papal aggression." At the other extreme, the Anglo-Catholics, considered by the Evangelicals crypto-papists, condemned the Orangemen as bigots and blasphemers, "men whose sole confession of faith is to curse the Pope and eat meat on Friday. They call herrings 'Popish chickens' and 'two-eyed-beef-steaks.' "[7] They saw little difference between them and the followers of John Kensit, fanatical antiritualists given to rioting in church, shouting down bishops, and covering the chasubles of celebrants with spittle.[8] Yet not even disdain for the Orangemen and their methods could persuade Anglo-Catholic dignitaries like Lord Halifax, dubbed Anglo-Catholicism's "lay pope," to sanction the imposition of Home Rule at the point of the bayonet.[9]

The archbishops of Canterbury and York worked diligently behind the scenes to inject an element of rationality into the Irish problem. The primate himself acted as the intermediary between Mr. Asquith and Andrew Bonar Law, the official leader of the Unionists in the Commons;[10] but rationality was in short supply that spring and they were unsuccessful. Voices grew shriller as the situation continued to deteriorate with each passing day. On March 3, a National Appeal declaring that if Home Rule became law they would sanction actions aimed at preventing the army from coercing Ulster was published over the signatures of (among others) Lords Roberts, Milner, and Halifax, Rudyard Kipling, and Dean Wace of Canterbury. Shortly thereafter, the "mutiny at the Currah," the resignation of army officers whose regiments would be charged with enforcing Home Rule, and the landing of 35,000 Mauser rifles at Larne the next month,[11] brought Ireland to the brink of civil war. The events of July nearly forced her over the brink. On Sunday, July 26, the Nationalists of the Catholic south, emboldened by the success of their adversaries, successfully landed 1,500 rifles at Dublin. At Bachelor's Walk, a detachment of the King's Own Scottish Borderers, frustrated by their failure to apprehend the gunrunners, and provoked by the taunts and brickbats of a large crowd, turned and fired, killing three and wounding many others. The next morning found Irishmen north and south mobilized and ready to kill one another.[12]

The fate of Ireland, though the most pressing, was by no means the sole cause for alarm. In *The Condition of England* (1909), C. F. G. Masterman had divided the population into three categories: the "conquerors" who owned the largest share of the nation's wealth, the "suburbanites" who served them as managers and white-collar workers, and the "prisoners" who kept the wheels of the economy turning. The prisoners had become increasingly restless since the publication of his book; so much so, that by the summer of 1914 they were openly rebellious. Men spoke of a repetition of 1848, only worse. Prophets of doom, always in plentiful supply, predicted great disorders, "something like the French Revolution," in the near future.[13]

In the three and a half years preceding the war, the number of workers represented at the Trades Union Congress had increased by 60 percent. Confidence in numbers, the failure of wages to keep apace of the cost of living, intractable local issues, and the growth of syndicalism and industrial unionism combined to make the unions, especially those representing the newly organized general workers, more aggressive. The number of strikes increased dramatically, from 857 in 1912 to 1,497 in 1913; with 937 strikes in the first half of the year alone, 1914 promised to break all records. A most dangerous situation began to take shape in July, when the Scottish coal owners announced a reduction in the minimum wage in most areas from 7s to 6s, a substantial sum to the workingman. Loyal to its northern brethren, the Miners' Federation of Great Britain announced it would strike if the reductions were put into effect, thereby compelling the transport and railroad unions to support their associate in the "Triple Alliance." September, October at the latest, promised to find England in the grip of the first general strike in its history.[14]

The "labour unrest," as it was euphemistically called, though not a matter of immediate concern to the church, produced in ecclesiastical circles a decidedly hostile reaction, which in turn must have compromised the efforts of the Christian Socialists to infuse the labor movement with Christian ideals. Dean Inge voiced the sentiments prevailing among his associates when he denounced the unions as criminal combinations whose leaders deserved to be executed as rebels against society.[15]

The battle of the sexes, however, excelled in tone and occasionally in actual violence the quarrels of Orangemen and Nationalists, labor and management. During the nineteenth century, the middle-class woman had achieved impressive, if hard-won, victories. Economically, she was winning her independence. The Married Women's Property Acts (1870, 1882, 1893) had released her from dependence upon her husband by guaranteeing her right to hold and dispose of property without his consent. The opening of the universities, the teaching profession, and certain branches of the civil service enabled her to develop her capabilities and become self-sufficient. In the political sphere, there was also reason for encouragement. Given her eligibility to vote in municipal elections after 1868 and for county councils after 1888, it seemed only a matter of time before she would receive the parliamentary franchise as well.

Paralleling women's slow progress toward economic and political emancipation was a demand for what, in effect, amounted to psychological autonomy from, and parity with, men. Unwillingness to live in a man's world on man's terms, frustration with the empty lives imposed upon them by the conventions of gentility, and resentment of the sexual double-standard combined somehow[16] with the ongoing and essentially peaceful agitation for the franchise. Whatever their reasons for fastening upon the vote, by 1914 the Women's Social and Political Union under Mrs. Emmeline Pankhurst and her daughter Christabel, the leading group, had undergone a transformation. It was no longer in the mood to be patient and act according to accepted norms; indeed, its actions, far from being ladylike, actually became criminal. Beginning in the spring of 1912, the members of the W.S.P.U., or simply the suffragettes, intensified their agitation. Clashes with the police, noisy demonstrations, and window breaking became the order of the day. One suffragette went so far as to insult the king, calling him a "Russian Czar" for ignoring the women's cause. Harassed members of Parliament, hitherto content with jokes about pregnant prime ministers and installing special conveniences for their would-be colleagues, now demanded strong repressive measures. But mass arrests, accompanied often by unnecessary brutality on the part of the police and male onlookers, provoked the militants further. More women were imprisoned, and if they refused to take food, it was forced down their throats. Loath to furnish them gratuitously with a martyr, Parliament passed in 1913 a "Cat and Mouse Act" enabling the Home Secretary to release starving women and rearrest them when they regained their health.

The implementation of the Cat and Mouse Act, represented pictorially on the cover of the *Suffragette* and in posters as an enormous "Liberal" cat holding a limp young woman in its blood-smeared jaws,[17] touched off an orgy of senseless destruction. Mrs. Pankhurst's shock-troops, no longer satisfied with harassing ministers and petty vandalism, resorted to attacks on the institutions of society. Letter boxes were set on fire, castles put to the torch, and the National Gallery forced to shut down after the Rokeby Venus by Velazquez was slashed and Sargent's portrait of Henry James mutilated. Suffragettes learned to make bombs. Irene Casey, a pretty wisp of a girl from Bradford, was sentenced to fifteen months in jail for possession of explosives intended to blow up the Royal family.[18]

Even if it had wanted, it was impossible for the Church of England, the oldest and easily the most vulnerable pillar of the Establishment, to dodge the suffrage issue. Sentiment in favor of women's suffrage, especially among those clergy involved in the Christian Socialist movement, developed early. In 1912, it became concentrated in the Church League for Women's Suffrage. Consisting of over 5,000 Anglican men and women, plus the bishops of Kensington (Maud) and Lincoln (Hicks) and Henry Scott Holland, the C.L.W.S. advocated the enfranchisement of women as the next logical step in the democratization of England. Regarding the way the police treated demonstrators, and the way elements of the religious press condoned and even encouraged their excesses, that was contemptible. "A gentleman," Holland chided the *Church Times*, "should remember that he is speaking of girls. A Christian should never forget the bond of common humanity. But from your tone one would suppose it was a matter of knocking rats on the head in the back yard."[19] Though they deplored the treatment accorded these "girls," several of Holland's colleagues neglected to apply their principles uniformly; they refused to condemn militancy on moral grounds, because recourse to extra-legal measures were sometimes the only way to right a still greater wrong.

Notwithstanding the oft-repeated argument that women should be denied the franchise because they fall easily under the influence of priests, for the most part the priests of the Established Church viewed the matter differently. It went without saying that the "new woman," cigarette-smoking and with a devil-may-care attitude—let alone the likes of H. G. Wells' free-loving *Ann Veronica* (1909)—offended their sense of propriety. Their "ideal" woman, the stock woman of the Victorian treatises of family life and the public school sermons,[20] was a delicate, all-suffering, self-effacing creature whose prime concerns might be summarized by the German *"die Küche, die Kirche, und die Kinder"*—kitchen, church, and children. The Christian religion, according to this view, regarded her as a "weak vessel," but one whose very weakness entitled her to special consideration. Inherently sentimental and flighty, she was incapable of exercising the same political functions as men. She had privileges instead of rights, notably of being protected and treated with honor and respect. Make her man's equal, take away her privileged position, and the mutual sympathy between the sexes would evaporate, as would the moral restraints against her exploitation by the physically stronger sex. Besides being undignified—"Can we imagine the Blessed Virgin Mary wanting a vote in Parliament, or to harangue vulgar listeners?"[21]—enfranchisement would destroy her femininity and turn the Home, man's haven in a stormy world, into a pandemonium of political argument. The desire of some ultra-militants to remove "obey" from the marriage service, as well as their advocacy of family planning, was proof-positive that they had taken leave of their senses and should be kept from tampering with the electoral process.[22]

The passage of the Cat and Mouse Act signalled a downward course in church-suffragette relations. Immediately the church, as the keeper of the national conscience, became a focal point for their appeals. Archbishop Davidson received scores of letters, petitions, and delegations demanding he throw the resources of the church behind the women's cause. An early supporter of votes for women, it was his policy never to commit the church officially in questions where fundamental moral issues of right and wrong were not involved. Here was the rub; for the treatment of the militants by the authorities, which he thought a strictly administrative and police matter, enthusiasts regarded as the deliberate torture of innocents.[23] To bring home their point, women students of church history turned the ancient (and obsolete) custom of sanctuary into a device for embarrassing Davidson and the church. In May, 1914, Mrs. Pankhurst sent a trusted lieutenant, Annie Kenney, to demand sanctuary at Lambeth Palace until women won the vote. After meeting Mrs. Davidson and having a long, heated argument with her husband, she was arrested, the suffragettes having taken care to notify the press and the police of her whereabouts.[24] As planned, the *Suffragette* and the letter writers responded in their characteristically abusive manner. "If Annie Kenney dies," one wrote in a woman-centered version of the Incarnation, "surely you cannot acquit yourself of the awful responsibility of her death! The sin of Pilate is being repeated again by you. In refusing sanctuary to Annie Kenney, you have driven away your Lord from your doorstep."[25] Miss Kenney weathered Holloway Prison with flying colors, descending soon after her release on the bishop of London. He was more fortunate; for when she presented herself, bag and baggage, at Fulham Palace, he asked her with his disarming naiveté whether, given his bachelor status, people might not wonder about her spending the night in his house.[26]

The bishops' personal inconveniences, however, were insignificant, compared with the reign of terror Miss Kenney's friends initiated against the church. Angered by refusals of support, and bent upon gaining the most publicity for their cause, they interrupted bishops' sermons and stopped the chanting of the Litany. On several occasions women chased preachers from the pulpit, haranguing their congregations until removed bodily by the police. Churches were disfigured, bombed, and burnt to the ground. A bomb was discovered in St. Paul's, another placed under the Coronation Chair in Westminister Abbey; Wargrave Church, in Berkshire, was totally destroyed; and the interior of Birmingham Cathedral painted with the slogans "the Church has a great responsibility towards women," "the clergy must rise on our behalf," and the ubiquitous "Votes for Women." Things had reached the point where one never knew what to expect in the house of God, or what protective measures to adopt. The Ulstermen,

fearful of neither the forces of militant Catholicism nor the Imperial
Parliament, prudently insured their churches against the ravages of
these Amazons. In certain English churches, the clergy, their patience
exhausted, employed strapping teenagers, members of the Church
Lads' Brigade, as guards.[27] But events were to spare worshippers the
spectacle of boys and women brawling in the aisles of buildings consecrated to the worship of the Prince of Peace.

PEACE IN THEIR TIME

Critics have maintained that, once war begins, the Church of England, protesting its incompetence to rule on complicated matters of
policy, unquestioningly accepts the decision of the government of
the day; or what is more reprehensible, consecrates the national
cause regardless of whether it is right or wrong. "Where," asked
J. A. Hobson, the author of a classic work on *Imperialism* (1902),
"have the priests ever failed to bless a war supported by authority
and popular passion? . . . In England the State Church has never
permitted the spirit of the Prince of Peace to interfere when statesmen and soldiers appealed to the passions of race-lust, conquest, and
revenge."[28]

Hobson's basic premise is correct. In a nationalistic age, the mass
of clerical opinion has consistently and vociferously supported the
foreign adventures of the government, as has public opinion in general. Yet his censure is unfair, inasmuch as it is indiscriminate, im-
plying a unanimity that was not in fact the case. The Church of
England has never been a monolithic institution in the sense that it
requires its communicants and functionaries to subscribe to an orthodox interpretation of current events; indeed, no church has ever had
such a requirement, it being rather a characteristic of the absolute
secular state. On occasion, some of the church's most respected personalities have defied the opinion prevailing in church and state.

In the matter of the Bulgarian Horrors of 1876, practically the
entire episcopal Bench denounced the government for not condemning Turkey.[29] Twenty years later, Bishop Percival was still belaboring
the government for courting and propping up the throne of the despicable Turk.[30] During the Boer War, which was the occasion for
Hobson's attack, the church's leadership was divided, although the

majority supported the official policy. Every view had its defender.
There were those who, like the archbishop of Armagh, waxed poetic
about the ethereal qualities of war:

> They say that 'War is hell,' the 'great accursed,'
>   The sin impossible to be forgiven—
> Yet I can look beyond it at its worst
>   And still find blue in heaven.
> And as I note how nobly natures form
>   Under war's red rain, I deem it true
> That he who made the earthquake and the storm
>   Perchance made battles too! [31]

Long-time friends and collaborators disagreed on matters of principle. Bishop Westcott, the champion of arbitration in industrial disputes, was adamant when the issue involved England's imperial
obligations. Expressed in Kiplingesque phrases, these obligations
were "to bear patiently the thankless burden of the white man and
train the uncivilised races to a noble life." [32] Henry Scott Holland, on
the other hand, disagreed with Westcott, risking the obloquy of his
colleagues to protest the Government's policy in South Africa. As
founder, editor, and chief contributor to the *Commonwealth*, the
monthly magazine of the Christian Social Union, he turned its columns into a soundingboard for antiwar propaganda. As canon of St.
Paul's, he delivered from its pulpit a stream of "pro-Boer" sermons.
"How do we pity those whom we so hopelessly outnumber, struggling
for an independence so passionately loved, and so fatally wrecked,
on whose little state we are bearing down with the entire weight of
an enormous Empire!" [33] A particularly scathing sermon, coinciding
with bad news from the garrison besieged in Ladysmith, was not
calculated to endear him to the press; naturally his sermons remained
as biting as ever.

   In view of these and other divisions over the Boer War, and in
order to understand the background of unanimity of Anglican opinion in the summer and early fall of 1914, it is well to pause here to
examine the relationship of the churches to the peace movement that
emerged in the decade or so before the Great War. Their activities
may be traced through the published reports and membership lists of
the numerous conferences, congresses, and societies that flourished
during this period.

These sources provide the researcher with scant reward indeed.[34] It is perhaps ironic that, in the century since the founding of the first peace societies in England in the wake of the Napoleonic wars, the churches should have been so backward in preaching to the world the Gospel text of which they are the custodians. Instead, the peace movement was led and organized by humanitarians and philanthropists such as the American publisher Edwin Ginn and Andrew Carnegie, as well as by men from the socialist and labor movements —men often divorced from religion. Only the Society of Friends, the backbone if not very nearly the entire body of Christian representation in the peace movement, bore a consistent and continuous *corporate* witness to the ideal of peace on earth.

There was ample opportunity for the churches to seize the initiative; yet they allowed their opportunities to pass. Take the first British National Peace Congress, composed of representatives of the peace societies of the United Kingdom, and held in Manchester in 1904. Its 240 delegates represented 24 nonreligious peace societies, 27 secular organizations of various kinds, 32 Friends' quarterly and monthly meetings, and a mere 9 religious bodies of unspecified denomination.[35] Down to 1910, only one of the high officers of the congress was affiliated with a church: Bishop Percival was president in 1905. Whereas the number of peace societies and other organizations affiliated with the National Peace Council grew from 68 in 1910 to 95 in 1913, only 4 religious societies (exclusive of the Quakers) were added: the Catholic Peace Association; the Knights of the Prince of Peace, whose denominational affiliation and activities I have been unable to trace; the Church of England Peace League, to be discussed below; and the Jewish Peace Society.[36]

The Hague conference provided further opportunities for bringing the peace issue before the religious public. Apart from a few bland leading articles in the press, the First Hague Conference (1899) caused hardly a ripple on the surface of ecclesiastical affairs. The Second Hague Conference (1907), called at the suggestion of President Theodore Roosevelt in 1904 but postponed on account of the Russo-Japanese War, attracted more attention. Purely a diplomatic gathering and therefore restricted to the plenipotentiaries of the participating states, church people as such were excluded from participation. Nevertheless a deputation representing the English churches arrived at The Hague bearing wishes for Godspeed and resolutions distinguished above all for the skill with which their generalities were phrased.[37] The Representative Church Council and the Convocation of Canterbury passed resolutions in the same vein.[38] Their effect on the conference was nil. W. T. Stead, the renowned peace advocate and crusader against the white slave traffic, doubted whether twenty out of the two hundred delegates ever darkened the door of a place of worship. "So far as I could discern there was no possible difference in the moral standpoint of Christians or of non-Christians . . . . The Conference was opened and closed without religious ceremony of any kind. In none of the debates was there even the most distant allusion to the existence of a Supreme Being."[39]

The Second Hague Conference, however, was not without some consequences in the religious world. J. Allen Baker, the Quaker president of the Free Church Council of London and M.P. for East Finsbury, was one of those very lovable and very persistent Victorian cranks possessed of an *idée fixe*.[40] In Baker's case, it was the conviction that the prerequisite for world peace was the union of the Christian churches for this desirable goal. While at The Hague as a delegate of the committee bearing the memorial from the churches, he conceived the idea of an exchange of visits between German and English clergy and laymen. This would forge the first link in the world alliance of Christian forces. Accordingly, he set up a joint committee including, for England, himself as chairman, and Archbishop Davidson, the bishops of London, Southwark and Kensington, Lord Robert Cecil, Lloyd George, Henry Scott Holland, Arthur Henderson, and Basil Wilberforce, archdeacon of Westminster and the youngest son of a former bishop of Oxford. The German delegation of 130 visited England from May 26 to June 3, 1908, to register an "appeal to all classes in both nations to promote . . . a mutual spirit of goodwill and friendship." Allowing for the good cheer of the participants (fostered doubtlessly by the repeated "hochs" and "heils" toasted at the banquets), it is certain that, as far as they were concerned, the emblem of the tour represented the sentiments of both sides at this time: the emblem consisted of the Imperial Eagle and the Lion and the Unicorn, each surrounded by a wreath and these intertwined; above, hovers a white dove; below, a garland with a ribbon bearing the inscription *"Pax Mundi."*[41] The following year, an English delegation of similar size, including six Anglican bishops and eleven members of Parliament, returned the visit and was warmly received by the kaiser at Potsdam.[42]

The peace-related activities of 1908 were capped by the Seventeenth Universal Peace Congress held in London from July 11 to August 1. Composed of representatives of peace societies throughout the world, the first of these congresses had been held in 1889 under the leadership of Frederick Passy and the Englishman Hodgson Pratt. Delegates had assembled regularly thereafter in various cities on the Continent, England, and the United States.

This congress attracted more church participation than any heretofore, having among its vice-presidents J. Allen Baker, John Clifford of the Baptist World Alliance, Cardinal Bourne of Westminister, Bishop Percival, J. E. C. Welldon, and the Rev. Samuel Barnett. For the first time an Anglican group, the Oxford branch of the Christian Social Union, was represented at a peace gathering; it had to share the hall, however, with the Rationalist Press Association, also devoted to peace.[43] The formal opening of the congress was preceded by a Christian Conference on Peace presided over by Bishop J. W. Diggle of Carlisle, of whom we shall hear more in subsequent chapters. The Pan-Anglican Congress, whose meetings were taking place simultaneously, sent a delegation bearing the usual message of greeting, temperate and noncommittal. The Anglican episcopate, "while firmly acknowledging the moral gains sometimes won by war," rejoiced in the growth of "higher ethical perceptions" as manifested by "the increasing willingness to settle difficulties among nations by peaceful methods."[44]

The foregoing summary is, admittedly, not a definitive index of the participation of the churches in the peace movement. Nevertheless it sheds light on a condition well-known to contemporaries and deplored by them. The Christian Conference on Peace, for example, left onlookers with the feeling that corporate Christianity was largely unconcerned about peace. At best, its participation was regarded as a token; all the more because the Anglicans were constantly excusing themselves to attend the Pan-Anglican meetings. Led by Mr. Asquith, several speakers lectured the churches on their apathy.[45] A few overstepped propriety. During a Congress-sponsored labor demonstration in Trafalgar Square, Ben Tillett, soaring on the wings of his own rhetoric, denounced them with facile and spurious arguments. "The churches were strong enough to prevent war if they chose," he is reported to have said, "but they were supported by capitalists, war-mongers, scare-mongers, and people of that kind, and so long as that state of hypocrisy continued peace would never be attained."[46] Cooler heads shared the platform that day; yet not a word of contradiction was uttered by J. Ramsay MacDonald; by Mrs. Charlotte Despard, a leader in the women's suffrage movement; or by the Baroness Bertha von Süttner, holder of the Nobel Peace Prize and author of the pacifist classic *Lay Down Your Arms*. They may have thought that the English workingmen, whose choruses sang the "Angel of Peace" and who carried placards bearing the Commandment "Thou shalt not kill," were more in the spirit of the Gospel than the clergyman in the pulpit.

Not until the time had run out did the churches lend support to the peace movement by setting up their own international organization. Here again, J. Allen Baker was the driving force. As an outgrowth of the exchange visits of 1908–1909, he set about creating a worldwide Christian peace movement. At a meeting in the Albert Hall (February 2, 1911), with the archbishop of Canterbury presiding and leading German religious figures in attendance, including Adolf von Harnack, the Associated Councils of Churches in the British and German Empires for Fostering Friendly Relations between the Two Peoples was launched. By 1913, the "British Council," with Baker as chairman and Archbishop Davidson as president, was claiming a membership of 10,000 in the British Isles and a circulation of some 60,000 for its journal, *The Peacemaker*.[47] The American Peace Society was formed shortly after the Albert Hall meeting, and early in 1914 the Swiss churches invited the churches of the world to a conference at Constance. Representing fourteen countries, the Protestant sections met on August 1, brought the World Alliance for Promoting International Friendship through the Churches into being at a hasty meeting, and dispersed while return transportation was still available.[48]

The efforts of the churches on behalf of peace were, therefore, too little and too late. Yet, in terms of the high personages and publicists who lent their names and sometimes donated their labors to the cause, the Church of England did better than most. The question of the Church's duty in furthering international peace and its relationship to war was taken up at five church congresses: 1885, 1896, 1900, 1911, and 1913. The Lambeth conferences of 1897 and 1908 issued encyclicals advocating arbitration and other peaceful means of resolving disputes between nations.[49]

The activities of a handful of clergymen ranged beyond the formalities of congresses and resolutions. In October, 1910, a group of former "pro-Boers" joined other interested churchmen in founding the Church of England Peace League. Nonpacifists save for a small segment of lay people, they had banded together for the purpose of keeping before their church the ideal of peace as part of the Divine ideal of human society and to promote international goodwill through working for the adoption of arbitration and conciliation.[50] Judging from the published lists of subscriptions and donations, the League was never large. In its best year, 1914, receipts totalled just under £69; it published no membership lists. The League nevertheless managed to carry on an active propaganda program, in addition to sponsoring lectures by its officials. These were well-known figures: the president was Edward Lee Hicks, bishop of Lincoln and a respected Greek scholar; serving as vice-presidents and on the executive committee were, among others, Bishops Gore and Percival, Hastings Rashdall, George Lansbury, William Temple, and the Rev. T. J. Lawrence, rector of Upton Lovel, Wiltshire, author of several textbooks on international law, and the only man in Holy Orders to be elected to the Institute of International Law. As to whether the League and like-minded persons succeeded in awakening the Anglican conscience to the urgency of disarmament and other measures, W. L. Grane, canon of Chichester and the author of a well-received book, *The Passing of War*, was certain that it did not. Viewing the situation in 1912, he dismissed the claim that the churches of Britain had "laboured earnestly" for peace. "I am quite sure that the Church of England has not. Among the multitudinous Societies and Organisations for every imaginable propaganda, no sort of association for promoting either the Peace of the World or any other kind of Peace Ideal, ever existed until about a year ago, and perhaps a hundred names would nearly exhaust its present membership."[51]

Viewing the events of 1914–1918 with the vantage of hindsight, it is tempting to admire the prescience of the Cassandras who warned about the impending holocaust and to condemn the shortsightedness of the apathetic. But to judge the prewar situation exclusively from the standpoint of the Cassandras would give a distorted picture of opinion at the time. There is plenty of evidence from men equally intelligent and far-sighted discounting the likelihood, if not the possibility, of a world war. Aside from genuine apathy and preoccupation elsewhere, the explanation of a good deal of ecclesiastical unconcern for the peace movement lies in the fact that peace was taken for granted and a world war was unthinkable. With all the small wars in the Far East and the Balkans, all the war-talk, invasion scares, and saber rattling, humanity did seem to be improving and becoming more rational. From churchmen and nonchurchmen, we repeatedly encounter such phrases as friendship and brotherhood "are in the air" (Archdeacon Wilberforce), internationalism "is in the air" (John Clifford), and "the *Zeitgeist* is on our side" (the Rev. J. M. Rendall, headmaster of Winchester College).[52] The 1914 edition of the *Peace Yearbook*, the National Peace Council's directory of organizations engaged in promoting international understanding, reveals unbounded optimism about the prospects for humanity:

Peace is no longer the tender infant of the Peace organizations . . . but has become the problem of the world. Peace, the babe of the nineteenth century, is the strong youth of the twentieth century; for War, the product of anarchy and fear, is passing away under the growing and persistent pressure of world organization, economic necessity, human intercourse, and that change of spirit, that social sense and newer aspect of worldwide life which is the insistent note, the *Zeitgeist* of the age.[53]

During the first decade of the twentieth century, the older humanitarian arguments based on the horrors of war were giving way to arguments more congenial to the time. Men learned from Prince Peter Kropotkin's *Mutual Aid* (1902) that war was contrary to the principle of human association. They learned from the Marxist journalist H. N. Brailsford that war was practically impossible in a world where the international economy was organized along capitalistic lines; the leaders of finance capitalism who controlled the foreign policy of their respective governments were greedy, wicked men, but they were not fools. His *The War of Steel and Gold*, published in March, 1914, contains the famous gaffe: "the frontiers of our modern national states are finally drawn. My own belief is that there will be no more wars among the six Great Powers."[54] Norman Angell's *The Great Illusion* (1910), one of the most talked-about books of the time, taught that the nations were inextricably bound together economically, so that a major war would paralyze them, forcing them to conclude peace within a few weeks or months. Even if one power emerged victorious, it would not enjoy the fruits of victory for long, since its booty would be drained off by the economically more efficient states.

These ideas, so naive to later generations, were then accepted and applauded by knowledgeable men, whether at church congresses or peace congresses or in cabinet offices. Free trade means peace, proclaimed the chancellor of the Exchequer, David Lloyd George. Disputes arise from misunderstanding of another's intentions. Peace is in the rational order of things; war is the supreme irrationality—and it hurts business.

Do nations hate each other; do the people hate each other? (Cries of 'No.') In Germany you have a number of labourers who are producing beet. They sell masses of it to us. Well, why should they kill their best customers? This is the worst way of getting on in business. (Applause.) We buy tens of millions worth of goods from Germany. Why should the Germans kill us? They buy thirty million pounds worth of goods from us. Why should we want to kill them? Really, when a man comes to your shop and does a good trade with you, you don't knock him down with a cannon ball. That is not the way to get on with him. It is not the way to increase your trade. What folly, what stupidity this is![55]

Nations were in fact settling their disputes peacefully, through arbitration. Between 1820 and 1880, 82 cases were settled by this method; between 1880 and 1900, there were another 90 cases of arbitration. In the fifteen years since 1900, over 150 arbitration treaties were signed, and the trend showed every indication of continuing.[56] Granted, most settlements involved matters of minimal importance and with little potentiality for war. But some did; there is no telling how many lives were saved by the successful arbitration of the Alabama claims (1872) and the Venezuela boundary dispute (1896).

Settlement of disputes through arbitration, however, hardly implied universal disarmament. Despite the arguments for disarmament, it was thought that if nations were armed, and provided they did not make serious miscalculations, their armaments guaranteed that unreasonable people would think twice before disturbing the peace of the world. Business aside, the Edwardian armaments-makers, surveying the longest period of peace in modern history, were utterly convinced of the deterrent capabilities of their product.[57] So was the archbishop of Canterbury. Nations must be armed, he told the Covocation of Canterbury, quoting with approval the remark of an American statesman during the great naval review of 1897: "Look there!" he exclaimed as the steel Leviathans steamed past, "By heaven, that means peace."[58]

ON THE EVE OF WAR

In view of the disorder and militancy disturbing church and state, as well as their confidence in the essential rationality of the international order, English people understandably paid scant attention to events on the Continent. The murder of the heir to the Austrian throne, the Archduke Francis Ferdinand, and his consort passed quickly across the front pages, failing to dislodge the escapades of the suffragettes and other matters of more immediate concern. Save for the usual obituaries and expressions of condolence, save also for a certain amount of fumbling with the atlas to locate Sarajevo in Bosnia, interest in the tragedy soon flagged. Only toward the end of July, after the Austrian ultimatum to Serbia, did the public pause to recognize that the unthinkable, a general European war, could start momentarily.

With the exception of the *Record*, the only paper failing to mention the assassination, the Anglican press affirmed unanimously its sympathy for the ill-starred House of Habsburg. The Emperor Francis Joseph, "the patriarch of Europe"—he had ascended the throne in 1848—was universally pitied. He seemed always to be in the shadow of some new tragedy. First the execution of his brother, the Archduke Maximilian, in Mexico; then the suicide of his son; and finally the assassination of his own wife were really more than any person should have to bear. The response of the *Church Times* was typical. After receiving the news from Bosnia with "a thrill of horror," it recovered in time to express a "passionate feeling of pity for the aged Emperor-King in his crowning sorrow."[59]

Unanimity in condemning the assassination failed to carry over into interpreting its significance. On this, two schools emerged. One saw it as a racially inspired murder, the outgrowth of the age-old conflict of Teuton and Slav; the other took a more philosophical approach. That the archduke should be slain by a Slav was, according to the first, a grim irony, as he had favored a tripartite division of power in the Empire between German, Magyar, and Slav. His forward-looking policy was, however, counterbalanced by his support of Bulgaria against Serbia in the most recent Balkan war and by the continued resentment by the Bosnians of the Austrian occupation of their country.[60] The *Church Times* took a different view, seeing the tragedy as part of a Europeanwide malaise manifesting itself in political murder. The archduke, it maintained, had been murdered for irrational motives, religious fanaticism, and a morbid hatred of the man and his policies. It concluded with the reflection that, however bestial, regicide was self-defeating because it improved the image of its victims; after all, "a man whose duty it is to be shot at gains respect."[61] But irrespective of how they interpreted the assassination, the prevailing mood was one of relief that for once there was an issue that did not concern England.

The tempo of English life continued as before. July was a delightful month, sunny and warm; one could forget for a moment the upheavals in society. The daily papers contained page after page of pictures of Boy Scouts on their way to camp, factory girls splashing in the surf at Brighton, and crowds of tourists bound for the Continent. In Convocation, in the ecclesiastical journals, and in their sermons the clergy of the Church of England allowed foreign affairs to recede into the background. The various conferences held between June 28 and the end of July turned their attention exclusively to problems of Establishment, changing moral standards, and the relation of religion to industrial problems; everyone had an opinion about Kikuyu. The Convocation of Canterbury spent its time discussing the position of women in the councils of the church and the revision of the Lectionary. The crusade against the Welsh Church Bill, news of General Huerta and the latest Mexican revolution, pleas for funds to assist the Church of England Mission to Hop-Pickers, and problems of parochial finance provided the main topics in the leading article columns of the weekly press.

Apart from the unpleasant news from Ireland, there seemed every reason to be hopeful about the international situation. The Agadir Crisis of 1911, though "decidedly disconcerting," had passed without a shot being fired.[62] And even if Adolf von Harnack unburdened himself to correspondents about English duplicity and an anticipated descent on the German coast in 1912,[63] relations between the two Great Powers were better than they had been for some time. The archbishop of Canterbury thought so, writing in June, 1913, to his friend Dr. Ernest Dryander, the court chaplain to the kaiser: "At this moment everything is tending toward a truer understanding of the essential brotherhood of Germany and Great Britain." At year's end, the liberal journal *The Nation* corroborated his appraisal: "Nothing more than a memory is left of the old Anglo-German antagonism."[64]

Powerful contingents of the British and German navies lay side by side at Kiel on the very day of the assassination. The crews had been enjoying races and salutes, fraternal strolls and banquets. The kaiser's spirits were never higher, his mood broken only long enough to scold the harbor police for arresting Lord Brassey, a man of seventy-eight and an expert in naval affairs, when he rowed too close to the Imperial Dockyard. He recovered immediately, and during a visit to the *King George V*, the British flagship, hoisted his ensign as an admiral in the Royal Navy, joked with everybody, and graciously accepted the cheers of the sailors. On July 17, a week before the Austrian ultimatum to Serbia, Lloyd George remarked to a group of bankers at the Mansion House that, "In the matter of external affairs the sky has never been more perfectly blue."[65] On the 23rd, the day Austria presented her ultimatum to Serbia, he urged the House of Commons to cut armaments expenditures because of the "altogether better feeling" between Germany and Great Britain, and because the points of cooperation between the two countries were "greater and more numerous and more important than the points of possible controversy."[66] On the 27th, the day before they went to war, the *Manchester Guardian* acknowledged that the situation was ominous. Yet its mood hardly matched the gravity of the situation. Since large-scale fighting could not begin for at least another two weeks, diplomacy would have all the time needed to localize this latest Balkan war where it belonged, in the Balkans.

The religious press, dependent on the mass-circulation dailies for its items of political news, reflected the general optimism. The visit of France's President Poincaré to Russia was bound to have a calming influence on Germany, convincing her of the folly of encouraging Austria in its newest Balkan adventure. The crises of the last fourteen years had demonstrated repeatedly that the Powers were guided by men determined to get all they could for their countries, but sensible enough to back off when they had overplayed their hands. There might be war in the future, but it would come when least expected and arise from a minor occurrence![67] War seemed so unlikely that on the 29th, the day following Austria's declaration of war on Serbia, the archbishop of Canterbury was "amazed" on being told by Margot Asquith that she had stopped her sister from going to paint in France and telegraphed her daughter to return without delay from Holland.[68]

Since they were published on Thursday and Friday, all Anglican papers appeared too late to record the assassination of Jean Jaurès, the French socialist leader, and the declaration by Germany of *Kriegsgefahrzustand* (prewar mobilization) on the 31st. Despite Germany's unwillingness to avail herself of Sir Edward Grey's offer of a conference of the Powers in London, there was still no reason to question her intentions; indeed, she was believed to be exerting pressure behind the scenes on Russia to localize the conflict. The kaiser, later branded the supreme war criminal, was the man of the hour, the champion of peace. "The Kaiser," said the *Church Family Newspaper*, a paper inoffensive in tone, central in churchmanship, and read chiefly in suburban and rural England, "is using his great influence for peace, while making—naturally enough—every preparation to fulfill his obligation to Austria."[69] Whereas these preparations gave the diplomats less room to maneuver, they would at least encourage them to work harder.

Published on the previous day (July 30), the *Guardian* was the first to suggest that England would be obliged to fight if Germany attacked France. True, the *Entente Cordiale* was only an informal understanding; nevertheless, it placed England under the moral obligation to defend the French Channel coast, especially since the capital ships normally assigned this task had been transferred to the Mediterranean by agreement with Britain. Concerning Belgium, neither the *Guardian* nor its competitors was concerned about a violation of her neutrality. Its leading article writer, confident that the treaty of 1839 afforded all the protection she needed, thought the most feasible route for an invasion of France lay through the lightly defended Meuse Valley.[70]

This dream-world atmosphere permeated the highest councils of state. Reporting on an interview with Mr. Asquith (July 31), the primate agreed with his evaluation of the European situation. The Great Powers, they believed, were averse to fighting over "the vagaries of a wild little state like Serbia, for which nobody has a good word, so badly has it behaved." England, the one state capable of preventing a general conflagration, must keep her intentions secret, because France and Russia would never act against the Central Powers unless assured in advance of her support. Germany, meanwhile, ever sensitive to the balance of power in the world, "shrinks from aggressive action—e.g. through Belgium [sic!], because it does not know whether or not we should immediately oppose; and, if we did, their task would be doubled in difficulty." Asquith closed the interview by begging Davidson to exert his influence in preventing the circulation of memorials and the holding of demonstrations in favor of nonintervention, as these might lead the quarreling Powers to misread the intentions of the government and overestimate the passivity of the populace. In this Davidson presumably complied.[71]

Raised in a country where Russia rather than Germany or Austria was the traditional villain—children were told the Czar would bundle them off to Siberia if they misbehaved—how many clergymen uttered "amen" on reading the denunciations of Russia for seeking to bully Austria? As late as 1904, when the Russian Baltic Fleet, steaming toward its rendezvous with the Japanese Fleet in the Straits of Tsushima, mistakenly fired on English vessels fishing off the Dogger Bank, ministers of religion joined in the outcry for immediate compensation or immediate war.[72] They now found it difficult to accept the prospect of their country's having to fight alongside of the most backward and autocratic state in Europe. As "An Appeal to Scholars," an open letter signed by university professors and theologians —F. J. Foakes-Jackson, Kirsopp Lake, F. C. Burkitt—put it: "War upon [Germany] in the interests of Servia or Russia would be a sin against civilization."[73]

Of the thousands of sermons preached on Sunday, August 2, most were never reproduced at all; fewer than one hundred were summarized or reprinted in the provincial press. Those that are accessible, however, are remarkably devoid of chauvinism, as a rule combining a tendency to recoil from the very thought of war with resignation as to its inevitability. Yet here and there, especially in the industrialized North, where the church had to contend with a strong Nonconformist element, an occasional Anglican preacher denounced the policy of intervention. The Rev. J. J. Wilson, rector of St. Michael's, Manchester, went so far as to beg the German consul to acquit him personally "of any participation in this great sin if my country should so far err as to fight with yours."[74]

There are also several instances of clergymen participating in demonstrations against intervention or working for local branches of the Neutrality League, an ad hoc committee of intellectuals: Gilbert Murray, Ramsay MacDonald, G. M. Trevelyan, J. L. Hammond, and others. A neutrality manifesto, drafted apparently on August 2, appeared in the *Manchester Guardian* on the following day.[75] Two bishops, Hicks and Percival, added their signatures to a long list of those trying to impress the government with the strength of neutralist sentiment. Intervention, they reckoned, would necessitate abandoning England's time-honored policy of maintaining the balance of power. Once again, Russia was portrayed as the stumbling-block to peace. An Allied victory, purchased with God knew how many lives, would be in reality a triumph for Czardom, raising thereby the specter of Russia's emerging as the premier power in Europe, possibly "the dictator both in this continent and in Asia."[76]

Far and away the most important sermon on that last Sunday of peace was by Randall Davidson. He was solemn. As he began to speak, cries of "votes for women" from suffragettes who had chained themselves to the seats rent the silence of Westminster Abbey. The suffragettes expelled by the police, he began to speak. His task was difficult. On the previous day he had written in reply to Dr. Dryander's inquiry whether the Church of England would consider taking part in the Jubilee of the four-hundredth anniversary of the Reformation in 1917, that war between two great Christian nations "is, or ought to be, unthinkable in the twentieth century of the Gospel of the Prince of Peace."[77] He now had to find words for the nation's bewilderment at this grave moment. He could offer little encouragement. What was happening was "fearful beyond words." This "thing," as he called it, was the work of the Devil, not of God's making. Nevertheless, a last minute reprieve was always possible; but whatever happened, he wanted everyone to know that the discipline of war had been imposed upon England for her own good. God's purpose might be detected even in the present tragedy, and "we have to take heed that it is not wasted."[78]

THE LIGHTS GO OUT

In the weeks following Davidson's sermon, the attitudes of his countrymen underwent a transformation of unprecedented completeness and rapidity. The Karl Barths and the Reinhold Niebuhrs would later denounce the easy optimism of their mentors, the men of the prewar generation, as secularized versions of a bankrupt theological liberalism. They would say that their predecessors had constructed a utopia out of their dreams, ignoring all the while the element of sin rooted in human nature. To a certain extent they were correct; their own "theology of crisis" was, after all, the product of the frustrations of that generation. As we have seen, the men of the early twentieth century were frequently more optimistic about a dawning age of peace and plenty than might be suspected with the advantage of hindsight. Herein lies the key to their initial response to the war. When it came, it burst upon them as a bolt from the blue. It frustrated their expectations and shattered their world; to be sure, not a few had the physical sensation of dizziness or of being cast adrift. Recording his initial impressions, the Rev. R. H. Lightfoot, vice-principal of Wells Theological College, noted: "The complete and absolute break-up of everything in which we hitherto have felt secure: of all that we truly trust in: of all that, as we say, we take for granted in this world: suddenly we feel it give, begin to go and slip from beneath our feet."[79] "Can life ever be again for us, who are old or middle-aged, what it has been?" the fifty-two year old Hensley Henson asked a friend. "All the pilot-stars of my political thinking seem to have fallen out of the sky, and I have not the ghost of a notion where we are all driving to."[80] Without warning, reason had ceased to operate in the cosmos, or at least it had momentarily fled from a part of it. One need not look to the superpatriots to see the reaction; everyone knew where *they* stood. It is the peace advocates, the champions of liberalism in religion and politics, who epitomize the revolution in attitudes.

Almost every denomination mentioned thus far as playing a part in the peace movement "went over" to the war. The August and September, 1914, issues of their journals—*The Catholic Herald, The Tablet* (a Jesuit publication), *The Baptist Times and Freeman*, and *The Methodist Times*—contain leading articles and editorials supporting British actions. For the Congregationalists, Sir William Robertson Nicoll's *British Weekly* carried on a vigorous anti-German propaganda. Initially strong for neutrality, its first editorial after the declaration of war, "United We Stand," supported the war completely.[81] John Clifford, "pro-Boer" and hammer of militarists, announced in a famous pamphlet, *Our Fight for Belgium and What It Means* (1917), that support for the Allied cause was a religious obligation: "The path of duty shone out in clearest light, and wherever it might lead us we had to go. It was a pillar of cloud by day and a pillar of fire by night. We must follow."[82] Even the Quakers wavered, albeit momentarily. The war was scarcely two months old when *The Friend* stated editorially that "the nation has entered this struggle in a just cause and has a right to claim the cooperation of her citizens." It went on to say that when force had met and conquered force there would be time enough for spiritual influences to come into play. There were, it concluded, "far worse [things] than to take part in this struggle."[83] The editors' point, however, that, while England's participation was ethically justified, Quakers must remain true to their historic abstention from war, was lost on a handful of younger Friends. By 1915, these, risking ostracism from their meetings to follow the promptings of the Inner Light, had enlisted in the army.[84]

The reaction was as intense among Anglicans. Among the signers of the neutrality manifesto of August 3, Bishops Hicks and Percival shared similar interests, came to similar conclusions about the war, and may therefore be considered representative of the moderate elements that came to favor intervention.

As president of the Church of England Peace League, Bishop Hicks had long worked in the cause of peace. In 1900, when still canon of Manchester, he had been a member of the Manchester Transvaal Peace Committee and author of a tract, *The Mistakes of*

Militarism (1901), denouncing the South African War as a sordid, imperialistic venture. The crisis of 1914 took him by surprise. War he had always regarded as a tragedy; war with Germany was plain fratricide.[85] Now he expressed himself in an eloquent sermon (August 3) warning that Britain had no formal alliance with either France or Russia, or quarrel with Germany. Rushing into war without reason would tempt Providence.[86]

Realizing that all his work and prayers and hopes had come to naught, during the next few days Hicks's feelings went the gamut from stunned disbelief at what the world had brought upon itself, to gloom at the apparent bankruptcy of organized Christianity, to anger at the invincible stupidity of "rational" men. Yet his anger abated almost as quickly as it had come; for after wrestling with his conscience, and seeing his son enlist (to die soon after), he concluded that the war had been forced upon England by "a nation gone mad, a nation possessed of a horrible idea . . . a nation that should have been our friend but has become our bitterest enemy."[87]

His associate, Bishop Percival, had done more than any single churchman to promote the peace movement. As early as 1896, he had denounced "that bastard patriotism" which gloried in oppressing others and which it was the duty of the church to eradicate.[88] He later earned a reputation as a "pro-Boer," opposing the government's South African policy because he feared it would demand the unconditional surrender of the Boer republics.[89] During the "mafficking" in Hereford following the peace treaty, a mob had marched on his palace; fortunately an alert coachman saved the day by closing the gate in the nick of time.[90] Besides serving on the executive committee of the Church of England Peace League and as president of the School Peace League, an organization devoted to enlisting the support of teachers and infusing into curricula the ideals of the peace movement, Percival found time in a crowded schedule either to be present at, preach to, or preside over various peace congresses. Upon rising to deliver the keynote address at the Boston Peace Congress of 1904, he had received a tumultuous ovation. In 1909, he had been the ornament of the delegation visiting Germany. Upon returning, he told the Convocation of Canterbury of the "overflowing kindness and hospitality" the delegation had received from all seg-

ments of German life from the kaiser downward. The German workers, he said enthusiastically, were "solid" for peace.[91]

August, 1914, found Percival horrified by what seemed man's
incapacity to control events. Publicly, he called for restraint, joined
a committee to counter the war-mongering section of the press, and
wrote every incumbent in Hereford to hold parish meetings for the
purpose of sending neutrality resolutions to Downing Street; privately, he admonished his friends to persuade local government authorities to follow suit. Although his immediate reactions to the
declaration of war are unknown, given his background, they were
probably similar to Hicks's; his statements certainly were. On August 12, the *Times* published his statement on the crisis in the form
of a letter. In reply to implications in certain quarters of disloyalty on
the part of those active in the peace movement, he defended his associates but lashed out at German cynicism and duplicity. When this
stern moralist spoke of duty, those who had been schoolboys under
him at Rugby knew what he expected of them: "Such a war is a
heavy price to pay for our progress towards the realisation of the
Christianity of Christ, but duty calls, and the price must be paid for
the good of those who are to follow us."[92]

His last and most important public statement on the war was made
in his Charge to his diocesan clergy in 1915. In it he made no mention of the tragedy that had befallen his family. But everyone knew
that he was devastated in that way peculiar to old men who have
seen their sons die; for in October, 1914, the apple of his eye, Colonel
Arthur Jex Blake Percival, was killed leading his troops at Ypres. His
words must have been painful to him, yet he was firm, insisting that
the Allies were "the predestined instruments to save the Christian
civilization of Europe from being overcome by a brutal and ruthless paganism." He concluded in a more ominous vein, calling upon
the nation to fight until complete victory was won "and the law of
Christ firmly established as the paramount authority in all national
and international affairs."[93]

A similar pattern quickly developed among the various factions of
the Christian Socialist Movement. Continental socialists had affirmed
repeatedly the solidarity of the workers of the world. Denouncing
war as the outgrowth of capitalism, they had even discussed the

feasibility of the socialist parties and the trade unions preventing war by a series of crippling general strikes.[94] These strikes never came to pass. When war actually began, national loyalty being stronger than class solidarity, socialist legislators voted war credits and their constituents dutifully reported to their regiments. In England, the reasons put forward by Ben Tillett typified the prointerventionist position of labor. Writing in *John Bull*, the most jingoistic and hate-filled of the mass-circulation papers, Tillett called the workers to arms because capitalism, with all its evils, was preferable to enslavement under kaiserism.[95] In certain respects, the major socialist groups within the Church of England faced a worse dilemma than their secular counterparts. Whereas they were spared the responsibility of having to decide on war credits, they had to reconcile their religious beliefs and socialistic ideals with the realities of world war.

Henry Scott Holland, as we have seen, had no qualms about taking governments to task when he thought them to be in error. In August, 1914, he was adamant about nonintervention, writing to the papers to plead ("with all my soul") for neutrality. It was to no avail. Then, with a violence uncharacteristic of this gentle, considerate scholar who enjoyed corresponding with children, he lashed out at the mass insanity that impelled rulers and subjects alike to cast civilization into the cauldron, all for the sake of a despicable little state like Serbia.[96]

As with the others, we can follow in outline the stages of his conversion. By September he was writing to a friend that "every day reveals the black blind horror of Prussianism. It is the very devil. It has to be fought: and killed. It is the last word in iniquity. I could not have believed that men could be so diabolical"—this was an early manifestation of the process of diabolization that would poison public opinion and make a negotiated settlement impossible.[97] By the end of the year, he had come to believe that England was not merely duty-bound to fight, but that the war involved issues of ultimate right and wrong. "We are eschatologists. God *must* win. We cannot have anything else."[98] Finally, by January, 1915, he had reached the point where he could portray the declaration of war as England's response to a summons from the Beyond, a fleeting glimpse of the Infinite:

And under the sway of such a direct spiritual emergency we seemed for
the moment to catch a sight of the eternal challenge which is the creative
power behind all history—which is always there, always will be. Now it
had blazed out, flung off all accretions and accumulations of time and
chance, and we stood face to face with God, and we made our answer in
His eyes. And we saw in an instant what He wanted, and so we took our
place within His purpose. 'Come up hither,' so the voice cried, 'and I will
show you things that shall be.' And the world-drama was laid bare, and we
saw the looms of God at work. We felt astir with the pressure and the tu-
mult and the heat of those tremendous forces by which the energy of God
is always driving our human story forward toward its great culmination.[99]

From this time until his death three years later, Holland supported
the war effort, using at the same time his considerable literary talents
to persuade Englishmen to observe their traditional standards of fair
play and humanity in its conduct.

Unlike the Christian Social Union under Holland, which came out
early and unequivocally for the Allied cause, the Church Socialist
League could never make up its mind. This was due in large measure
to its heterogeneous membership. Certainly an organization consisting of some holding opinions not commonly associated with the
tenets of Christian Socialism was ill-prepared to take a firm position
on the war. The Rev. Egerton Swann of St. Mary's, Paddington
Green, a theological modernist and a Fabian, trembled lest the
Labour Party displace England's natural rulers, the landed classes;
Paul Bull used to give homilies likening the British Empire to the
Kingdom of Light.[100] In any case, serious in-fighting among the executive board delayed a formal statement of policy until April, 1915.
That statement, still indecisive, was prefaced by an admission that
insoluble differences existed within the organization. The only point
everyone could accept was that war was evil, having its roots in
human sinfulness and the irreligious conditions arising from the rejection of the Gospel.[101]

Aside from a middle group that hoped participating in the national
effort would give socialists a claim to a voice in determining the
peace, the League was torn by conflicting enthusiasms. Egerton
Swann, whose hatred of Germany verged on the pathological, was
the natural leader of the prowar faction. The conflict, he asserted,
was both inevitable and desirable: "it would have been a thousand

pities that it should not have been." For a man who had never heard
a shot fired in anger, he had unbounded confidence in war as an uplifting experience, a "splendid," "magnificent," "divine" experience.
Humiliating defeat would do Germany a world of good, knocking
the conceit out of her once and for all.[102]

Swann's blood-lust found its match in pacifist intransigence. An
anonymous article appearing in the *Church Socialist*, "Murder in
the Thieves' Kitchen," admonished the workers to think of themselves first and to "remember that the private quarrels of the sons of
Mammon are not ours, for we are enrolled in the Catholic Army of
the Kingdom of God."[103] Equally divisive was the response of George
Lansbury. There seemed no chance of compromise when Lansbury
moved at the League's annual conference a resolution to the effect
that wars would cease only when groups of men and women ("peace
armies") would stand willingly between the opposing lines, offering
themselves as sacrifices for the love of God and their fellowmen.[104]
In the face of fascist aggression twenty years later, a similar stand was
to provoke from Ernest Bevin one of the most scathing denunciations
ever uttered by one labor leader against another.

Not everyone was as definite in his views as Lansbury. Clerical
utterances during the early days of the conflict frequently manifest
contradictory feelings. In practically the same breath as they condemned war as the antithesis of the Gospel message, "hell with the
lid off,"[105] the most unmilitant individuals implied it was not necessarily an unmitigated evil. After considering the disasters so narrowly
averted, there was a broad consensus in favor of the proposition that
a short, victorious conflict was an acceptable price for restoring
national unity. Until Christmas, 1914, and then intermittently for
the duration of the war, a favorite gambit of preachers was the "holy
interlude"[106] when the voice of faction became stilled and the spirit
of brotherhood diffused throughout the land. In restoring national
unity, war had wrought a miracle, or so it must have seemed to those
weary souls who now heard the Pankhurst women denounce Hun-
coddlers, arm-chair strategists, and pacifists of every description. Better still, one can imagine their relief on hearing Mrs. Pankhurst
proclaim: "If we women, with all our grievances against men, can
hold our tongues, I think other people might do so."[107] Labor became
quiet for the time being, and on August 3 John Redmond, leader of

the Irish party in the House of Commons, promised to join hands with the Ulstermen against the common enemy. Well might Henry Scott Holland become elated by this turn of events: "God save England! God save Ireland! The great reconciliation is achieved. A new era in English history has dawned."[108] Other clergymen, impressed by the unexpected alliances brought about by fear of a common enemy, looked forward to an era of peace and cooperation. God had "miraculously" united old enemies: England aiding France a century after Waterloo; Russia allied to England and France sixty years after the Crimean War; and most miraculous of all, Russia and Japan comrades a mere decade after Port Arthur. Exultation, a confidence that, even with the world fast going to ruin about them, God was preparing a better world, pervades the early war sermons. "May the guns ring in a new age of wider charity, a bigger God and a larger heaven."[109]

And so the clergy of the Church of England went to war. They had neither wanted nor expected a European war; but when it came, it furnished an issue upon which all could agree. Whereas a majority undoubtedly favored England's role in the South African War, a respected and vocal minority opposed it, becoming the nucleus of the peace movement that took shape afterwards. In 1914, representatives of both groups opposed involvement in a general war until the moment their country committed herself irrevocably. Once war became a reality, they united to support England in her moment of need. Although it is unlikely that the clergy supported the war with absolute unanimity, the Anglican newspapers, periodicals, diocesan magazines, theological journals, and the regular provincial newspapers—at least the ones I have seen—never mentioned any who opposed it. They may have adopted a policy of self-censorship. Yet I have come across nothing to indicate that this was indeed the case. Certainly the few organizations opposed to the war would have welcomed endorsements from clergymen of the Established church. These were never forthcoming. With the exception of laymen like George Lansbury, whose Anglicanism and religious-based pacifism made him unique among labor leaders, even Christian Socialists approved of their government's actions; for this time they were convinced that England had right, as well as might, on her side.

III. THE NATURE OF THE ENEMY

Having become involved in a catastrophe that daily unfolded the potentiality for evil locked within the human heart, the first order of business was to sort out and explain the reasons for its having broken out in the first place. Christianity places great emphasis of self-examination. In times of stress the impulse of the devout Christian is to look inward and to ask what he personally, or the society of which he is a member, has done to bring down the wrath of God. This was true of the clergy of the Church of England, as well as those of other denominations, during the first weeks of the Great War. Anglo-Catholics, Evangelicals, modernists, and Christian Socialists all shared a feeling of shame and guilt at the moral failings of their country. Yet, despite their having certain ideas in common, each assigned special significance to one factor as being primarily responsible for the conflict.

The most popular and easily intelligible explanation of a purely religious nature was advanced by long-time opponents, the Evangelicals and the Anglo-Catholics. If they agreed on anything, it was that the war represented a judgment from Heaven, a calamity "sent" by the Lord to punish the nations of the West, and especially England, for their sins. The root of the evil lay, of course, in a misdirected faith: faith in God had been replaced by "faith in progress," an umbrella term covering all the false values cultivated by the materialistic, industrialized, urbanized, secularized civilization of the early twentieth century. Church people had for years warned that the nation, cut loose from its spiritual moorings, was drifting away from God. One after the other, they saw the traditional outward expressions of reverence decline or disappear almost entirely. Bible reading and family prayer had become rarities, practiced only among the old-fashioned; church attendance declined from one religious census to the next, while the circulation of Sunday newspapers and the profanation of the Sabbath by trading, excursions, and a host of vulgar entertainments continued to increase. It seemed as though no earthly force was capable of stemming the tide of sin, revealed in the steady increase in drunkenness, gambling, prostitution, and the divorce rate.

The views of Bishop Winnington-Ingram were typical of this mode of thinking. Since his early days as head of Oxford House in the East End, he had worked closely with the Public Morality Council of London, an interdenominational organization devoted to lobbying for stronger legislation against immorality. England, he said, deserved God's wrath; for despite all his efforts, the use of the parks for immoral purposes, the output of salacious books and films, and the dissemination of birth control propaganda and appliances continued to flourish.[1] One of his diocesan clergy, the vicar of All Saints', Margaret Street, was more vehement, asserting that in prewar England "the race was going from bad to worse; the worship of God was disappearing from our land. Hard, godless women were springing up in multitudes about us, increasing numbers of them refusing to bear children, and increasing numbers who had families were incapable of bringing their children to the feet of Christ. . . . Well, the patience of God is exhausted, and the angel of death has appeared over the land, his sword in his hand."[2]

The government, which should have been the outstanding example of obedience to God's Word, was possibly the worst offender. Spurred by an alliance of secularists, Nonconformists, and Welsh nationalists it had introduced in April, 1912, the Welsh Church Bill, dubbed by its opponents "the Church Robbery Bill." Sponsored by the religious press, a Million Shilling Fund was begun and demonstrations and protest marches, sometimes numbering ten and twenty thousand participants, held to protest the threatened disestablishment and disendowment of the Episcopal church in Wales. The coming of war less than three months after its passage into law seemed an unmistakable sign of divine displeasure. For the remainder of 1914 the newspapers printed scores of letters warning against being too sanctimonious; for the spoliation of the Welsh church was worse than even the burning of Louvain and the bombardment of Rheims by the Germans. England had no right to pray for victory until she repealed the Welsh Church Act; indeed, God would send disaster after disaster until England made amends.

Proponents of this theory seldom confined themselves to reciting

England's sins. All the belligerents, they thought, were suffering for specific acts of commission. France's separation of church and state, Germany's injustices in Poland, Austria's withholding of the God-given right of nationality from her Slavic minorities, and Russia's persecutions of the Jews were all worthy of punishment. Even "poor little Belgium" had the Congo atrocities between herself and God.

The difference between the modernists and other groups was illustrated by the conclusions they derived from their evaluations of the same evidence. From the very beginning, strong reservations, occasionally outright hostility, marked their attitude toward the punishment theory. On the second anniversary of the war, B. H. Streeter described it as merely a panic-reaction to the suddenness of the catastrophe, and therefore inadequate to explain the causes of the war; after all, a judgment sent by God should have some justice in its working.[3] Hastings Rashdall was less generous, insisting that, as far as England was concerned, divine punishment could not be a factor because the war was "neither a judgment, nor a punishment, nor a sin, but the finest piece of national righteousness of which this nation has ever in modern times shown itself capable."[4]

Members of the Christian Social Union and the Church Socialist League also tended to minimize the divine agency in Europe's tragedy. When they spoke of punishment, they meant the self-in-flicted suffering occasioned by faulty institutions and the values they fostered. All modern wars were, according to this definition, only indirectly wars of "policy," being in reality "the full blood-red flowers of Capitalism."[5]

The Rev. Paul Bull, an officer in the Church Socialist League, exemplified the Christian Socialist attitude. Beginning in 1904 with *God and Our Soldiers*, his recollections of his chaplaincy during the South African War, and in *Manuals for the Million*, a series of homiletic pamphlets, Bull warned that as long as society was organized on the principle of unrestrained competition and individualism, so long would there be war. He saw the prospects for the capitalist system as gloomy indeed: either it would be overthrown by its wretched wage-slaves or perish in a war arising from its need for ever-expanding markets. Bull was not surprised by the outbreak of the Great War; what did surprise him was that capitalistic civilization had managed to survive for so long.[6]

To others, however, attributing a catastrophe of such immense proportions to a single theory of human sinfulness or of economic causation was too simple, failing to account for all the known facts. There was sufficient material available to allow for a more broadly based interpretation. There also developed, as we shall see, the need for a new interpretation, one that would place the blame exclusively on one Great Power: Germany.

NAMING THE GUILTY

In doing the research for this section I was, to my surprise, unable to discover anti-German sentiment in the prewar church that would account for the intensity of the hatred that surged up after August 4. Quite the contrary; for throughout the nineteenth century, clergymen, indeed the English ruling classes generally, were given to a pro-Teutonic, if not always to a definite pro-Prussian, bias. Although Bismarck's early wars, with Denmark and Austria, were denounced as aggressive, the cause of a united Germany under Prussia never lacked influential supporters. At the outbreak of the Franco-Prussian War, several of the major literary figures of the day lauded the God-fearing, duty-loving Prussians. Once again France, Tennyson's "red fool fury on their Seine," would get a well-deserved drubbing. The Rev. Charles Kingsley, to mention the prime example from the ecclesiastical world, saw the Germans as the descendants of virile, noble savages. It was their ancestors, the Gothic warriors he portrayed in *Hypatia* (1853)—also a favorite with German readers[7]—and the heroic *Hereward the Wake* (1866) who had rejuvenated the decadent Roman world and championed Anglo-Saxon freedom against William the Conqueror. "Were I a German," he wrote during the battle of Sedan, "I should feel it my duty to my country to send my last son, my last shilling, and after all, my own self to the war, to get that done which must be done, done so that it will never need doing again."[8]

The picture of Germany that emerged as the century progressed revealed a nation bound to England by both racial and dynastic ties; a nation which, like England, had thrown off the "papal yoke" in the sixteenth century; a nation of teachers and scientists and chivalrous warriors. The Germans were held up by public school headmasters as a people of the highest moral standards. To illustrate an appeal to young people to remain pure, F. W. Farrar, headmaster of Marlborough and subsequently dean of Canterbury, told how those assigned to bury the dead after the battle of Sedan discovered that, whereas the knapsacks of the Germans contained pages from Holy Scripture, the French knapsacks contained books "tainted through and through with the leprosy of uncleanliness." Lecturing on "The Kingdom of God and the Ideals of Manhood" to a meeting of Anglican youth, J. E. C. Welldon held up the elder von Moltke as the exemplar of the union of character, courage, and intellect.[9]

The speeches during the 1908 visit of German church people lend further insight into the attitudes prevailing in religious circles a few years before the war. During the various meetings, speakers stressed that Germany had been the home of English democracy, an interesting example of how the findings of scholarship diffuse among the general public. Beginning in the early 'seventies, the works of Bishop William Stubbs, notably his three volume *Constitutional History of England to 1485* (1873–1878), one of the monumental works of nineteenth century historiography, set forth the thesis that the English constitution originated in the laws and customs of the Germanic successors of the Roman Empire. A popularized "Stubbsism" was rife during the meetings of 1908. According to J. E. Ellis, a member of Parliament and a well-known figure in the peace movement, "since the olden days, when our forefathers stood and watched together and fought together for their freedom in the days of the Roman Empire, they carried with them their love of freedom and liberty. Since those days, we of the Teutonic stock have been distinguished for two things, our love of liberty, and our devotion to religion."[10] At that same meeting, Bishop Winnington-Ingram, the Germans' London host, was effusive. Having spent eighteen months in Germany after graduating from Keble College in the early 'eighties, he considered himself an authority on Germany. His welcoming speech, laced with guide-book expressions like *"Wunderbar hübsch!"* and *"Ach die schöne luft!"* praised the Germans for their music, industriousness, and family life. In view of his anti-German tirades six years later, it is worth quoting a portion of his peroration:

If you want to love Germans and Germany, go and live as I did in Germany. I will tell you some of the things that will make you love Germans

and Germany. You will find there such kindly feelings toward England.
. . . I carried away first—and you would if you visited Germany—a sense
of the genuine friendship of the people towards our country. . . . I say,
should we not love a nation like that? Why, it is akin to our own! We are
cousins, nay, we are brothers to the Germans, and therefore, as a nation,
I say, '*Wir alle lieben Deutschland und die Deutschen.*'[11]

Germany's challenge to England's supremacy at sea and her ex-
pansionistic policies failed to alter this flattering picture appreciably.
When the German naval building program began in the 'nineties,
several Anglican newspapers asserted that she should be allowed to
develop her military potential, since only the eventual alliance of
the Germanic powers of Central Europe, England, and the United
States could save civilization from being overwhelmed by the tide of
oriental and Slavic barbarism.[12] Lloyd George himself affirmed (at
the Seventeenth Universal Peace Congress no less) that it was England's determination to maintain a ratio of two-to-one in capital ships
that had touched off the armaments race. Furthermore, Germany
had as much right to her army as England had to her navy. "Her
army is to her what our navy is to us—her sole defence against invasion. Yet she has not got a Two-Power Standard."[13] As to German
expansion, as late as 1913 Anglican bishops, professors of theology,
and newspapers saw it as a natural and in certain respects a laudable
development. Expansion promised continued peace rather than crisis
and confrontation. Far from threatening England, the growth of the
German merchant marine and colonial empire were in reality hostages to peace, guarantees of her continued good behavior.[14]

In view of the amiable tone prevailing in the relations of English
and German churchmen, it is hardly surprising that, with the advent
of war, efforts should have been made to see the conflict through the
eyes of the enemy. As the weeks passed, this approach became increasingly unpopular, as was to be expected; yet even by the end of
September, 1914, one might occasionally hear qualified defences of
the German position.

The *Commonwealth* and the *Church Socialist* maintained that the
German people wanted to fight neither England nor any other country, but had been forced by Russia to draw the sword in self-defence.
"Russia, with its autocratic ideas, with its backward civilizations,
with its blinding police-tyrannies, builds up a vast dread on the eastern

frontier. Its pressure is menacing and hateful. It is against this monstrous weight that Germany flung itself."[15] The *Church Socialist*, admitting that the Social Democrats had proven themselves Germans first and socialists second, nevertheless applauded their good sense in voting war credits. It also supported the official German contention that Russia was bent on a war of conquest.[16] Germany was therefore to be forgiven her animosity toward England. By intervening on the side of the "Big Barbarian," England had committed what in German eyes amounted to racial treason.[17]

It was not unusual for clergymen to praise the Germans' good qualities. Henry Scott Holland admired the bravery and the good manners of the average German soldier and hoped his countrymen would control their hatred when reading of atrocities; they should open their pianos and play tunes from *Das Deutsche Geistliche Leid*, "the most beautiful, tender, and beseeching book in the world."[18] If one found nothing to praise, he could at least call for moderation and Christian charity. In keeping with this precept, the *Challenge*, a reform-minded newspaper founded and edited by William Temple early in 1914, announced its intention of publishing evidence that the "Hymn of Hate," Ernest Lissauer's musical diatribe against England, was repugnant to the majority of Germans.[19] Meanwhile, the Rev. Edward Lyttelton wrote from Eton asking why, in the name of love, if England had any nurses to spare, should they not be sent across the lines to work for the wounded Germans.[20]

Others reacted quite differently, however. It was a commonplace of the prewar period, embodied in the phrase "civilized warfare," that whereas dum-dum bullets might be necessary to stop Afridi tribesmen who, unlike white men, continued charging after being wounded, such things "are not done" when Europeans make war on one another. Although impossible to abolish the horrors of war entirely, they had been ameliorated by the International Red Cross, by the Geneva and Hague conventions on the laws of war, and, most importantly, by the diffusion of the "humanitarian spirit." As the editor of the *Church Times* remarked during the Spanish-American War, "outside Turkey children are no longer murdered for sport, nor are women violated; the rights of noncombatants are respected . . . and altogether war is no longer a name for indiscriminate slaughter and destruction."[21] This confidence was shattered sixteen years later; between August 25 and Christmas, 1914, events occurred that showed the humanization of warfare to be wishful thinking and the enemy to be something less than human.

During the last week of August, the Germans, charging atrocities by *francs-tireurs*, initiated a campaign of terrorism culminating in the burning of the magnificent library of the University of Louvain. It would be difficult to overestimate the impact of this seemingly gratuitous display of Teutonic fury on educated opinion the world over. More than anything else, Louvain was the decisive factor in convincing waverers of the wisdom of intervention. The Rev. H. D. Rawnsley, canon of Carlisle and an official of the Church of England Peace League, captured the public's mood in the poem "Louvain":

> Nothing can wipe away this dastard stain
>   As unforgiveable as unforgot;
>   Kaiser! on your black battle shield this blot
> A darker blot for ever shall remain;
> Religion, books, carved stone, and storied pane
>   Pleaded as vainly as the men you shot,
>   Wherefore our indignation burns red-hot
> Above the fiery ashes of Louvain.[22]

To make matters worse, the Advent season began badly, when Admiral Hipper's cruiser squadron bombarded the East Coast towns of Scarborough, Whitby, and Hartlepool (December 16), causing heavy civilian casualties. For the first time since 1667, when the Dutch raided Sheerness, Britain itself had become a theater of operations. The continuation of the war into the New Year came, moreover, as a profound disappointment to those who had convinced themselves it would end with the first snow. The published sermons and articles reveal an increasing uneasiness and depression. It gradually became clear that as sinful and as deserving of punishment as the Allies were, they hardly deserved such a terrible scourging. As clergymen recognized that the existing theories were inadequate to explain what was taking place, or to sustain the level of morale needed for a protracted contest, their view of the war and of the enemy changed.

The theory that the war had its origin in divine punishment was well-suited for adaptation to the changed circumstances. Whereas the notion of sin was retained, the emphasis on self-examination and

retributive justice was modified to a large degree in favor of concentrating on the sins of Germany. Earlier impulses to credit her with
at least some positive qualities, much less to praise her, were suppressed. In 1917 there appeared a book by Frank Weston, *Conquer-
ing and to Conquer*, wherein this process of laying the burden of
guilt on the shoulders of Germany is illustrated clearly. "In each
nation," said Weston, "you will find some or other of these sins; but
she has them all, and glories in them. She is the most perfect and
thorough expression of the sins of all Europe."[23] Germany, as other
of his colleagues put it, had "perfected" sin, thus making herself the
moral "plague spot" of the world.[24] The bishop of London did an
about-face, affirming that the war must not be called a punishment
for England's sins, "for if we had been more sinful, adding cowardice
to our other faults, we might have avoided it altogether."[25]

With Germany established as the most sinful nation, it now became possible to blame her exclusively for the war, a premeditated
crime "engineered by fiends incarnate, and fought by a nation of
lunatics."[26]

The myth of German premeditation grew in part out of a miscon-
ception about the sequence of events leading up to modern wars.
Governments rarely if ever make the decision to begin a war on a
certain date and then proceed to build a military machine. Yet every
war between great powers is in a sense "premeditated," inasmuch
as logistical considerations impose the necessity of identifying a
potential enemy and formulating contingency plans years in advance. Once formulated, however, these plans may never be put into
operation.

The performance of the German army during the first weeks of
the war lent weight to the charges that it was the product of a long-
matured scheme. It was difficult to believe otherwise, especially in
light of the fact that the plans of the Imperial General Staff (the
very name of which had a ring of efficiency to it) had been executed
with such precision. That thousands of railroad trains should be able
to move millions of soldiers to their destinations with unerring ac-
curacy, that it was possible to feed, even shave, these men as they
were marching, and that naval vessels should be at their stations well
before the actual declaration of war was obviously not the result of

a few days of emergency planning. The conclusion seemed inescapable: for forty years the kaiser's government had been plotting and preparing, arming and working, for the conquest of Europe, perhaps of the world.

Once people began to search, they easily discovered evidence of German planning. Nothing had apparently escaped the planners in the Wilhelmsstrasse. Russian munitions factories; Belgian, Chinese, and Italian banks; Wall Street; and the Cumberland coke industry had all been taken over by German financial interests. The army had used the years of peace to infiltrate spies and military planners disguised as traveling salesmen into the countries of their intended victims.[27] During the spy-mania that raged on and off throughout the war, clergymen were among those urging the immediate deportation of enemy aliens. The hundreds of overworked and underpaid Austrian and German waiters at seaside hotels were immediately suspect, as was many an old maid governess suddenly shunned as a menace to the British Empire. "We ought to make a clean sweep of them," proclaimed J. E. C. Welldon.[28]

Having warned in 1912 that "Germany strikes when Germany's hour has struck,"[29] the war confirmed Lord Roberts as England's foremost soldier-prophet. It was now clear that certain seemingly unrelated events were actually elements in a carefully thought out strategy. With the completion of alterations on the Kiel Canal in June, 1914, Germany had brought her naval preparations into harmony with the plans of the army. According to the Rev. T. T. Norgate, a former secretary of the Clergy Friendly Society whose interest in military affairs led the *Challenge* to commission him to write nearly a dozen war-related articles, even the kaiser's departure for his annual Norwegian cruise after the assassination of the archduke had a purpose, to throw dust in the eyes of Europe while Germany prepared to get in the first blow. In addition to her own plans, it was said that the Allies had unwittingly provided a number of incidents highlighting their weaknesses and convincing Germany that *Der Tag*, the day of reckoning toasted for so long in ship's wardrooms, had arrived. The Caillaux trial divided the French public and pointed to deep-seated national weaknesses; labor unrest and sporadic rioting in Russia gave the impression that that vast empire was about to dis-

solve in revolutionary chaos; finally, and worst of all, England was
immobilized by the Irish troubles. The Allies were off balance, incapable of resisting Germany's well-tuned war machine.[30]

Name-calling in young children, focusing usually on the elimina-
tive functions, is a normal technique for getting attention and re-
leasing anger. On the other hand, the images and expressions employed against adversaries by a group or an entire society, far from
indicating its immaturity, may provide insights into its latent assumptions. After all, we denounce our enemies for lacking those
qualities we most value, as well as for embodying those we most
despise.

As might be expected from men of religion, the anathemas pronounced against Germany and her leaders were charged with religious imagery, the rhetorical style they knew best. Whereas they
seldom went into the gutter with the journalist Horatio Bottomley,
who referred to Germany as "Verminy" and "Germhuny," the language they did employ rivalled in virulence that of the Reformation.
Germany, variously portrayed as the twentieth century's equivalent
of the Roman Empire, Babylon, and Assyria, was also the sworn
enemy "of Christian civilization, of moral progress, of spiritual enlightenment," a veritable "curse and hissing amongst the nations."[31]

At first, there was general dismay and inability to explain why
the Germans, with whom they had had so much in common, should
become without warning the "Zulus of Europe," a people capable of
being transformed at a command into a horde of Huns. Interest in
this tribe of barbarians became so intense that the religious press
published in the early months of the conflict capsule histories of the
Huns and of "The Kaiser's Model: Attila, the Hun."[32] The word
Hun became a popular malediction. Used as a noun (as in "You
Hun!"), it was an insult; as an adjective, it signified anything typi-
cally low, German, or un-English; it might even be substituted for
the sanguinary expletive of the working classes. In any case, it seemed
to the Rev. C. R. Ball, vicar of All Saints', Peterborough, that Germany, afflicted with a national insanity, "perverted of moral sense,
possessed of national dementia, sunk in the depths of moral infamy,

shrinking from nothing in its mad lust and worship of the will to power,"[33] had become the enemy of the human race.

Whether through private initiative or official encouragement, every means of disseminating information and forming attitudes, including the pulpit, was mobilized to blacken the image of Germany. Compounded of ignorance, fear, and hatred, the stereotype that emerged as a result of these efforts was certainly appropriate to "the hideous enemy of righteousness." German humor, German morals, even German table manners were held up to derision and unfavorably compared to the higher standards prevailing among the Allies. Germany's faults, however, differed from ordinary human weakness of character in that they sprang from the sins of pride, covetousness, and hypocrisy.

The typical German, according to G. A. Studdert-Kennedy, an extraordinarily popular chaplain nicknamed by the troops "Woodbine Willie," was a person of bovine placidity, "dumb and stupid and blind." In temperament, he was the complete opposite of the Englishman. "The individual German is the most easily governable, easily biddable, do-as-I'm-toldable, get and get underable person in the world. The individual Briton is the most independent who-the-devil-are-ye-talking-tosh, I won't-be-made-a-doormat-of-for nobody-ish person in the world."[34] And no wonder, for the German's was a half-formed personality, one stunted by a lifelong process of regimentation beginning in the home. Every institution—home, school, factory, army, church—had its assigned part in turning him into a "marionette" incapable of self-direction. Descendants of free-born warriors, the companions of Armenius, the terror of the Roman legions, the modern Germans had become a race of helots, a total reversal of the earlier view of the German as a virile, muscular Christian.

Aside from the obvious pejorative value, it is significant that expressions with mechanical connotations—marionette, pawn, cog, tool—should have been chosen to describe the German character. For nearly a century, German intellectuals had tended to think along lines contrary to the liberal-democratic ideology prevailing in western Europe. Unlike the West, where individual liberty consisted in having rights *against* the state, in Germany nationalistic philosophers like Arndt, Fichte, and Hegel idealized the state, maintaining that freedom for the individual meant his right fully to realize his potential, in reality to become truly human, by submerging himself *within* the collectivity.[35]

From a religious standpoint, it was bad enough that the state claimed jurisdiction over the individual's body; it was outright blasphemy, a denial of the essence of Christianity, to assert rights over his mind as well. God had created man in His own image, entrusting him with the ability of choosing between good and evil. "It is a man's right to be led and not driven, to be persuaded and not compelled," said Studdert-Kennedy in a sermon to the troops. "In other words, it is man's right to grow . . . [for] the necessity of Freedom is the basis of the Christian Faith."[36] By denying that spark of divinity in every man, the German system robbed him of the essence of humanity, thereby inverting the values of the universe and turning man himself into a machine. William Temple, a moderate in questions of theology and certainly no Germanophobe, feared that after having ascribed Godlike qualities to the state, the Germans would end by proclaiming it was God Himself.[37]

With the possible exception of the philosopher Nietzsche, the kaiser, as the living embodiment of this autocratic system, was denounced more vehemently than any German in history. Feelings about William II in Anglican circles had always been rather mixed, depending more on the current political situation than on a universally accepted characterization. But on the whole, Anglicans had a favorable impression of him. As an amateur theologian, he carried on a correspondence with his old friend William Boyd Carpenter, a former bishop of Ripon and chaplain to three English monarchs; so distinguished a church figure as W. M. Sinclair, the archdeacon of London, cited his opinion to prove a point of theology.[38] As an amateur preacher, he took pleasure in regaling his guests on the royal yacht *Hohenzollern* with sermons of his own composition, translations of which were published and favorably received in the Anglican press. A sermon on the Boxers, cunning and bloodthirsty orientals intent upon obstructing the advance of European commerce and the Christian religion, is at least comparable to English pulpit oratory of the same *genre*.[39] His efforts on behalf of world peace did not go unnoticed or unappreciated. As Archdeacon Wilberforce told the German visitors in 1908. "Your nation [is] ruled by a sovereign unique in

European history for the loftiness of his ideals, the variety of his accomplishments, the earnestness of his religion, [and] the intensity of his patriotism. . . ."[40] Three years later, the German peace-advocate Alfred E. Fried won a Nobel Prize for *The German Emperor and the Peace of the World*, a book praised by Norman Angell and devoted to the thesis that the kaiser "is a lifelong pacifist."[41]

There was another side to the Anglican view, of course. "Mineself und Got!", a poem published in 1901 and republished in 1914, indicates that his preachments ("Got pulls mit me, und me mit him") were not always appreciated.[42] His garrulousness, generosity in self-praise, and tactlessness had long been a source of irritation. His *Daily Telegraph* interview of 1908 was roundly condemned in the press as the "impulsive folly of a mercurial monarch swayed by the over-mastering sentiment of the moment."[43] His intemperate statements, particularly the famous speech of July 17, 1900, telling the soldiers embarking to quell the Boxer Rebellion to emulate the Huns, were cited before and during the war as proof of his unfitness to rule a great military power.

The war confirmed the unfavorable image once and for all. William II was pictured throughout the war as a weak, vain, gullible, even degenerate man. Phrases such as "tawdry, theatrical personage," "arrogant apostle of German Culture," and "man of commonplace abilities and of distinction purely histrionic" rang from pulpits throughout England. Analogies between the kaiser and the wicked personages of the past were constantly drawn. Attila, Antiochus Epiphanes, Nebuchadnezzar, Sennacherib, Louis XIV, Napoleon, Pontius Pilate and, oddly enough, Jezebel were compared to the kaiser, always to his disadvantage. Students of prophecy, Evangelical laymen for the most part, were quick to identify Germany with the scarlet colored, seven-headed, ten-horned Beast portrayed in Revelation 17:3 and the kaiser with the mighty king in Daniel, 11:3. To certain writers, he was none other than Antichrist, a fact proven by a complicated series of mathematical computations, or by the simple observation that he was 666 months old when the war began: 666 is the number traditionally assigned to the Beast of the Apocalypse.[44]

One incident may be cited to illustrate the extent to which Englishmen came to loathe the kaiser. In November, 1914, Archbishop

Lang of York provoked an uproar that must have taught a lesson to any of the kaiser's would-be defenders. Since August 4, the kaiser had been the subject of scurrilous abuse. His mustachios and way of holding his withered left arm, a birth-defect, made him an ideal subject for music hall comedians. According to *The Encore*, the trade journal of the music hall artistes, no program was complete unless enlivened by a joke, a skit, or a song ("Lord Have Mercy on the Kaiser," "To Hell With the Kaiser") about William II.[45] Cartoonists and poster artists delighted in representing him as Herod. A widely circulated cartoon, captioned "God (and the Women) Our Shield!" shows him, sword in hand, driving a Belgian mother with a baby in her arms before him. *Punch* later published a cartoon depicting the kaiser as Satan mixing "The Elixer of Hate," while an infant is affixed to the wall behind him with a spike through its chest.[46]

Lang took the opportunity of a patriotic gathering in York's Empire Music Hall to deplore the personal abuse being heaped upon the kaiser. To drive home his point, Lang told of the "sacred memory" he cherished of the German emperor kneeling beside Edward VII at the bier of Queen Victoria, his grandmother.[47] Not even the archbishop of York could find shelter in the storm that ensued. His residence at Bishopthorpe was inundated by a flood of letters, postcards, and newspaper clippings. One devout layman, a churchwarden and communicant for twenty-five years, described his daily prayer that the kaiser might rot eternally in hell. Canon Tupper-Carey later recalled that his friend received twenty-five Iron Crosses in the mail.[48] Protest meetings were held in provincial towns and London boroughs; ruridecanal conferences sent resolutions condemning his statement; and Hastings Rashdall commented, unkindly and unfairly, that "for once Cosmo's sycophancy got the better of his usual astuteness."[49]

Doubts about the sincerity of the kaiser's religious faith were inevitable. He was variously portrayed as an heresiarch fighting against the truth, or as an apostate who had secured the Turkish alliance by secretly converting to Islam. Bishop Stileman of Persia told a meeting of the strongly evangelical Church Missionary Society that German propaganda presented him as the "Huge Mohomet Guillaume," and the Hohenzollerns as descendants of Fatima, sister of the Prophet. Others referred to him as "William the Wicked," the pagan chieftain who offered Satan, the Prussian tribal deity, libations of blood. As Studdert-Kennedy told his congregation on the Western Front, "the god that the German leaders worship is the idol of the earth—a cruel and crude monster who lives on human blood."[50]

GERMANY'S WAR-INSPIRERS

The preceding picture contains certain elements that we shall have to examine separately, namely the popular conception of the relationship of German cultural and religious life to an absolutist state. At this point it seems well to pause for a moment to glance at the clergyman in a capacity that enabled him to play an important part in shaping public opinion, that of an intellectual of a special type.

The person actively engaged in wars, bitter strikes, and other social upheavals may be called upon to withstand prolonged and intense psychological strain and physical suffering. To make his sacrifices bearable, and to mobilize greater energies for the fight, he needs an all-embracing, yet easily intelligible, explanation of what is happening and why.

It is a phenomenon familiar to sociologists that the intellectual, instead of viewing the struggles of the world with the detachment popularly attributed to inhabitants of ivory towers, may actually assume a vital role in conflict situations. It is precisely because the man dedicated to truth for its own sake and to humanistic values may also be intensely patriotic, that in time of war he is likely to be torn by conflicting loyalties. Yet it is no paradox that he who cherishes human life and cannot sanction the taking of it for any but the weightiest reasons, should be among the first to step into the arena of conflict; for only by presenting the issues in terms of the society's dominant, though not necessarily articulated, ideas, assumptions, and values can he resolve his inner tensions. In effect, he utilizes the society's ideology first to verbalize the cause, then to assert for it a validity transcending considerations of self-interest and expediency. It only remains for the propagandist to translate these ideas into the catch-words, the slogans, and the visual images appropriate for mass consumption.[51]

Once perceived in an ideological context, a conflict invariably assumes a broader significance. If one side is the exemplar and the champion of "pure principles," it follows that the other side must be motivated by their opposites. When dealing with the ideology of the enemy, therefore, it becomes incumbent upon the intellectual to assume a predominantly destructive role. "We fight not to destroy a nation," wrote H. G. Wells in the first flush of national self-righteousness, "but to kill a nest of ideas. . . . Our business is to kill ideas. The ultimate purpose of this war is propaganda, the destruction of certain beliefs, and the creation of others."[52] To be sure, it no longer suffices merely to call the other side names, to impugn its motives, integrity, and objectives. Its entire *Weltanschauung*, its world-view, must be demolished. This approach, it should be noted, is seldom expected to bring victory through shaking the enemy's confidence in his world-view; rather its aim is to further arm one's own people psychologically. Nothing can be good or true in the enemy's position because his operating assumptions and formal philosophy are totally fallacious. In resorting to this method of negative indoctrination, the intellectual, as Karl Mannheim so aptly put it, transforms conflicts of interest into conflicts of ideas, thereby imparting to them an altogether new dimension.[53]

If we pursue this idea a step further, we find that the minister of religion or the devout layman is capable, given the right set of circumstances, of radicalizing a conflict to a degree impossible for the secular-minded. Besides idealizing an issue, his training and general outlook predispose him to "theologize," to cast it in terms of absolute, divinely sanctioned moral imperatives; he may even go so far as to conclude that one side is in league with Antichrist, the other fighting in company with God and the Angelic Host.

Throughout the conflict, but especially during its early stages, no sermon, article, or pamphlet dealing with current affairs was complete without its ritualistic denunciation of Friedrich Nietzsche, Heinrich von Treitschke, and General Friedrich von Bernhardi. The extreme nature of their opinions, presented usually in the form of short, easily quoted aphorisms, lent themselves for use by Allied propagandists as illustrations of the perversion and brutalization of the German intellect. These three men, a philosopher, a historian, and a soldier came to personify a kind of anti-Trinity, the three "lying prophets" whose teachings had instigated and sanctioned actions contrary to all civilized norms. As the council of the evangelical Church Association proclaimed, "the poisonous explosives discharged from

the howitzers of German philosophy had produced their dread results."[54] But although their doctrines did reflect something of the
intellectual climate of Wilhelmian Germany, clergymen as a rule
lacked the intellectual equipment to assess the true nature and extent
of their influence.

However much the educated Englishman might romanticize the
qualities of his Teutonic forebears and admire the victor of Sedan,
in reality he knew and cared to know little about modern German
history, institutions, and political theory. None save an elite of university professors and theologians read the German language with
facility. The study of German, indeed the study of modern languages
generally, was retarded on all educational levels by a combination of
parsimoniousness, conservatism, snobbery, and legal restrictions. In
1900, for example, Mr. Justice Wills ruled that local school boards,
given control of elementary education by the Act of 1870, lacked the
authority to expend public funds in such "extravagant" (i.e. addi-
tional and advanced) subjects as higher mathematics, advanced
chemistry, French, and German.[55]

The public schools, institutions where the overwhelming majority
of England's future leaders received their education, were notorious
for these failings. Several of the old boarding schools did in fact offer
German on "the modern side," but since Latin and Greek were required for university admission, since these subjects took up more
than half of the instructional day, and since the classical masters
stubbornly resisted innovation, Virgil and Horace triumphed over
Goethe and Schiller. Arthur Christopher Benson, a prolific writer
whose father had been headmaster of Wellington College before becoming archbishop of Canterbury, and who had himself become a
successful housemaster at Eton, was a self-proclaimed "victim" of
the classical curriculum. Only after taking his degree at Cambridge
did he realize his educational shortcomings, and by implication those
of the governing class as a whole. "I knew a very little French, a very
little mathematics, a very little science; I knew no history, no German, no Italian. I knew nothing of art or music; my ideas of geogra-
phy were childish. . . . My only accomplishment was the writing of
rather pretty Latin verse."[56]

Besides offering little in the way of German history and literature,
the universities were experiencing difficulty in finding students will-

ing to study German. At Cambridge, where Benson spent the last years of his life as master of Magdalene (1915–1925), the number of students presenting themselves for the local examinations in German, never substantial, had dwindled to zero by 1911. The number of students destined for the army who visited Germany to learn the language at first hand had fallen to an insignificant number; so small in fact that Sir T. Vezey Strong, the Lord Mayor of London, feared England would be unable to keep up with the latest developments in military science.[57]

There is nothing to indicate that knowledge of things German was any more diffused among the clergy than among the population at large. Skill in the German language certainly was not. All that the church required of a candidate for ordination in 1914 was a university degree or a diploma from a theological college—Professor A. C. Headlam believed that insisting on just a pass degree tended to attract second-raters[58]—enough theology to pass the examination for deacon, and a knowledge of Greek and Latin. Few apparently possessed modern languages; indeed, it was said that some candidates were such poor linguists that they crammed for the examination by memorizing translations of entire passages in the classical languages.

Clerical reading habits were another problem. Unless one became a full-time scholar, the tendency was to fall behind steadily in those areas that make for an educated man. Critics of clerical education reported finding on the shelves of the vicarages they visited more seven penny novels than works of scholarship, German or otherwise. The fault, chided the authors of one study, all acknowledged authorities in the field, lay with the clergy training institutions. More often concerned with propagating the viewpoint of a particular party in the church than with giving a solid education, they failed to instil in their students a love of learning. The result, they concluded, was to be seen in their home libraries and in the innumerable curates who were incapable of sitting down with a book for so much as an hour at a time.[59]

The critics may have been overharsh in one respect. The life of the clergyman was inimical to self-improvement through reading. For the parish priest, poverty, family obligations, and the routines of work in an urban area left neither the money for purchasing books nor the energy for reading them. Bishop Winnington-Ingram spoke from personal experience when he advised students at the Cambridge Divinity School to read as much as possible while they still could; later "you will fight for an hour's reading as one that fighteth for a breath of air."[60] The same applied to the bishops, whose hectic pace was proverbial. Winnington-Ingram's predecessor, Mandell Creighton, a famous historian, lamented to the London Diocesan Conference that he had become conscious of mental deterioration since being translated to the see of London. "I have no time to read a book; I have really not had time even to think."[61] The archbishop of Canterbury was busier still. Randall Davidson normally put in sixteen or seventeen hours a day discharging his own immediate responsibilities, leaving little time to form opinions on such pressing matters as unemployment, let alone the intricacies of German political theory.[62] Even had he wanted to inform himself on this subject, he would have learned little from the standard English periodicals. To take one example, *The Hibbert Journal*, an internationally renowned review of religion, theology, and philosophy, devoted scarcely any space to developments in German thought. Anglican scholars limited their writings to religious and controversial topics, as was to be expected.

The sudden outbreak of war places the average clergyman in an awkward position with respect to his traditional role in the community. As with all men of higher education, he is expected by his associates and, more importantly, by those looking to him for guidance, to have an opinion on the great matters of the day. Unfortunately, however, the knowledge needed to deal with highly complex problems in an intelligent manner cannot be acquired as soon as the need becomes apparent. To make matters worse, the information media may actually create more confusion by bombarding him day after day with masses of "facts" about situations that change with kaleidoscopic unpredictability. Chances are, the unifying principle will not emerge from the facts, but be imposed from another source.

Faced with the predicament of being expected to have an opinion, and at the same time well aware of his educational deficiencies, the clergyman turned to a species of propaganda tailored to meet the needs of men in his position. Commentaries published soon after the war began, among them the *Oxford Pamphlets* and short pieces by Lord Bryce, Gilbert Murray, Spencer Wilkinson, Paul Vinogradoff, G. M. Trevelyan, H. A. L. Fisher, and Ernest Barker bore the stamp of some of the greatest minds of early twentieth century England. Their chief defect was that they were hastily assembled productions by scholars whose main interests lay outside the field of contemporary German studies. Nor were they intended to serve as serious institutional studies. Their purpose, in the words of the *Report of the Central Committee for National Patriotic Organizations*, the body sponsoring them, was to justify "both historically and morally England's position in the struggle."[63] A number of these pamphlets, including the influential book-length *Why We Are At War, Great Britain's Case* (1914) by six members of the Oxford Faculty of Modern History, stressed the intellectual origins of the conflict. One feature they all had in common was the considerable space devoted to the writings of Nietzsche, Treitschke, and Bernhardi, which may account for the paucity of references to other German writers.[64] In any case, as superficial and biased as they were, these works furnished the basic factual framework for a thoroughgoing attack of Germany's intellectual and religious leaders. Clergymen, ironically, became at the same time the targets, the creators, and the disseminators of propaganda.

Of the three writers in question, only Allen H. Powles's translation of Bernhardi's *Germany and the Next War* was available in a complete edition when the war began. The first printing had been ignored by the book reviewers for the religious press, and the book does not seem to have been discussed widely before October, 1914, when Lord Roberts noted that it was only then being read by English people.[65] Priced at two shillings, its publisher, Arnold, must have turned a handsome profit during the first year of the war. Treitschke, on the other hand, was practically unknown to the reading public. In 1913, J. A. Cramb, Professor of History at Queen's College, London, complained that not a single page of his multivolume *History of Germany in the Nineteenth Century* had been translated.[66] The same was true of *Politics*, his most important theoretical work, which did not appear in a complete translation until 1916; by then, however, attitudes had hardened and the public mind had become absorbed with other issues. Nietzsche's *Complete Works*, in Dr. Oscar Levy's expensive eighteen volume edition, became available just a few weeks before the war. Though this edition is a labor of love, representing a great expenditure of time and energy, many of the translations are totally unreliable.[67] Only *Beyond Good and Evil* was available in a cheap 1914 "war edition," priced at one shilling.

The sign placed next to the *Complete Works* of Nietzsche displayed in a Piccadilly bookshop, "The Euro-Nietzschean War. Read the Devil in order to fight him better,"[68] contains at least a kernel of truth: few had actually read "the Devil." One cannot be certain whether all the critics of the "lying prophets" read their works, or read them with sufficient care to do justice to their ideas. A comparison of the passages quoted in innumerable pamphlets and sermons reveals a striking similarity; coincidence, perhaps, or an indication of extensive borrowing from each other as well as from the pamphlet literature and compendiums of suitable quotations. M. A. Mügge's *Friedrich Nietzsche, His Life and Work* (1911), an otherwise undistinguished work, furnished a mine of incriminating quotations. With the exception of John Neville Figgis, the only Anglican scholar to publish a full-length study of Nietzsche, *The Will to Freedom* (1917), German editions and commentaries by German scholars were never cited—at least in none of the works I have seen. If worst came to worst, one could always get ammunition from the daily press; in September, 1914, Bishop Winnington-Ingram confessed to taking all the quotations for a powerful series of sermons from an article, "The Pan-German Creed," in the *Daily Mail*.[69]

In wartime England, as in prewar Germany, where Fritz Stern has shown there was no academic exegesis of Nietzsche, everyone had his own interpretation of "the real Nietzsche."[70] It is, therefore, less important for the purposes of this study to discuss what Nietzsche actually taught, than to describe what people *thought* were his teachings.

There existed within the Church of England a polarization of opinion about Nietzsche. At one end of the spectrum was the minority, men with independent reputations as philosophers, who felt that, despite the potentially dangerous elements contained in his philosophy, these were counterbalanced by its positive aspects. By December, 1914, Dean Inge, formerly a critic of his arrogance and ungentlemanly attitude toward women, had changed his mind sufficiently to defend him before a meeting of the Clergy Home Mission Union. Nietzsche's doctrine, he affirmed, was a plea for individualism and "the Eugenic man" (a cause Inge himself espoused), not a justi-

fication of militarism and race hatred.[71] Inge was supported in this
view by F. R. Barry, canon of Westminster and later bishop of Southwell, who noted that Nietzsche's philosophy had more in common
with religion than he realized and owed more to Christianity than
he dared admit even to himself. "Nietzsche's whole outlook is dominated by what is perhaps the source of all religion—the insatiable
craving for the Beyond."[72] Nietzsche, like Christ, loathed the obscu-
rantism of priests and so-called wise men; technicians he described
as "super-chimpanzees," the German professoriate as "learned Philistines" and "scholarly oxen." The *Übermensch*, the overman or
superman, represented anything but an idealization of the Prussian
Junker, of whom Nietzsche was contemptuous; rather he embodied
the best in the Christian tradition, the eternal yea-sayer, the lover
of life who overcame the limitations of his humanity and achieved
spiritual strength through suffering. "Even people imbued with the
ethics of Nietzsche," said John Neville Figgis, "are nearer to the
Kingdom of God than men stricken with gold fever, because he
teaches you to be noble for its own sake."[73] Nietzsche was therefore
the greatest opponent of Darwinism and the ethic of dog-eat-dog in
the nineteenth century.[74]

The vast majority of Anglicans, however, damned him as the most
evil German next to the kaiser. For them, he was the apostate son of
a respectable Lutheran family, "the great immoralist," "the mad
philosopher." None could deny the power and originality of his intellect, but it was easy to devalue his accomplishments by showing them
as manifestations of the insanity that made him an invalid. Nietzsche
was brilliant, but a lunatic; a prophet, and a degenerate; a genius,
"an unbalanced genius of Slavonic blood . . . whose mind became
unhinged before he was fifty, and who has apparently been successful in unhinging the brains of a large proportion of his fellow
countrymen."[75]

The man who inspires new ideas has little power in his lifetime,
and none after his death, to restrict their application to the area of
his original intentions. Like Nietzsche, he may realize this and warn
against the idiots or, as his friend Jacob Burckhardt termed them, the
"terrible simplifiers" using them to destructive ends. Yet, whatever
influence Nietzsche may have had on prewar German thought, research has thusfar been unable to modify Crane Brinton's conclusion

that his doctrines were largely unknown to the kaiser and his immediate circle of advisors.[76] Such doubts, however, never troubled the popular preachers, including several bishops, who were convinced that Nietzsche had exerted a powerful influence in his lifetime, his philosophy so captivating educated Germans that they reduced his principles to a blueprint for world domination.

The outstanding characteristic of anti-Nietzsche pulpit oratory was an emotionalism bordering on hysteria. Nietzsche, it was said, stood for everything a Christian abhorred and must fight against. His exultation in the name Antichrist, his proclamation that God is dead, and his scorn for Christian "slave morality" was but one side of the equation; the other consisted of his application of the Darwinian concept of the survival of the fittest to human society. The *Übermensch* was truly a "blonde beast," a raging two-legged tiger who knew no law except the law of the jungle. The triumph of his ideas would mean the reversal of the evolutionary process, the return to chaos. The choice before the world, reiterated constantly in the titles of sermons and poems, was simply (in the words of a lay correspondent with the *Challenge*) "Christ or Nietzsche?"

> Christ or Nietzsche? Cross or sword?
>   Love of kind or lust of power?
>   Choose O man. God strikes the hour.
> Choose thy symbol. Choose thy lord.
>
> Christ or Nietzsche? Love or hate?
>   Life in death or death in life?
>   War for peace or war for strife?
> Choose thy future. Choose thy fate.[77]

Ideas by themselves are harmless; they become deadly weapons when men of action adopt them as a basis of policy. From Frederick the Great to Bismarck, German militarism, though a predatory, selfish system, was nevertheless a system governed by the realities of a situation. Wars of "limited liability" have at least the virtue of being waged for defined, attainable goals. The teachings of Nietzsche, on the other hand, were credited with having introduced into German policy an element of boundless fanaticism, providing the militarists and Pan-German imperialists with a kind of philosophical motor to power the Prussian Juggernaut; and providing the English with a

reason to fight to the death. "The German military war lords," proclaimed the Rev. C. L. Drawbridge, secretary of the Christian Evidence Society and a popular speaker in Hyde Park, "have adopted
the Nietzschean idea and have inculcated [it] into their military machine, which acts upon the principle: the violent shall, by means of
the mailed fist, acquire glorious reputation for greatness, that greatness which is the only true foundation for empire."[78] The superman
had grown into the supernation; its handiwork was to be seen at
Louvain.

In view of Nietzsche's outbursts against the Germans ("It is part
of my ambition to be considered the despiser of Germans *par excellence*"[79]), it is all the more surprising that his name should be linked
with that of Heinrich von Treitschke, the most nationalistic of historians. Yet many critics, forgetting that Treitschke's major ideas
had been set forth in lectures at the University of Berlin well before Nietzsche began writing, believed that "the nineteenth century
Machiavelli" had actually applied Nietzschean ideas to real grievances. Treitschke exemplified Germany's self-pity and resentment
that she, a nation destined to fulfill a world-historical mission, had
achieved nationhood too late to acquire colonies, which, like battle-
ships, were symbols of prestige in the late nineteenth century.[80]

Rich, powerful nations are seldom loved; and Treitschke's resentment of Britain's ill-gotten empire, as evidenced by the subsequent
outcry over the South African War, was shared by people throughout
Europe. The case against Treitschke, however, was made to rest on
a far more substantial base than his glorification of war and hatred
of England, the chief obstacle to Germany's attaining her "place in
the sun." Treitschke and his followers were held responsible for conditioning the German people to behave as strong, spoiled, frightened
children. On the one hand, by making the self-interest of the *Macht-
stadt*, the power-state, the yardstick in everything, and by conjuring
up the apparition of "a bogy England" on the other, Treitschke had
prepared the ground for the growth of a parallel myth, that of a
Germany begirt by enemies. An irreversible cycle was thus set in
motion: Germany increased her army estimates annually and built
a magnificent fleet; feeling themselves threatened, other nations followed suit, in turn reinforcing German nationalism and xenophobia
and creating pressures for a new round of arms spending.[81] William

Sanday, who probably knew as much about Germany and the Germans as any cleric, saw the war as the tragic unfolding of a self-fulfilling prophecy. England never wanted war with Germany, but Treitschke had helped create such a fear of foreigners, that his countrymen became doubly suspicious when approached with the sincerest assurances of friendship. When a genuine crisis finally did come, they reacted with predictable haste, irrationality, and violence.[82]

Treitschke died in 1896, well before the deterioration in Anglo-German relations reached an acute stage. Between then and 1911, when the first German edition of General von Bernhardi's *Germany and the Next War* appeared, his worst fears about England seemed confirmed. The Boer War, the Moroccan Crisis of 1905, Germany's diplomatic defeat at Algeciras the following year, and finally the Agadir Crisis of 1911, which prompted Bernhardi to prepare his partially completed manuscript for publication, were taken by certain segments of German opinion as proof that "perfidious Albion" would stop at nothing to thwart Germany's aspirations.

Bernhardi, who as a young lieutenant of Hussars had been among the first officers to enter Paris in 1871, became known shortly after the outbreak of the Great War as the satanic genius of German militarism. So thoroughgoing a campaign was waged against him by Allied propagandists that their distortions and exaggerations live on in works of popular history and in text-books published a half-century after the Armistice. During the war, he resented his notoriety to such an extent that he wrote *Germany and England* (1915) as a rejoinder to his critics. He would now be equally upset at hearing himself mentioned, with no compliment intended, as "the leading military theorist of his day," or to learn that he had been an "influential military writer" whose pronouncements "carried great weight" with the war party.[83]

Since *Germany and the Next War* was the only recent work by a German military figure available when the war began, and since it combined arrogance and self-righteousness with a pseudoscientific rationale for violence—passages proclaiming war a biological necessity and prolonged peace a disaster abound—educated men generally fastened upon it, assuming it represented the thinking of the entire German military class. It is true, as his critics always mention and as he boasts in his memoirs, that, in addition to being translated into most of the languages of the civilized world, the book also went through six editions in Germany. But he fails (and modesty does not seem to be a factor here) to specify the number of copies in each edition. One thing is certain, however, the book was never circulated by the million in Germany, as alleged by the propagandists and preachers. Many educated and socially prominent Germans never heard of Bernhardi or of his book, some seeing it for the first time in England or in the United States. Nor was he ever an accredited spokesman for the General Staff, having been retired in 1909 while still under the age limit because of his outspoken criticism of the army's leadership.[84] The Foreign Office was so embarrassed by his rantings that it considered suppressing *Germany and the Next War* entirely.[85]

The fact that Bernhardi became famous in England at a time when Nietzsche and Treitschke were being widely discussed encouraged the belief that he, and through him the "Potsdam militarists," had fallen under the influence of their theories. Actually, *Germany and the Next War* betrays no awareness whatsoever of Nietzschean ideas; and although Treitschke is cited about two dozen times throughout the 288 page book—Goethe and the poets of the War of Liberation are cited as frequently—Bernhardi may have been less a follower of Treitschke than hitherto imagined by his critics. Unlike his reputed mentor, an outspoken anti-Semite, Bernhardi mentions nothing about the Jews; nor did he hate the English, whom he credited with doing great, civilizing work for humanity. It is also significant that the superpatriot who lectured so eloquently on the right and the duty of the state to make war, insisted that war was a serious business to be undertaken for only the weightiest of reasons, and then fought for limited objectives: possessions, power, sovereignty. He also advised belligerents to conduct themselves in keeping with accepted usages, shunning atrocities, political murder, and preconcerted political deception. "A State which employed deceitful methods would soon sink into disrepute. The man who pursues moral ends with immoral means is involved in a contradiction of motives, and nullifies the object at which he aims, since he denies it by his actions";[86] hardly an assertion that the end justifies the means. Yet these qualifications escaped those who recommended Bernhardi's book as required reading for anyone desirous of understanding what Bishop Diggle of Carlisle called "The Inner Meaning of the War."[87]

Germany's war-inspirers had been identified and refuted: Nietzsche had formulated the basic philosophical justification of violence; Treitschke had refined it, made it respectable in the academic world, and related it to long-standing grievances; Bernhardi had, so to speak, merely dotted the i's and crossed the t's, adding the practical touches of the professional soldier.

THE TREASON OF THE PASTORS

Referring to the leaders of organized religion in Germany, Henry Scott Holland asked early in the war several questions that were to be repeated innumerable times during the succeeding four years: "But why, in the Name of God, have these peace-lovers allowed their rulers to be what they are? Why have they tolerated the policy, the diplomacy, which has made Germany a byword in Europe? Why have they allowed militarism to create another Germany which is the ironical confutation of the Germany which they portray to us?"[88] Although the answers were as varied as they were numerous, they agree in essence that the success of the warlords and of the war philosophers was explicable only when considered within the broader context of the failure of the German churches.

Germany's theologians were themselves responsible for questions being raised about the state of religion in their country. Led by Adolf von Harnack, Adolf Deissmann, Ernest Dryander, and Rudolf Eucken, eighty of the most renowned members of the religious and academic communities issued in September, 1914, an *Appeal to Evangelical Christians Abroad*, a statement enthusiastically supporting their country's policies and defending "the inner right of us and our Emperor to invoke the assistance of God." The Germans, they insisted, were fighting to save the West from Russian barbarism. Knowing this, England nevertheless deliberately misrepresented the issues and endeavored through its worldwide propaganda network to place the burden of guilt exclusively upon Germany. Germany, the *Appeal* continued, was fighting for its existence against a hostile congeries of powers. "No scruple holds back our enemies, where in their opinion there is a prospect of seizing for themselves an economic advantage or an increase in power, a fragment of our motherland, our colonial possessions or our trade. We stand over against this raging of the peoples, fearless because of our trust in the holy and righteous God."[89]

Hardly a tribute to the German sense of timing, the publication of the *Appeal* in England within days of the burning of Louvain and the massacres at Dinant and Tremonde, where scores of defenceless civilians were machine-gunned in reprisal for guerrilla activity, served to inflame public opinion further. *To the Christian Scholars of Europe and America*, the Anglican reply, was drafted in part by the archbishop of Canterbury and signed by scholars representing every shade of theological opinion. Henry Scott Holland, Dean Inge, William Sanday, Charles Gore, Hastings Rashdall, B. H. Streeter, Walter Lock (warden of Keble College), and T. B. Strong (dean of Christ Church) and a host of others displayed greater unanimity in countering the German claims than they had ever shown in their theological debates. They examined the German contentions point by point, refuting them in polite but uncompromising language. Finally, in the most telling blow of all, they noted how Germany's actions spoke louder than all her paens to *Kultur* and humanitarianism. In view of Louvain, "will not the Christian scholars of other lands share our conviction that the contest in which our country is engaged is a contest on behalf of the supremest interests of Christian civilization?"[90]

The newspapermen were not as even-tempered as the dons. For weeks, epithets like "this ineffable document," "cynical audacity," and "nauseating to a degree" studded the pages of the Anglican press. The leading article writer of the *Guardian* was astonished by the hypocrisy of men who could unashamedly profess the Christian faith while at the same time pledging loyalty to a regime that honored Nietzsche and adopted as gospel the doctrines of *Germany and the Next War*.[91]

These attitudes became ingrained as the war progressed, opening a breach in the relations of the clergy of Europe's largest Protestant countries that remained unclosed long after the shooting had stopped. But if the sentiments expressed in the *Appeal* opened the eyes of those who had hitherto failed to appreciate the extent of German chauvinism, subsequent statements revealed streams of depravity that ran deeper than the worst outpourings of the lying prophets. Ministers of religion in all the warring nations said contemptible things, things absolutely at variance with the law of love; and in this the Germans may have been no worse than anyone else. Given the scope of this study, it is impossible to determine the extent to which the war sermons quoted in the religious press were true reflections of opinion in the German churches. Undoubtedly editors with an eye to circulation selected the most appetizing morsels for their readers' consideration. As might be imagined, when published these showed Germany in the worst possible light; understandably so, since some preachers positively revelled in descriptions of slaughter and pillage. Rheinold Seeby, professor of theology in Berlin, pronounced the slaying of the unworthy an act of charity. Pastor Zoebel called for the extermination of the unregenerate:

It is this deep consciousness of our mission that permits us to congratulate ourselves, and rest content with a heartfelt gratitude, when our guns beat down the children of Satan, and when our submarines—instruments to execute the Divine vengeance—send to the bottom thousands of the non-elect. We must fight the wicked with every means in our power; their sufferings should give us pleasure; their cries of despair should not move German hearts. There ought to be no compromise with hell, no mercy for the servants of Satan—in other words, no pity for the English, French, and Russians, nor indeed for any nation that has sold itself to the Devil. They have all been condemned to death by Divine decree.[92]

If the pastors, whose profession it was to preach the Gospel, could without censure utter such blasphemies from their pulpits, then the ultimate source of the German malady, and therefore of the war itself, must be sought in her religion, or, more properly, in her lack of the right religion.

To ask about the failures of organized Christianity in Germany meant asking about Lutheranism which, though not dominant in all the states, was the faith of Prussia, the strongest and most aggressive. The resulting reinterpretation of German history, based on the corruption of religion and its subservience to the state persisted, coloring the thought of certain highly placed ecclesiastics during even the Second World War.[93]

Luther, to paraphrase the famous epigram about Erasmus, was widely regarded as having laid the egg that future generations of his

countrymen hatched. The story of his life furnished ample illustration of how he had set Germany on the wrong path. Led from one
extreme to the other by the powerful example of his scepticism, contempt for authority, and conviction of his own rectitude, his successors ended by exalting force as the supreme arbiter in human affairs.
What is more, the reformer's flagrant disregard for covenants solemnized in the sight of God, manifested by his marriage to a runaway
nun and acquiescence in the bigamy of Philip of Hesse, became
precedents for Germany's later disregard for treaties.[94]

It is quite true, as the clerical commentators maintained, that after
shattering the religious unity of Europe, Luther failed to create a
church capable of standing without external supports. Luther, who
believed that the secular power was sanctioned by God and that the
godly magistrate was commissioned to support true religion, nonetheless opposed secular intervention in spiritual matters. Yet circumstances beyond his control, among them the increasing radi-
calization of the Reformation and the disorders resulting from the
Peasant's War of 1525, compelled him to turn to established authority
to help reorganize the church and preserve the peace necessary for
preaching the Gospel. Though placing his movement under the tute-
lage of the secular prince ("God's sword on earth") was probably
the only way of keeping it alive in the sixteenth century, by the
twentieth century the Lutheran state churches had become the virtual
prisoners of their protectors. They had lost what the historian Golo
Mann has called the capacity for "creative unrest."[95]

Beyond this point, however, the accepted historical interpretation
becomes clouded with misconceptions and wishful thinking. The
human failing of using selective memory to obscure what is incon-
venient to one's argument is evident in what follows. The subservience of Lutheranism to the state (it was said without explaining
why it should have been different in England, where the Church of
England was also subservient) had initiated a series of chain reactions involving every aspect of German thought and feeling. The
first indication that something was amiss with Lutheranism was the
withering of that corporate sense of responsibility normally signified
by the designation "church." The churches, powerless to influence
policy, ceased performing their function as critics of current institutions and morality, gradually forfeiting the right to criticize.

Eventually they became scarcely more than ecclesiastical propaganda bureaus, preaching to the masses the official line of "slavish Kaiser-worship."[96]

The most significant consequence of the misalliance of church and state was to be seen in the diversion of German theology and philosophy into unproductive and ultimately dangerous channels. Prohibited from playing a meaningful role in the national life, Lutheranism turned inward, accentuating a tendency, inherent according to some authorities in the concepts of the indwelling Christ and the priesthood of all believers, to separate personal religion from theology, theology from morality, and morality from politics.[97]

As a result of separating personal religion from theology, Germany's spiritual leaders, whose overemphasis on the factual details as opposed to the spiritual significance of the Scriptures had in the nineteenth century made Dr. Arnold and Bishop King of Lincoln uneasy,[98] adopted an outlook amounting to theological adventurism. Though generally accepted among Anglicans, this interpretation nevertheless appealed to them for different reasons. Opponents of modernism hoped that by tracing the failures of German Protestantism to liberal theology, they could discredit the new tendencies within the Church of England. Able to agree on little else, Evangelicals and Anglo-Catholics maintained that the German mind had been poisoned (as the English mind was being poisoned) by modernism and the higher criticism. In a typical description, a review of Sir Robert Anderson's *The Higher Criticism and the War* (1915), the editor of the *Record* accused the German theologians of leading "the infidel crusade of the sham Higher Criticism . . . which in a single generation has led to the dethronement not only of the Bible but of the Christ of the Bible in Germany"; elsewhere, they were likened to disgusting microbes swarming over the pages of the Bible.[99]

Not content with discrediting modernism, Anglo-Catholic extremists helped reinforce doubts about the loyalty of their party to the Church of England by transforming this issue into an attack on Protestantism itself. Protestantism, said the advertisement placed in the *Church Times* by the Catholic Literature Association, was among the more inferior articles made in Germany; the Rev. H. R. Baylis described the war as a struggle between Catholicism, a faith teaching obedience to constituted authority, and "the same Protestantism, or own brother to it, that invaded this country in the sixteenth century, and tried, very nearly successfully, to dominate our national religious life." On occasion, it was even charged that the doctrine of justification by faith had inspired the Germans to ravage Belgium and France.[100]

These examples have been cited to illustrate the range of Anglican opinion on this issue. Closer to the mainstream was the Rev. F. J. Foakes-Jackson, dean of Jesus College, Cambridge, who asserted that, in adopting an overcritical and overintellectual approach to the sources of the Faith, the Germans had altered its essential character, creating in its place something akin to an up-to-date version of Deism with its unrevealed god.[101]

This development, Foakes-Jackson and like-minded people affirmed, was bound to have repercussions in spheres that at first glance seemed far removed from those effected by rationalizing the articles of the Christian faith or highlighting certain factual errors in the Scriptures. For these facts have served to place the source of morality outside this world, moving it beyond the reach of reason alone. Upon them are based religious doctrines, and for nearly two thousand years these doctrines have been both the source and the sanctifier of those moral imperatives—to do good, to love justice, to respect the law—upon which the survival of the social order depends. The liberal theologians reaped more than they bargained for when they set about cleansing the German mind of its religious misconceptions by challenging these facts wholesale and without considering the long-term consequences. Rationalism proved too strong a purgative. Besides depriving the German mind of its natural defences, thereby leaving it vulnerable to the power-philosophies of the late nineteenth century, it undermined the moral foundations of society by depriving them of their religious and metaphysical sanctions.[102] With these gone, nothing remained to prevent Nietzsche and his disciples, passionate men driven by hatred and national pride and armed with a pseudoscientific rationale for violence, from teaching what preachers characterized variously as the doctrines of the "God-State," "political atheism" and "moral agnosticism."[103]

The choice of such phrases implied that the treason of the pastors had enabled the Germans to go clear contrary to the Natural Law, the existence of which has been a basic presupposition of Western

Civilization. Originating in classical antiquity, from whence it was taken over by the Christian church at an early date, the concept of the Natural Law rests upon the assumption that, because God has engraved upon the hearts of men certain general principles of morality, discernible by reason, all are bound by the same rules. Deny this, admit that righteousness is on the side of the heaviest battalions, and the earth becomes a pandemonium, humanity lapses into savagery.

Violating the Natural Law, though fraught with danger, did not exhaust the evil potentialities opened by Germany's apostasy; but beyond this point, explanations tend to be less coherent, as the clerical mind was evidently beset by crosscurrents. For example, the choice of phrases like "moral agnosticism" seems also to express in an unconventional form one of the most persistent problems of western philosophy: Realism as opposed to Nominalism. Basically, in view of the first, "universals," general concepts—church, state, beauty—and generic ideas—chair, cow, man—have a reality of their own, being reflections of perfect forms in the mind of God. To the Realist, "man" refers not merely to a specific person, but to a quality, "manness," common to all and therefore more real than anything perceived by the senses. According to the Nominalist, on the other hand, universals are merely convenient mental classifications, abstractions having no existence outside the mind of the thinker. Apply the Nominalist argument to art, and beauty becomes only what pleases the beholder; apply it to religion, and there is no room for concepts such as "the sins of man" because only the individual is real.

It is, moreover, impossible to restrict these doctrines to metaphysics and theology; for as the saying that everyone is born either a Platonist or an Aristotelian implies, they represent not so much matters of formal philosophy as mental habits and predispositions.

Applied to political theory and questions of morality, it is apparent that these ways of thought are irreconcilable. What is the measure of good and evil? Is law merely a political act, an expression of the needs, the ambitions, and the will of the community and its rulers; or is it a reflection, however incomplete and imperfect, of the Divine Wisdom? Religion can give but one answer. Law and Justice and the principles of Morality are not merely implanted by God in the bosom of man, they are built into the very Frame of Order. Indeed, we find in certain theologians of the period echoes of the age-old dispute whether something is right because willed by God, or willed by God because it is right. Historically, people as diverse as Grotius, Milton, and Hooker have held that even God, omnipotent and possessed of absolute freedom of will, is nonetheless constrained to act rationally and rightly, in fact "lawfully." Thus Hooker declared in the *Laws of Ecclesiastical Polity* that above all the laws is "Law in general . . . . that law which giveth Life unto all the rest which are commendable, just and good, namely, the Law whereby the Eternal himself doth work."[104] By the same token, during the Great War W. C. E. Newbolt, canon of St. Paul's and author of several works on pastoral theology, affirmed "It would seem that there is an abstract right and wrong, the violation of which involves chastisement. Not even God, it appears, can justify these [moral] faults."[105]

Law, then, at the same time the creation of God and binding upon Him, pervades the cosmos. Now it is one thing to sin against the right; it is quite another to deny that there is a right to sin against, as the Germans were supposed to have done.[106] This goes a long way toward explaining why the utterances of the leaders of Germany's political and intellectual life were seized upon and quoted so often and with such vehemence, regardless of how they were obtained initially or the real influence of their authors upon the German mind. They were all of a kind, Nietzsche's mystical reverence for the superman and doctrine of the "transvaluation of values," summed up in the motto "Nothing is true, nothing is forbidden";[107] Bethmann-Hollweg's tirade over the "scrap of paper" guaranteeing Belgium's neutrality; and Bernhardi's assertion that, inasmuch as Christian morality is based on the law of love, it is inapplicable to the affairs of nations.[108] As understood by the clerical community generally, in denying the existence of a supreme moral law of universal validity, they had introduced an intolerable relativism; intolerable because, if pursued to its logical conclusion, the will (whether of the individual or of the state) would be elevated above the Law of God, and God Himself relegated to the status of a cipher.

More serious still were the implications of another, related, concept. According to A. O. Lovejoy, the authority on the subject, the medieval conception of an ordered, hierarchical universe created by and culminating in God the Father, and expressed metaphorically as the Great Chain of Being, was held by most educated men down to the eighteenth century.[109] This is doubtlessly so, as far as literature, science, and philosophy are concerned. But in religion it persisted in its traditional sense much longer. Charles Kingsley, for instance, became elated upon contemplating "that divine and wonderful order, by which God has constituted the services of men, the angels, and all created things; the divine and wonderful order by which sun and stars, fire and hail, wind and vapour, cattle and creeping things fulfil his word."[110]

During the Great War, too, we find traces of this idea in sermons, where it is related to the sins of Germany. Here, however, there seems to be an assumed relationship, never explained clearly, between the natural world and the laws governing it, and the moral order. Just as Hooker predicted that "the frame of that Heavenly Arch erected over our Heads should loosen and dissolve itself"[111] if nature disobeyed its own laws, and Pope observed in the *Essay on Man* that the elimination of one link in the chain would bring chaos or the dissolution of the cosmic order, so certain clergymen evidently believed that the same would result from rebellion against the moral law. Bishop Diggle of Carlisle, a participant in peace congresses and a frequent contributor to the quarterlies, expressed this idea shortly after the tragedy of Louvain:

There runs through the universal system of created things . . . an illimitable series of recurrences, sequences, antecedents, and resultants which we are in the habit of calling causes and effects, sources and streams, seeds and fruits. But for this infinite chain which links prior causes and subsequent consequences, the whole creation would cease to be a cosmos and become a disjointed chaos. The universe, instead of being sealed with the impress of law and order, would be a mass of confusion, an insoluble riddle, with no workable hypothesis for us to build and act upon.[112]

What follows would, as far as the entire Church of England is concerned, be forcing the evidence to bear too great a weight; but some of Diggle's colleagues (and not isolated individuals either) went so far as to assert that, in preaching political atheism, or, in a manner of speaking, moral-political Nominalism, the Germans were "fighting against God and the Divine order of the Cosmical curve."[113] And the consequences of their disobedience, at times set forth in the most frightening language, were just as serious in the twentieth century as in the sixteenth century. In the opinion of the bishop of Kensington, if the principle that might is right prevailed, "we believe it would be the very destruction of the world."[114] Studdert-Kennedy was more emphatic, saying shortly after the Armistice, "If you preached that doctrine, and convinced all men of it . . . you would kill God, shatter the stars, and put an end to the universe. You would, in fact, quench the unquenchable fire."[115] Studdert-Kennedy was a passionate man, a poet often careless with words, and this is a rhetorical flourish perhaps. But rhetoric can have hypnotic and destructive powers of its own.

A last touch must be added to complete the picture of a thoroughly evil enemy. The view became widely accepted that the "hunnish" behavior of her armed forces branded Germany as the apostate, a nation that had abandoned an obsolete Christianity and revived the worship of the ancient Teutonic war gods, a religion more congenial to its true character. The poet Heine's prophecy that one day Thor would awaken, rub the sleep of centuries from his eyes, and smash with his hammer the Gothic cathedrals had come to pass; only now, all of civilization was shuddering under the blows of, in Canon Rawnsley's words, "the vile barbarities of Berserk rage whose fury broke the Cross."[116] In fact, the outline of the German religion of the future could already be discerned. It would be an amalgam of Nietzschean philosophy and the ethics of the warrior gods; its symbol would be the inverted cross of Thor's hammer; its prayers, exalting the proud of spirit, the subtle of heart, the merciless, and the warmongers would be chanted as a blasphemous burlesque of the Beatitudes.[117]

IV. FROM THE JUST WAR TO THE APOCALYPTIC CRUSADE

Writing in a pamphlet *Against a Premature and Inconclusive Peace*, Canon Rawnsley, the poet, asserted, "this is a war to the knife for the freedom and existence of democracy against the pretensions of autocracy—a war of contrasted spiritual ideals—a war in the dominion of the soul."[1] Statements of this sort, revealing as they do several interpenetrating layers of meaning, involving political systems, ideology and religion, should caution us against easy generalizations. The Anglican response to the Great War was a complex phenomenon, presenting a variety of facets, each an aspect of the whole, yet each having its own peculiar characteristics. For purposes of analysis, therefore, we must treat these separately, remembering all the while their relationship to the larger whole.

England's participation in the Great War presented people of all denominations with a dilemma. Granted, Germany and her Myrmidons represented militarism, a false, anti-Christian philosophy, and a religion barely distinguishable from Devil worship; but from a religious standpoint, could even this justify a Christian in slaying his fellowmen? The early Fathers of the church—Justin Martyr, Tatian, Irenaeus, Tertullian, Origen, Athanasius, Cyprian, and uncounted martyrs—would have had no difficulty answering this question. They would have denied absolutely that recourse to the sword was permissible to the follower of Christ, and cited dozens of passages from the New Testament to prove their point. War is incompatible with Christianity. The Christian is bound in all things by the law of love, the heartfelt desire to sacrifice oneself for another's "true good." It is his lot to bear persecution and if need be to suffer martyrdom, not to make martyrs of others. Lactantius (d.320), tutor to the son of the Emperor Constantine, was by all odds the most uncompromising, refusing to allow killing under any and all circumstances. "Therefore in this precept of God no exception whatever ought to be made; but that it is always unlawful to kill a man whom God willed to be a sacred animal."[2]

With the triumph of Christianity in the Roman world in the fourth century, the church began to accommodate itself to the demands of the secular order. The church accepted the state, which now sought to protect it and to promote Christianity as a stabilizing, civilizing influence. Hardly had toleration been proclaimed in 313, when the synod of Arles, called the following year to deal with the Donatist schism, declared that those who threw down their arms were to be excommunicated. Finally, in 416, Theodosius II made the Imperial Army a Christian monopoly, closing it to persons "polluted by the profane and false doctrine of pagan rites."[3] Henceforth pacifism within the church was transformed into a principle of personal conduct exclusively or, in the case of the clergy, who must perform the sacraments free from the taint of bloodguiltiness, made a prerequisite for their calling. By the sixteenth century, pacifism, whether held by Cathari, a Peter Chelciky of the Hussites, the Anabaptists, or even someone like Erasmus was deemed subversive to good order.

From Augustine in the fifth century, to Aquinas in the thirteenth century and Luther and Calvin in the sixteenth century, to the fathers of Vatican II in the twentieth century, Christian thinkers have been in essential agreement in laying down the minimal conditions under which one might rightfully engage in war.[4] This, naturally, is not meant to imply that war was ever regarded as a good in itself. Insofar as it springs from and fosters the base passions—hatred, cruelty, pride, revenge, ambition—it is offensive to God. At best, the theory of the just or justifiable war is (to borrow a Barthian term) hardly more than a *Grenzmoral*, a "borderline morality" for rationally determining rules for a fundamentally irrational activity. According to the classic formula, therefore, to qualify as a "just war" a conflict must be consistent with three principles: (1) It must be declared and conducted by a proper authority, that is, by any corporate body or person exercising legitimate sovereignty. If this condition is lacking, the warriors may be regarded and treated as brigands. (2) It must be waged for a just cause, such as to defend oneself or a weaker power, to take back that which has been seized, to punish an aggressor, or to exact compensation from him. (3) It must be undertaken with a right intention, namely the furthering of some good or the preventing of some evil. It is, for example, wrong to use a slight injury as the pretext for seizing an advantage long coveted. Even if a right intention is present, however, war must be undertaken only after everything else has been tried and failed, and then only if there is the moral certainty of success; if not, the injury must be sustained.

To these formal guidelines is usually added a fourth, taken largely from Francisco de Vitoria, a sixteenth century Spanish theologian and jurist interested in the moral implications of the conquest of the New World. Since war is a moral act undertaken by a moral agent, the state, it ought to be conducted *debito modo*, in a proper manner and with moderation. Basic to fighting in the proper manner is the principle of proportionality, the striking of a balance, necessarily a rough and ready one, between ends and means. No matter how righteous a cause or honorable the conduct of hostilities, to draw the sword without hope of victory, or to fight to the last ditch against obviously impossible odds, has long been considered sinful because it compounds human suffering to no purpose. Likewise, employing insufficient force, or sufficient force ineffectively, is sinful because it prolongs suffering needlessly; conflicts should always be ended as quickly and humanely as possible. Finally, since the days of St. Augustine Christian ethicists have insisted that justice in warfare means eschewing acts of an intrinsically immoral nature: rape, massacre, looting, and incendiarism are always sinful. One should not inflict needless suffering and destruction disproportionate to that required for obtaining satisfaction or winning victory. The lives and property of noncombatants are of course to be respected whenever possible; nor are they to be attacked directly as a military target.

The major Protestant denominations recognize the validity of the just war, incorporating it in their basic confessions of faith: the Lutherans in Article XVI of the Augsburg Confession of 1550, the Presbyterians in Article XXIII of the Westminster Confession of Faith of 1647, the Congregationalists in Chapter XXIV of the Savoy Declaration of Faith and Order of 1658, and John Wesley throughout his writings. The just war theory, expressed in a terse, simple statement, is also embodied in the Anglican Articles of Religion,

Article XXXVII stating "It is lawfull for Christian men, at the com-
maundement of the Magistrate, to weare weapons and serue in the
warres"—why the word *iusta*, which appears before *bella* in the Latin
version of 1552, was omitted from the Elizabethan recension is a
mystery.

The foremost Anglican divines of the nineteenth century—Charles
Kingsley, Frederick Denison Maurice, J. B. Mozley, Bishop Westcott, J. M. Wilson—as well as James Martineau, the Unitarian leader,
and P. T. Forsyth, the Congregationalist theologian, held views differing in no significant way from the traditional concept of the just
war.[5] War, they maintained, is of course incompatible with the
teaching and ideal of Christ, and would be impossible in a world
ordered along the lines of the Gospel. But this cannot be the last
word. As Bishop Westcott indicated in language with a decidedly
Platonic ring, evil was impressed upon human nature at the Fall, and
the wars resulting from this blemish "are a blurred image on earth
of the war in heaven."[6] The Christian must acknowledge the fact of
sin and take the world as it is. Since no power exists that can judge
between nations and enforce its decisions, the option to go to war
must always remain open as the *ultima ratio*, the last reason or the
last recourse in obtaining justice.

J. B. Mozley, whose sermon was widely considered in the Church
of England as an authoritative statement on the subject, carried this
doctrine further, viewing war as an essential ingredient in human
progress, and conflict as inherent in the nature of things. Inspired
evidently by the Franco-Prussian War, in 1871 he told an audience
at Oxford University, where he was Regius Professor of Divinity,
that, whereas self-defence is a primary criterion for the just war,
there are other, equally important, reasons for fighting.

. . . self-defence by no means exhausts the whole rationale of war. Self-
defence stands in moral treatises as the formal hypothesis to which all
justification of war is reduced; but this is applying a considerable strain
to it. When we go further, we find that there is a spring in the very setting
and framework of the world; whence movements are ever-pushing up to
the surface—movements for recasting more or less the national distribution of the world; for establishing fresh centres and forming States into
new groups and combinations . . . . There is doubtless an instinctive
reaching in nations and masses after alteration and readjustment, which
has justice in it, and which arises from real needs. . . . But such just needs

when they arise must produce war; because the *status quo* is blind to new necessities, and does not think such an alteration to be for the better, but much for the worse.[7]

Mozley's sermon, together with those of his contemporaries, were cited and reprinted during the early days of the Great War. Yet just war criteria, though utilized at the beginning and doubtlessly taken for granted throughout the conflict, were gradually superseded by less reasoned, albeit emotionally more satisfying, interpretations. For the concept of the just war is, after all, fundamentally rationalistic, applying specific logical criteria to a given situation. It is a concept best suited perhaps to a society like Italy in the *Quattrocento*, where a number of states, sharing a common culture and matched fairly evenly in wealth and power, vied for mundane objectives.

Save for the period of the religious wars in the sixteenth century, these conditions persisted throughout Europe until the eighteenth and nineteenth centuries. It was then still possible to consider war as a phenomenon akin to a natural disaster. A misfortune for those concerned directly, it left even the vast majority of those in the belligerent states untouched in their daily lives. One scarcely realizes in reading the novels of Jane Austen that the scene is set at a time when England was fighting for its life against Napoleonic France.

The theory of the just war, however, is ultimately unsuited to the conditions of "total war," being neither intended nor designed to apply to conflicts where technologically sophisticated societies, armed with the most frightful instruments of destruction, struggle continuously for years on end. Although undertaken for ostensibly rational ends, the major wars of the twentieth century have been in practice fundamentally irrational in the broadest human terms. Of course men are killed and suffer in war, no matter what the weapons employed. But unlike the wars of the past, those who returned from the trenches described their experience as a surrealistic nightmare almost impossible for human nature to cope with—the paintings *We are making a New World* by Paul Nash and *La Mitrailleuse* by C. R. W. Nevinson capture this quality successfully. Significantly, a new term, "shell shock," had to be invented to describe the mental disorganization arising from the combined effects of noise and nervous strain. As we have already suggested, war on such an immense scale, demanding sacrifices which are by just-war standards disproportionate to the hoped-for ends, must be waged for the most exalted interests of the human race. It is easier to pay the tariff in blood, to send one's sons to a Verdun or a Passchendaele, if one believes that the enemy seeks to enslave the world; easier still when convinced one's own side fights for the eternal verities.

Appeals to idealism have always been important in mobilizing energies for the fight, witness the hundreds of thousands of young men who flocked to the recruiting offices after August 4. Yet there are limits even to the idealism of the young. If war reaches a point where it becomes psychologically intolerable to large numbers of people, especially civilians, then the meaning assigned to it may change altogether. In certain instances, there may in fact occur a flight from reason to the irrationalities of apocalyptic thinking.

Resounding through the Old Testament stories of Deborah, Joshua, Gideon, and the Maccabees, and mentioned in several places by St. Augustine, one type of war, the holy war, has played a significant role in the history of Western Christendom since the close of the eleventh century. The holy war, or crusade, is not unique to Christianity, although the word "crusade," derived from the Latin verb *cruciare* (to mark with the Cross), has a definitely Christian connotation. Islam has its jihad, wherein the faithful are enjoined by the Koran (v. 37) to cast out, slay, crucify, and cut off on alternate sides the hands and feet of unbelievers; Judaism has the struggle with Amalek.

The crusade differs from the just war in several respects. As with the just war, the crusade has its proper authority and object, only these are infinitely more exalted. *Deus Vult!*, "God wills it!" cried the knights assembled at Clermont to hear Urban II proclaim the First Crusade. The crusade is God's war, willed by Him, proclaimed by His church, and conducted under its aegis to defend or extend true religion. (We may note parenthetically, that the term has also been used in a wider sense for secular causes undertaken with religious fervor: Wilberforce's antislavery crusade and Winnington-Ingram's crusade against vice exemplify this type.) Unlike a regular war, in which the soldier serves as a legal obligation, the crusader volunteers to fight as a religious obligation.

Although capable of accomplishing great things against great odds, the crusading mentality is characterized by pigheadedness, self-righteousness, and fanaticism, unwholesome qualities at any time, extremely dangerous in time of war. The crusader is a moral absolutist who reverses the equation Might is Right. For him, Right is Might simply because God is the essence of righteousness; and as surely as day conquers night, the righteous must ultimately prevail. The crusader's confidence in the final victory of his cause, if not for himself personally, serves to radicalize a conflict by raising the level of violence and ruining chances of a sensible, magnanimous peace. All weapons are permissible, all stratagems are legitimate in the battle against the earthly representatives of cosmic evil. And he who has wrestled with the enemies of the Lord is unlikely to settle for anything less than their unconditional surrender and humiliation.

There is a depth of truth in the remark by R. H. Tawney that "War is either a crime or a crusade."[8] In it is summarized the English experience in 1914–1918. True, the English have had other crusades in their history; and Napoleon, Czar Nicholas I, and others have been cast in the role of Antichrist. What distinguishes this phenomenon in the Great War, however, is the degree to which it became part of the imagination of religious people. For a great many Anglicans—we shall never know precisely how many—clergy and laity alike, the conflict that began as a necessary, if somewhat idealized, campaign to safeguard national interests and rid the world of a military despotism was transformed under the pressure of events into a holy war, ending as a frenzied crusade against the Devil incarnate.

BELGIUM

The process of abandoning just-war concepts in favor of defining the war as a purely religious struggle is illustrated by the changing attitudes toward England's comrades in arms. If Germany was evil, it followed that by the mere fact of opposing her the Allies bore witness to their devotion to the contrary system of values. Their sins notwithstanding, an aura of holiness was made to surround the Allies, and they were cast in the role of a Sir Galahad, or more appropriately, St. George doing combat with the Teutonic dragon. But war, like politics, makes strange bedfellows; and before the Allies could become proper subjects of reverence, their reputations, by 1914 somewhat tarnished in British eyes, had to be refurbished.

Needless to say, the name of Russia conjured up images of knout-wielding Cossacks, Siberia, and pogroms. But as the Czar's "steam-roller" began its westward movement, "Holy Russia" became the dominant theme. Though none could deny the many black marks against her name, the shortcomings of Russia were easily dismissed by attributing them to her pro-German bureauocracy and aristoc-racy. Because the Christianity of the bulk of the Russian population, consisting of simple, childlike peasants led by saintly Orthodox patri-archs, had remained free from the corrupting influence of western rationalism, she would always be a trustworthy ally; an ally, more-over, that knew how to fight. "The present war will undoubtedly bear to the Russian masses the aspect of a crusade, and the alliance of the German with the hated Turk, his hands ever red with the blood of martyrs, will stamp the Kaiser for them as the Beast of the Apo-calypse."[9] From August 1914 until 1918, when practically the entire Anglican press demanded the overthrow of the Bolsheviks (secret German agents) for having made a separate peace, scarcely a harsh world about "Our Great Ally" is to be found even in Christian Socialist publications.[10]

The reaction to the invasion of Belgium is by all odds the best example of how the secular considerations—treaty commitments and strategic necessities—first put forward in support of aiding an unpopular ally later became consecrated as moral imperatives, finally being replaced altogether with religious arguments.

Memories dating from the Boer War of vicious Belgian anti-British propaganda, as of the personal abuse heaped upon the royal family by the French press—in 1903 *L'Assiette au Beurre* published a car-toon entitled *L'Impudique Albion* portraying Albion, his toga hiked up around his waist, bent over and thrusting his buttocks, in the image of Edward VII, into the face of the world—still rankled. To make matters worse, there appeared in February, 1904, a report by Roger Casement, a British consular official, proving that the agents of King Leopold II of Belgium had committed horrible crimes against the natives of the Congo Free State, his personal domain. Casement's work struck a responsive chord, setting off a moral crusade reminis-cent of Wilberforce's campaign against the slave trade or Gladstone's denunciations of the Bulgarian horrors. The following month, E. D. Morel founded the Congo Reform Association to mobilize public opinion against Belgium's violation of the free trade clauses of the Berlin Act (1885) and the evils of the "rubber system," vividly brought home by publications featuring photographs of "lazy" plantation workers contemplating the severed limbs of their children.[11]

Led by Randall Davidson, the Anglican community responded with generosity to the calls of the Association. In a deservedly acclaimed speech before the House of Lords, the primate protested that the Congo situation was a disgrace and insisted that the government take practical measures to remedy "this terrible matter."[12] His speech made so profound an impression that the *Daily Chronicle*, normally no friend of the Established church, confessed it "did something to justify the presence of Bishops in the Legislature."[13] The Aborigines' Protection Society, plus various church-affiliated and denominational missionary organizations, lent their facilities to publicizing the cause of the oppressed Congolese.[14] In Parliament, meanwhile, Keir Hardie, Sir Edward Grey, Charles Dilke, and Herbert Samuel launched, in Elie Halévy's words, a "campaign of aggressive humanitarianism."[15] These denunciations, predictably, produced a rift in Anglo-Belgian relations. The Belgian government, indignant at the meddling of a country that permitted the virtual enslavement of Chinese coolies in its own South African territories, initiated a pro-German foreign policy which it pursued until the eve of war.

The invasion of Belgium, often expressed metaphorically as a sexual assault, so shocked Englishmen's sense of decency and fairplay as to make them forget their former resentments. For many a preacher, the initial response to the "rape" of Belgium must have been conditioned less by considerations of national self-interest than by the "public school spirit," the moral outlook inculcated by the great public schools and their less prestigious imitators. Perhaps the briefest and most insightful appraisal of the aims and ideals of the English public school in the prewar period is to be found in a lecture by J. E. C. Welldon delivered in Tokyo in 1906 at the invitation of the Japanese minister of education. The aim of the public schools, he affirmed, was not so much to cultivate the intellect and prepare for a career as to build character. Through school songs, boyhood rituals, patriotic sermons and other activities, England's future rulers had inculcated in them the values and discipline of the Christian gentleman. Field sports, about which there clung the mystique of the "muscular Christian," were especially important in the process of socialization: "For learning, however excellent in itself, does not afford much necessary scope for such virtues as promptitude, resource, honour, co-operation, and unselfishness; but these are the soul of English games."[16]

The epitome of English boyhood was Tom Brown, the hero of Tom Hughes's panegyric to boys and Rugby. Appropriately enough, the characters of Tom Brown, the champion of the underdog, and Slogger Williams, the bully, were drawn from life; their famous fight was also based on an incident witnessed by Hughes at Rugby: both antagonists later took Anglican Orders, undoubtedly to Hughes's great satisfaction.[17] Given their background, therefore, it is hardly accidental that the main issue of the war was first perceived by many, Welldon included, as simply an unprovoked, cowardly assault by a "big bully" upon his tiny, inoffensive neighbor. Studdert-Kennedy was appalled by Germany's behavior, attributing it to improper upbringing and disdain for the Sporting Spirit.[18]

German heavy-handedness succeeded where all the blandishments and public relations devices of Leopold II's Press Bureau failed; for the Anglican press withdrew its charges against the regime in the Congo almost immediately after the invasion of Belgium. Furthermore, Roger Casement's unsuccessful attempts at persuading Irish war prisoners to help free Ireland by serving their German captors, as well as his involvement in the Easter Rebellion of 1916, played into the hands of those wishing to refurbish the reputation of Belgium by smirching that of her chief accuser. The report of 1904 was denounced as a fabrication prepared by Casement, a paid German agent, to bolster the German position in Africa. "It is now beyond question," proclaimed the *Guardian*, "that the [Congo] horrors were greatly exaggerated by German agents; the very British Consul who certified to their truth is at this moment an active sympathizer with our principal enemy."[19] Bishop Talbot and a handful of interested persons petitioned the government for a reprieve on account of his humanitarian work; Archbishop Davidson wrote to various officials advising them that it would be impolitic and unjust to hang a man so obviously insane.[20] Needless to say, those advocating the supreme penalty for "that recreant knight," "that most contemptible of all traitors, Roger Casement," carried the day.[21]

The courage and tenacity displayed by the Belgian people in defending their homeland evoked praise from all quarters. Music halls rang with the catchy tune of Mark Sheridan's, "How Belgium Put the Kibosh on the Kaiser"; dabblers in poetry turned out reams of verse (mostly awful) lauding "Belgium, the Noble and Self-Sacrificing!"[22] Clergymen were gratified by Belgium's refreshing, if totally unexpected, reminder that the ideals of chivalry were still alive in Europe. In this connection, the newspapers often praised the "magnificent exploits" of the tiny Belgian army, occasionally going so far as to compare them with the deeds of Sir Galahad. As was to be expected, the popularity of the Belgian royal family rose along with that of its subjects', a fact illustrated by the references made throughout the war to a cartoon in *Punch*. The kaiser is depicted here standing amid the smoking ruins of Belgium: "So," he says, taunting King Albert, "you see—you've lost everything," to which the noble king replies, "Not my soul!"[23]

Among the first Anglican dignitaries to equate Belgium's righteousness with holiness, Hensley Henson devoted a long sermon, "Judaea and Belgium," to comparing her tribulations with those of ancient Israel under the tyrannies of Egypt and Babylon.[24] Many of his compatriots, however, were quick to draw specifically Christian analogies, thereby broadening the significance of Germany's aggression. Belgium came to symbolize for them the Christ of the nations; to be sure, certain preachers ventured still further, transmuting the symbolism into startling word-pictures. The Rev. Hewlett Johnson, later famous as the Communist "Red Dean" of Canterbury, vividly portrayed the prostrate nation: "through her tears Belgium may look up. Her prayer is answered; her victory is won. Crushed and bleeding she lies beneath the German's heel, but on her head, and not on his, there rests the crown, even if it is a martyr's crown."[25] Belgium became the personification of the Allied cause, God's cause, because it was there, in Flanders, that the new Nebuchadnezzar had set up not a golden idol, but a howitzer, an idol of iron. "And a false prophet has been found to sing its praises, this huge and bloodstained embodiment of the superman, man freed from the contemptible weaknesses of truth, and chivalry, and honour, man mighty with the gigantic strength of the elephant, cruel with the ferocity of the tiger, cunning with the slyness of the fox. . . ."[26]

BRITAIN JUSTIFIED

Another manifestation of the subordination of just war concepts to a religious interpretation may be seen in the way certain church figures perceived their country's cause.

The arguments at first put forward in favor of intervention need no elaboration here; they were the commonplaces normally employed by governments to vindicate their warlike policies. Suffice it to say, as did the headmaster of Eton in a sermon published as a pamphlet by the authorities, that intervention was necessary because England's worldwide interests, ultimately her national survival itself, depended upon keeping Belgium's deep-water ports out of unfriendly hands.[27]

As reasonable as this assessment was, it offered small comfort to those who believed that the morality of a policy must rest on something more substantial than one nation's interpretation of its own interests; after all, a "necessary" war need not be a just war. Even the case of Belgium, cited as the ideal example of the just war, lent itself to an interpretation favorable to Germany. True, Belgium's granting a right of way to Germany would have amounted to a declaration of war on France; but might it not also be said that her refusal was tantamount to aggression against Germany, as it weakened her overall strategic position.[28] Or one could take a different tack entirely, following A. Maude Royden, the foremost woman evangelist of her day and a leading pacifist, in repudiating as blasphemous the claim that England was rescuing Belgium: "Look at Belgium now!"[29] The problem, then, was to reconcile self-interest with recognized standards of justice and, most importantly, with Divine precept.

The concept of Christendom has traditionally denoted more than an area of the world adhering to a particular body of religious teachings; rather it has signified an ordered unity, that common outlook and culture Burke meant when he wrote of men and nations being bound together despite conflicting interests and emnities by "a secret, unseen, but irrefragable bond of habitual intercourse."[30] The functioning of this world order, this cosmos so to speak, depends upon the willingness of the nations to conduct themselves in accordance with a body of assumptions, principles, and unwritten understandings. Resilient to a point, it is nonetheless an extremely fragile order, being vulnerable to fanatics—Jacobins in the eighteenth century, Germans in the twentieth century—who refuse to be bound by the rules.[31]

Respect for a treaty, an expression of basic trust between nations, was regarded by those raised in the public school tradition as a matter of honor equivalent to a gentleman's word of honor. "In nothing perhaps is the character of a gentleman more strikingly seen than in his shirking from a breach of trust," said J. E. C. Welldon;[32] indeed, whatever his suspicions, a master should always take a boy's word, lest an atmosphere of distrust be created between two gentlemen.

First and foremost, treaties, like oaths in the Middle Ages, represented obligations undertaken in the sight of God and therefore sacred in His eyes. To evade them or to abrogate them unilaterally for whatever reason would create international anarchy, compelling each country to mount perpetual guard against its neighbors. And since a good offense is the best defense, why not steal the first march on a prospective foe? While the origin of the phrase "sanctity of treaties" is obscure, and is probably of secular derivation, it became a staple of pulpit oratory. The rhetoric of the Rev. F. Y. Leggatt was typical in this respect. Treaties, he declared, were actually "God's demand notes, endorsed by His Divine hand"; to disregard them necessarily involved eternal damnation.[33]

The invasion of Belgium aside, few things damaged the reputation of the German leaders so badly as the published reports of their eleventh-hour meetings with British diplomats. The most shocking example of German cynicism and lawlessness was laid to the highest official next to the kaiser, Theobald von Bethmann-Hollweg, the chancellor. On one occasion he attempted to buy British neutrality with a promise to annex no part of metropolitan France; on another occasion he flew into a rage in the presence of Sir Edward Goschen, His Majesty's ambassador, denouncing the government for betraying a kindred people "just for a word—'neutrality,' a word which in war time is so often disregarded—just for a scrap of paper. . . ."[34]

Whether Bethmann-Hollweg's proposal was sincere (Germany had everything to gain if it was), or his words chosen more for effect than meaning, is irrelevant for our purposes. What is important is their profound influence on British sensibilities. Clergymen wrote Sunday School plays about "A Scrap of Paper,"[35] and the "infamous proposal," as it came to be called, was taken as an invitation to share Germany's guilt through sanctioning her crime. Analogies between the offer of peace in return for tolerating evil and the life of Christ came easily to mind. He had been betrayed by a false friend, as had Belgium; He had been tempted by the Devil, as had England.[36] At stake in England's response to the infamous proposal was more than international righteousness and justice, important as these were. "If we had consented," said Paul Bull, "faith and honour would have perished from among the nations, and the soul of Europe would have died."[37] In resisting the temptation, England had found her soul, something he thought should be remembered thankfully at every Eucharist.[38]

From this standpoint, then, the nation had been under a threefold obligation to go to war: the code of honor of the English gentleman; the need to protect the European community from an outlaw; and the duty to uphold the Word of God as embodied in treaties. The Bishop of London, Hensley Henson, and others thought this obligation so compelling as to warrant reinforcement through preaching on appropriate texts, invariably from the Old Testament. Judges 5:25 was among the most popular:

We could not stand by inactive while treaties were trampled under foot, and nameless outrages wreaked on an innocent people. We could not suffer that noble heritage of Liberty and Empire, which we have received from our forefathers, to be stolen from us by the brutal aggression of the German autocracy. Our way was straight: our obligations were evident. To flinch at this dreadful crisis would have been to merit the malediction of the Prophetess: 'CURSE YE MEROZ, SAITH THE ANGEL OF THE LORD, CURSE YE BITTERLY AND THE INHABITANTS THEREOF: BECAUSE THEY CAME NOT TO THE HELP OF THE LORD, THE HELP OF THE LORD AGAINST THE MIGHTY.'[39]

Mark Twain once remarked sardonically, referring to the British race, that there is a passage in Scripture mentioning them specifically: "Blessed are the meek, for they shall inherit the earth." Yet for all their bluster, indeed, for all their downright foolishness, Anglicans believed sincerely in their country's sacred mission. As in the nation as a whole, the war fostered in the national church an atmosphere in which strange ideas could flourish. Not that these were necessarily new; on the contrary, some had long found favor in certain quarters,

the war merely bringing them to bear on new issues. For example,
the partisans of the British Israelite theory, Low Churchmen mainly,
proclaimed the Anglo-Saxon race a chosen people, the bulwark of
the Saints.[40] The Rev. G. H. Lancaster, vicar of St. Stephen's, North
Bow, argued in a well-received volume on *Prophecy, the War, and the
Near East* that "the Anglo-Saxon Race, Great Britain and America
—the former Ephriam and the latter Manassah—is the Redeemed
House of Israel, and therefore invincible."[41] Without ever claiming
that God is English, it was easy enough to imply that He had a special
relationship with His Englishmen:

> God of England! God Almighty!
> God of England's children free;
> God of England's wondrous story;
> England's God, we cry to Thee.[42]

Those who were quick to denounce the notion that the English
were the covenant people of God might themselves profess comparable doctrines. Bishop Winnington-Ingram, loudly seconded by
his colleagues in the colonies, preached with assurance the duty of
the English to shape the non-European world in their image, an
argument that would take on added significance when the time came
to decide the fate of the German colonies. God had bred Christian
ideals into the very fiber of their race. God had chosen them to hold
up before the world the example of morality in every sector of life.
God had entrusted them with the largest, most diversified empire in
history in order to spread the Word among the backward races and
raise them to true freedom. "We have been the mother of free countries. We have grown free nations. There is no country in the world
that can make people happier under its rule than our country. We
seem to have a knack, a genius for creating free nations, who love
their mother . . . . We are the mother of the free; but more than that,
we are the children of Freedom! England is the child of the free"[43]—
Ireland had evidently slipped from the bishop's mind.

When set against this background, the history of England became
the record of an all but unbroken chain of triumphs in God's name.
Save for the few times when she had paid dearly for violating His
trust, England had humbled the bullies, defended the underdogs, and
championed liberty the world over. This high valuation of England's
mission confirmed enthusiasts in the belief that God not only favored

the Allied cause, but that He was actually on "our" side. England was the Sword of the Lord. He had selected, trained, and commissioned England as the instrument of His retributive justice. "We believe," wrote S. C. Carpenter, Winnington-Ingram's biographer and a future Dean of Exeter, "that we have been divinely commissioned to end Prussian militarism. So we have."[44]

Confidence in England's mission was a source of encouragement, as well as an awesome responsibility. It was a responsibility, however, sustained by the faith that, God willing, mankind might at last attain the supreme goal, peace. Though there were some pessimists, as there always are, the overwhelming majority thought their generation was striking the mortal blow at war itself. God works in strange ways, and who would be so bold as to say definitely that a disastrous war was not His way of bringing humanity to its senses? In this, people as different in background, interests, and temperament as Gilbert Murray, the Oxford classical scholar and peace-worker, and the Bishop of London were on common ground. Both saw the struggle as a war to end war; both urged its vigorous prosecution; both were delighted to hear about enemy casualties, the higher the better. "For my own part," wrote Murray, who together with other scholars had recently signed a letter urging neutrality, "I find that I do desperately desire to hear of German dreadnoughts sunk in the North Sea. . . . When I see that 20,000 Germans have been killed in such-and-such an engagement, and the next day that it was only 2,000, I am sorry."[45]

If the Allies "exterminated" German militarism—an idea that was to have lasting and disastrous consequences—they were sure (in Hensley Henson's words) to "break the Empire of Force, and establish in its place the Kingdom of Goodwill."[46] Interpreted in this self-righteous way, the war proved that England was sacrificing the flower of her manhood out of love for Germany. Germany would some day bless England for having defeated her. No longer prey to the kaiser and his gang, free from the burden of swollen armaments, the German people would have a chance of attaining true freedom. Even the lowly *Hausfrauen*, hitherto regarded as drudges and breeders of soldiers, would be emancipated. Besides, victory would harm the German character further, as it would harden their belief in a false philosophy.

In view of the prevailing attitude toward the enemy and the Allied causes, it is hardly surprising that special significance should be assigned to the anniversary of England's entry into the struggle. August 4, 1914, became for a time a holy day in the calendar of the English Christian. It was solemnized as the day when God called upon England to decide between peace and its soul. It was a day depicted in the symbolism of the Crucifixion and the Resurrection. "On that day the whole nation renounced its past, was born again, died to self and rose again for others."[47] The sword had been thrust into England's hands; and, if we are to believe Studdert-Kennedy, it had been put there by the Lords of Hosts Himself. "In August, 1914, God called in a voice like thunder. He called to England across the narrow stretch of sea, 'Come out! Come out! Come out from home and comfort. Come out to right the wrong. Come out to share my sorrow and help to save the world.' God called and England answered. Thank God England answered, and simply said, 'I come.' "[48]

ENGLAND'S HOLY WAR

We must now complete the picture with a discussion of the holy war phenomenon itself. While it is evident that clergymen displayed a marked tendency to identify England's war aims with the Divine scheme, hardly any clergymen, regardless of denomination, were prepared to go so far as the Jesuit Hugh Benson. The convert son of a former archbishop of Canterbury, Benson announced when the war began: "It's extremely like Armageddon, and why shouldn't the Kaiser be Antichrist? Besides, there's an eclipse of the sun tomorrow. It all fits in. 'The sun shall be turned to ashes. . . .' "[49] Among the Nonconformists, John Clifford and J. H. Shakespeare, another Baptist leader, pronounced at a meeting of American Baptists: "We are fighting for Christianity against paganism, for right against might, for liberty against cruel tyranny; for humanity against the works of the devil."[50] Yet these seem to have been rare outbursts. I have been unable to discover the holy war phenomenon as it will be described below among the leaders of Roman Catholicism or Nonconformity, or manifested to any great extent in their respective periodicals.

On the Anglican side, the conflict was first declared a crusade (for reasons best known to themselves) by laymen of varying degrees of religious commitment. Lord Halifax, the Anglo-Catholic leader, issued in November, 1914, one of the first proclamations of a holy war. His call was echoed shortly thereafter by Mrs. Henry Sidgwick, sister of A. J. Balfour and principal of Newham College, Cambridge, and by Viscount Haldane.[51] Although practically the entire Anglican press and possibly a majority of the clergy eventually decided their country was engaged in a genuine holy war, this aspect of war psychology came to the fore only as a result of the interaction of several factors: events, popular superstitions, religious beliefs, personalities.

There is in all societies a substratum of mystical, miraculous, and prophetic beliefs that come to the foreground and gain respectability in times of crisis and distress. Unfortunately, the kind of study which would have enabled us to measure the extent to which beliefs of this sort were prevalent in the England of 1914 was not carried out at this time. On evidence from a later period, however, we do know that superstitions about the spirit-world are still widespread among English people, especially among the less educated. The sociologist Geoffrey Gorer estimated in the mid-'fifties that at least one-sixth of the population believes in ghosts, while another 44 percent have consulted a fortune teller at some time in their life. Soldiers, whose lives may be saved or lost by the merest chance, have always been prone to superstition. In addition to the ubiquitous rabbit's foot, the infantry in both world wars have prized Bibles as amulets; with some reason, as there are authenticated (and well-publicized) cases of pocket testaments stopping bullets.[52]

These beliefs, although not specifically religious in nature, blend easily with the eschatological portions of Scripture. Scripture speaks of two kinds of war: those of the past, waged by the Chosen People at the behest of God, and, in the Last Days, the denouement of history when Good will vanquish Evil at Armageddon (in its secularized form variously known as "the final clash" and "the battle of destiny"), the dead shall rise to be judged, and the messianic kingdom established. Jewish apocalypticism, the expression of the yearnings of a persecuted people for divine intervention in its affairs, was taken over in toto by the Christian church during its own time of tribulation in the first century. Mark 13:7 speaks of the necessity of wars and rumors of wars; Paul speaks in 2 Thes. 2:7 of the time when the wicked shall be revealed "whom the Lord shall consume with the spirit of his mouth." The theme of messianic warfare permeates Revelation, where it is prophesied that the Messiah, a sword issuing from His mouth, will return to conquer the Beast, inaugurate the millennial reign, overthrow Gog and Magog, until finally the New Jerusalem shall descend from Heaven (Rev. 21:2).

The Great War, with its attendant bereavements and uncertainties, heightened interest in the occult and created an ever-growing clientele for mediums, crystal gazers, palmists, and the like. Less than a month after England's entry into the conflict, tales of unusual happenings purporting to prove the intervention of supernatural powers in the earthly conflict began to circulate.[53] Cases of churches destroyed completely save for an ancient relic or a sacred picture, stone crosses standing unscathed at shell-swept crossroads, and alleged appearances of Joan of Arc were reported in the press and discussed with gravity by the religious public. For a year after the battle of Mons (August 23–24), people talked about how the sorely pressed army had been saved at the last moment through the intercession of an angelic host mounted on white horses.[54] The government was also interested in this story for its own reasons: *The Real Angels of Mons* (1915), an emotional telling of the tale by the Rev. A. A. Boddy, vicar of All-Saints', Monkwearmouth, Sunderland, was published with the permission of the official censor as a spur to recruiting.

Viewed in conjunction with evidence from the Bible, these "phenomena" assumed portentous significance. Millenarian and apocalyptic interpretations of the conflict flourished. Clergymen of all parties, but especially Evangelicals, turned to their Bibles, seeking to predict the future in terms of the symbolism of Daniel and Revelation. After surveying the "signs of the times," the conclusion was inescapable that the world was on the verge of momentous changes. It had arrived at "the hinge of the age," the last days of the present dispensation and the prelude to the Lord's return. As 1914 drew to a close, references to Armageddon appeared with increasing frequency in sermons and religious poetry. Typical in this respect was H. C. Beeching, a former professor of theology and Dean of Norwich, who wrote in *Armageddon*, a pamphlet published by the S.P.C.K., that "we are fighting for others as well as for ourselves, for the weak against the strong, for right against might, for Christ against anti-Christ. And so the battle is not ours, it is indeed Armageddon. Ranged against us are the Dragon and the False Prophet; but the issue is sure."[55] "Armageddon," a play by the renowned dramatist J. M. Martin-Harvey, brought a secularized version of this message to the audiences at the New Theatre.

The events of the early spring and fall of 1915, one of the most trying periods in the war, were of critical importance in whipping this restlessness, expectation, and sense of impending doom into a crusading fervor. The year began quietly enough, all things considered; and after the indecisive battle of Neuve Chapelle in March, large-scale operations ceased. In a sentence reminiscent of the closing lines of a great war novel, at the end of March a dispatch from the British sector of the Western Front noted briefly, "there is nothing special to report."[56] Then hell broke loose and disaster followed disaster. On April 22 the Germans launched with deadly effect, near Ypres, the first poison gas attack of the war. On May 7 a German submarine sent the liner *Lusitania* to the bottom off the west coast of Ireland, claiming nearly 1,200 lives. Six days later, British sensibilities were further shocked by the Bryce Commission's *Report on Alleged German Atrocities*, a chilling document by even the standards of the nuclear age. May ended as it had begun, with tragedy; the Germans began sending their Zeppelins against the Home Counties. Things then became relatively quiet for a time, but after a summer of desultory fighting in the West, the public was outraged in mid-October, when the Turks began slaughtering the Armenians and the Germans executed Nurse Edith Cavell, the daughter of an Anglican clergyman, for helping Allied soldiers escape from Belgium.

These events startled the Anglican community as nothing since the declaration of war and the burning of Louvain. The archbishop of Canterbury was deeply moved, writing to Mr. Asquith:

The last few weeks have shown us afresh the nature of the fight we have to wage against the unbridled force of cruelty and wrong. The unscrupulous defiance of international promise by the studied use of poison gas, inflicting [the] acutest suffering upon soldiers in the field, or by the ruthless sinking of a huge passenger ship with its living freight of non-combatants, gives us new evidence of the spirit which in the earlier stages of the War inspired the shameless horrors perpetrated upon helpless civilians under the authority, as we now know, of the officers of the German Army.[57]

Davidson's remarks, biting and to the point, were those of a man who could keep tight reign on his emotions. There were those of his colleagues, however, who were transported with rage, indulging themselves in extravagant violence of thought and expression. Indications of a changing attitude toward the war began to appear in sermons, always a barometer of clerical thinking. On May 21, for example, the *Challenge* published excerpts from the annual visitation charge of Archdeacon Blakeway of Stafford: the war, he declared, had passed from a crisis into a crusade. Six days later, the *Guardian* reported that Archdeacon Basil Wilberforce, at this time chaplain to the House of Commons, had paused in the midst of a speech against Lord Kitchener's detractors to announce that the war "has been recognized solemnly as the Battle of the Lord."[58]

Shortly after the gas attack at Ypres, Bishop Winnington-Ingram, proud of his nickname "the Bishop of the Battlefields," returned from a visit to the London Rifle Brigade ("my regiment"), his first since its departure for France the previous September. A man of fifty-seven, he was a vigorous, outgoing personality who, when he put aside lawnsleeves and gaiters for a natty chaplain's uniform, looked more the part of a dashing subaltern than the bishop of London. Having learned his profession at Bethnal Green and Stepney in the 'nineties, he was a popular and effective mission preacher;[59] a favorite activity, stemming from an abiding interest in apologetics, was debating atheists on Sunday afternoons in Victoria Park. By 1915, he had earned a reputation for being able to understand and express in picturesque language the feelings of his comrades. This he did in the first of a series of appeals to the church published at the beginning of June. "I think the Church can best help the nation first of all by making it realise that it is engaged in a Holy War, and not be afraid of saying so. Christ died on Good Friday for Freedom, Honour and Chivalry, and our boys are dying for the same things. . . . MOBILIZE THE NATION FOR A HOLY WAR!"[60]

It is always risky to assign to one man either exclusive credit or blame for an important shift in group attitudes. The fact that holy war rhetoric was taken up by preachers soon after Winnington-Ingram's declaration neither proves that he inspired their enthusiasm nor that they "borrowed" the idea from him. What does seem likely, however, is that he, together with several others whose activities are documented less adequately,[61] acted as a catalyst, clarifying at a crisis in the war hitherto vague, ill-defined ideas and verbalizing their feelings. It should also be noted that this reaction was largely a civilian phomenon. There is always the tendency for the civilian, bombarded with horror stories, concerned about his loved ones, and feeling helpless in the face of vast, impersonal forces, to be more prone to this kind of hysteria than the combat soldier. Many a soldier, knowing "poor 'ole Fritz" to be a man like himself, very human and very frightened, was inclined to view the furor over the *Lusitania* and Nurse Cavell as so much nonsense, the holy war as clerical cant.[62]

Be that as it may, clergymen of all ranks, representing all shades of opinion in the Church of England, took up the call for a holy war. While it would be pointless to multiply quotations indefinitely, the following passage, by the Rev. Basil Bourchier, rector of St. Anne's, Soho, and a friend of Winnington-Ingram's, recaptures something of the holy war frenzy as its height.

We are fighting, not so much for the honour of our country, as for the honour of our God. Not only is this a Holy War, it is the holiest war that has ever been waged. The cause is the most sacred that man has been asked to defend. It is the honour of the most High God which is imperilled. Our enemies have done despite to His Name. The Christian man never has had less cause for misgiving for being a soldier. This truly is a war of ideals. Odin is ranged against Christ, and Berlin is seeking to prove its supremacy over Bethlehem. Every shot that is fired, every bayonet thrust that gets home, every life that is sacrificed, is in very truth 'for His Name's sake.'[63]

Similarly, F. Holmes Dudden, the author of the standard biography of St. Ambrose, preached "An Extraordinary Call," a sermon proclaiming that "We are fighting not only for our hearths and homes, we are fighting for our altars, for our holy religion and for our God."[64]

In tracing the development of ideas within a group, we can detect at times nuances so fine and subtle that, notwithstanding our sense of their importance, it is difficult to measure their overall impact with any degree of certainty. This is the case with a mode of thought lying at the base of the crusading mentality, and which must have played a key role in determining how the Bourchiers and the Duddens perceived the conflict. Persons inspired by violent enthusiasm for an ideal, particularly those whose outlook has been conditioned by religious training, tend evidently to be moral absolutists, to see a radical antithesis running through all creation. We might almost say that their thought displays certain Manichaean qualities, that is, the heresy, a Christian offshoot of Persian Zoroastrianism, postulating an eternal struggle between two fairly balanced forces: absolute goodness represented by the god of light, and absolute evil represented by the god of darkness. Yet spirits though they may be, their combat takes place on several planes; it is never restricted to the shadow-world alone. Viewed in these terms, the Great War represented nothing less than an aspect of the eternal struggle of supernatural powers. Good and Evil, God and Lucifer, sometimes using Britain and Germany as their surrogates on the material plane, sometimes personified in them, were doing battle. This seems the only explanation for the rash of statements like the following, made by Bishop Diggle of Carlisle. According to him, the war was not merely a conflict with a despotic state holding an anti-Christian ideology:

On both sides this war has more the nature and attributes of a crusade than of an ordinary war. No doubt in this war the ordinary elements of commonplace war may be found in abundance—greed, envy, lust of power and preeminence, commercial and industrial advantage . . . . But in this war there move and work spirits deeper, stronger, more revolutionary than any or all of these—spirits of good and evil, powers of heaven and principalities of hell, invisible spirits of goodness and wickedness of which men are the instruments and the world the visible prize. . . . this present war is essentially a spiritual war; a war waged on earth but sustained on either side by invisible powers.[65]

This perhaps sheds light upon comments, occasionally entire speeches, that would otherwise appear to be the rantings of madmen. It gives some insight into what Colonel Granville Smith meant when he told the Church Pastoral Aid Society that at the Front, one could hear the spiritual warfare going on all about, and sense that God and the Devil were drawing up their legions; or what a young officer had in mind when he wrote to his sister comparing the sensation of going to war with that of entering some vast cathedral full with the Divine presence.[66] The Great War had become for these people quite literally a war of spirits, although the visibly wrestling hosts were of flesh and blood.

Opposition to the crusading-apocalyptic war hysteria can be dealt with briefly; it was weak, unorganized, and late in developing. Bishop Gore stood out amid a generally apathetic or hostile episcopate in denouncing what, to his mind, represented a shameful, unchristian upsurge of fanaticism. In an article published in the *Oxford Diocesan Magazine*, Gore chided the enthusiasts for resorting to language associated historically with the Crusades, not the most glorious period in church history. Certainly England had been duty-bound to enter the struggle against Germany; but since the history of England was hardly immaculate, national penitence rather than national self-righteousness was more in keeping with the spirit of the times. Protests were also registered by the Rev. Walter Lock of Keble College, Oxford, and Henry Scott Holland, both of whom maintained that, their crimes notwithstanding, the Germans remained God's children; clergymen should remember their calling as His servants, and not go about as "Mad Mullahs preaching a Jehad."[67]

What effect apocalyptic preaching had upon the popular imagination, or how effective it was in moblizing energies for the war effort, one cannot say. Nor can one properly assess how far such language reflected the feelings of the clergy as a whole. Yet if the sermons, editorials, and letters published in the religious press between May and December, 1915, and intermittently thereafter for the remainder of the war, indicate anything, it was that a numerous and articulate group of zealots heeded the extraordinary call to preach a crusade. It is certain, however, that the critics of the holy war were pilloried as over-intellectual prigs by every Anglican newspaper except the *Challenge*—a tribute to its editor, William Temple—and soon lapsed into silence. The High Church, High Tory *Guardian* on the one extreme, and the *Record*, ever-loyal to the Reformation Settlement on the other, agreed in words that could easily have been lifted from each other's editorial pages. "If this is not a 'Holy War,' we do not know what war could be so considered . . . . This is the holiest war in history, and every soldier of the Allies who strikes a blow in it performs a religious duty."[68]

V. THE CHRISTIAN AND THE SWORD

Not every Englishman saw the Great War as a struggle to save Christian civilization from Teutonic savagery, much less as a conflict of the children of light against the children of darkness. There were from the very beginning a number of groups, small and determined, whose dissent from the prevailing view and refusal to behave as society thought they should taxed English tolerance to the utmost, at the same time compelling the more thoughtful to define further their attitudes toward violence.

People opposed the war for various reasons, usually unrelated to a rejection of violence in principle. Anarchists denounced it as the supreme expression of the organized and therefore of the unfree society (although Prince Kropotkin supported the Allied *states* against the German *state*); some socialists and trade unionists, who furnished far and away the largest contingent of conscientious objectors, saw it as the fruit of capitalism and a threat to labor's hard-won gains; still others, among them the members of the Union of Democratic Control, led by E. D. Morel, maintained it was the result of an undemocratic diplomacy.

There were those, however, who were motivated primarily by religious considerations. As we saw in the previous chapter, pacifism predominated among Christian thinkers until the triumph of Constantine, the just war then being accepted by the Roman church and by the major denominations that emerged from the Reformation. Yet from time to time pacifistic minorities have appeared within the various communions. Pacifism has always remained (theologically) an alternative to war, defensible on several levels within the context of Christian ethics. The so-called "historic peace churches" of Dutch and German origin, together with their offshoots in Great Britain and the United States—Mennonites, Hutterites, and Brethren—have carried forward the nonviolent, nonresisting tradition of the early Christians. They have affirmed that the state, albeit a legitimate institution given by God for the sins of man, has no claim to their services; for the world and anything associated with it was literally the dominion of Satan. As the True Church of the Saved, and although still alive in the flesh, they considered themselves as already living according to the absolute law of the Gospel and practicing the disciplines of the hereafter. Their pacifism, therefore, was "legalistic," resting on the literal interpretation of the Sermon on the Mount. A sixteenth-century spokesman for the Swiss Brethren explained their position succinctly: "In Matthew 5 Christ forbids believers to use all force." When confronted by their critics with the wars of the Israelites, their normal tack was to dismiss the Old Covenant as superseded by a newer, better revelation. Hence they would suffer, resisting evil neither on their own behalf nor on behalf of others, however unoffending or innocent. That was the Lord's will. Lastly, to their legalistic approach to the Scriptures they added the conviction that the self-sacrifice of the nonresistant was redemptive, repeating the original act of redemption upon the Cross, a concept taken up in the twentieth century by advocates of unilateral disarmament and the "martyr nation" theory.[1]

The Quakers form a bridge between the quietistic pacifism of the Reformation sects and the nonviolent activists, Christian and non-Christian, as in Gandhi's case, of recent times. Perhaps because their sufferings never approached those of the Anabaptists, burned as heretics by Catholics and drowned as heretics by Protestants, perhaps also because their doctrine of the Inner Light (the Divine light in the hearts of men) led them into closer communion with their fellowmen, they easily accommodated themselves to the world. William Penn, after all, planted a colony in the New World, where the settlers served on juries, in the constabulary, and as magistrates.

The Quaker rejection of war rests less on proof-texts (a fact frequently overlooked by their critics) than on the conviction that the experience of the Inner Light, by making a man new through permitting him to join spiritually with Christ, removed the ground for enmity and led to a better way in human relations. As with the pacifistic sects of the Reformation, the Quakers accepted their sufferings; unlike them, they accepted them as a way of *resisting* evil. Whereas the others suffered without hope or intention of transforming the world within historical time, they viewed their sufferings as a vehicle for change. To the Quakers and those subsequently influenced by their ideals, violence is as inconsistent with the spirit of Christ's teaching as it is incompatible with human nature. Whereas the exponents of the just war viewed Christian love primarily in terms of charity and a concern for the victims of wrongdoing, the Quakers viewed love primarily in its redemptive-rehabilitative aspect. They hoped to change the heart of the wrongdoer and set him right with God, thereby rescuing him from the consequences of his sin and, in the long run, protecting the innocent more effectively than the strongest fortifications. But you cannot change the heart of the wrongdoer by blowing him to bits. Like calls forth like. Violence breeds violence, and hatred, hatred. The hardest of hearts, however, will ultimately melt if approached with gentleness and the willingness to suffer all it has to offer. Robert Barclay, the Quaker's foremost theologian of the seventeenth century, described this ideal in operation in his *Apology* of 1676. When soldiers came to disperse their meetings, they refused to move, forcing the intruders either to kill them on the spot or remove them bodily—after which they promptly returned to their meeting houses, or held their services on their ruins. They eventually won the respect of, and toleration from, their persecutors: "as this patient but yet courageous way of suffering made their persecutors' work very hard and wearisome unto them, so the courage and patience of the sufferers . . . did secretly smite the hearts of their persecutors, and made their chariot-wheels go on heavily." The strong man armed was, to them, strong because strengthened through suffering and armed with the weapon of the spirit, that gentleness which is the product of strength and self-mastery.

The outbreak of the Great War found the Quakers, who would eventually supply the largest contingent of religious conscientious objectors, the largest, wealthiest, and most influential body of Christian pacifists in the world. Save for a few individual defections at the outset, they wavered not a jot from their time-honored position. Immediately upon England's entry into the conflict, the Society issued in the form of a paid advertisement in the major national newspapers what comes as near to being an official statement of policy as we have. This manifesto applauded the government's efforts to avoid war and acknowledged the justice of the nation's cause; nevertheless, it concluded by asserting that, since war necessarily involves killing men and maiming the human spirit, not even a just war warranted fighting.

Next to the Quakers, pacifism was strongest among the Congregationalists. During the war, two well-known and highly respected Congregationalist ministers, Leyton Richards and Nathaniel Micklem of Withinston were forced to resign their positions because of their antiwar attitudes. In May, 1916, F. H. Stead was instrumental in founding a Congregational League to Abolish War. At Mansfield College, Oxford, where C. J. Cadoux, author of several respectable histories of the early church and the standard *The Early Christian Attitude Toward War*, preached against the war, Congregationalist students became involved in pacifist activities.[2] W. E. Orchard, another leading Congregationalist, was a convinced pacifist, comparing the conflict to a struggle between Sodom and Gomorrah. Orchard's pamphlet, *The Real War* (1914) in the *Papers for War Time* series edited by William Temple, was the only widely circulated work by a nationally known religious figure to brand as unadulterated nonsense the idea that the war was the product of the thought of the lying prophets. Their evil doctrines cut across national boundaries, he affirmed; for the real war was the good and evil contending within each man's spirit.

Dissatisfaction with the attitude of organized religion concerning war generally drew pacifist members of the various denominations together in interdenominational groups. The most important and long-lived of these, the Fellowship of Reconciliation, was formed at Cambridge in the closing days of 1914. Composed of people like W. E. Orchard; Leyton Richards; Richard Roberts, a Presbyterian minister; and Henry T. Hodgkin, a well-known Quaker physician, the Fellowship represented (and still does) an effort to unite the pacifist outlook with Christian philosophy.[3] Christians, its "Basis" states, are forbidden absolutely to wage war; only through love can evil be overcome. At the risk of life itself, the follower of Christ must never raise so much as a hand to defend himself. Nor must his nation. According to A. Maude Royden, at the height of the August crisis England should have disarmed completely and unilaterally, and, clad only in the cloak of righteousness, dared the Devil to do his worst. If that meant national death, then God's will be done. "Will no nation be found ready to die for peace? Or is peace too small a thing to die for? Had we been willing, for the peace of the world, to risk all, and had we suffered for it, our suffering would, like the Crucifixion, have been redemptive and outward failure truest victory."[4]

Despite the activities of these individuals, and with the exception of the Quakers, pacifists have always represented the tiniest minority within Nonconformity. Sir William Robertson Nicoll exaggerated but slightly when, writing in 1916, he claimed that Nonconformity's "resistance to the interpretations and arguments of Pacifism has been absolute."[5] The same was true—truer—of the Church of England. With the exception of A. Maude Royden, an early member of the F.O.R. who became active in the Life and Liberty Movement, a campaign initiated in 1917 to win self-government for the Church of England, and George Lansbury, also a leader in the F.O.R. and its president in the 'thirties, pacifists played an insignificant role in the life of the nation and its church. Of the more than four thousand conscientious objectors imprisoned in early 1918, the largest group consisted of men refusing to serve for ideological and economic reasons. Very few based their objection exclusively on Christian ethical teaching, and of these fewer than one hundred were members of the Established Church. A leaflet published at this time by the Friends' Service Committee calculated that Anglicans composed 7.50 percent of the total number of conscientious objectors, lower than the figure for professed atheists (12 percent), higher than the last-placed Roman Catholics (3 percent).[6]

If Anglican laymen were poorly represented in the pacifist ranks, their spiritual leaders were absent altogether. A survey of the ecclesiastical press, biographies of the leading divines, and peace literature of the period has failed to reveal a single man in Anglican Orders who denounced war for the reasons traditionally advanced by Christian pacifists, whatever their orientation (not quite: Paul Jones, the Episcopal bishop of Utah, resigned under pressure in 1918 because of opposition to his pacifist beliefs). As a phenomenon within the Church of England, a pacifist movement developed and reached its peak in the interwar years; but its exponents were commonly dismissed as cranks and exhibitionists. These same pacifists held church appointments and supported the Allies during the Great War. Dr. E. W. Barnes, master of the Temple and subsequently bishop of Birmingham, defended the conscientious objectors, recognizing all the while England's need to take part in the struggle.[7] Dr. Hewlett

Johnson edited *The Interpreter*, a theological journal favorable to the Allied cause. One is puzzled by the claim in his memoirs to have always been "ninety per cent pacifist" (never defined); for the sting lay in the remaining nonpacifist ten percent, which enabled him to denounce the kaiser and support with enthusiasm the Soviet Union against Nazi Germany and Red China against the United States in the Korean War.[8] H. R. L. "Dick" Sheppard, the popular vicar of St. Martin-in-the-Fields, volunteered for noncombatant service in France, was disgusted by what he saw there, and returned home when his health, always delicate, failed. Yet Sheppard, who as president of the Peace Pledge Union became an international figure in the 'thirties, refrained from criticizing the war publicly. His fellow worker in the Union and a leader of the F.O.R., the Rev. Charles Raven, canon of Liverpool, applied for a combatant commission when the war began, was rejected on medical grounds, eventually serving in France as a chaplain; he did not become a pacifist until the "Christ and Peace" campaign of 1930.[9] Evidently the experiences of each of these men during the Great War, coupled with their disillusionment with the peace and fear of another holocaust, rather than their reading of Scripture, were the critical factors in their change of mind.

Drawn, as we have seen, from the same sociointellectual milieu as the nation's leaders in politics, business, and the professions, the episcopate and higher clergy of the Church of England have served the state in capacities ranging from justices of the peace to advisers to the king, from ambassadors to foreign courts to members of royal investigating commissions. A few have found that the road to preferment lay through the armed camp. During the Civil War, John Dolben, later archbishop of York, was wounded while serving with the Royalist forces at Marston Moor; Peter Mews, later bishop of Winchester, was taken prisoner at Naseby and at the age of sixty-six helped move the cannon at Sedgemoor for the forces of James II. In recent times, Archbishop Maclagen of York (d.1910) drew for fifty years a pension as an ex-officer in the Indian army. Certainly involvement in the mainstream of national life, plus the control exercised over the church by the government, have fostered a tendency for ecclesiastical and governmental opinion to converge. But sociological factors, the life histories of its bishops, and the church's own self-interest really fail to get at the assumptions behind its opposition to pacifism or explain the rationale for denouncing it as infidelity to humanity and apostacy from Christ—in fact heresy.

Part of the explanation must be sought in the nature of Anglicanism itself. By the mere fact of its legal position in the state, the Church of England, unlike several of the sects, neither has nor can have a doctrine concerning the separation of the faithful from a corrupting world. It is coextensive with a majority of the nation, whereas the sect aims at a small, select membership. It deliberately leaves certain of its basic formularies ambiguous, to the exasperation of rigorists, whereas the sect aims at precise definition. Save for the aggressive minorities at either end of the spectrum, it has succeeded in avoiding major schisms: the Methodists left largely against their will; and those following Newman to Rome created a sensation disproportionate to their numbers. To preserve a basic minimum of peace within their church, Anglicans have by and large preferred to be guided by tradition and usage, tacitly avoiding long, emotional debates on the basic tenets of the Faith. During the war, pacifists were, predictably, denounced as knaves and fools. But while their knavery could be dealt with by the law, their "foolishness" seemed to involve an approach to religion antithetical of those norms and accommodations with the world deemed necessary by Anglicans for preserving their church.

Before discussing their objections to pacifism as an ethical system, a word is necessary here about the role of personality, style, and social status in shaping attitudes. A source of irritation complained of constantly by those having dealings with pacifists was that they were stubborn, self-righteous people who exuded moral superiority. Notwithstanding the advances toward political democracy, England in our period was still a society where deference was expected by and paid to a man according to his station in life.[10] Pacifists, however, generally rated no such deference from the clergymen of the Established church. Sociologically, they consisted for the most part of semieducated tradesmen, artisans, and white-collar workers to whom clung the odor of socialism; they were "not gentlemen."[11] If they claimed a religious basis for their pacifism, they were almost invariably Nonconformists (epitomized by the leadership of the F.O.R.), about whom clung the odor of the meeting and the conventicle; although, given the overall contribution of Nonconformity to the war effort, pacifists were always attacked for their erroneous principles rather than for their denominational affiliations. What is more, for pacifists, they were more militant than might be supposed, making it difficult for opponents to get a word in edge-wise. This trait stung Bishop Gore, never the most patient of men, into remarking that they were among the most exasperating people with whom he had ever had to deal. The female pacifist, like the suffragette, tended to abuse the prerogatives of her sex. The Rev. R. J. Campbell, a leading Nonconformist until he became an Anglican in 1916, so resented being lectured by one matron that, gentleman though he was, he interrupted her, warning that if ever the Germans, "those hounds of hell," invaded England, pacifism would save neither her nor her loved ones from death or worse.[12]

A major theme in the polemics of the early period of the war stressed that pacifism was a perverted spiritualism arising from pride. The good Christian, as we have seen, accepts the world for what it is, imperfect and filled with sin; then, guided by his faith, he sets out to put things right. But the pacifist, convinced of his personal infallibility, will have no truck with a world incapable of living up to his absolute standards. The idealism of the proud, a pitiless perfectionism divorced from the real world of flesh and blood, inevitably degenerates into materialism and hedonism. For if, as was pointed out by John Neville Figgis, an implacable foe of pacifism, the suffering and death of war are the worst calamities, then only the material is real and we must therefore live for the moment. To adhere to this "voluptuary theory of the universe" would mean sacrificing righteousness and justice in the name of peace, prizing life above holiness and charity.[13] In the long run, then, pacifism was self-defeating. By pursuing peace at any price, it ends by forcing the innocent to pay the supreme price. Pacifists, in the blunt phrases of Studdert-Kennedy, who knew war at its worst, "cry out against war not because it is wrong, but because it is so damned uncomfortable. They want peace not because it is right, but because it is pleasant. Such sloppy talkers and thinkers about peace are ministers of war."[14]

Important though the above criticisms were, they merely set the stage for the assault on what was taken as the central core of pacifist teaching, its use of the Bible. Of the innumerable sources setting forth the Anglican position—the press for 1916 and 1917 has at

least one sermon, essay, or leading article a week on the matter—
none is as thoroughgoing or argued with more conviction than *Peace
and War*, a collection of addresses, some of which were delivered to
captive audiences of pacifists and conscientious objectors. The work
of Paul Bull, a former chaplain to Sir John French's cavalry division
in South Africa, these pieces reveal the thinking of a unique man
who was simultaneously an admirer of the British soldier and the
military life, an imperialist, a socialist, and a staunch Anglo-Catholic
and ritualist.

Bull's attitude toward the standards of authority in religion, and
hence toward pacifism, has a great deal in common historically with
the Anglican opposition to radical Protestantism. For Bull, as for
Richard Hooker, the Bible is not the whole source of religious truth.
Divine Wisdom has other modes of teaching beside the Bible that
warrant attention, namely the customs and usages of the church, the
inner light, and human reason. All are valid, though neither is in
itself a sufficient guide for Christians; together they deepen the understanding of the Mind of God.[15] Unfortunately, in their longing
for certitude, pacifists, latter-day Puritans, repudiated all standards
of authority, substituting instead their uninformed opinions.

Bull maintained in this connection that pacifist fundamentalism
and bibliolatry perverted the meaning of Scripture, transforming a
dynamic, living force into a sterile legalism hostile to the spirit of
Christianity. To be consistent, pacifists found themselves compelled
to cite only those texts suitable to their purposes and to exclude everything else. They were, moreover, hypocrites. Professing to approve
of the injunction to "Resist not him that is evil," their wealth testified
to a blind spot as far as other, equally important, admonitions were
concerned. For instance, how attentive were Quaker shipowners and
cocoa manufacturers to the injunction to "Lay not up for yourselves
treasures upon the earth?" To emphasize this point, Bull chose several
texts and demonstrated how a literal interpretation would lead to
absurd conclusions. "But are you really sure that you are sincere?" he
asked. "Have you obeyed literally all the other commandments of
the Lord in the Gospels? When an eye or hand or foot has caused
you to stumble (i.e. led you to sin), have you plucked it out or cut it
off, literally and without evasion or explanation?"[16]

One must guard against building systems on isolated passages of

Scripture. Every heresy is armed with its favorite text. To arrive at the truth, the Bible should be seen in its historical context. Christ exercised His ministry at a time when a single power, Imperial Rome, ruled the world. The Sermon on the Mount, Bull asserted without realizing that he was utilizing an argument favored by Bernhardi for his own purposes, was intended as a guide to the Christian in his personal relationships rather than as a standard for secular governments. When the Lord said His kingdom was not of this world and admonished the disciples to resist not evil, to love their enemies, and to turn the other cheek, He was merely instructing them "to behave with kindness and meekness when they are persecuted and oppressed. He is not legislating for national and international relationships. . . . He is simply teaching Christians not to nourish personal feelings of revenge." [17]

Those holding these views were apt to discountenance pacifism for other reasons as well. Through the centuries Christianity has portrayed the Saviour in seemingly contradictory terms. On the one hand, He is gentle, merciful, a loving Father; on the other, He is stern, strong, a sharp-tongued Judge. Similarly, the Christian church has portrayed itself under various guises; sometimes as a community of brothers united in love and at peace with all men, at other times as the Church Militant, sword in hand. When a child is baptized, he is dedicated body and soul to confess without shame the faith of Christ crucified and, in the words of the Prayer Book, "manfully to fight under His banner against sin, the world, and the devil, and to continue Christ's faithful soldier and servant to his life's end." In language rich in the imagery of Ephesians, 6:13–17, comfirmation was presented by popular preachers as the clothing of the Christian knight with "the girdle of Truth, the shield of Faith, the helmet of Hope, the breastplate of Righteousness, and the sword of the Spirit." [18]

For the young man growing up in the liberal (one could say anthropocentric) atmosphere of the Victorian church, the militant aspect was kept in the foreground. The image of Christ became fused with the public school ideal of manliness. Thomas Hughes's lectures on *The Manliness of Christ* (1879) are the natural sequel to the earlier *Tom Brown's School Days*. [19] Military metaphors, representing in the New Testament the Christian's internal, spiritual warfare, were used incessantly, almost casually, in the pulpit oratory of the period. The Prince of Peace was referred to as "The Man's Man," "the Great Commander," "the Infinite Commander," "the *Krieg-herr*," "the most perfect and knightly character in the whole history of chivalry"; His church as "the oldest fighting regiment in Europe"; even a small prayerbook or hymnal might be transformed into a "pocket pistol."[20] His use of a whip of cords to drive the money-changers from the Temple proved that His wrath might spill over into violence. Small wonder that men reared in an environment where the speech pattern was permeated with military phraseology and who routinely used this in their daily lives should have been tempera-mentally as well as intellectually incapable of sympathizing with the pacifist position. How many agreed with the parson who cried that, if Christ returned today, he would expect to see Him using a bayonet; or with Archdeacon Wilberforce when he proclaimed, "To kill Ger-mans is a divine service in the fullest acceptation of the term"?[21] The Church Militant with a vengeance!

Rhetoric of this sort reinforced tendencies to see pacifism as in-consistent with the traditional concept of man as a social being, a concept deriving ultimately from the Augustinian view of the two cities. The Christian citizen was regarded as belonging simultane-ously to two divinely ordained moral orders. Membership in the Church Universal, represented imperfectly on earth by its various branches, binds him to a worldwide brotherhood, to God, and to the supernatural order; living in the world, however, places upon him inescapable responsibilities. Ideally, he should live as if already in the Celestial City, devoting all his energies to the religious life; impos-sible in reality, as material needs must be met. As a practical matter, therefore, he cannot divide his life into water-tight compartments, separating the church from the world. He is obliged to assume secular responsibilities and to perform in capacities unrelated to religion.[22]

There are fundamental differences in nature and function between the church and the state. The church is a union of men as Christians, assigned by the Lord the special task of preaching the Word and preparing its members for the life hereafter. This work cannot be accomplished with force, nor can violence advance the Kingdom of God. The state, on the other hand, is essentially a union of men as men, concerned with the well-being of its citizens in this world only.

As long as human nature is marred by the old Adam, the state will have to employ force in restraining evildoers. Unless the state is armed, it cannot preserve order; and without order there is no security for life, property, or religion; indeed, the work of the church presupposes the existence of the armed state. To preserve society from its wouldbe destroyers, policemen and judges are needed, as are executioners. Loving and killing are thoroughly compatible; for "He who kills in obedience to God's commandments is showing his love of God, and, therefore, to the children of God."[23]

Though the state exists by divine appointment, and though all Christians are citizens, not all citizens are Christians. The state as such is under no obligation to act in accordance with the principles governing the private life of the Christian and his relationship with God. "To the State *qua* State Christ did not pretend to be a lawgiver," said the Rev. William Lowndes, a clergyman stationed in the West Indies, in a book published by the Society of SS. Peter and Paul. "The religion of Christ cannot be applicable as a mere set of precepts to worldly organizations, 'Society' or the 'State,' any more than the political constitution of Mars, even if we knew it, could be made applicable to English life."[24] Not that the state is free to act immorally; on the contrary, it exists to serve a moral purpose, possessing as a corporate entity all the attributes of a "moral person." Besides defending its citizens, it must cultivate the natural virtues: truthfulness, honesty, fidelity. But holiness and nonresistance can be no part of this. The error of the pacifists, then, consisted in their conferring upon the state the attributes of the church.

Commentators were willing to acknowledge, on grounds of an ancient Christian tradition, that nonresistance under certain circumstances might be an acceptable mode of conduct for the individual. In a tradition, extending some would say from Jesus Himself, but certainly from St. Ambrose of Milan through St. Augustine to Luther, the Calvinists and beyond, moralists have affirmed the praiseworthiness of the good man's refusing to defend his life and property with violence. Said Ambrose, "I do not think a Christian, a just and a wise man, ought to save his own life by the death of another; just as when he meets a robber he cannot return his blows, lest in defending his own life he should strain his love toward his neighbor."[25]

Anglicans, however, held with these, their forbears, that pacifism on the part of the individual must be limited by the extent to which it brings harm to the innocent. It is one thing, went the standard argument, for a man to permit an aggressor to kick him to death; quite another if the victim happens to be a helpless child—Tolstoy would allow the child to die, reason and the interposition of his own body having failed to dissuade the assailant.[26] Not to resist the evil-doer in such a case, indeed to allow oneself to be killed, would be a breach of love on two counts: first, because it is not good for the evildoer to go unchecked in his iniquity; second, because it ignores the obligation of charity and mercy toward the helpless of the earth. A similar situation might arise in the affairs of nations. As the state is made up of all kinds of men, so the world community consists of all kinds of states. By analogy, the obligations of the state toward its own subjects apply equally to its neighbors. Participation in a just war is actually an extension of its domestic peacekeeping responsi-bilities, an idea supported also in specifically religious terms. Accord-ing to M. G. Glazebrook, a former headmaster of Clifton and canon of Ely, once one is committed to acting in accordance with the con-cept of the brotherhood of man under the fatherhood of God, his "neighbour" becomes in reality everyone whom he has the ability to succour.[27]

The Church of England has always recognized and honored the proffession of arms. As St. Augustine wrote to Count Boniface affirm-ing the worthiness of his calling in the sight of God, so, fourteen centuries later, Frederick Denison Maurice wrote of the soldier to his son: "I believe the Spirit of God as really calls him to his duties and fits him for them as he calls me to mine."[28] Like judges, police-men, and clergymen, soldiers are essential to the life of the com-munity. Unlike pacifists, who occasionally denounced soldiers as murderers and instruments of evil masters, the Anglican clergy were unanimous in defending them as servants and instruments of the Lord. Nothing could be further from the truth as understood by Christian apologists over the centuries than the definition of war Thackeray puts into the mouth of Henry Esmond: "Murder done to military music." Killing in war and murder are in different universes morally. The primary element in murder involves a private person slaying another for private ends. The soldier, of course, is a public functionary forbidden to act on his own initiative; he executes the law when ordered by, and as an agent of, the legally constituted authority in the state. Secondly, just as the soldier does not act in a private capacity, neither does he fight against individuals. The cause served by the foe rather than the foe himself is the object of attack. Thirdly, each opponent takes basically the same risks in warfare, whereas the murderer insures himself of an unfair advantage. Finally, the soldier's willingness to submit to discipline, undergo physical hardship, and risk death and mutilation for the commonweal testified to the sacrificial nature of his calling. It is this sacrifice that ennobles an otherwise degrading phenomenon. "Remember," Hensley Henson bade those who would scorn the warrior, "physical force becomes charged with moral energy when it is the servant of justice. The battlefield becomes radiant with moral witness when its carnage is transfigured with unselfish devotion and its anguish is mitigated by ministries of love."[29]

The theory of the state and the concept of citizenship prevailing among Anglicans at this time derived ultimately from St. Paul's admonition to the Romans: the powers that be are ordained of God, and every soul is subject to them for conscience's sake. No allowance was made for the individual, whatever his qualms, to abstain completely from the national effort. The Englishman might freely disagree with the government and exhaust every legal means to prevent a given course of action. But once war was declared, he could not rightly separate himself from the fortunes of his country. The good Christian was by definition a good citizen, a loyal subject, and a patriot. His duty, a word then charged with the deepest religious significance, consisted of subordinating not only his private interests, but also his private judgment, to the authority of the state.[30] In his own sphere, Caesar was supreme. He could neither grant salvation nor require its surrender; however, since he safeguards his subjects' property, he may claim it, every bit of it; since he protects their lives, he has a right to them as well.[31] To deny this, to resist the magistrate, constitutes rebellion, which, having its model in the rebellion of Lucifer, will be punished with hellfire.[32] William Temple presented the issue if the Christian, the state, and the sword in terms of a moral equation. "The Nation," he wrote to Archbishop Davidson, "has real rights: it exists by Divine appointment; it is subject to moral law. I believe England was morally bound to fight—and England means

Englishmen."[33] Temple, it should be recalled, was regarded by pacifists before and during the Second World War, when he began his tragically brief primacy, as their strongest theological opponent. They understood their antagonist only too well, and he they. In 1943, he wrote to one war protester about what lies at the root of the rejection of pacifism by the great institutional churches. While granting that there is much to say in favor of the Christian's refusing to fight, he warned that unqualified pacifism would bring in its train the establishment in England of the Nazi regime, Gestapo and all.[34] The implication is clear: whether the foe be nazism, kaiserism, or communism, if it triumphed, what chance would there then be for building a Christian civilization?

THE CONSCIENTIOUS OBJECTORS

The issue of pacifism ceased being a theoretical matter the moment Parliament passed (January, 1916) the first of a series of military service acts. In addition to authorizing the conscription of unmarried men between the ages of eighteen and forty-one, this act directed that special tribunals, established under the Derby Scheme of the previous year to hear appeals for exemption on grounds of economic and personal hardship, were to determine the validity of "conscientious objections" to military service. Those who had denounced pacifists for their erroneous beliefs and for refusing to serve their country voluntarily were now confronted with new problems, involving issues as weighty as the Christian endorsement of force itself. Under what circumstances, if any, could a citizen defy the law if it demanded actions incompatible with his conscience? To what lengths could the state go in forcing compliance with the law and in punishing dissent?

The would-be conscientious objector—later in the war he was called simply "conchy"—had to run a dreadful gauntlet of persecution, legal and otherwise. His first encounter with authority came in the form of a face-to-face meeting with a local tribunal, a panel composed of clergymen, prominent citizens, and retired army officers who were likely to reflect the public's contempt for "shirkers." To make matters worse, they were often neither compassionate nor well informed about matters of conscience; actually, they might be positively ignorant. There are on record numerous cases which would be quite humorous, had they not involved intense suffering on the part of those involved. At Oxford, the military representative, an elderly Colonel Blimp-type who thought Tolstoy the name of a place, asked in all seriousness whether "an eye for an eye and a tooth for a tooth" was not a precept of Jesus. When an applicant reeled off a New Testament passage in Greek, in itself a provocation, the chairman of another tribunal snapped: "Greek, you don't mean to tell me that Jesus Christ spoke Greek. He was British to the backbone!" In the last instance we shall cite, a clergyman asked: "Since when has the Spirit of God prevented a young man like you doing his duty to help his country and his friends?"[35] To put it mildly, the law, while allowing for conscientious objection to military service, failed to provide impartial, let alone knowledgeable, judges.

If the applicant succeeded in satisfying his interrogators of the legitimacy of his claim, he could be excused from military service altogether. In most cases, however, he was merely exempted from combat duty and ordered to choose from among several duties unrelated to killing: ministering to the wounded, working in the Non-Combatant Corps, or minesweeping, a dangerous occupation by any standard. As a rule pacifists in the Quaker tradition accepted service on these terms without protest. Well aware that the end result of their choice might be the saving and mending of lives to be put back into the war, they argued that the duty of saving life immediately endangered transcended every other consideration. There was, in the last analysis, no way of determining for certain that *this* life, saved at *this* moment, would in the end take the life of another; even if the certainty existed, allowing it to perish would mean depriving it of the chance of being reclaimed for God. Nevertheless, about one-seventh of all conscientious objectors (mostly on nonreligious grounds), about 1,350 men, became "absolutists," refusing to take the king's shilling under any circumstances. Their position, considered a reductio ad absurdum of pacifist teachings even by those supporting their right to dissent, was based on the premise that participating in anything connected with the war effort, including hospital work, meant compromising with evil and thereby tainting themselves. To teach them the error of their ways, the government, equally uncompromising, placed them in the custody of the military authorities.

Few Englishmen were subjected to more physical and mental torture than the absolutists; enemy prisoners were usually treated with more respect and consideration. An early group, consisting of thirty-four men, was shipped to France, sentenced to death for refusing a command in a war zone, and, after the order was countermanded by the prime minister himself, sentenced to ten years in prison. Those flaunting the symbols of military authority, especially saluting and wearing a uniform, were beaten, degraded publicly, housed in nasty quarters, and given what passed for food out of a slop bucket. The toll was heavy. By November, 1918, ten had died in prison, another sixty perishing soon after release; thirty-one lost their reason as a result of their experiences.[36] As a further measure of public contempt, hundreds were left to languish in jail after the Armistice, and all were disfranchised for five years under the Representation of the People Act of 1918, which brought full manhood suffrage to England. Yet severe as these punishments were, they were gentleness itself, compared to the treatment meted out to pacifists in France. There, many were shot and their next-of-kin sent a curt notice that so-and-so had "died as a coward."

The worst abuses were quickly ended by Army Order X (May, 1916), which decreed that objectors were to be remanded to the civil authorities. But their troubles did not end in civil prison, where a regime of solitary confinement, enforced silence, and harsh discipline further undermined the health of men weakened by the rigors of the barrack-yard. In desperation, prisoners refused to eat unless conditions improved. Of hunger strikers, J. E. C. Welldon said it should be no concern of the state what prisoners did with their food.[37] Welldon, however, failed to mention that hunger strikers were treated as had been the suffragettes; they were fed through rubber tubes forced down the throat.

Non-Anglican objectors complained that prison authorities were inattentive to their appeals for services by ministers of their own faiths. Nor did they care for the attitude of the Anglican chaplains, paid prison officials; an understandable feeling when one has been told he ought to be drowned for cowardice. Services in the Church of England chapel were reported as being cold and comfortless, the sermons unedifying. Naturally, conditions varied from prison to prison, but if conditions at Wandsworth Prison were anything like typical, things must have been pretty grim: there the chaplain preached that St. Paul, an army tent contractor, had been a patriot "proud to do his bit for his Empire."[38]

Despite their opposition to pacifism in principle, it was rare for clergymen to demand the same treatment for all pacifists. As a rule, even the most outspoken critics tried to differentiate between the objector whose religious scruples, however mistaken, entitled him to consideration, the malingerer, and the agitator whose primary objective was to disrupt the war effort.

The last type, of course, raised the greatest storm, the belief prevailing in the press that the concentration of hundreds of absolutists at Dartmoor posed a threat to national security. Archibald Robertson, bishop of Exeter, was acclaimed by the press for exposing the Dartmoor "scandal." The "conchies," he wrote, "draw their rations, conduct a pacifist, not to say a revolutionary propaganda through the post, and do not work. . . . They should be made to work, or not allowed to eat." To impart to them a truer view of the national emergency, he concluded with the suggestion that they be transported to those parts of England visited frequently by the German airplanes.[39]

Indictments of the absolutists' patriotism, though exaggerated, should not be dismissed entirely, as they contained an element of truth. Led by Clifford Allen and Fenner Brockway, the No Conscription Fellowship actively counselled young men in how to behave before the tribunals and advised them about ways of avoiding military service. After the war, Stephen Hobhouse, a leading Quaker absolutist, boasted of how industrious his compatriots had been. While imprisoned in regimental guardrooms, fairly comfortable quarters by earlier standards, they spread verbally and by leaflet antiwar propaganda among the troops. The Fellowship of Reconciliation, not content to protest the war, issued circulars calling upon the workers to protest by refusing to work in the arms factories.[40] These activities persuaded otherwise sympathetic people that they were abusing their privileges under the law. The Englishman's vaunted tolerance, warned Henry Scott Holland, was wearing thin: "The Objector must not try our patience too hard."[41]

Given the gulf between them, it is all the more to their credit that, from the moment they were apprised of the situation, leading church figures went before the public to denounce the abuse of conscientious objectors as irrational, cruel, and a stain on English civilization. Acting as spokesmen for their fellow bishops, the archbishop of Canterbury and Bishop Gore constantly reminded the House of Lords, and through it the nation, that crimes committed in the name of national survival were crimes nevertheless. Several petitions, a list of whose signatories reads like a *Who's Who* of English Christianity, were presented to the authorities. Nonconformists of the stature of John Clifford, W. E. Orchard, and W. E. Selbie, a leading Congregationalist, joined John Neville Figgis, William Temple, and other Anglicans in denouncing the existing system. Within the space of two weeks, one petition gained the support of both archbishops, twenty-five bishops, and one hundred and fifty clergymen.[42]

Humanitarian considerations aside, the defenders of the conscientious objectors rested their case on two principles: the inviolability of conscience and the supremacy of law. Though bound to the nation by ties of interest and sentiment, they thought (one might almost say they *felt*) there was a point beyond which not even an established church could tolerate secular interference without forfeiting its credentials as a religious society. True, conscience needs to be cultivated and instructed, as original sin predisposes man to self-deception; yet that spark of divinity in each man may, after all, express itself as a dictate of conscience. Could a Christian dare grant that the vote of a majority, even the vote of a Parliamentary majority, was a more infallible test of truth than the individual conscience? An opinion might be wrong and contrary to the best interests of the state and the teachings of the church, yet the often tragic history of Christianity demonstrated that the state was unworthy as the custodian of conscience. Said a writer in the *Commonwealth*, probably Henry Scott Holland: "The earthly State is *not* the ultimate and absolute category of conscience. To say this is to be guilty of the very 'Prussianism' which we abhor. The individual conscience has that in it by which it looks beyond all the divisions of peoples and nations, and breathes the air of a higher patriotism in loyalty to the Kingdom of God."[43]

From the legal standpoint, the most serious complaint against the tribunals arose less from their errors in judgment, inevitable when interpreting the law's vague definition of what constituted a conscientious objection, than from their way of administering the law.

In too many cases the tribunals had obviously been operating on the assumption that, since those avoiding military service were unpatri- otic, they had forfeited their rights under the law. Taking this as his text, Bishop Gore pointed out the inconsistency of England's claim- ing to champion freedom while at the same time persecuting Quakers and others who had rendered valuable services to society. The na- tion had done well to repudiate their ideas; it had shamed itself by denying them the protection of the law.[44]

Three months before the Armistice the *Challenge*, a persistent and outspoken critic of the tribunals, reported that hundreds of men had been court-martialled repeatedly and sentenced to prison for refus- ing national service.[45] To those who denounced the Cat and Mouse Act, the procedure whereby conscientious objectors were court- martialled, imprisoned, released, called to the colors, and then court- martialled again, violated a cardinal principle of English law: nobody should be punished more than once for the same crime. One could argue, of course, that refusal to comply after release from prison technically constituted a new offence, an argument commonly met by asserting the injustice of inflicting punishment for what was in reality and abiding state of mind. For the state to avoid this funda- mental issue, meanwhile allowing its agents to violate the rights of some of its citizens, was an implicit denial of its own nature as a "moral person."

From his position as head of the ecclesiastical hierarchy, and there- fore as the chief intermediary between church and state, the arch- bishop of Canterbury could see the problem in all its complexity. There are in the Davidson papers at Lambeth Palace files containing hundreds of items of correspondence that passed between him, the conscientious objectors, their families, political leaders, and the gov- ernment. Time and again he spoke personally and wrote to the high- est officials about improving procedures and living conditions. In certain cases, where flagrant miscarriages of justice had occurred, he intervened directly, going out of his way to badger the authorities until they put things right. Yet, to his disappointment, he soon learned that when enthusiasts contend, anything a moderate man might say (or not say) is bound to give offence. People like Charles Boothby were always ready to denounce him for wasting time on "these puny things"; people like Dr. Alfred Salter, a Quaker and a socialist, upbraided him for supinely watching while "these splendid young men" were persecuted for their religion.[46]

Except for the handful of individuals he and his associates were able to help, Davidson's efforts were on the whole bound to fail. Plenty of men in high places were willing to do something for the absolutists; unfortunately the issues dividing them from the nation were irreconcilable. This dilemma comes across clearly in Davidson's account of an interview with Dr. Salter:

> This last interview was very depressing to me as showing the apparent spread of what I regard as the perfectly hopeless position of men who under the leadership of cultivated and capable people like Salter are absolutely refusing any kind of public service, direct or indirect, which would facilitate the carrying on of the War by placing the country in a stronger position. Salter would make no difference between fighting and—e.g. making boots or digging potatoes [if useful in the war effort]. . . . It is this which appears to me to weaken our cause when we are appealing against imprisoning men for conscience sake. The conscience of the man seems to me in these cases to mean simply his abdication of the duties of a citizen to the corporate life of the community to which he belongs and whose civilized order he enjoys.[47]

One side or the other had to yield. The absolutists, having set their consciences above questioning, above criticism, above the law, could not accept national service, however disguised. No less conscientious, the government felt bound by the mandate conferred upon it by the electorate to demand of them tangible compliance with the law; lacking this, its only alternative was to punish them. Churchmen saw their role as referees, guaranteeing that this punishment was carried out lawfully and decently.

THE CHRISTIAN COMBAT

As he who preaches nonresistance must assume responsibility for the consequences of his doctrine, so he who preaches the legitimacy of war cannot escape responsibility for *its* consequences; for to desire a certain end is to a degree also to will the means of achieving it.

Since the object of war is to force the adversary to submit by inflicting upon him loss and suffering, it would seem that the greater and more widely extended the loss and suffering, the better the chances for a satisfactory conclusion. In the Christian view, however, means are as important as ends. Justice in the application of force, as we have seen, must be present simultaneously with the other criteria of the just war: a proper authority, a good intention, a righteous cause.

Though not always recognized as a formal code, the rules for the right conduct of war were reinforced for Anglican Christians by the gentleman's code of honor. Here, as elsewhere, it would be difficult to overestimate the importance of "the public school spirit," "the sporting spirit," and "muscular Christianity" in forming group attitudes. To the men raised in this tradition, war was something in the nature of a fair fight, a kind of deadly football game between evenly matched teams. And rough as it was, the "game" of war, like rugger, should be played by the rules and with a generous spirit. It is no accident or sign of bravado that the terminology of public school games —"play up," "play the game," "play with a straight bat," "fair play and foul"—permeated pulpit oratory during the early years of the war. An English soldier, Tom Brown in khaki, would never deign to abuse a fallen foe. The war must be a "White War," said E. E. Holmes, canon of St. Paul's and a Boyle Lecturer; "We'll thrash this mean lout into another mood," echoed his colleague at St. Paul's, S. A. Alexander, "but we'll not dirty our hands to hit him once below the belt, or shame our feet once to kick him when he is down. The Christian character is what it is in spite of un-Christian enemies. They shall never dictate to us what we shall be, and, in this war, our war lord is Jesus Christ."[48]

In the eighteenth century, Kant, working from different premises, came to conclusions similar to classic just war doctrine. Every war, he wrote in his essay, *Perpetual Peace*, in which belligerents do not impose upon themselves restrictions in the use of possible means, must pass inevitably into a war of extermination.[49] Though Kant's maxim is undeniably true, no sane European in his day envisioned wars of extermination; neither did the contestants during the Great War. Kant wrote during one of those rare moments in history when Christian principles coincided, however incompletely and accidentally, with the practice of armies. Notwithstanding Voltaire's scathing commentary in *Candide*, or Carlyle's in *Sartor Resartus*, the warfare of the Enlightenment and throughout the nineteenth century was about as "civilized" as warfare has ever been. Nations *did* refuse to employ all available means. Granted that the device had still to be perfected, but the men to whom Robert Fulton showed plans for a submarine exclaimed, "without reflecting or from attachment to established and familiar tyranny," it is barbarous to blow up a ship with all its crew.[50] Although Napoleon's Spanish campaigns were marred by ghastly crimes committed by and against guerrillas, there took place nothing comparable to the enormities of the Wars of Religion. In the Crimean War, the War Office in London rejected a plan to use sulphur fumes against Sebastopol because "an operation of this nature would contravene the laws of civilised warfare."[51] Outside Europe, where the Ten Commandments did not always run, descents into barbarism might still be steep, as in the Indian Mutiny, the Maximilian episode in Mexico, and the suppression of the Philippine insurrection. But on the whole, post-Napoleonic Europe enjoyed (if this is the proper word) a period of comparative peace and comparative humanity in warfare.

Throughout this period, however, forces were operating below the surface to transform the nature and, eventually, the rules of warfare. The forty years since the creation of the German Empire saw the art of war mechanized, industrialized, and democratized. Composed of professional cadres training annual classes of conscripts, and these supported by masses of reservists, the armies that faced each other in the Great War became the prisoners of their very size. Aside from food and medical services, they could function effectively only as long as they were assured a regular supply of the new or improved engines of destruction. High explosive shells by the million, mobile artillery, machineguns, airplanes, ships, chemical warfare agents poured from the factories and workshops of Europe and America as from a devil's cornucopia. The Great War became a struggle between societies, not merely between their armies. The millions of workers who produced these articles, though technically noncombatants, and the places where they worked, though legally private property, now became as important as the soldiers in the field. By the rules of its own perverse logic, war made combatants even of schoolchildren, who collected fats for explosives and bought with their pocket-money War Savings Certificates. At the same time as these socioeconomic developments blurred the distinctions between civilian and soldier, technological developments overcame physical barriers, bringing the home population directly under the guns of the enemy.

Adherence to commonly accepted rules, whether embodied in formal codes, the customs of civilized man, or "trench law" (the unwritten code of the fighting man) serves to give war the semblance of predictability through providing a standard to which the contestants may refer in assessing the consequences of their actions.[52] By 1914, however, neither the general staffs of the various countries nor those who had drafted the Hague Conventions of 1899 and 1907 could predict accurately how the established rules and usages of war would be modified by the advances in military technology and organization; the psychological impact they never stopped to think about at all. After Louvain, certainly after the crisis of the spring of 1915, they realized that the changes had been for the worse, and that the laws of war were in fact being widely disregarded. Regarding civilians, a new note, a note that was to become the dominant one in the twentieth century, was struck by Lord Montague of Beaulieu, a pioneer in motoring. Addressing the House of Lords a week after the worst air raid on London, he said:

It is absolute humbug, in my opinion, to talk about London being an undefended city. The Germans have a perfect right to raid London. It is defended by guns and squadrons of aeroplanes, and it is the chief seat of industry for the war. We are only deluding ourselves when we talk about London being an undefended city of no military importance, and say that the Germans are carrying out some act in attacking it which is not worthy of a civilised nation. . . . This is a war of nations, and not alone of armies, and you must endeavour to bear the casualties that are caused in the same way as the civil population of France and Belgium are bearing the casualties inflicted by this kind of warfare.[53]

All life within a given area became a potential target. Though lacking the phrase, Montague of Beaulieu and his listeners certainly had the concept of "total war."

As the strain of war compelled many devout people to abandon the just war for the crusade, so the conditions of modern warfare created a moral dilemma resolved, frequently after agonizing self-examination, by abandoning another aspect of the just war. Even though the conflict had been undertaken in accordance with the traditional criteria, they found it increasingly difficult to conduct it with justice. For the just war is in reality incompatible with total war, since the principles of proportionality and discrimination between combatants and noncombatants cannot be applied consistently. They had come to a logical impasse. If the enemy resorts to immoral means, those on the side of righteousness must either adopt these means themselves or resign themselves to throwing away lives needlessly, which is contrary to just war concepts. Similarly, if the force to be applied must be proportional to the force to be overcome, then it would be killing people unnecessarily to insist that the armed forces make do with less. The author of an anonymous memorandum on the use of poison gas, condemned universally as immoral, pointed up this dilemma when he wrote: "To meet force with inadequate force is the final futility."[54] Lastly, a problem came to the fore during the Great War that has been stated in its most extreme form by the development of thermonuclear weapons: given weapons of mass destruction, there is no practicable way of distinguishing and separating the innocent from the guilty. These were issues that every morally conscious person needed to concern himself with.

Could the Christian sanction England, the world's premier naval power, using its advantage to blockade Germany, and in the process threaten innocents with starvation, if the war could thereby be shortened? Anglican opinions was divided from the beginning. One segment, representing supporters as well as opponents of the war, disagreed with the official policy for moral and political reasons. Every nation, they asserted, had the right to prevent its enemies from importing arms, munitions, and other war-related materials; but it has no right to cause babies to be born dead or deformed from what A. Maude Royden termed "economic pressure" on their mothers.[55] Besides being immoral, a hunger blockade might in the long run be self-defeating: by alienating neutrals, uniting the Germans behind the kaiser, and provoking a desperate people into unprecedented atrocities it would actually prolong the bloodletting. Worst of all, the German army could always be fed by cutting the civilian food ration.[56]

Such arguments evidently fell on deaf ears. Because it involves no overt violence against the enemy's civil population or armed forces, clergymen in general saw the blockade as a humane method of waging war. Compared with the way the Germans made war, and especially in view of the *Lusitania* disaster, the blockade appeared to be positively lenient.

But was it legal? According to international law, a blockade must be effective—blockading forces must be on station continually—and applied equally to all neutrals. From a legal standpoint, therefore, German charges of illegality were well-founded: since Allied naval power was ineffective in the Baltic, and since certain neutrals received preferential treatment, the blockade was "illegal." In answering these charges, clergymen employed a casuistry rivalling at times that of the much-maligned Jesuits. England, claimed A. J. Balfour, maintained the spirit of international law even when she appeared to be violating its letter; for discrimination between neutrals was more a matter of geographical accident—he failed to explain why this should matter on the high seas—than of official policy.[57] Besides, the Germans could not "decently complain of the starvation plan,"[58] as they had resorted to a similar tactic during the siege of Paris in 1871; anyone versed in international law knew that a blockade was merely a siege on a larger scale.

Convinced that England was fighting for God and civilization, the bulk of the religious press urged the expansion of the list of contraband goods to include anything useful to sustaining Germany's economic life. The *Church Times*, for instance, lent its editorial support to demands that the navy be given a free hand to do whatever it deemed necessary to tighten the blockade. Its logic was outwardly consistent with just war principles, except that it had lost sight of the need to balance ends against means. If the end of war is peace, then, it reasoned, the speed with which peace is obtained should be the determining factor in any strategy; and since "our only way of effecting peace is to bring the Germans to their knees, the more tightly we press the blockade the sooner will peace come."[59] The tone of the *Guardian*, however, was hardly calculated to bring peace closer. When the neutral Dutch objected to England's high-handed methods of enforcing the blockade, it replied that "no power can talk to us in that strain."[60]

Whereas one could only guess at the misery inflicted by the blockade, the ghastly accounts of Tommies blinded and choked by chlorine gas left nothing to the imagination. Writing from the vantage point of 1927, B. H. Liddell Hart, the military analyst, suggested, over optimistically it seems, that "gas may well prove the salvation of civilization from the otherwise inevitable collapse in case of another war."[61] Yet in 1915, gas represented the ultimate perversion of science. Public indignation, whipped up further by the press, reached a fever pitch. At first glance it may seem strange that, after nearly a year of terrible slaughter, people should be any more squeamish about the effects of gas than of other weapons. Splinters from an old-fashioned shell can mangle a man and cause more suffering than gas. The difference is that it is possible to hide from a shell or a bullet. Before proper masks became available in sufficient numbers, the bravest of soldiers felt helpless against the "loathsome, noiseless wall of filthiness." Like the knights who were indignant about being shot at by lowly peasant harquebusiers, clergymen as well as soldiers believed gas was a "dirty" weapon, unworthy of the Christian gentleman. The use of gas, in the opinion of the *Challenge*, "because it reckons on a chance wind and not on the courage and skill of either attacker or attacked, is not—in our English phrase— 'playing the game.' "[62]

Everyone agreed gas was immoral; the disagreement developed over what to do about this new threat. As a practical matter, if by employing gas the enemy stood to gain a major tactical advantage, perhaps even to win the war, could a Christian in all good conscience consent to retaliation in kind? In the emotionally charged atmosphere of the holy war, some clergymen answered with shrill cries for revenge. In the opinion of the Rev. E. W. Brereton, rector of Hollinwood, Essex, whose sermon Horatio Bottomley, a patriot in his own right, thought worthy of publication in *John Bull*, "we are fighting for dear life against enemies who are not Christian, not human beings, but reptiles. We claim the right to fight these fiends not with kid gloves. I scorn the humanitarians who object to reprisals."[63]

Fearing the implications of England's following suit, a more temperate man, Randall Davidson, sought to lead the church and to keep the government true to Christian principles. On several occasions he wrote privately to Lord Stamfordham, the king's private secretary, and others pleading for their help in discouraging talk about reprisals. On May 7 he wrote a moving letter to Mr. Asquith, published shortly thereafter, reiterating that Germany's having sunk to a new low was hardly a reason for England to follow her lead. If England replied in kind, a process of escalation, as it is called nowadays, would begin; and God alone knew where it would end:

It seems to me that international agreements for securing the honourable conduct of war would then be obliterated in a brutal rivalry as to the horrors which can be perpetrated on both sides. The result would be a tangle, that the world would soon be saying, and history would say thereafter, that there was nothing to choose between the nations who were at War, and it would become a matter of small importance, and probably of disputed fact, who it was who began the general course of adopting these vile usages.[64]

Every precaution should be taken to protect the troops from the ill-effects of gas, but the dishonor for adopting such a weapon should be left to Germany alone.

The primate's forthright statement attracted criticism, a good deal of it vicious and vulgar; indeed, the English Church Union, through the duke of Argyll, denounced his stand.[65] Yet dozens of Anglicans, clergy and laymen, wrote to convey their appreciation for his having voiced their feelings to the nation. It made no difference; for a few days later (May 18) Lord Kitchener pronounced gas a "diabolical" weapon, and in the next sentence announced "His Majesty's Government feel that our troops must be adequately protected by the employment of similar methods."[66] The Devil was to be called in to exorcize the Devil.

Coming from Kitchener, idolized as the fount of military wisdom, the decision to resort to admittedly immoral means met with grudging acceptance rather than open opposition. In deferring to the professional judgment of the soldiers, those who had initially joined Davidson in condemning gas warfare came to see the matter in a different light; in fact, Davidson himself was no longer outspoken on the subject. If England used gas, the sin rested entirely on Germany's soldiers; regrettable as it might be, there seemed no alternative short of throwing away the lives of the men in the trenches. Nevertheless, the military were admonished, as a sop to conscience, to act with moderation, employing gas when absolutely necessary, and then only those types that produced unconsciousness, or, at the worst, brought a speedy, painless death.[67]

The gap between the ideal of justice in war, the traditional rules of war, and the tactics imposed by the new technology of warfare is perhaps best illustrated by the debate on reprisals for civilian casualties suffered during German raids on "military" targets in England. For the first time in centuries, English women and children were being killed in their homes by a foreign foe. The attacks that began with the naval bombardment of Scarborough, Whitby, and Hartlepool in December, 1914, were followed intermittently by air raids culminating in the tragedy of June 3, 1917, when hundreds of Londoners, including schoolchildren, were killed or wounded.[68] These casualties, small in comparison with those sustained during the Blitz, were enormous by the standards of the time; they showed that the front was now wherever the enemy chose to strike.

Whenever the death toll rose sharply, the outraged citizenry, besides looting "German" stores in the East End, invariably demanded that the "aerial murderers" and "the baby-killers of Scarborough" (Winston Churchill's phrase) be given a generous helping of their own *Schrecklichkeit*. Always on edge, their tempers short, people were easily roused to paroxysms of rage by circulation-hungry newspapers. Taking a leaf from *John Bull*, the *Globe* and the *Daily Express* sponsored open-air rallies to demand reprisals against German civilians; the Corporation of London, the lord mayor of London, Lord Willoughby de Broke, and the earl of Rosebery urged upon Parliament a no nonsense policy.[69] Pemberton Billing's advocacy of indiscriminate bombing of population centers earned for him the dubious title of "member for air": he favored a rule of dropping six bombs for one, and "To Hell with pacifists, praters, Party politicians, peace-mongers! We're out for War—let it be War to the death!"[70] Sir Arthur Conan Doyle, the creator of Sherlock Holmes, caused a stir when, in a letter to the *Times* on "The Uses of Hatred," he insisted that, since England must win the war whatever the cost, reprisals and a well-orchestrated campaign of hatred against Germany were necessary to sustain public morale: he closed with unkind words about "platitudinous Bishops and gloomy Deans."[71]

Few war-related issues were more divisive, engendering more ill-will within the Church and more public criticism of the church, than the question of reprisals. No one denied that fighting in populated areas necessarily involves risks to noncombatants; but in such cases the intention of the act, rather than the act itself, determines whether it is in keeping with Christian principles. Reprisal or retaliation against the enemy's forces is the essence of war; an attack aimed deliberately against civilians, whether for revenge or as a tactical objective, is plainly contradictory to all principles of justice. As Conan Doyle said, the higher clergy of the Church of England, bishops and deans, tended to reject his view of reprisals altogether; and since they dominated Convocation, in February, 1916, a resolution condemning reprisals, moved by the archbishop of Canterbury, was carried unanimously. The church put itself on record as believing that, aside from lowering the standard of honorable conduct between nations, harming noncombatants deliberately, even in response to barbarous outrages, was murder.[72] By all means let there be massive reprisals—against the makers of war and their machines, not against their children and womenfolk. *Lex Talionis*, a poem by one G. P. Leonard, expresses the horror felt by most thoughtful Anglicans better than volumes of sermons:

> In London our women and children lie
> Murdered out of a summer sky,
> And men say, 'Let *their* children die!'

> 'Let our sons soar in the German air
> And fling down death on the children *there*,
> And children—dear as our children were!'

> High were our hearts when we sought the fight,
> 'Mercy' we said, 'is better than might,'
> And we chose for our battle cry, 'God and the right!'

> And now? Great God! have we fallen so low
> That we may learn *this* damned thing from the foe?
> Christ! by Thy cross and passion, 'No.'[73]

Those protesting the bombing of open towns, especially Freiburg, pulverized in April, 1917, in reprisal for the sinking of two British hospital ships, evoked stern criticism from the public and their fellow clergymen. Archbishop Davidson, who together with Bishop Talbot had denounced the raid in the Lords—during the Second World War Bishop Bell of Chichester, Davidson's biographer, denounced in the same place the policy of obliteration bombing—was amazed at the number of letters he received demanding the slaughter of innocent

Germans. A fair idea of the mood at this time may be gleaned from the following letter received at Lambeth: "LET THE GUTTERS RUN RED WITH GERMAN BLOOD! Those who survive have been spared to see this carried out and very soon our brave airmen, trusting in Almighty God, will be smashing to pulp the German old men, women, and children. . . . Every shilling we can spare must buy a Bomb to smash-in-pieces a German Kindergarten."[74] Nor was the primate immune from personal abuse. *"Gott sei dankt!"* wrote another correspondent, mimicking a German woman, "Our Kaiser's God has raised up fool friends for us among the English themselves. They have two old women, the Archbishops of Canterbury and York, who have ordered that their young men shall stay in safety at home and that their Government shall make no reprisals."[75]

Those clergymen who approved of reprisals, and there were a lot of them, did so not necessarily because they relished the thought of killing German civilians. As in the case of the blockade and poison gas, here, too, they had a strong case, justifying their stand by appealing to the selfsame principles as those advocating moderation. The Germans, they maintained, bombed civilians to terrorize them and to break their will to resist. English reprisals, on the other hand, would in the long run save lives. When the Germans realized the futility of their tactics, they would stop killing English civilians and Englishmen would then stop killing theirs in reprisal. Admittedly, England could not plead its cause before God with the blood of "murdered" children on its hands; but to say this and nothing else seemed to represent a dangerous sentimentalism. Why only German children? "Our" children were just as innocent and had just as much right to live as theirs; perhaps more, since their fathers were fighting for civilization. The logic of this argument was pursued to its ultimate conclusion in a statement remarkable for its candor. Writing on the third anniversary of the war, the Rev. H. D. A. Major, a leading modernist theologian and editor of the *Modern Churchman*, announced:

The strongest moral argument against reprisals is that some are punished by them who are not actually guilty. In so far as unarmed Germans approve of the atrocious methods of their government they are guilty of its crimes, as guilty as though they themselves actually bombed London or torpedoed the *Lusitania*. In the case of others, particularly children, they are not guilty, and those who undertake reprisals would spare them if they could separate them from their guilty countrymen. This they are hardly able to do . . . . But the question is this:—If the innocent cannot be separated from the guilty, ought the guilty therefore to be spared and allowed to continue unpunished their evil ways? It is not for the good of humanity that the guilty should be spared even though the innocent should suffer with them. . . . If the only way to protect adequately an English babe is to kill a German babe, then it is the duty of the authorities, however repugnant, to do it. More particularly is this so when we reflect that the innocent German babe will in all probability grow up to be the killer of babes himself, or at least an enthusiastic advocate of that horrible policy of frightfulness of which the killing of babes is one of the features. Whereas the English babe whose life is saved by this means will, we may reasonably anticipate, grow up to be a protector of babes, and a detestor of those who would slay them.[76]

The Majors had gone clear contrary to every precept of Christian teaching and every principle of justice evolved over two millennia. In short, it had become legitimate to prevent an evil by doing that same evil; to kill someone, even a child, for a crime that lay in the future and might never take place at all.

It was almost as if everyone born between the Rhine and the Polish frontier had been tainted with a double dose of original sin. The Germans were so evil as to be incapable of understanding anything but force, and responding to any emotion save fear. Things had come to such a state that by mid-1917 the leading Anglican newspapers were advocating actions unthinkable three years earlier. When the Germans captured Captain Blaikes of the *Caledonia* and threatened to try him for attempting to ram a submarine, the *Church Times* supported the *Times* in suggesting that a German prisoner of equal rank be set aside as a hostage with the expressed intention of meting out to him the exact treatment accorded to Captain Blaikes.[77] When rumors of German mistreatment of English prisoners circulated in the press, a number of clergymen put forward plans for placing German prisoners in the front line trenches or shipping them in freighters to the United States: "it might do their souls good to be afraid lest one of their country's submarines might inadvertently send them to the bottom."[78] The depths were finally reached on the fourth anniversary of the war, when the *Church Times* advocated using dum-dum bullets on the Western Front. "We have got past the stage of splitting hairs over words like reprisals, having found by bitter experience that the homeopathic treatment of treating like with like is the only kind that suits the German patient."[79]

Demands for reprisals grew louder as the Armistice approached. With the German army disintegrating as an effective fighting force, there was the likelihood that the High Command, desperate for a means of saving face, would threaten the destruction of occupied towns to coerce from the Allies more favorable armistice terms. If this was indeed their plan, said Hastings Rashdall, the Allies should then select certain German towns "of no exceptional beauty or historic importance, and regard them as hostages for Ghent and Antwerp."[80] The *Church Quarterly Review* proposed much the same thing, insisting that "if [the enemy] destroys Brussels we must destroy Berlin; if she destroys Ghent we must destroy Cologne. No sentence short of this will prevent the brutality of the German."[81]

Roland Bainton quotes in his study of *Christian Attitudes Toward War and Peace* a few lines from a sermon illustrating the "brutal candor" with which the bishop of London exhorted his countrymen to kill Germans. In this sermon, entitled oddly "A Word of Cheer," he cried:

... to save the freedom of the world, to save liberty, to save the honour of women and children, everyone who loves freedom and honour, everyone who puts principle before ease and life itself before mere living, is banded in a great crusade—we cannot deny it—to kill Germans, to kill them not for the sake of killing, but to save the world, to kill the good as well as the bad, to kill the young as well as the old, to kill those who have shown kindness to our wounded as well as those fiends who crucified the Canadian soldier, who superintended the Armenian massacres, who sank the *Lusitania*, and who turned the machine guns on the civilians of Aerschot and Louvain; and to kill them lest the civilization of the world itself be killed.[82]

A horrible statement to be coming from a Christian minister; yet it was this same Winnington-Ingram who preached understanding of the enemy during the Boer War and told an audience at Guildhall at the very beginning of the Great War that they should never forget, even in the heat of the fight, that they were Christians and gentlemen.[83] Maybe this was hypocrisy; unlikely, knowing Winnington-Ingram.

There is nothing to indicate that he, or Major, or Rashdall, or the vast majority of those demanding reprisals of various kinds were hard-hearted men. Like the absolutists, they were men of principle; unlike them, however, they found that some of the principles by which they lived seemed to conflict with one another as well as with military necessity. It is hard for a man to have to bury by the dozen children killed in air raids, as did Winnington-Ingram, who in prewar years had been the recipient of awards from orphanages as "the child's friend." They did not want revenge, in fact they were careful to caution against allowing a Christian sense of justice to degenerate into a soul-destroying hatred; but they cried for the slaughter of innocents to stop. In doing so, they lost their sense of proportion, failing to see where their principles were carrying them. Randall Davidson, whose primacy exemplified the church's function as the conscience of the nation, could see what was happening. The danger, as he always tried to emphasize, is that if men are prepared to use any means to achieve a valued end, they must in the end ride roughshod over all values. The great tragedy of modern war, as he well knew, is that, once the first links have been forged in the chain of horror and hatred, the barbarous act is the natural outcome of the barbarous weapon and the determination to take total war to its logical conclusion.

VI. THE CHURCH IN THE WAR

FILLING THE RANKS

Elie Halévy once observed that during the Great War state control of thought took two forms: one negative, aiming at the suppression of all opinion deemed contrary to the national interest; the other, aptly termed "the organization of enthusiasm," aimed at generating and directing emotion into channels useful to the war effort.[1] This system, however, was less rigid and well-organized than might be supposed. Though only the British government had the authority, granted under the Defence of the Real Act (D.O.R.A.), to impose censorship and to suppress "dangerous" publications, it used these powers in an erratic fashion. Antiwar journals like the *Labour Leader* and the *Tribunal* were suppressed temporarily, as was the conservative and prowar *Globe*; even Lord Northcliffe's *Times* was prosecuted under D.O.R.A. Nor was the government the sole agency engaged in shaping public opinion. Until 1917, when a Department of Information was created to oversee its various undertakings, the production and dissemination of propaganda remained largely a matter of private initiative. Organizations boasting on their executive committees celebrities in politics, business, the intellectual world, and religion sprang up all over the country. Under the vice-presidency of A. J. Balfour and the earl of Rosebery, the Central Committee for National Patriotic Organizations, founded late in 1914 to coordinate the efforts of all committees engaged in patriotic work, promoted meetings, supplied speakers, and subsidized propaganda. Similar programs were instituted by the Fight for Right Movement, which included Sir Francis Younghusband, the Himalayan explorer, and Evelyn Underhill, the mystic; the Rural League, under Lords Roberts and Milner; and the Imperial Maritime League. Even the London Electric Railways Company commissioned a series of war posters.

Convinced of the righteousness of England's cause, and believing that Christianity was concerned as much with the discharge of civic responsibilities as with the religious life, patriotic clergymen resolved to do their "bit" for king and country. Both convocations, every diocesan conference, and innumerable parish meetings passed resolutions to the effect that, in its dual role as the servant of God and of the state, the Church of England must aid the nation with every resource at its command. As a servant of God, it was incumbent upon the church to take the lead in humanitarian enterprises. Aside from the obvious need to provide military chaplains and to cope with the anticipated increase in the demand for its ministrations at home, various organizations, already overburdened with their normal tasks of distributing religious literature and working among the poor, were called upon to shoulder heavier responsibilities.

The concentration of large numbers of men at training centers in England and at base camps in the war zones provided organizations such as the Pocket Testament League, Religious Tract Society, British and Foreign Bible Society, and the Society for Promoting Christian Knowledge with ideal conditions for placing their wares in the right hands. Taking full advantage of their opportunities, they distributed during the first two years of the war over forty million Bibles, hymn books, prayer books, and tracts. The S.P.C.K., the oldest and best financed, led the field in distributing all forms of religious literature. Its presses were kept busy throughout the war turning out vast quantities of material of a religious nature as well as timely war-related materials. Besides publishing *War-Time Tracts for the Workers*, a series devoted to explaining the spiritual implications of the conflict, the Foreign Translations Committee undertook tracts for German prisoners, devotional books in Xosa, Zulu, and Sesuto for the native South African troops in France, and in Maori and Cree for the New Zealanders and Canadians.[2]

Church organizations ministered to the material as well as the spiritual needs of soldiers and civilians. A complete list of their services to war-torn countries would fill several pages; suffice it to say that charities as worthy as the Belgian Relief Fund, Great Britain to Poland Fund, Serbian Prisoner Fund, and Russian Jews' Relief Fund benefitted from having enlisting the support of the Anglican church. Nor was domestic relief neglected; for while continuing their regular activities as best they could, the Church of England Men's Society, the Church Army (the Anglican answer to the Salvation Army), and an array of women's organizations expanded their services. Among other things, they assisted the families of servicemen, explaining to their wives their rights under the system of allowances, and helping them fill out the complicated claim forms. When men departed for or returned from the front, they were treated in church-run temperance canteens, as were their womenfolk who worked in the munitions factories. If they were captured, they sometimes received parcels of supplementary food rations, note paper, tobacco, shaving utensils, and other creature comforts. Church workers served the wounded by raising money for the purchase of ambulances, stretchers and hospital beds, writing letters for the bedridden, and perhaps most important of all, bringing to France the wives and mothers of seriously wounded men. Soldiers' orphans were housed and cared for by the Waifs and Strays Society; in return, the older children volunteered to guard local bridges and reservoirs, or to act as orderlies and messengers.

Humanitarian work, however, far from exhausts the list of activities; to be sure, many a clergyman would have rated this as secondary in relation to the church's contribution to the warlike side of the national effort. Clergy and laity alike took it for granted that, as a servant of the state, the church would contribute directly to the Allied cause by explaining to the people the causes and the meaning of the war, maintaining on the home front a high level of morale, and preaching what the Rev. W. T. Elliott, vicar of Ingrow-with-Hainsworth, Leicester, called "a lofty, burning, inflexible, sterling patriotism."[3] Translated into practical terms, this meant that the primary obligation of the patriot was to enlist in the armed forces of his country.

An exculpatory myth is as untrue as a defamatory myth. After the Armistice, various churchmen, uncomfortable about their wartime activities and anxious to reestablish themselves in the public's esteem, sought to dissociate themselves from the recruiting mania. As late as 1966, Canon Roger Lloyd, author of the only general account of the Church of England in the twentieth century, asserted: "The number of bishops and other church dignitaries who flung themselves into the campaign to persuade young men to join the army seems to have been very small."[4] As might be expected, some were more active than others; but on the whole, Lloyd's judgment is a gross understatement. More than even the religious press, which was unanimous in emphasizing the duty of the clergy to encourage enlistments, diocesan publications and provincial newspapers indicate there was hardly a bishop or church dignitary who did not participate in some way in the recruiting drives.

As head of the church, the archbishop of Canterbury took an early stand on recruiting; the fact that he was unwilling to ask the clergy to turn their pulpits into recruiting platforms, or to join himself in an appeal sponsored by the Parliamentary Recruiting Committee, hardly indicates, as his biographer implies and as Canon Lloyd asserts, his opposition to clergymen acting as recruiters.[5] In the first instance, he was not opposed in principle to clergymen preaching recruiting sermons—St. Thomas Aquinas said they could do that;[6] rather he refused Lord Derby's request to encourage this officially because he thought it unwise, tending possibly to have the opposite effect.[7] Davidson himself had early gone on record, declaring his position in a pastoral letter of December, 1914. "The well-being, nay the very life, of our Empire may depend upon the response which is given to the call for men, and I think I can say deliberately that no household or home will be acting worthily if in timidity or self-love, it keeps back any of those who can loyally bear a man's part in the great enterprise on the part of the land we love."[8] During the next four years these words were echoed, and amplified, by his colleagues on the episcopal bench. Again and again we read of bishops, regretting that age and pastoral duties prevented them following their inclinations to enlist, exhorting their subordinates to use without stint their powers of persuasion. Addressing the clergy of his diocese, Bishop Moule of Durham observed prophetically that, since an army of two million would be "none too large" to curb Teutonic aggression, each must "take frequent opportunities of reminding your people, your young men of all ranks, and their friends of the real nature of the call of King and Country."[9]

Surrounded by copies of Alfred Leete's famous poster of Lord Kitchener staring and pointing his finger at "YOU," the representatives of church and state shared the recruiting platform. Hensley Henson repeatedly gave time from a crowded schedule to tour the Durham countryside with Lord Derby, the head of the Parliamentary Recruiting Committee, to rouse the miners.[10] While the primate sidestepped all requests to appear with recruiters, Archbishop Lang seems to have enjoyed presiding at recruiting rallies. "My brothers," he told a meeting of the Church of England Men's Society, "don't live and look back on the year 1915 with a cause of shame, to know yourself and to be known to be one of the men who failed. Here is the plain, straight thing to do—rise up and do it."[11] Christian Socialist leaders, several of whom enjoyed national reputations, plunged into the campaign with the same enthusiasm of their conservative compatriots. Paul Bull, Stewart Headlam, and John Neville Figgis encouraged those with whom they came in contact to enlist. Although a supporter of the Independent Labour Party, James Adderley nevertheless scolded it for opposing conscription when it ought to have been encouraging its members to join the forces; it executives, he suggested, should be compelled to write their manifestos amid the ruins of Ypres.[12]

The bishop of London was far and away the most indefatigable, and the most successful, of clerical recruiting sergeants. A popular, outgoing man, wherever he went Winnington-Ingram preached on the same text: better to die than see England a German province. His most successful foray took place at the very beginning of the war. While visiting the Burgess Hill and Hayward Heath encampments of the Territorial Army, General Smith-Dorrien, later commander of the Second Army, asked him to "put a little ginger in your sermon, Bishop, as some of these men have not volunteered as yet for foreign service." He did, his sermon, "A Call to Arms," being credited with inducing two brigades to go overseas. He later boasted of having been thanked officially by the War Office for having added ten thousand men to the fighting forces of the crown; soon thereafter a grateful king appointed him K.C.V.O.[13]

In view of the clergy's functioning in a society where the influence of organized religion had been declining for a least a half-century, their success in recruiting fighting men is all the more remarkable. Certainly, the publicity carried on by the mass circulation newspapers and the Parliamentary Recruiting Committee reinforced the appeal of religion; but it should also be noted that the Hensley Hensons, the Paul Bulls, and the Winnington-Ingrams were experienced preachers who had spent years in refining their techniques and studying their listeners. They were adept at using emotive words, and a few of their recruiting speeches, embellished with a phraseology calculated to appeal simultaneously to religious feelings, love of country, and the emotions are masterpieces of the salesman's art. Nor should we overlook the position of the clergyman as one of the natural leaders of his community. This was especially so in the rural districts, where that keen sportsman, the fox-hunting parson, might on occasion be seen in the forefront of the chase. Like his eighteenth and nineteenth century ancestors, in certain areas he was still the resident gentleman, an authority-figure who by virtue of his education and standing in the hierarchy of local society commanded the respect of simpler folk. Rural clergymen occasionaly had astounding success as recruiters, as when the Rev. Richard Huggard, vicar of St. John's, Barnsley, proudly announced having enlisted two thousand men.[14]

Those bidding their parishioners volunteer might stress any of a number of points. Some began with a simple declaration of "fact": God, speaking through His church, expected every man to do his duty. "God wants you," proclaimed Canon Newbolt, echoing Kitchener, "He is summoning you to put all your powers at His disposal."[15] Fighting for England and fighting for Christ were one in the same thing, a truth represented symbolically by the crosses on the Union Jack:

> Fight for the colours of Christ the King,
> Fight as He fought for you;
> Fight for the Right with all your might,
> Fight for the Red, White, and Blue.[16]

So-called "recruiting texts" were quoted to lend divine sanction to their appeals. Lord Kitchener needed every available man, and nobody should risk the curse of Meroz by ignoring his call. In *Repentance and Strength*, a collection of sermons emphasizing the last part of the title, the Rev. A. W. Gough, vicar of Brompton and prebendary of St. Paul's, proclaimed that every Englishman worthy of the name should don with pride the khaki uniform, "the festal garment which God is offering to us to-day, which He is insisting that we put on."

The cowardly, the indolent, and the selfish were denounced from the pulpit for sinning against God and their fellowmen, as were the fair weather patriots who satisfied themselves with wearing a patriotic button and displaying a patriotic picture, when what they really needed was a "patriotic kicking."[18] "Is there a man who can go that

chooses to sit down and reckon himself unfit?" asked the master of
St. Catherine's College, Cambridge, "It is a pity we cannot brand
that sort of man 'Made in fear of Germany.' Would to God we had
known when they were born that they would eat our bread and grow
and live amongst us, trusted and approved, and yet cowards. We need
not have prayed and worked for them."[19] Among the harshest criticisms were those directed against the sportsmen, insensate creatures
who enjoyed their golf and their football while others died keeping
the enemy from their door. In November, 1914, the *Challenge* reported that thirty-four thousand men, the equivalent of several regiments, had watched Chelsea beat Bolton: what would have suited
them best, remarked the editor bitterly, "was a shrapnel shell in their
midst, some simple sign that England is at war and needs them."[20]

Instead of appealing to the prospective recruits directly, recruiters
used to aim their remarks at their relatives, particularly their female
relatives. They reminded parents that it was better for their sons to
fall in battle than to live out their lives in dishonor. "Oh, Christian
mother," gushed one preacher, "would you not rather that your son
lay dead at your feet than that he should live in dishonour?"[21] Such
pleas initially met with a degree of success, women themselves join-
ing in the effort. Suffragettes as well as bishops' daughters urged
women to stir the hearts of their men. Girls, egged on perhaps by
clerical advice to apply the pressure of contempt to malingerers, presented eligible-looking youths with white feathers and petticoats;
Anglican women's groups assisted in the early recruiting drives. The
Mothers' Union, for example, published before fighting began in
earnest a small pamphlet *To British Women, How They Can Help
Recruiting* (1914): needless to say, it was never reprinted.

Of critical importance in creating the atmosphere of the holy war,
atrocity stories served also as stimulants to recruiting. Propagandists,
both private and official, went to great lengths to frighten their countrymen. Wherever he turned, the citizen encountered reminders of
German bestiality. His newspapers, evidently adopting the War Office dictum that "essential" truth rather than literal truth would govern its news releases, were filled with exaggerated reports, doctored
photographs, and savage cartoons, notably those of Louis Raemae-
kers, the artist for the Amsterdam *Telegraaf*. Atrocity museums were
opened, and the music halls, a form of entertainment popular with

the working-classes, staged atrocity reviews. In a typical piece, entitled appropriately "By Jingo, If We Do—!" the cruelties of a band of Uhlans were depicted so realistically as to prompt *The Encore* to caution against frightening audiences too much. Recruiting sketches abounded, "The Rotter" and "The Slacker" acting out their message in explicit terms.[22]

The clergyman, like everyone else, was a target for this kind of propaganda, but with a difference; if he chose, he could use his unique position to feed it back into the mainstream of popular thought, attaching to it in the process the moral authority of the sacerdotal office. Finding it hard to believe that the Germans, civilized people like himself, could so quickly sink into savagery, he tended at first to shy away from unauthenticated atrocity stories. Yet Louvain, the Bryce report, and the *Lusitania* were decisive in dispelling whatever doubts he might have had. It became easy to believe anything of the Germans; indeed, whatever atrocity story happened to be in vogue at the moment, it was picked up and broadcast by clergymen. The crucified Canadian sergeant; babies tossed in the air and caught on bayonet points; Burton Mayberry, the ship's engineer whose cheeks had been tattooed with Cobra heads; the factory for converting the bodies of dead German soldiers into fats for explosives and food for hogs; germ warfare; and the dropping of packets of poisoned sweetmeats to French children represent a small sample of the enormities related from the pulpit.

Of all the appeals to human emotion, none was more deeply rooted in the collective consciousness or exploited more ruthlessly than the fear of sexual outrage. The church, the suffragettes, and various civic groups had long campaigned against sexual immorality, particularly as manifested in the growing number of assaults on young girls. As late as 1913, A. Maude Royden had held the audience at the annual church congress spellbound with a description of prostitution, vice, and sweating in the great cities of Europe and America.[23] The conditions portrayed in *The Maiden Tribute of Modern Babylon* (1885), W. T. Stead's exposé of the international white slave traffic, were still too much in evidence. When the war began, therefore, the public was already sensitized to crimes of a sexual nature. This theme, elaborated at first in the press and by the propagandists, was taken up by zealous clerical recruiters. They painted the German soldier, with his spiked helmet and long bayonet, as a slobbering, libidinous brute, the incarnation of Eros run wild. If ever the Germans came to England, the atrocities inflicted upon the women of the occupied territories would be multiplied tenfold:

To be shot dead is bad, but there is a worse fate for them. Our mothers and grandmothers would have gone crazy at the thought of their men tamely submitting to the imposition of a mixed race in England. Yet that would, we know, be the result of a German invasion. Half the children born next year in a town occupied by German troops would have a German soldier for a father. That is what it means when the poor Belgians tell with utter anguish and shame of the order to leave every door open at night to the German soldier. Can any woman be so indifferent to her prospects as not to shudder when she reads the papers? Let every woman resolve to have nothing to do with a man who can enlist and fight for the protection of his home and will not. Better the German soldier than such a pretty tailor's lay figure [sic]. I cannot speak plainer than I do.[24]

There are other instances where the fear of sexual outrage was utilized as a stimulant to recruiting. The bishops of London, Lichfield, and Chelmsford recommended that their diocesan clergy tell churchgoers about what the Germans were doing to the women of France and Belgium.[25] A common motif dealt with the German's supposed penchant for cutting off women's breasts; indeed, one group of stories had them hacking off the breasts of wooden statues of the Virgin Mary. Paul Bull once told a congregation about a Yorkshire lad who overheard returning soldiers tell about seeing such atrocities in Flanders. As he looked at his mother and sister, the young man cried, "They shalln't do that to mother and Nelle," and ran off to enlist.[26]

Unlike the German soldier, Tommy Atkins was depicted as the exemplification of manliness. This had not always been the case, as may be ascertained from Kipling's Barrack-Room Ballad about "Tommy." As long as England could get along with a small volunteer army, with scarcely better than the dregs of society serving in the ranks, the red tunic was a stigma barring its wearer from public places open even to ill-mannered civilians. Soldiering was commonly deemed synonymous with loafing. To have a son "go for a soldier" was as humiliating for a respectable working-class family as "going into trade" had been for its social superiors at an earlier time. The Great War made soldiering respectable; for the first time in English history the army became in reality the nation in arms.

To get as many as possible to take arms, it was necessary to transform Wellington's "scum of the earth" into Christians and gentlemen. Prospective recruits and their womenfolk were advised not to worry about the moral well-being of the British soldier. At a time when venereal disease was rampant, they were told that Tommy's "instinctive desire is to be clean in body and soul"; like the lovable characters in a Bruce Bairnsfather cartoon, "Tommy is wonderful . . . Tommy is gay . . . Tommy laughs and sings. . . ."[27]

Led by brave, devoted officers, the boys of England, milksops lately freed from their mothers' apron strings, were becoming seasoned veterans, men in every sense of the word. Better still, the "comradeship of the trenches," the "beautiful brotherhood of the trenches," was held to have brought about the spiritual rebirth of many a sinner. "The most encouraging feature to all Christians," claimed the Rev. James Bent of the Salford Dock Mission, "is the glorious fact that thousands of men are finding even in the trenches a sanctuary, a very Bethel."[28] His faith strengthened, Tommy, always high-spirited, faced whatever war held in store for him. Without underestimating the hideousness of the wounds inflicted by modern weapons, there were those who maintained that Tommy retained his sense of humor despite his wounds. "The wards of a military hospital," according to one chaplain, "are not 'sad aisles of pain,' though pain has been in full evidence. They are homes of happy laughter, and of fun which has never been careless, or bitter, or cruel."[29] Given the enthusiasm with which the clerical recruiters threw themselves into their work, it is no wonder that marching soldiers remembered them in their songs: "Yes, Kitchener loves me, the Bible tells me so."[30]

MOBILIZING THE CLERGY

Save for a handful of Christian Socialists, the overwhelming majority of Anglican clergymen considered it a duty and a privilege to aid the nation in its moment of need. Throughout the conflict, the religious press published innumerable items proclaiming that the clergyman, no less than the ordinary citizen, must be ready to give without stint, and without flinching, the blood of his sons to the national cause. That generosity with words was matched by generosity in deeds is amply attested by the weekly obituary columns. By the time conscription became law, the most idealistic young men had long since joined the colors; and of those granted commissions, the lay sons of the clergy supplied an estimated 30 percent of the officers of the army.[31] The casualties they sustained, and the honors they won, were proportionally high. As of February, 1916, thirteen bishops' sons had died in combat or of wounds; the bishop of Buckingham led the episcopal mourners, having lost both of his sons. Noel Chavasse, son of the evangelical bishop of Liverpool, died the only soldier in the war to win the Victoria Cross with bar.[32]

Emulating the sons of the clergy, the members of church-affiliated organizations, altar servers, and scouts were also among the first to enlist. The Church Lads' Brigade, one of the more successful Anglican organizations for youths, sought to attain its religious objectives within the context of a paramilitary organization. Whereas its spiritual accomplishments were not always apparent, its military methods —camping, drilling, military exercises—proved a national asset, as it contributed 120,000 of its current and past membership to the fighting forces.[33] Winnington-Ingram was especially proud of the Church Lads' Brigade; under his presidency, its London branch recruited a battalion of 1,000 men which subsequently earned a personal commendation from Lord Kitchener.[34]

In eulogizing a former student, Gilbert Murray paid homage to all the promising young scholars who in the earliest days of the conflict put aside their studies to enlist—more than a thousand Oxford undergraduates had been nominated for commissions by the end of August, 1914.[35] Resolving not to be outdone by their students, some of the foremost intellectuals of their time, men too old to fight but still young enough to enjoy learning to fight, joined various paramilitary volunteer units. The sight of Murray himself charging across the Oxford meadows, or F. M. Cornford giving instruction in musketry, or Hastings Rashdall and the rector of Exeter turning out at seven o'clock on a chilly morning to drill with "Godley's Army" (after A. D. Godley of Magdalen College) must have tickled many a new lieutenant of infantry. Yet he would have understood why his middle-aged mentors were tramping the countryside. The English university man and the public-school boy prided themselves on belonging to a privileged class. They were the products of an education designed, in the words of Edmund Warre, one of the great headmasters of Eton, to create "the best baronets ever seen, loyal and true and kind, the salt of the earth . . . honest secretaries of state, open-handed village-squires, broad-minded bishops."[36] They were gentlemen who, despite their snobbery and class pride, had nevertheless imbibed a sense of noblesse oblige. Rank carries privilege, and privilege is justified by service to one's school, to one's inferiors, and to one's country, the defense of which is the service par excellence.

The divinity student responded in exactly the same manner as his secular counterpart. Well might the *Official Year-Book of the Church of England* lament that the number of students resident at colleges and seminaries had been "seriously depleted" by the war.[37] Of the 1,274 students enrolled in the thirty-two Anglican theological colleges, nearly four hundred withdrew immediately, a staggering blow to the church, given the roughly six hundred ordinations in normal years.[38] Ordinations fell steadily during the war: 610 (1914), 453 (1915), 330 (1916), 167 (1917), 114 (1918), 161 (1919);[39] the church would miss this "lost generation" of priests for decades to come. All colleges had to curtail their programs drastically; some went out of existence altogether, as did Bishop's Hostel, Farnham, a promising endeavor under B. K. Cunningham, an outstanding teacher of theology.[40] Other Anglican activities suffered as a consequence. For example, by 1915, 2,700 men who had either been teachers in Church of England elementary schools or enrolled in teacher-training colleges were in the forces.[41]

In the universities and theological colleges, certain teachers yielded nothing in skill or enthusiasm to the nonacademic recruiters. Because the conflict had broken out during the summer vacation, several colleges thought it fitting to reward those who had already enlisted, and to take steps to encourage the remainder to emulate their classmates. Dr. Alfred Caldecott, dean of the faculty of theology at King's College, London, promised special classes and examinations for any student upon his return from service.[42] Others, however, saw no need to sugarcoat the pill. Bishop Gore testified that he knew from personal contacts of students who, if left to themselves, would not have enlisted, but who were pressured by the authorities of the theological colleges and other responsible persons.[43] In this connection, Gore may have had in mind a statement by the Rev. W. E. Barnes, Hulsean Professor of Divinity at Cambridge. "Sir," he informed the editor of the *Church Times*, "in about five weeks the October term begins at this University. May I say that I hope to meet in my lecture-room no man between twenty and thirty (who can pass the medical test) who has not either offered himself for active service or submitted himself to military training? There is a time for everything, and the present time is a time for bearing arms. A new Waterloo must be won over a new foe . . . ."[44]

Four bishops went further than professor Barnes, placing in effect a premium on physical incapacity in the ranks of the priesthood. To encourage divinity students to enlist, the bishop of London let it be known in June, 1915, that he intended to deny ordination to any man of military age not certified unfit for military service.[45] His pronouncement applauded in the press, Winnington-Ingram was joined eventually by the bishops of Carlisle, Chester, and Manchester in declaring to the Convocation of Canterbury their ban, effective on June 18, 1916, on ordinations for men in condition to serve.[46] Their decision, however, failed to win wide support from their colleagues, prompting the *Modern Churchman*, seldom patient with a moderate course where the war was concerned, to reprove the bishops for adopting a niggling policy bound to harm the church.[47]

Whether those already ordained should enlist or be compelled to serve was another matter. Since the Middle Ages, canon law, supplemented by the vows taken at ordination, has expressly forbidden the cleric to bear arms or engage in war. Though often honored more in the letter than the spirit, the fact that high ecclesiastics circumvented the law by wielding a heavy club in battle was a tacit acknowledgement, albeit of little consolation to their victims, of the principle that the clergyman must not shed blood. Throughout its history, the Anglican episcopate, always favorably disposed to priests urging laymen to fight in just wars, opposed anyone in Holy Orders serving as a combatant. In their formal gatherings and pastoral letters, the bishops followed the lead of the primate: a clergyman could with a clear conscience and with their blessing become a chaplain or serve in another noncombatant capacity; he should not bear arms.[48]

Significantly, however, none of the diocesan bishops—at least none that I know about—either formally prohibited his clergy from enlisting or opposed clerical combatancy exclusively on the grounds of canon law; actually, they preferred to base their case on pragmatic grounds rather than fundamental principle. The major argument, constantly reiterated, was that the clergy were needed at home, and that they could best further the national effort by performing their accustomed duties. Yet their official pronouncements often contain, all but hidden amid the surrounding verbiage, brief phrases such as "at present" and "as yet," escape clauses indicating that, whereas clerical combatancy was inappropriate for the present, circumstances might later dictate another course. Canon law notwithstanding, there might come a time when the ordinary rules would have to be suspended; the survival of the nation, and with it the survival of the church, must ultimately be the overriding consideration. Writing privately to the bishop of Salisbury sometime at the beginning of the war, Archbishop Davidson emphasized this point: "I do not believe that an ordained man ought to be a combatant in the Army. For the Minister of Christ to serve as a *fighting soldier* is to my mind to disregard unduly the special Commission which is his. I do not of course say that this should be applicable in the moment of supremest urgency in the Nation's life, or if the country were invaded, or the man's parish being attacked."[49]

Had Davidson and the others said this openly and plainly from the outset, chances are that a good deal of misunderstanding, let alone heartache, would have been avoided. For the first year of the war, there was some grumbling, emanating largely from Bottomly and his sort, as to why the French should be conscripting Roman Catholic priests for the trenches while strapping young Anglican curates were still to be seen at parish teas. Yet there was no general outcry until the clergy of all denominations were excused from attesting under the Derby Scheme, and, the following year, 1916, exempted from the Military Service Act. At this point the mood changed perceptibly, organized religion as a whole, and the Church of England in particular, becoming the target for wholesale abuse.

Whereas the man in the trenches was usually quite definite about the incompatibility of his profession with the parson's, civilians, clerical and lay alike, tended for different reasons to be intolerant toward "shirkers." The House of Commons became a storm center. Philip Snowden, M.P. for Blackburn, linked his pacifism and opposition to conscription with an abiding antipathy toward jingoistic clergymen. In 1915 he sought to embarrass the episcopate by having it prosecuted under D.O.R.A. on charges of preventing clergymen from enlisting.[50] When the Military Service Act became law, he demanded its amendment to include clergymen because, judging from their statements, "I am quite certain that there is no class in the community who are so anxious to engage in combat service as ministers of religion are."[51] His views were shared by John Dillon, the Irish nationalist leader who later joined Sinn Fein in resisting conscription in Ireland; Dillon thought it indecent for clergymen to clamor for conscription, while at the same time insisting that it not be applied to themselves.[52] By 1916, the clergy had become so unpopular in Parliament that when Colonel Sir A. Griffith-Boscawen, a defender of their exemption, asked how many could be spared without detriment to the spiritual welfare of the nation, the Honourable Members replied in unison, "All of them!"[53]

Unhampered by parliamentary conventions, and carrying a grudge against the church ever since the dock strike of 1889, Ben Tillett delivered an impassioned attack on clerical exemptions. He was incensed at the prospect of his brethren dying while clergymen painted army life in rosy hues. In September, 1916, he introduced at the annual meeting of the Trades Union Congress at Birmingham a resolution condemning exemptions in highly uncomplimentary terms. This resolution embodied all the old suspicious of a political church. The clergy, Tillett said, were hypocrites. They favored conscription as long as they were unaffected personally, but when it looked as if *they* might be called, "these cowardly creatures" evaded their responsibilities by going through the back doors of Parliament. "Why," he continued, "should these men who are so fond of talking about heaven be so afraid to go through its gates?" His resolution carried by nearly two hundred thousand votes.[54]

There is absolutely nothing but Tillet's word to confirm the charge of episcopal influence behind the scenes; on the contrary, the primate took pains to establish that the excepting clause in the Military Service Act was not the result of episcopal influence.[55] Tillett and Snowden, both Nonconformists, were not especially well-informed about the Anglican community. Had they followed the weekly press they would have learned that considerable numbers of deacons and curates disagreed with their superiors and expressed a desire to fight along side their parishioners. A small number of extremists argued that, in view of the religious nature of the conflict, it was absurd to hold men to vows never intended to apply to such extraordinary situations: "If a man wants to go and fight for his country no Bishop ought to stop him because he has taken certain irrelevant vows."[56] Others defended clerical combatancy by maintaining that if it was proper for the ordinary Christian to kill a German, then it must be proper for the priest who encouraged him to do likewise.[57]

A recurrent theme (one to which we shall have to return in more detail) stressed the war as providing the church with a signal opportunity to reverse the trend of public opinion and recover its lost prestige. To leaven the armed forces with priests, or with men possessing the vocation for the priesthood, would help create such a reservoir of goodwill, such a community of interest and understanding between minister and ministered, as to usher in a golden age for the Church of England. If, on the other hand, the church muffed its opportunity and allowed the impression that the younger clergy were skulking behind the bishop's apron, then it would deservedly lose the respect of men everywhere. It was becoming increasingly evident that their exemption was having a detrimental effect, hampering them in performing their pastoral duties. This was especially true in the populous industrial districts, where parish priests were accosted on their rounds by gangs of small boys who, thumb to nose, followed them down the street chanting "Kitchener wants *you!*"[58] Things had come to such a state that Winnington-Ingram himself was interrupted during an address on Tower Hill by jeers and questions about his holding back curates from taking their place in the trenches.[59] By sitting on the fence and allowing matters to go from bad to worse, the bishops were sowing the seeds of disestablishment and worse, seeds that would begin to germinate with the restoration of peace.

Younger clergymen, perhaps cherishing memories of athletic triumphs, were wounded by the slurs on their manhood. Like the Rev. C. E. Wormell, the tall, muscular curate of St. Paul's, Stafford, Essex, who challenged anyone in a group of railwaymen to accuse the clergy of cowardice, they resented being in a position of feeling obliged to advise others to enlist, while at the same time being prohibited from doing what they urged.[60] Difficult to measure, but certainly present, were also the elements of envy and boredom. The men of their generation, their school chums, were visiting distant places and doing exciting, dangerous things; things that must have held out an alluring appeal when contrasted with their own workaday world of visitations, Sunday school classes, and personal obligations. It is therefore not surprising that in December, 1915, one thousand junior clergy of the diocese of London should petition Winnington-Ingram to organize the life of the diocese so as to permit them to do work related to the war, to invite all those of military age to offer themselves for those branches of national service he deemed suitable, and to consider waiving the rule prohibiting clergymen from becoming combatants. The great recruiter of fighting men refused, saying that the diocese could not afford their loss, while the army could so far do without their services.[61]

The bishops held to this view until the spring of 1918. Then, on March 21, the Germans began a series of all-out offensives aimed at destroying the Allies before the Americans arrived in strength sufficient to break the deadlock on the Western Front. By April 5 they had pierced the British lines near St. Quentin to a depth of forty miles; on April 9 they delivered a second blow south of Ypres, took Armentiéres, and opened a wide breach in the British front; on April 13 the cumulative effect of these thrusts prompted Field-Marshal Haig to issue his famous order of the day: "With our backs to the wall, and believing in the justice of our cause, each one of us must fight to the end." The government, however, determined to hold on despite the loss of an entire army, introduced a new military service bill (April 9) which raised the military age from forty-one to fifty and abolished the clerical exemption. The archbishop of Canterbury immediately gave his blessing to the inclusion of the clergy; but six days later, Parliament reversed its decision because it feared another Irish Rebellion if Roman Catholic priests were conscripted.

This sudden about-face placed every clergyman up to the age of fifty-one in an ambiguous position. No matter how genuine his personal reasons or religious scruples, these were bound to be questioned, and probably misconstrued, if he did not come forward voluntarily. To clarify the position of the Anglican church, the primate delivered before the Lords a speech stressing that neither he nor his associates had anything to do with excluding the clergy from the bill. As evidence of the church's good faith, he promised "to see what we can do voluntarily under conditions so different—and this is the real point —from those of 1915–1916 as to justify a different attitude on our part from that which we took at that time."[62]

To implement his pledge, Davidson convened on April 22 a conference at which the seventeen diocesan bishops present agreed to give their clergy the opportunity under a voluntary system to place themselves in the same position as would have been theirs under conscription. Everyone was now free to follow the dictates of his conscience. He could offer himself for noncombatant service or fight in the ranks. To be sure, Winnington-Ingram was carried away, taking the decision as a warrant to "call up" and "comb out" all the eligible clergymen in his diocese. On April 24 the *Times* published his "invitation" to them: now that "we are at the crisis of our fate," he urged them to enlist for noncombatant service, adding that he was prepared to grant a "special dispensation" (whatever that meant) to those wishing to bear arms.[63]

The results of the bishops' action must have been disappointing in the extreme to those who had envisioned legions of cowardly curates marching off to their just deserts, or enthusiastic young men getting their wish. Actually, large dioceses like London, Southwark, Oxford, and Birmingham contributed as a rule fewer than fifty fighting men apiece. The reason for this poor showing is readily apparent: many were overage, while the eligible younger men had already enlisted as chaplains, were working in church-sponsored recreation huts, serving with the Royal Army Medical Corps, or doing other forms of national service. By the summer of 1918, the clergy were spread thinner than they had ever been before. The Church of England had been scraping the bottom of the manpower barrel long before the bishops' call up; it was now scraped clean through. The call-up hurt the church all along the line. It compounded the loss of ordinands from the colleges and seminaries, guaranteeing that the clergy who remained in England, especially in the crowded urban parishes, would be working harder and longer hours than heretofore. That their flocks, despite the leakage to the forces, were now tended with less care is evidenced by the Bishop of Birmingham, who wrote to the primate complaining that, with one priest for every five thousand people, the quality of their work had deteriorated markedly. London was worse off, with 761 men in Orders—incumbents, curates, and missioners—to cover its six hundred parishes.[64]

THE CLERGY AND THE WAR EFFORT

By taking part in recruiting drives, and themselves occasionally enlisting as combatants, clergymen became involved in highly visible and inherently controversial activities. Yet they were also well aware that many mundane, unglamorous tasks needed to be done before the final victory; for the issue depended as much on having the most efficient system of producing and paying for the tools of war as on having the soldiers to use them. Here, as in the other activities discussed thusfar, they thought it the duty of the church to teach by its own example that, through service, sacrifice, and self-discipline, those remaining at home could make as valuable a contribution to the sacred undertaking as the men at the front.

The conflict had scarcely begun when reports appeared of ministers of religion undertaking war work of various types: making sandbags, acting as drill-instructors, home defence duty. During the furor over the shell shortage in 1916, solved eventually by creating the Ministry of Munitions, leading churchmen, among them the archbishop of York and the bishops of Bangor and Pretoria, thundered against the nation's unpreparedness. Upon returning from a tour of the Ypres sector, bishop Furse of Pretoria denounced the dearth of shells as "little short of murder," and demanded that production be increased at all costs, if necessary even by mobilizing every man, woman, and child for work in the munitions factories. Only in this way would the enemy, whom he was certain was the Devil incarnate, be smashed.[65] Shortly after the episcopal outcry, the press began carrying stories about, and articles by, clergymen working for armaments manufacturers, particularly Vickers Ltd.[66] They put in a hard week, working six days and returning to their parishes for services on Sunday; a few suffered physical breakdowns.

These were the activities of individuals, undertaken largely on their own initiative. By the winter of 1916, however, the drain on England's manpower reserves had become grave indeed, compelling certain governmental departments to bid against one another for an ever-dwindling resource. The army, recently weakened by the slaughter in what was euphemistically called the Somme "offensive," demanded the conscription of all nonessential workers. The departments responsible for running the war industries resisted, maintaining that exemption of their workers was the only way of meeting production quotas on time. To satisfy both sides, Lloyd George created in December the ministries of Labour and National Service, and launched a publicity campaign to encourage citizens to undertake work to release others for the front.

With the exception of the Church Socialist League, several of whose members labelled National Service "National Serfdom" because it seemed to foreshadow labor conscription, the scheme was received with enthusiasm in Anglican circles. Only through such service, asserted the Rev. Christopher Cheshire, Scott Holland's successor as editor of the *Commonwealth* and an opponent of military conscription, could a man justify his existence and claim to a place in the community. "If he will not work . . . for the common good, then he has no right even to eat: he could not justly complain if he was tied in a bundle and tossed into the nearest fire." [67] The press as a whole praised the scheme in extravagant terms. For the clergy remaining at home, sheltered always from the ultimate realities of life and death, national service would be at least a kind of postgraduate education, a means of infusing vitality into the tired Establishment. [68]

There were special problems that needed to be overcome before the church could play its part fully. As the bishop of Kensington informed his colleague at Lichfield, "Numbers of clergy in parishes are eating their hearts out longing to be of service, and yet of course they are tied to their parishes. It does seem as though at this abnormal time, we are challenged as a Church to be up and going." [69] Soon thereafter, the archbishops furnished Neville Chamberlain, the director-general of National Service, with a plan whereby the diocesan bishops themselves would be the "responsible employers," enquiring of the clergy what work they wished to undertake. The bishop could then enroll them for "special service" as chaplains to the forces and hospital workers, or "general service" as munitions, office, and agricultural workers. [70] A Clergy National Service Committee, with offices at the Church House, Westminster, was set up to promote volunteering and process applications. By May, the committee was able to announce with pride that nearly four thousand clergymen had offered themselves for special service, while another two thousand were rendering general service. Lichfield, a model diocese in this respect, contributed five hundred of its six hundred priests to various National Service projects.[71]

The summer of 1917 found men in Holy Orders serving in such uncharacteristic occupations as auto mechanics, stokers on merchant ships, coal miners, postmen, engineers, and tax collectors. In Birmingham, where Bishop Wakefield urged his clergy to assume duties as policemen, sixty-five donned uniforms as special constables. Whether at the behest of his bishop or on his own volition, one clergymen, unnamed unfortunately, took on a most extraordinary form of national service. Wrote Wakefield to the primate: "one of our clergy—a delicate man—a very distinguished experimental chemist, is now a leading research worker at the greatest gas (poisonous) factory we have, and has I suppose more German victims of his brain than any other ordained man in the world!"[72] Though not as far reaching in consequences, clergymen in other areas volunteered for work directly related to the war: producing and transporting munitions, building airplanes and ships, patrolling the coasts, and code ciphering. Hastings Rashdall had evidently put his time with Godley's Army to good use. After becoming an expert marksman at the age of fifty-nine, he joined the staff of the Admiralty Intelligence Department.[73]

Early in 1917, the high point of the German submarine offensive, coinciding as it did with a late frost which caused a delay in plowing, involved the religious community in still another aspect of the war effort. Unless sowing was done on Sundays as well as weekdays, the nation faced a critical food shortage in the coming year. Recognizing the emergency, Anglican and Roman Catholic prelates—less so Nonconformist officials—endorsed plans for allowing their people to do farm work on the Sabbath. In a letter to R. E. Prothero, the distinguished historian and president of the Board of Agriculture, Archbishop Davidson noted that, inasmuch as food supplies were in a precarious state, he could without hesitation advise Anglicans to work in the fields on Sundays with a clear conscience.[74] His position, however, met with opposition. Led by the *Record*, Evangelicals deplored the "desecration" of the Lord's Day, registering their disapproval with a flood of petitions, letters, resolutions, and editorials. Nevertheless, his colleagues in dioceses with large farming populations appealed to their clergy to encourage Sunday labor. Sometimes country parsons, aided by contingents of their colleagues from the towns, worked in the fields themselves; sometimes, like the bishop of Exeter, they helped alleviate the food shortage by granting permission for potatoes to be grown in consecrated ground. Nor was it unknown for their wives to lend a hand; and although few went so far as Mrs. Rawstorne, wife of the bishop of Whalley, in taking daily lessons in plowing, more probably emulated Lady Derby in serving as part-time potato pickers.[75]

Assuming every eligible man became a soldier, and every ablebodied priest offered himself for national service, England would have been in dire straits had she been unable to mobilize her economic resources. Somehow the money had to be found to buy the tools of war and to pay the workers who made them. He might have qualms about stumping the countryside for recruits; he might hesitate about working in an armaments factory; here, however, was an opportunity for the most fastidious of clergymen to make a contribution to the war effort.

Whatever device the government chose to employ, from increased income and excise taxes to long-term War Loans and inexpensive War Savings Certificates, the church stood ready to lend its support at every turn. In addition to associating itself with the work of the War Savings Committee on the national level, and cooperating in innumerable local undertakings, the church put itself on record as favoring tying in its own fund-raising machinery with that of the state. Unlike recruiting, where he hesitated about encouraging appeals from the pulpit, in this case the primate was quite explicit about the "sacred duty" of those with influence, clergy and laity alike, to stimulate interest in the War Loans. "It needs but a little thought," he told the Canterbury Diocesan Conference, "to see how to bring home in simple words to simple folk the truth that they are materially and solidly helping their country by investing in the new War Loan whatever savings are at their command, and that they must—positively must—increase the investible money by every economy which they can devise."[76]

As usual, the activities of Winnington-Ingram were the most flamboyant, attracted the most attention, and were therefore the most frequently reported. Taking advantage of his position as the spiritual leader of the wealthiest and largest diocese in the land, he wrote the government offering to place the "entire machinery" of the church in London at its disposal for the Second War Loan drive (1915). Shortly after this, he participated in ceremonies at which the prime minister inaugurated the Loan with a stirring call to Englishmen to give to their last farthing, to their last ounce of strength, to their last drop of blood.[77] Once again the bishop volunteered the "whole organization" of the church in his diocese; only this time he supplemented his offer by having distributed a half-million leaflets bearing "A Message from the Bishop of London to the People of London." Every Londoner, he proclaimed, must tell himself constantly that, "however small it may be, I must save what I can and invest it in the War Loan to help my country. I cannot 'have a good time' at home while the lads at the front go through what they call 'a hell.' "[78] His work in this area was crowned with success in 1917, when he played an instrumental role in organizing a mammoth War Loan demonstration. The spiritual and the worldly were united that day, as the crowd overflowing Trafalgar Square listened to sermons and patriotic speeches, recited the Lord's Prayer and sang "O God, Our Help in Ages Past" to the accompaniment of massed military bands.[79]

Aside from the obvious need to finance the war and, for psychological reasons, to persuade the enemy of the foolishness of fighting a nation with inexhaustible resources, references to specifically religious considerations figured in the rhetoric of fund-raising. Perhaps the most popular theme dealt with the wholesome attitudes and the spiritual benefits to be derived from lending money to the nation. By investing money that would otherwise have gone for luxuries, particularly those of the alcoholic variety, the individual was actually contributing to his own salvation. If he trained himself to do with fewer material things, he would then not be so tempted to sin to get them; he would also be showing his Lord his devotion to his fellowmen. Admittedly, a man unwilling or unable to serve in the forces might make a fortune by staying at home and investing in profitable securities; nonetheless, investing in the War Loans was presented as an appropriate, if only a symbolic, substitute for the blood-sacrifice of the soldier.

These arguments, supplemented by imaginative publicity devices and personal influence, proved highly effective. From every corner of England came reports of children in Anglican day schools bringing in their pennies for War Savings Certificates, of small rural congregations devoting the whole of their Sunday collections to the War Loans, and of wealthy bishops and poverty stricken curates scrimping and saving to purchase shares in their country's future. The war accomplished what critics had long complained of: it caused to be shut down for at least the time being several overlarge, overexpensive, ostentatious episcopal palaces. Archbishop Lang, for instance, closed up most of Bishopthorpe, cut his living expenses in half, and put the remainder into the War Loans. Some went to extraordinary lengths to press their case. Bishop Wakefield of Birmingham borrowed a thousand pounds from a local bank and offered to advance a small amount to any clergyman wishing to subscribe to the War Loans. Yet this was not as great a personal sacrifice as that of the country parson who announced he would supplement out of his own pocket the interest on low-yield certificates.[80]

Church organizations specializing in assisting needy clergymen, providing pensions for retired clergymen, and investing church funds saw a chance to serve the nation and at the same time acquire safe, remunerative securities. A close inspection of their accounts, unfortunately unavailable, would no doubt yield valuable information about the church's involvement in the war effort. Even the fragmentary figures published in the press to advertise their patriotism suggest something of the magnitude of their commitment. Minute in comparison with the total cost of the war, nonetheless, between June 1915 and February 1917, the Clergy Friendly Society, Ecclesiastical Insurance Office, Church Benefit Society, Clergy Pensions Institution, Ecclesiastical Commissioners, and Governors of Queen Anne's Bounty invested over £4,500,000 in government securities.[81]

Clergymen recognized that all their efforts would be for nothing unless prices remained stable. Unfortunately, the government, which could have averted serious inflation by drastically increasing taxation at the outset, chose to finance the conflict largely through borrowing. As a result of its heavy expenditures on economically unproductive war materials, coupled with the diversion of raw materials and industrial plant to military uses, the amount of money in circulation increased to the point where it could not be absorbed by the existing consumer goods. Consequently, in Great Britain food and retail prices more than doubled, the index of real wages falling thirty-two points between 1914 and 1917.[82]

Resolved that the war would not be lost through laxity on the home front, the highest officials of the Church of England urged their people to combat inflation by restraining their impulses to buy unnecessary commodities and by moderating their demands for higher wages, prices, and profits. Inasmuch as butter, sugar, lard, and margarine, the scarcest food items, remained unrationed until 1918, the archbishops took it upon themselves to remind the nation of the "imperious necessity" (Davidson's phrase) of economizing. Since bread had become as vital as bullets, they denounced the glutton, the hoarder, and the waster of food as a sinner against God and man. Though it is impossible to gauge precisely the effectiveness of their appeals, the fact that women's groups and all religious newspapers published hints on wartime shopping and cookery—recipes for such culinary atrocities as haricot-bean fritters abound—and the fact that many parishes discontinued church teas, parties, school treats and other functions involving the consumption of food, must have contributed something toward easing the shortage and keeping prices down.

During the first two years of the war, the consensus among churchmen of all parties and theological position was that the authorities had been remiss in placing the economy on a war footing. "It is pitiful," lamented Prebendary Gough, "that the people should be content to go in blinkers, and that the Government should guide it without whip, or bit, or bridle."[83] As far as the economy was concerned, it was imperative that it should assume dictatorial powers, powers that in the years before the war they would have denounced as illegal and immoral infringements of the liberties of the Englishman.

It is doubtful whether those denouncing "economic criminals" actually wished to see them physically harmed; yet the quality of their rhetoric made it clear that profiteers and strikers were enemies of society who deserved to be treated none too gently. Studdert-

Kennedy, a champion of the working man's rights and after the war a regular speaker for the Industrial Christian Fellowship, thundered against their selfishness. "The master who would make a fortune out of his country's loss, and the man who would imperil his comrades' lives to make a higher wage, are both traitors and murderers, and ought to be shot."[84] William Temple, president of the Workers' Educational Association, demanded the state take over the entire wealth of the nation, outlaw strikes, and regulate the economy in the same way as the generals regulated the army. "Let us not merely submit to orders, but demand them, so that if we fail the nation in our appointed task—whether that task be to fight or to manufacture or to administer or to uphold men's spiritual life—we may be shot by our own command."[85]

SUSTAINING THE SPIRIT

Before examining the methods employed by the clergy to sustain the morale of soldiers and civilians, we must note that they did not impose these tasks upon themselves for patriotic reasons alone. Patriotism coincided with self-interest. As indicated in connection with the recruitment of clergymen for war work, the war presented the church with an opportunity to do more than just its "bit" for a good cause. By associating itself with the national effort, it hoped to win England back to God and to itself. This objective was revealed nowhere more clearly than by Hensley Henson. Carried away by the enthusiasm of the early days of the war, he predicted that the name of England would emerge from the struggle with fresh titles to veneration, and that the church was bound, if it cooperated, to benefit from its historic connection with the nation.

Men will be disposed to give it a fair trial, willing to admit its right to express the Christian religion to and for Englishmen. The ancient churches, where the flags of the regiments have been treasured, and whose walls will carry many names of comrades sleeping on the battlefields or beneath the ocean, will seem natural homes of religion to the soldiers and sailors returning at last from the long war. A new link between the Church and the nation will have been forged in the furnace of affliction.[86]

Henson's predictions seem to have been confirmed at the outset. Glowing reports of men overcoming their shyness about religion, of a spontaneous revival at the front, were common coin.[87] There are indeed indications, impressionistic rather than statistical in nature, that the territorial forces and those responding to Kitchener's call in the first period of the war were more attentive to religion than the mass armies of the second half of the war.[88]

Yet, judging from the history of religion in the pre-1914 army, pessimists had grounds for their warnings that it would not last, that this "revival" was too good to be true. As early as the Boer War, clergymen had noted how little Christianity influenced the service-man. In 1900, army chaplains reported to the Convocation of Canterbury that in regiment after regiment, there was not a single communicant, not one. The situation in the navy was little better, as evidenced by the fact that services on shipboard were usually attended by only two or three officers.[89] Whether the increase in men attending services and coming forward for confirmation represented a genuine revival in 1914 or not, hopes for one faded as the old pattern reasserted itself in the following years. Despite a few bright spots—Winnington-Ingram's London Rifle Brigade for one—the army was, if we count heads, mostly pagan. At a time when 70 percent of the men were registered as "C of E," one might find twenty in a camp of five thousand, or twenty in a big battleship, attending communion services.[90]

The full extent of the failure of the churches in the army (all the churches, that is, with the possible exception of the Roman Catholic, universally recognized as doing splendid work) was brought home by a study carried out over a period of three years beginning in 1916. In that year, while staying in the great base camp at Rouen, Professor D. S. Cairns of the United Free Church College, Aberdeen, became disquieted upon realizing that the British soldier was out of communion with the churches. To investigate this phenomenon and the reasons for it, he proposed to the heads of the Y.M.C.A., the Rev. Tissington Tatlow of the Student Christian Movement, and Bishop Talbot of Winchester a full-scale interdenominational study. Eventually, no fewer than eleven churches, besides the Y.M.C.A. and a strong Church of England contingent, were represented in the project.[91] Based on a painstaking evaluation of chaplains' reports and thousands of questionnaires submitted by everyone from front line soldiers to the chaplain-general in the War Office, their final report, a thick book published in 1919 as *The Army and Religion: An Enquiry and its Bearing upon the Religious Life of the Nation,* is the most thorough and comprehensive source we have for the religious picture in the army; it is a pity that nothing comparable exists for the population at large. Its conclusions, previewed by Bishop Talbot for his son, Neville, an army chaplain and in the 'forties bishop of Pretoria, may be summarized in a single disheartening sentence: "Christianity and the Churches have failed, are out of it, are dis- liked, and *not* for righteousness' sake."[92]

Tommy, before the war the man in the street, brought his attitudes toward the churches into the mass armies after 1915. The army was England in microcosm; there was no reason why the mere act of donning khaki should have made Tommy in the "loomp" a different person. Yet there was a difference. Here, in the war, was the kind of opportunity the churches had longed for. Living amid the blood and the fear and the filth of the trenches, men reached out instinctively for something more than human support. That they were open to religious influences is demonstrated by the discussion in *The Army and Religion* of the "natural religion" of the soldier. Tommy, like the slum dweller, "had" religion, albeit it not necessarily the Christian religion. But if he was to be reached by Christianity, it would have to be presented in terms meaningful to him. The tragedy was that or- ganized religion, and not least of all the Church of England, was never quite able to use its opportunities to advantage. Motivated by the sincerest intentions, in terms of its primary spiritual mission the National Church seemed dazed, indecisive, and overtaken by a pa- ralysis of initiative on every level. When action was taken, it was often characterized by amateurishness and maladroitness—evidently a per- sisting fault, if we are to believe *Crockford*'s Preface for 1964: "There is in the Church of England a deliberate cult of amateurish- ness which is responsible for the futility of much that it tries to do." Churchmen themselves recognized the problem, without being able to suggest a solution. Occasionally they reacted with bitterness, as when Bishop Gore, on hearing that the Y.M.C.A. was doing more for the soldiers in certain areas than the parallel Anglican organiza- tion, the Church of England Men's Society, shot back: "I don't know. It's only another failure of the Church of England to seize an op- portunity. I hate the Church of England." Gore's solution was to send his generation to the trenches for cannon fodder and start the church over again from scratch.[93]

From Tommy's standpoint, the difficulty lay in the fact that religion had become more a matter of Christianity *and* the churches rather than Christianity *in* the churches. For too many soldiers Christianity, if they knew anything about it (and 80 percent of the recruits from the Midlands were reputed never to have heard of the Sacraments),[94] meant "churchianity," the cold, official outlook of the Anglican church. The war, according to the bishop of Kensington's report for *The Army and Religion*, had changed nothing. All the time-worn arguments against the prewar church were being cited afresh by the soldiers: the party spirit; lack of fellowship; pew rents; a "classy," socially exclusive priesthood; the enemy of labor and the friend of nobles and capitalists.[95] The bishop's view is confirmed in part by Donald Hankey, a brilliant, young, and attractive churchman soon to die. Writing in *A Student in Arms*, a best seller on both sides of the Atlantic, Hankey described his comrades as men with genuine religious instincts repelled by religiosity and religionists.

He [the soldier] thinks that Christianity consists of believing the Bible and setting up to be better than your neighbours. By believing the Bible he means believing that Jonah was swallowed by a whale. . . . This is surely nothing short of tragedy. Here were men who believed absolutely in the Christian virtues of unselfishness, generosity, charity, and humanity, without ever connecting them in their minds with Christ; and at the same time what they did associate with Christianity was just on a par with the formalism and smug self-righteousness which Christ spent His whole life trying to destroy.[96]

From every theatre of operations came reports from chaplains, confirmed after the war by a spate of memoirs, to the effect that the troops resented formal religious functions and the men supervising them. Compulsory Church Parade, the army's version of the traditional "English Sunday," led the list; the troops considered it just another inspection. The preaching at Church Parade was a perennial sore point. Whereas the recruiters had developed an interesting style, the sermons in the field or in the base camps were condemned as deadly dull. One can imagine hundreds of sweating men, their buttons shining in the Mesopotamian sun, fidgeting as the padre preached interminably on the death of Socrates, the cruise of the Argo, or the commutation of tithes. Speaking through one of his Tommies, Studdert-Kennedy drew a none too complimentary picture of his comrades as spiritual leaders:

> Our Padre were a solemn bloke
> We called 'im dismal Jim.
> It fairly gave ye bloomin' creeps
> To sit and 'ark at 'im,
> When 'e were on 'wi Judgment Day
> Abaht that great white throne,
> And 'ow each chap would 'ave to stand
> And answer on 'is own.
> And if 'e tried to chance 'is arm,
> And 'ide a single sin,
> There'd be the angel Gabriel,
> Wi' books to do 'im in.[97]

The chaplains were Christianity's first line in the forces. When the war began, 113 chaplains of various denomination were serving with the forces. Not every denomination was represented, the War Office providing only Church of England, Roman Catholic, Wesleyan, Presbyterian, and Jewish chaplains. Before long, however, the United and Primitive Methodist, Baptists, and Congregationalists established a United Army Board to nominate chaplains to the War Office. From then on, everything moved along smoothly, there being little difficulty in finding men to undertake this service. The ranks of the chaplains swelled, reaching a total of 3,480 by the Armistice. Of these 1,937 were Anglicans, a total of 3,030 Anglican priests having received commissions as chaplains in the four years of the conflict; 88 of these were killed in combat or died of wounds and disease.[98]

Although the history of the chaplains in the Great War remains to be written, it is clear that, for the Anglican clergyman, motivated by the evangelistic spirit or by his bishop's suggestion, becoming a chaplain might be more difficult than for any other denomination. The appointment of Anglican chaplains was marked at first by the same party spirit and smallness as marred the church in time of peace. Bishop Taylor Smith, the chaplain-general, had a profound aversion to Anglo-Catholics, "extremists," making it practically impossible for them to obtain commissions. Not until Lord Halifax was put on to this discrimination, and the *Church Times* embarked upon a high-powered publicity campaign, was the situation remedied.[99] To the complete satisfaction of no one, but to the complete dissatisfaction of no one either, Archbishop Davidson neatly circumvented Smith by appointing the well-liked Bishop L. H. Gwynne of the Sudan deputy chaplain-general in charge of the chaplains in France, where most of them were serving.[100]

It would be as unfair as it is untrue to say that the Anglican chaplains were an incapable lot, unresponsive to the spiritual needs of their flocks. Just as there are all kinds of men, so there were all kinds of chaplains, from the wretch court-martialled and sentenced to six months in jail (without hard labor) for immoral conduct,[101] to those men whose decency, sensitivity, and evangelical fervor were in the finest traditions of the Christian ministry. B. K. Cunningham, working at his "Bombing School for Chaplains," where rest and recuperation were combined with specialized training; Father King of Mirfield leading the assault troops in "Our Father" before going ashore with them at Gallipoli; P. B. "Tubby" Clayton scrounging to make Talbot House (from which sprang Toc H, a worldwide Christian fellowship) a fit place for those passing through Poperinghe—all set a standard of excellence unsurpassed at any time and in any army. His poetry, his endearing ways, and his hearty renditions of "Mother Machree" made G. A. Studdert-Kennedy the best-loved chaplain in the B.E.F.—loved that is by the troops; his superiors thought him a madman; would that there had been more madmen as Studdert-Kennedy! But these were exceptional personalities, as rare in the service as they had been in civilian life. And since men of their caliber probably numbered no more than a few dozen out of the entire corps of Anglican chaplains, of necessity they were spread thin, exercising only a local influence. By themselves, they were utterly incapable of taking their church out of the doldrums.

The chaplain's job was difficult under the best of circumstances. His first task was to bridge the social gap between himself and his charges, in certain respects the hardest task of all because the distance was even wider in the army than in civilian life. In language, bearing, and outlook he had little in common with the ranks. As a chaplain in the British army he was (and is today) a commissioned officer, holding on the lowest level a rank equivalent to captain, which entitles him to private quarters and the services of a batman. To further complicate matters, he was among the most overworked men in the

army. A chaplain newly assigned to a line unit discovered, frequently
to his dismay, that he was expected to be a jack-of-all-trades. When
not performing his pastoral duties, he could be found assisting in the
nearby Church Army recreation hut or canteen; into the small hours
of the morning he censored the mail. If he hoped to get anything like
pastoral work done, he had to ward off without giving offense superiors who would submerge him in trivia. As the only man with
"time on his hands," the chaplain automatically became a social
director; many a battalion owed its concerts and amateur theatricals
to the padre. Sometimes he acted as the unit's major-domo, being put
in charge of the mess luxuries, arranging menus, and seeing that the
hot water was ready for men returning "home" from the trenches. If
for some reason the prunes were badly stewed, or the lamps improp-
erly trimmed, he was promptly "told off."[102] If there was a battle
he might be called upon to drive an ambulance or help with the
stretcher cases. A prime example of official stupidity was the fact
that, if he wanted to go into no man's land to bring in the wounded
or minister to the men in the front-line trenches, he would have to
ignore the much-publicized standing order against Church of England chaplains going forward of brigade headquarters. Contrast this
with the Roman Catholic chaplain, who had better have had a good
reason for *not* being with his men wherever he was needed.

An important aspect of the chaplain's duty involved preparing the
men to go into action, a task requiring the utmost sensitivity to the
feelings of others. The vast majority doubtlessly did their best to con-
sole the troops and take their minds off the forthcoming ordeal by
discussing spiritual matters. Their best, however, was not always
deemed good enough. Here, too, the Roman Catholic chaplains received higher marks from the men, including Anglicans. Recalling
his experiences in *A Passionate Prodigality* (1933), a bitter book
but still a minor classic, Guy Chapman noted: "one felt a serenity
and certitude streaming from [the Catholic chaplain] such as was not
possessed by our bluff Anglicans. . . . The Church of Rome sent a
man into action mentally and spiritually cleaned. The Church of
England could only offer you a cigarette."

Things might have been different had the Anglican chaplain been
his own man, which was not always the case. Instances were reported
of chaplains receiving their sermon topics directly from the com-

manding officer. Speaking at a soldiers' dinner after the war, Major-General Sir William Thwaites recalled that before an engagement he would gather the chaplains together and preach *them* a sermon. "I told them on one occasion that I wanted a bloodthirsty sermon next Sunday, and would not have any texts from the New Testament. . . . On that Sunday I got hold by accident of a blushing young curate straight out from England—but he preached the most bloodthirsty sermon I had ever listened to."[103] Some, however, needed little encouragement to bellicosity. Loathing war as he did, Studdert-Kennedy nevertheless used to visit the troops in the field with a troupe ("the travelling circus") comprising a champion boxer, two champion wrestlers, and an N.C.O. who had killed eighteen Germans with a bayonet. When they had finished demonstrating methods of killing and self-defence, he would get their "tails up" and ready for battle with a twenty-minute sermon.[104] C. E. Montague, the journalist and dramatic critic, recalled that when the war was drawing to a close he overheard chaplains complain that a few more German towns had not been destroyed and that the latest type of poison gas had not yet had "a fair innings."[105]

Important as these activities were, they were seldom undertaken with the same sense of urgency as marked the effort on the home front. To sustain morale in England consisted not only of generating patriotic fervor, but involved also the more delicate task of combating a widespread loss of faith. At the outset, a "revival" similar to that in the army seemed to be under way, the churches being crowded with people seeking solace from religion. What is more, the pressures created by abnormal emotional conditions broke down inhibitions. Inhibitions against prayers for the dead, the bogy of sound Evangelicals, were swept away on a tide of grief; likewise, the demand grew for access to the reserved Sacrament, another area of contention in the prewar church. Yet, as the conflict dragged on, the ever-lengthening casualty lists and, ironically, the atrocity propaganda itself, helped create a mood of despair. Increasingly people found themselves incapable of deriving comfort from the thought of God in heaven; if anything, it angered them. The wonderful pictures of God, enthroned with His Son on His right hand, beaming while the angels sang to the saved, seemed a mockery of the sufferings on earth. "Has God gone mad?" cried a distraught woman; and the

answer, verbalized as one verbalizes for a child its pent-up sadness
and anger, came from the pen of Studdert-Kennedy:

> And I hate the God of Power on His
>   hellish heavenly throne,
> Looking down on rape and murder,
>   hearing little children moan.[106]

Such sentiments, often expressed in blunter terms, stung the bishops into "doing something." Ignoring warnings from Bishop Gore
and Peter Green, canon of Manchester and a respected commentator
on ecclesiastical affairs (his articles signed "Artifex" appeared regularly in the *Manchester Guardian*), that the nation was preoccupied
elsewhere, they launched in late 1915 and early 1916 a National
Mission of Repentance and Hope aimed at stirring the clergy to re-
dedicate themselves to their profession and to reevangelize the nation.[107] Despite the frenetic activity, the self-deprecating sermons,
and the vast quantities of literature put out by the S.P.C.K. and other
agencies, the National Mission was ill-conceived, poorly executed,
and marred by internal squabbles over such things as employing
women as speakers and the approach to be taken toward the labor
movement.[108] The epitaph of the National Mission was composed
years later by one of its organizers, F. A. Iremonger, William Temple's biographer and dean of Lichfield: "in spite of all that had been
said and done, there were no signs of a renewed desire on the part
of the people of England to identify themselves with the fellowship
and the worship of the National Church."[109]

We may go further than Iremonger and say that the loss of faith,
compounded by the irrationalism and bloodlust of the tub-thumping
German-haters, drove hitherto devout churchgoers from the fold and
prevented new ones from coming in. Whereas the Statistical Unit of
the Central Board of Finance of the Church of England confirms that
no attendance figures were gathered during the war, contemporaries
believed that they had either declined absolutely or remained stat-
ic, religious services attracting only those already attached to the
church: no one maintained that attendance had increased.[110] Lacking attendance figures, we may still gauge something of the damage
done to the church during the war years by referring to other indices.
Take baptismal figures, which indicate an ominous trend because

concerning the younger generation of potential church people. Baptisms fell from 700 per thousand live births in 1913 to 678 in 1918; after climbing erratically in the 'twenties (but never in proportion to the rise in population), they began an absolute decline that has persisted until the present. The figures for confirmations and communicants at Easter tell the same story. From a high point of 229,000 confirmations among the population aged 12–20 in 1914, they fell to 183,000 in 1919; the former figure has never been equalled since. Communicants at Easter, 2,445,000 in 1913–1914, were down a quarter-of-a-million by 1917–1918; this figure, too, has never recovered, dropping to 1,957,000 by 1964.[111] To arrest the already perceptible decay in the church's position, and at the same time prevent a loss of religious faith from undermining faith in the Allied cause, it became necessary to explain why the war was an argument against neither the Church of England nor the Christian religion.

Historically, certain Christians have regarded chastizing the body by fasting, flagellation, and wearing coarse, uncomfortable clothing as aids in cleansing it of sin, purifying the spirit, and experiencing a mystical union with God. However much they rejected the extreme forms of asceticism, apologists for the war nevertheless stressed the importance of pain and suffering for the uplifting of the human race. Suffering, by their definition, was in reality "joy in the making," a soul-purging trial ordained by a loving Father.[112]

The problem of suffering was also discussed in other than the traditional theological terms. Just as in the eighteenth century apologists for Christianity met the challenge of Newtonian physics by asserting, in Locke's words, the *Reasonableness of Christianity*, certain aspects of the theory of evolution became absorbed into the Christian worldview and the new insights then applied to the Great War. Without realizing that their arguments were in essence the selfsame ones attributed to the "lying prophets," various Anglican divines studded their works with the crudest pseudoscientific, pseudometaphysical allegations. War and suffering they proclaimed to be God's prod and leash. Through them He guided the evolutionary process along the road to ultimate perfectibility, allowing, all the while, man to explore (sometimes disastrously) alternate lines of development. According to the prevailing view, expressed by Archdeacon Wilberforce, "Creation is God evolving, under the overwhelming constraint of love, that which is involved in Himself, and the law of progress is the law of evolution. The law of physical evolution necessitates, both on the physical and moral plane, the fiery ordeal of war with the opposite of good, which is the only means of transition into higher, nobler life, and Infinite, Immanent Mind must share every pang that ever racks the individual soul or any part of animated nature."[113]

It followed, then, that the horrors of the war were merely necessary interim-horrors; they were "the stern and kindly taskmaster of the race," the stimulus to a new English renaissance, the source of all the gentle virtues: mercy, compassion, charity.[114] As for the suffering of innocents, that was a repetition of Christ's own tribulation, symbolizing a promise written in blood of a new world to be born out of the wreckage of the old. From their sufferings would emerge a revivified passion for justice, a new hatred of violence, a new impulse to fraternity among men. According to J. W. Diggle:

This war, though red in tooth and claw, is yet rich in the promise of a brighter world in which peace shall reign among men of good-will. It is the herald of a new rising Star of Bethlehem to the music of the angels' song: even though Herod in his rage and dread, slaughter the innocents in indiscriminate massacre, and cause weeping in innumerable, empty, darkened homes. It is the final ringing out of the Herods and a fresh ringing in of the Christ. It is the agony in the womb of the morning; of a new birth of mankind to a life of higher truth and nobler liberty.[115]

Well might Dean Inge describe the making of such assertions as rather like lavishing praise on cancer because it inculcates in its victims a spirit of patience and long-suffering.

But hundreds of thousands of England's best young men had already put the sorrows of the world behind them. Handling the problem of death properly is for the priest one of the supreme tests of his ministry; and there is no reason to doubt that the vast majority of clergymen of all faiths performed this function well. Yet it must also be said that there was never a dearth of preachers, some of them well-known Anglican personalities, who allowed their patriotic zeal to take precedence over their duty as ministers of the Consoling Word. There survive in the newspapers and in pamphlet form innumerable sermons devoted to proclaiming what Winnington-Ingram, with his unique way of turning a phrase, called "the bright view of death." It was stated repeatedly and in the clearest terms that, irrespective of the life he had lived in the past, when a British soldier fell in battle he (like a Moslem killed in a jihad) earned automatically a passport to heaven. There, surrounded by the seraphim and cherubim, he would stand "cleansed from the stain of sin, crowned and triumphant, looking unto Jesus in the unveiled splendour of Paradise."[116]

Although others might avoid such unequivocal claims, in sermons delivered on occasions ranging from recruiting rallies to services for the dead, the act of "flinging" away one's life on the battlefield was presented as a splendid, triumphant, even Christ-like act of "sublime grandeur." To die for England, in the opinion of Basil Bourchier, "is to taste the sweetest vintage of death that can be offered to English lips—yes, to drink the sweetest draught ever held in death's iron cup, and to pass to that which is to come in a veritable ecstasy. To die for England . . . for the young Englishman must be the glittering topmost peak of beatitude."[117] Those dying in this manner were more than heroes; they were martyrs crucified to atone for the sins of the world; they were "potential saints" who, released from the burden of the flesh, were awaiting reunion with their loved ones in Paradise. Until then, the bereaved would have to bear their sorrows as Christ bore the agony of the Crucifixion.[118] To help them over the worst of their grief, Lord William Gascoyne Cecil, elevated to the see of Exeter in 1916, called upon the congregation of St. Margaret's, Westminster, to let the mourners know how much they appreciated their sacrifice: "Yes, let us doff our hats to the parents of the brave dead, and offer them our humble congratulations."[119]

Mounting dissatisfaction with the progress of the war prompted the restatement in contemporary terms of the age-old question of why God, omnipotent and loving, tolerated evil: why did not God end the war with a quick Allied victory? This was a baffling question, and one senses from the literature that fewer clergymen tried to answer it, or answered it with less confidence, than other questions raised by the war. Nor were the answers always consistent with one another; indeed, they seem clearly contradictory. Of course God, the Creator of the Universe, could halt the carnage whenever and however He chose. Yet for Him to do so would be contrary to His nature; He could not interfere directly to rescue man from the consequences of misusing his reason without reducing him to an automaton.[120] Besides, nothing worth having comes easily; and an easy victory would

necessarily be at the expense of righteousness. Just as Germany
needed a sound thrashing to bring her to her senses, so victory for an
unrepentant England would merely encourage her in her sinful ways.
Believing this, certain individuals took the unusual step of imploring
God to allow the war to continue. "Lord," prayed the Rev. L. G.
Buchanan, vicar of St. Luke's, Wimbledon Park, "don't give us victory, until; don't send us peace, until—until the nation's heart is
ready for it, until the nation's character is ready for it."[121]

Another school stressed the more positive aspect of the equation:
divine justice rules the world, and the Allies were God's allies. His
righteousness could be discerned even when evil seemed to prosper.
If He allowed the Germans to succeed in their iniquitous schemes,
this was merely His way of raising them the higher so that He might
humble them the better. When they had gorged themselves on the
fruits of their wickedness, then—then the avenging arm of God Almighty would strike out from heaven to smash and pulverize and
sweep them away. In any case, whether one subscribed to the theory
of the delayed victory as a purgation for England's sins or as part of
God's scheme for punishing Germany, it was considered unseemly
and unworthy of the Anglican Christian to believe the issue anything
but certain.

During the Great War every mode of expression and communication served in some way to further the organization of enthusiasm;
indeed, the war penetrated into the heart of Anglican religious life.
The act of public worship itself became a means, if only a subsidiary
means, of getting across the patriotic message. As we have already
seen, the sermon was admirably suited to this purpose. By the same
token, other portions of the religious service could be used to teach
not only a theology of abasement, but a faith to strengthen men for
the fight and make them worthy to win.

Confident though they were in the final victory, clergymen did not
venture prophecies as to exactly how long it would take or how many
would die before the great day arrived. Nevertheless, they were convinced that prayer, if employed in the right spirit, would help bring
it closer. From the psychological standpoint, beside comforting the
mourners and asking God's mercy for the dead, prayer could also
strengthen confidence that, although far from the scene of action,

one might still exercise a measure of control over events. Not that they claimed prayer could change a destroyer into a battleship; rather they encouraged prayer as a means of strengthening the courage and resolution of the ship's company. In the occasionally simplistic terminology of men like Winnington-Ingram, prayer was transformed into a kind of "wireless telegraphy" (his term) to the Almighty. Ceaseless intercession demonstrated at once that a worthy end was desired and confidence in God. Lessening the amount of prayer indicated a lessening of desire and confidence, diminishing God's power to act, and thereby worsening the lot of the English soldier.[122]

Despite the initial complaints that the forms of prayer issued by the archbishop of Canterbury contained neither a definite statement of Allied righteousness nor a petition for victory, these deficiencies were soon corrected. In fact, one could almost write a history of the war on the basis of the prayers and hymns composed for special occasions. There were prayers for protection against air raids and submarines; prayers uttered at the "baptism" of tanks; prayers for the living, the dead, and those about to die; prayers to render inoperative German naval mines and to stop the northeast wind blowing, as it spread the poison gas; prayers to strengthen the arms of munitions workers and farm workers; and prayers asking God's favor for England's plans and to confound those of the enemy. In the spring of 1917, there was an outpouring of prayer on behalf of President Wilson and the Russian revolutionaries.

Even more than the prayers, Anglican hymnody reflected wartime attitudes and spread its rhetoric. The old favorites, "Onward Christian Soldiers," "Fight the Good Fight," and "Soldiers of Christ, Arise" were sung with renewed fervor. To these were added thousands of new compositions, performed probably no more than a few times and mercifully forgotten. Every theme touched on thus far became a fit topic. At the beginning, England's claim to be waging a just war, expressed in the words signalling judicial combat in the Middle Ages ("God defend the Right!"), became the theme of innumerable hymns. England had gone to war with clean hands and a pure heart, according to a work by the Rev. James Eckersley, rector of Weeford, Lichfield:

Not ours, O Lord, to wake the sword,
  Or cannon's deadly rattle;
But while we laboured long for peace
  Our foes prepared for battle.
Be with us, then, and keep us safe
  From all who sore assail us,
For justice, truth, and freedom's sake,
  Let not thine arm now fail us.[123]

This theme was superseded eventually by the holy war. Wrote a temporary chaplain to the forces:

Come, crush the hostile powers of sin,
  And Satan's stronghold gain,
That all may welcome Thee—the Christ,
  Whose right it is to reign.[124]

Finally, the dominant theme, summarizing the position of the Anglican clergy on the issues involved in the struggle and what they hoped to see the world gain from it, is expressed in an anonymous battle hymn, "God Send Us Fortune!"

Onward till the cause be won
For all oppressed humanity;
Fling wide the banner to the sun
  Of Justice, Honour, Liberty![125]

VII. FOR A JUST AND LASTING PEACE

PEACE THROUGH VICTORY

The distinctive quality of the approach of devout men to the war is illustrated nowhere more clearly than in their attitude toward peace. The concept of peace prevailing among church people at this time consisted of a blending of Christian idealism with the ideas that emerged as the conflict ran its course. In its religious sense, the word had several shades of meaning, none of them directly related to politics, although they might lend themselves to a political interpretation. Above all, peace signified an ideal state of *spiritual* harmony, unity, and concord existing simultaneously between man and God, man and man, and within each man. Defined by William Temple as "the twin of love and joy,"[1] peace was that all-pervading feeling of power and brotherhood that would emerge with the acceptance of the Gospel as the sole standard of men and nations, and the recognition of the unity of the human family in Christ. But beyond this, since nations are composed of individuals, the Christian standards and religious teachings upon which peace rests must remain so many empty formulae until brought to life by those at peace within themselves—in a sense the real supermen: each must come to God and become strong though overcoming his personal devil. Lastly, true peace, the peace of God, was a creative force. Once achieved, it would release the energies of humanity, enabling it to realize fully the potentialities of existence.

When those holding this exalted and essentially spiritual conception of peace sought to apply it to the question of the war, they often ended by rejecting the approaches favored both by pacifists and politicians. John Colet's maxim that an unjust peace is preferable to the justest war they dismissed as an absurdity because it gave a license to wickedness. Peace there must be at any price, even if that price be cataclysmic war. By the same token, they took exception to the diplomatist's view and indirectly also to the classic doctrine of the just war. At the root of the Christian apologetic for war is a legal presumption.

Just wars, according to St. Augustine, are defined as those "which avenge injuries, when the nation or city against which warlike action is to be directed has neglected either to punish wrongs committed by its own citizens or to restore what has been unjustly taken by it"; elsewhere, he says that the ultimate object of war is peace.[2] The object of war, then, is not to overthrow Satan and his vassals, but rather the termination of armed conflict through the restoration of rights. Yet for many, this view, too, was intolerable. Peace must be of a certain quality. If peace meant merely preserving a society wherein men might sin with impunity and worship Mammon, it was no peace at all; it was in reality a "*Pax Diabolica*," a soul-destroying as well as body-destroying form of warfare. Such a peace was unworthy of the Christian and hateful to his Lord.

With respect to the Great War itself, a problem of primary concern involved the best way of effectuating the Christian ideal of peace. Scarcely had it begun, when thoughtful Anglicans began discussing the eventual settlement. By common consent they pointed to the Congress of Vienna, which ended the Napoleonic Wars, as a model of precisely what future peacemakers should avoid; it was at Vienna, they believed, that the powder-train had been set for the explosion a century later. Moreover, judging from the tone of some of the rhetoric, it seems that conferences in general had an ungentlemanly aura about them, smacking of the haggling of tradesmen in the marketplace. There was no end to the admonitions that plenipotentiaries should avoid discussions of fine points or succumb to arguments of expediency. To fight a white, gentlemanly war was not enough. The peace must be one of "pure idealism," established on "the rocks of righteousness" rather than on "the quicksands of diplomacy."[3] Bishop Hicks went so far as to suggest that England take the lead in framing her armistice terms in accordance with the precepts of the Sermon on the Mount.[4]

A peace of pure idealism, however, need not be gentle or generous; if anything, it can actually be so harsh as to work against the cause of peace. Nor do the precepts of the Sermon on the Mount exist in a vacuum. When these combine in the minds of overwrought men holding a devil-theory of history, they are apt to give rise to fantastic war aims. As the struggle in Europe continued, the earlier disposition to view Germany as fighting for wrong but nevertheless rational objectives—land, loot, the readjustment of the power-balance—gave way increasingly to the process of diabolization already described. Attributing unlimited objectives to the enemy, clergymen responded by formulating a set of unlimited objectives for the Allies. Inasmuch as Germany had sold herself to Satan, or, as some alleged, actually embodied his spirit—"we are up against the forces of evil and a spirit loosed from hell" was the way Bishop Nickson of Bristol put it[5]—it was no longer a matter of honoring the nation's pledges or even defending England herself. The Allies were fighting a crusade against Antichrist, a "root-and-branch war" to kill war by eradicating the *doctrine* of state idolatry, the *spirit* of aggressiveness, and the *disease* of militarism. Quite early in the struggle, Allied war aims took on apocalyptic overtones. Wrote one evangelical poet, a regular contributor to the *Record*:

> Peace! Christendom! and close
> With thy supernal foes,
> The rulers and powers of darkness in the sky;
> Where sin's black flag is flown
> Strike for the Eternal Throne!
> And all the spheres shall thrill with that *last victory*![6]

It may sound very well to say one is out to destroy the seat of evil in the universe; the danger, of course, lies in people believing in and acting upon such grotesque claims. Since they bear no relation whatever to the real world, they are impossible of attainment, which in turn brings greater frustration. Yet the crusader, as Paul Bull recognized, cannot help himself. He must refuse to acknowledge impossibilities, strive after the unattainable, and attempt to overcome the world.[7]

How, then, to end the bloodshed? Since the combatants represented antithetical world-views, and were fighting for otherworldly objectives, it followed that the conflict was insoluble by the traditional methods of diplomacy. The diplomat and the moral rigorist begin from opposite poles. The diplomat commonly approaches his task with the recognition that negotiating with an opponent, whatever his beliefs and however wicked his actions, is first and foremost a political act. True, moral objectives are important in politics, but the political process is such that they can seldom be pursued directly. We cannot always make a bee-line straight for righteousness. Unlike moral judgments, political judgments are tentative and conditional. Negotiating involves at base determining priorities and then striking a balance, admittedly rough and ready, between power and goals, cost and value. The negotiator usually finds it necessary to compromise on what he would *like* to have in order to safeguard what he *must* have. He may have to settle for half-a-loaf simply because the whole loaf is not worth the price. There is something to ponder in the remark of Metternich that a diplomat should never permit himself the pleasure of a victory; for if he does, his triumph must be the product of another's humiliation. Especially in settling the conflicts of great powers, if the settlement is to close the issue, the defeated party should not leave the table with a rankling sense of injustice. For the sake of peace, it may even be desirable to acquiesce in injustice and allow the offence to go unpunished.[8]

Here is the rub. For while the clergy might commend such flexibility in disputes concerning wages, boundaries, and the like, they considered compromise totally unacceptable in issues involving the eternal verities; and in the case of the Great War this meant every issue. It almost seems as though certain individuals believed an unrectified evil was like an uncorrected accounting error, only infinitely more serious. If allowed to go unpunished, it would throw the cosmic order off balance. Time and again, important Anglican figures denounced the idea of a negotiated settlement, declaring it positively sinful to bargain with the kaiser, let alone with the likes of the sultan. Should the Allies seek to lessen their sacrifice by yielding an iota of principle, they would commit treason against God, imperil their souls, and betray those who had already fallen, an argument of tremendous power. The Christian must never consider peace as long as wrong continues. "Wherever evil is at work," proclaimed Bishop Diggle, "whether on earth or elsewhere, it is certain that God will not make peace with it: but will at all costs carry on incessant war. So will all God-like men"[9]—in effect a prescription, given human nature, for universal, unremitting war.

Cooler heads, while refusing to interpret the conflict in these absolute terms, frequently arrived at the same conclusion by a different route. As a strictly practical matter, neither arbitration through neutrals, the hope of the prewar peace movement, nor negotiations seemed appropriate. The success of both procedures rests less upon external guarantees than the contending parties retaining a modicum of confidence in each other's integrity. This element of basic trust had gone up in flames with Louvain. In proclaiming that might made right, that the law of nations, sanctified by the law of God, was subject to the higher law of expediency, the Germans had undermined the foundations of civilized order in Christendom. How could the Allied governments be certain that the Germans, pleading necessity, would not later repudiate a peace treaty as just another "scrap of paper"? What guaranteed that the Hohenzollern emperor would not give his word with tongue in cheek and fingers crossed? The archbishop of Canterbury, by nature a compromiser, was adamant on this point. "So long as they assure us that they are committed irreconcilably to principles which I regard as absolutely fatal to what Christ has taught us . . . I should look on it as flimsy sentimentalism were I to say that I want immediate peace."[10] There seemed but one safe, reasonable method of dealing with an enemy to whom sacred pledges meant nothing: destroy completely his mischief-making powers.

Four phrases, each indicating something of the mood prevailing in ecclesiastical circles, recur with regularity in the literature of the period. Whether one said "premature peace," "inconclusive peace," "patched peace," or "botched peace," he meant the same thing: never again must Germany be allowed to repeat her assault upon civilization. Any peace settlement that was not, in the words of Canon Alexander of St. Paul's, "final, decisive, and permanent" would contain the seeds of future wars.[11] To leave a proud people like the Germans unconvinced that they had indeed been overpowered on the battlefield would only encourage them to bide their time until they could exact retribution from those who had thwarted their ambitions.

Having thus taken the position that it was wicked for Christians to bargain with the minions of Antichrist, and that even if negotiations were possible, the Germans could never be trusted to keep their word, moral fundamentalists found they could accept neither a peace that reestablished the prewar *status quo* nor one that would end the struggle before the Allies achieved all their objectives. In short, they became entangled in a web of myth, partly of their own fashioning, partly the creation of propaganda. To advocate exploring a promising though unexpected proposal for a settlement would have necessitated a sudden and radical readjustment in thinking. This they could not do without feeling untrue to themselves and, more importantly, betraying a divine trusteeship. In pursuing peace, as in waging war, they abandoned the principle of proportionality. In this they were not alone, the statesmen, soldiers, and intellectuals gravitating toward essentially the same position. Whatever the cost, the struggle must continue until Good vanquished Evil. Addressing an Anglican women's group at the beginning of the war, Winnington-Ingram insisted that, "while one man is left in the world who stands for the New Testament against the Gospel of Power, for Christianity against the new religion of culture, that man must fight on." [12] This remark is an early symptom of a growing trend. For as it progressed, the war acquired a logic and a momentum of its own. Their emotional investment in the Allied cause was reinforced by an investment, steadily augmented, in blood. The dead cried out to the living to finish the job and vindicate their sacrifice, although this meant adding untold millions to their number. No alternative remained. The Allies must resolve to strive for nothing short of a total victory consummated by an unconditional surrender and a dictated peace. Bernhardi's slogan, "*Weltmacht oder Niedergang*" (world-power or downfall) applied also to England and her empire:

There must be no 'draw.' Either he or we must go under. . . . It is now evident that there can be no talk of peace until the mad-dog of Europe has been bludgeoned, till the snake has been scotched, till the enemy has been beaten to his knees, till the philosophical materialism of Prussia has been worsted, till Right has vanquished Might. Then let us talk of peace; but it must be a peace the terms of which are dictated at Berlin by the conqueror to the conquered.[13]

PROPOSALS FOR ENDING THE WAR

Between September, 1914, and November, 1917, there emanated from religious leaders two significant pleas for ending the conflict, and at least six definite proposals from neutral countries, British statesmen, and from the Central Powers themselves. Yet, given the universal antipathy against a nonmilitary solution, all peace proposals were foredoomed to failure. Virtually every one was denounced by the major organs of Anglican opinion as promoting war, and its author subjected to a cacophony of abuse matched only by the worst effusions of the Northcliffe press. What we must take note of here, however, is not so much the fact that they were rejected, but the special reasons, some related only incidentally to the war, advanced to justify the stand in each case.

Indications that attitudes had hardened beyond compromise became apparent quite early. Toward the end of September, 1914, Dr. Nathan Söderblom, the Lutheran archbishop of Upsala, wrote to religious leaders in Europe and America inviting them to sign a general statement in favor of peace. Although his "Appeal to the Churches of the World" bound signatories to no specific recommendations for a settlement, it did call upon all those in power and with influence to keep before their eyes the ideal of peace in order that the bloodshed might soon cease. Whereas leaders of various persuasions in America, Switzerland, and the Scandinavian countries signed without hesitation, no official of the Church of England saw fit to append his signature.[14] In rejecting the Appeal, the archbishop of Canterbury, who personally thought it a moderate and reasonable document, informed his old friend that "the conflict which has been forced upon Europe . . . must I fear, now that it has begun, proceed for the bringing to an issue the fundamental principle of faithfulness to a nation's obligation to its solemnly plighted word."[15] And the only way to do this, he later wrote to another correspondent, was to reduce the enemy to impotence through decisive victory on the battlefield.[16]

In contrast with the archbishop of Upsala, whose authority did not extend beyond the borders of neutral Sweden, the pope stood at the head of a worldwide organization having communicants and resident officials in all the warring countries. Three months after the death of the saintly Pius X (August, 1914), his successor, Benedict XV, issued the first encyclical of his pontificate. Touching briefly on the desirability of restoring the temporal powers of the papacy, *Ad Beatissimi* was primarily a religious document concerned with modernism and other matters of Roman Catholic doctrine and worship. With respect to the war, the new pope confined himself to a short description of its horrors and to a prayer for its speedy end. He said nothing about the Belgian atrocities.

This failure to denounce the German crimes, as well as his reluctance to place the guilt for the war squarely on Germany's shoulders, was regarded as a perverse type of impartiality. Nothing he said after this, including several strenuous protests against inhuman methods of warfare, could restore his credentials as a potential peacemaker. The Anglican community was, on the whole, shocked by the "studied nullity" and "moral supineness" of the papal pronouncement. Dean Inge, a relentless and not always a fair critic of the Roman Catholic church, condemned papal indifference toward the victims of Teutonic war-lust.[17] Whereas a nineteenth century pope had had the courage to excommunicate Napoleon, his successor was playing a "despicable" part in the Great War. "Not only has the moral authority of the Papacy been unexerted; not only has Rome refused to condemn the greatest crime in history—the wanton attack on Belgium; but no attempt has been made to protect its own priests and nuns from murder and outrage and its most venerated shrines from destruction . . . . A Papacy which has sold itself to Pan-Germanism can in the future enjoy neither credit nor influence."[18]

War encourages even the most intelligent people to search for (and those who seek, find) conspiracies where few would have thought to look before. Coincidences, apparently unrelated facts, and ambiguous statements suddenly take on a new significance when seen in the light of war. However simplistic, the notion that Benedict's reticence was due somehow to an arrangement with the enemy seemed plausible when considered against the background of papal political ambitions. According to this theory, ever since the Italian seizure of Rome in 1870 and the French separation of church and state in 1905, the Holy See had sought to regain its lost possessions through ingratiating itself with the Teutonic powers, especially Germany. In turn, these, intending all the while to wage aggressive war, grasped quickly the value of such an ally. It was no coincidence, said the Rev. C. E. Osborne, rector of Wallsend and author of a well-received book on religion and the war, that the ending of the *Kulturkampf* and the *rapprochement* between the Hohenzollerns and the papacy coincided with the formation of the Dual Alliance in 1879. From then on, the kaiser could rest secure in the knowledge that the Catholic hierarchy, as the Lutheran before it, would throw its prestige behind his every action. Dr. Hartmann, the cardinal-archbishop of Cologne, would vie with Professor von Harnack in appreciating the "moral beauty" of William II's policy and in condemning the criminality of the Allies in conspiring against it.[19] Cardinal Hartmann, it should be remembered, had well-earned the Englishman's disapprobation, as would anyone who announced that "we have confidence in our just cause, in our brave troops, and in our noble Kaiser, who combines in himself all the virtues of his ancestors of the House of Hohenzollern, but above all in our Lord of Battles."[20]

In certain quarters, regaining his temporalities was assumed to be merely of secondary importance, as the pope had far more sinister reasons for cultivating the Central Powers. Ever since the Reformation, England has experienced periodic bouts of "Romanophobia," leading sometimes to violent outbreaks. The example set by the church and king mobs of the eighteenth century was followed until well into the next century; their spirit has persisted to a degree until the present day. As late as 1852 in Stockport and 1867 in Birmingham, riots erupted during which scores were injured and several Catholic churches desecrated by Protestant mobs. From generation to generation, anti-Catholicism has been nourished on fear and hatred. The Catholics' supposed dual loyalty to the pope and the king; their beliefs, especially in the invocation of saints, veneration of the Virgin, transubstantiation, and miracles; the notion (maybe a form of wishful thinking on the part of their critics) that monasteries were little better than houses of assignation: all have been the stock items in the folklore of popular Protestantism.[21]

The nineteenth century was particularly productive in this area. The sheer bulk of new anti-Catholic literature, supplemented by inexpensive editions of classics such as *Foxe's Book of Martyrs*, replete with horrific tales and illustrations of atrocities against Protestants, testifies to the vitality of an ancient tradition. Incensed by the growth of ritualism, Anglo-Catholicism, and the fact that nearly one hundred Anglican clergymen, including Ronald A. Knox, the brilliant son of the evangelical bishop of Manchester, had been received into the Roman Catholic church since 1910,[22] extremists appealed further to popular prejudices. The cry of "the Church in danger" had never seemed more appropriate. Evangelical societies, among them the influential Protestant Truth Society, the Kensit Crusade, the Wycliffe Preachers, and the Church Association conducted a persistent campaign against crypto-Catholics within the Establishment and real ones outside it.

The cause of toleration was not advanced by the debate over Home Rule. If anything, the transformation of a basically political issue into a fullblown No Popery crusade brought the old prejudices to the surface and kept them constantly before the public in the two years preceding the war. After August 4, all the standard myths were merely brought up to date. The Jesuits, always associated in the popular imagination with disloyalty to England, were now singled out and accused of every imaginable crime and perversion. As a means of implementing the pope's grand design for world domination, they had taken prisoner the doddering old Francis Joseph, infiltrated the German government, and gained control of the Center party in the Reichstag. In England, meanwhile, they had helped build up through Catholic monastic and educational institutions a secret army. With Germany pressing from the outside (aided of course by Jesuit spies equipped with wireless apparatus) and subversion within, the British Empire would soon collapse, taking with it the Protestant religion.[23] In language reminiscent of Reformation diatribes, writers on prophecy went so far as to identify the papacy with the Whore of Babylon, the Great Harlot, and Gog. The beasts seen in Daniel's dream (Dan. 7), it was explained, were actually allegorical representations of the papacy. "The ten-horned Beast may sometimes be taken as referring to the Papacy; hence the second Beast, the False Prophet, is the Roman clergy and Babylon is Papal Rome."[24]

It is against this background that Benedict XV's most important initiative for peace must be viewed. On August 1, 1917, he sent to the governments of all the belligerent states the strongest appeal for peace ever to come from a religious leader during the Great War. "Is the civilized world," he pleaded, "to be only a field of death? Is Europe, so glorious and flourishing, to rush into the abyss as if stricken by a universal madness, and commit suicide?" Affirming that he regarded both sides with "perfect impartiality," he called upon the statesmen to consider their responsibilities to humanity as a whole. The pope also stated in general terms that, if ever there was to be lasting peace, moral might would have to be substituted for armed force and "the noble and powerful institution of arbitration" take the place of fighting. Finally, as a means of halting the present conflict, he admonished the warring states to accept the principles of disarmament, freedom of the seas, and renunciation of indemnities.

All occupied territories, including the German colonies, should be restored to their owners.[25]

Although several important Anglicans, notably the editors of the *Challenge* and the Rev. Walter Lock, believed the papal invitation, if not its specific proposals, warranted consideration as a basis for exploratory talks, memories of *Ad Beatissimi* and fears for the safety of Protestantism created an atmosphere inhospitable to any initiative originating in Rome. This latest appeal was, moreover, ill-timed to take advantage of whatever peace sentiment remained in England. Coming at the height of the controversy over the International Socialist Conference at Stockholm,[26] and two weeks after Erzberger's peace resolution in the Reichstag, it immediately fed suspicions of collusion with either the Germans, the Bolsheviks, or both. An article in the *Contemporary Review* implied that His Holiness was the cat's-paw of Germany, a theory to which the religious press largely subscribed. "The hand which signed the Papal document is the hand of Benedict XV. But the voice is the voice of Erzberger."[27] While the *Church Quarterly Review* deemed the proposals "profoundly unsatisfactory" because England would have to be mad to grant Germany freedom of the seas, the *Guardian* dismissed them with the curt statement that "no Allied Government will give them five minutes' serious consideration, more especially since they begin with the formula 'No annexations and no indemnities,' which was coined in Germany and put into circulation by the crazy Russian revolutionaries. . . ."[28]

Peace proposals emanating from nonecclesiastical sources fared no better. Shortly before Christmas, 1916, the Central Powers submitted to a number of neutral governments similar notes for transmission to the Entente Powers. Whereas these announced their readiness to enter immediately into negotiations, they contained nothing to indicate their willingness to discuss such outstanding issues as the evacuation of Belgium, the restoration of Alsace-Lorraine, and the fate of Serbia. The reaction of the English press was predictable; it greeted the approach with universal contempt. Lord Northcliffe's *Daily Mail*, never given to mincing words, set the tone by characterizing it as "The Empty Stomach Peace Whine."[29] Notwithstanding the protests of moderates like Henry Scott Holland, who denounced this attitude as absurd and wicked,[30] the religious press yielded to its secular counterpart nothing in rhetorical violence.

Dubbed the "Kaiser's peace kite," the note signified the last word in Teutonic arrogance. The offer to transfer the action from the battlefield to the conference table represented not the triumph of rationality, but rather the long-awaited sign that the enemy was weakening. A redoubling of the military effort, a "knock-out blow," would soon bring him to his knees. To make peace at this juncture would enable the war lords to save face, thereby averting an internal revolution. This was definitely not the time to make peace. Anyone desiring peace on terms different from the ideas set forth at the beginning of the conflict was not a patriot, but a dangerous sentimentalist. Anything less than total victory would be to repudiate a divine trust and condemn unborn generations to the hell of another war. As the *Church Family Newspaper* reminded its readers, "we cannot take peace as a boon from the hands of the great Antichrist. The law of right and the claim of conscience forbid our doing so. Better perish as an Empire than yield to the proposals of the enemy."[31]

Public indignation had hardly begun to cool when another proposal arrived, this time from across the Atlantic. Next to the pope and the kaiser, Woodrow Wilson was the person least likely to receive a sympathetic hearing in England. Beside regarding him personally as a supercilious, meddlesome prig, the average Englishman had few good things to say about the United States, a country where everything, including social prestige and a seat in the Senate, could be bought for hard cash.[32] The two great democracies of the West, related by ties of language, culture, and blood, were natural allies; or at least this was the message British propaganda sought to convey to the American people, particularly to intellectuals and religious leaders. So intent were they upon this task that the Department of Information at Wellington House, under Colonel John Bucan, solicited pro-Allied writings from Anglican bishops and composed special news stories for the benefit of American preachers. Certain groups in the United States were most amenable to pro-Allied influences. During the Great War, and again in 1940, England had a powerful friend in the Protestant Episcopal church. Episcopal clergymen, large numbers of whom had attended English universities and corresponded regularly with acquaintances in England, made no pretense at neutrality. Outstanding in this respect was the Rev. William T. Manning, rector of Trinity Parish, New York City, who on numerous occasions preached in support of British war aims and policies.[33]

Yet as the war progressed, the blunder of the butler who announced Bishop Brent of the Philippines as "the Bishop of the Philistines" seemed close to the mark. For the great neutral did not scruple to trade with the enemy and then, after its ships had been stopped and searched for contraband, to lecture England on the freedom of the seas. Nor did the United States see fit to say a word about Belgian neutrality, Louvain, or Germany's flouting of the Hague Convention, to which it was a signatory; indeed, gentlemen winced when its president replied to the outrages of the submarines with pious platitudes about being "too proud to fight." Not until those miraculous three weeks from March 15 to April 6, 1917, when the czar abdicated and Wilson brought his country into the war, did the image of the United States improve. Actually it was revolutionized, changing overnight from Uncle Money-bags the trader in blood, to "the United States of America—the greatest lovers of freedom in the world."[34] Needless to say, Wilson became the Presbyterian Moses leading the peoples to the promised land of peace, a role he found rather congenial.

In December, 1916, however, this development was still some months in the future. On the 18th, six days after the communication of the message of the Central Powers, the president dispatched through Secretary Lansing a peace note of his own. Later entitled "The Way to Peace," this message, worded to accent his disinterestedness, represented a sincere effort to find a common basis for negotiations. Observing that the long-range objectives of both sides were "virtually the same," and that this sameness had caused so much confusion, he suggested a method of blocking the deadlock. If each side stated its terms precisely, they might then find their positions less irreconcilable than hitherto imagined.[35]

His good intentions notwithstanding, Wilson's attempt at peacemaking was an unmitigated disaster. He had said all the wrong things. By seeming to place the Allied cause on the same level morally as the German, he offended even those who had always been friendly to the United States. Fearing dangerous expressions of anti-American sentiment, the government withheld publication of the note for several hours, thereby gaining time to soften editorial comments. Personal expressions of dissatisfaction were intense, however. The king, stunned by Wilson's statement, broke down in tears during luncheon at Buckingham Palace.[36] Sir Henry Wilson, British military representative on the Allied Supreme War Council, expressed his countrymen's reaction most succinctly: he confided to his diary his loathing for President Wilson, "that ass."[37] Ministers of religion said exactly the same thing, if in language more in keeping with their sacerdotal office. Devoting part of his Christmas sermon to Wilson's appeal, Bishop Ryle, dean of Westminster, must have spoken the mind of the overwhelming majority of his colleagues: "President Wilson has either, in a fit of mental aberration, sent the wrong note, or he has entirely misapprehended the European situation."[38]

Undismayed by the reception accorded his note, Wilson returned the following month to the theme of peace. During the course of a speech to the Senate (January 22), acclaimed by G. Lowes Dickinson, the classical scholar and originator of the name "League of Nations," as possibly the most important in history,[39] the president stressed that the future peace of the world depended on certain conditions: establishment of a League of Peace, freedom of the seas, arms limitation, and recognition of the principle of national self-determination. Unfortunately, here as elsewhere, Wilson's insensitivity to the feelings of others coupled with his uncanny talent for spoiling high-sounding pronouncements with a single ill-chosen phrase. Realizing a peace imposed on a humiliated loser would poison the atmosphere of the postwar world, he advised the belligerents to strive for "a peace without victory."[40] This was the last straw. Wilson the meddling idealist now had to bear the added stigma of Wilson the friend of the kaiser; to be sure, Walter Hines Page, the American ambassador to London, thought his chief had unconsciously fallen under German influence in his thought.[41] Once again, press and pulpit erupted with the familiar anti-American and anti-Wilson diatribes. This time, however, the furor subsided as quickly as it had begun; for on February 3 the United States government, after being informed of its intention to resume unrestricted submarine warfare, severed relations with Germany. The following week the entire Anglican press took the first halting, half-apologetic steps in rehabilitating a potential ally.

The last approach to peace we shall discuss originated from an unimpeachable source. In November, 1917, the *Daily Telegraph* published a long letter in which Lord Lansdowne, the negotiator of the Anglo-French Entente and a former member of the cabinet committee responsible for conducting the war, belittled the idea of winning with one last all out effort. Originally rejected by the *Times* because it represented no "responsible" segment of national opinion,[42] the Lansdowne letter struck a note of sanity needed at a time when everything seemed to be coming apart. It began by pointing out that, whereas England would certainly emerge victorious, to prolong the struggle further would spell ruin for civilization. Insisting that the restoration of Belgium and other territorial adjustments were essential to a durable peace, Lansdowne went on to propose that the government state clearly that England's war aims excluded the destruction of the German nation or the imposition upon her of a different political system. In closing, he asserted that if it could once be established that economic problems, freedom of the seas, and other problems were not insurmountable, then "the political horizon might perhaps be scanned with better hope by those who pray, but can at this moment hardly hope, that the New Year will bring us a lasting and honourable peace."[43]

Lord Lansdowne's prestige as an elder statesman, plus the fact that his letter coincided with the Italian debacle at Caporetto, the Bolshevik Revolution, and the end of the Passchendaele fiasco, contributed to its gathering more support in Anglican circles than any other proposal. The *Challenge* and the *Commonwealth* applauded his bravery in courting the abuse invariably heaping upon advocates of a negotiated settlement. In the first significant departure from the usual line, both maintained that while England should never accept a patched-peace, neither must she refuse to discuss even the possibility of negotiations.[44] The Rev. Tissington Tatlow, whose Student Christian Movement had members in Germany as well as in the Allied countries, welcomed the letter at the first ray of hope on an otherwise dismal horizon. Tatlow's support of the Allied cause was counterbalanced by the fear that the war had gone on too long, that people were allowing it to become an end unto itself. He deplored the tendency of his countrymen to rebuff any and all overtures without first reading them, let alone taking the trouble to explore their implications. "Germany and Austria have both said again and again that they want peace. Ought we not say as clearly and emphatically as Germany has said it that we, too, want peace, and ought we not to see whether an honourable peace can be achieved?"[45]

In relation to the Anglican community as a whole, these pleas for moderation were cries in the wilderness; if anything, they provoked stronger denunciations of "peace-mongers," by 1917 no less sinful than being a warmonger. On one occasion, T. B. Strong, dean of Christ Church and later bishop of Oxford, maintained the right of the Oxford Union to hear what the local M.P. had to say about the Lansdowne proposal. Lord Hugh Cecil, an active churchman and a staunch defender of the conscientious objectors, saw no need for discussion: "Moloch must be humiliated in the sight of his votaries if they are to accept a purer faith."[46] The two largest Anglican newspapers deplored the way so distinguished a man as Lord Lansdowne encouraged pacifists and undermined national unity by diverting its attention from winning the war.[47] Even the prudent Gore denounced the proposal, being convinced that the only security for peace was the decisive overthrow of militarism.[48] The lesson, as Lord Lansdowne learned, was unmistakeable: no matter what the source, the nation had become too committed to the war to think of peace in terms other than total victory. The church merely reflected this mood.

OUTLINE OF THE CHRISTIAN PEACE

It would be wrong to give the impression that the Anglican community was ever in absolute agreement on the specific terms of the peace settlement. One segment, comprising a number of outstanding personalities, opposed from the outset a harsh, vindictive treaty, however it was arrived at. "My objection to that program," wrote Edward Lyttelton to the primate, who agreed, "is that for the future everything depends on Germany being *converted* to a better frame of mind, and that it is impossible to convert a nation from belief in brute force by hammering her, and then leaving her future in the hands of the hammerers. In other words is there the faintest hope that Germany will see the truth merely by losing all her young men?"[49] But by far the largest number seem to have held the opposite view; and it is to these that we must turn our attention. Believing that loving kindness would be wasted on the Hun, they demanded not the generous readmission of the errant brother to the family of nations, but punishment—swift, condine, exemplary.

No aspect of the forthcoming settlement was endorsed more heartily than the restoration of Belgium. Inasmuch as the conflict had begun with her violation, the representatives of all denominations insisted that no armistice be concluded until the invader surrendered his ill-gotten gains, promising to make such recompense as was still possible to the people of that ravaged land. Nothing could revive the dead or mend torn bodies, but elementary justice dictated that German gold provide for the widows and educate the orphans, rebuild the towns and restock the libraries.

As a rule, those advocating a hard line went beyond what might be considered fair reparation. In terms of pounds and shillings, the First World War cost the victors nearly three times as much as the vanquished. Day after day, the wealth accumulated painfully during a century of economic progress was plowed with abandon into the Flanders mud. As the struggle drew to a close, an enraged public, taking stock of its debts, released its frustrations in cries for expropriation, cries to make Germany pay "until the pips squeaked." It seemed monstrous to allow them to make restitution only for the damage they had caused, while the Allied taxpayer, bled white to save the world from Antichrist, had to pay for everything else. Half-realizing that Germany's wealth was, after all, limited, and that reparations in manufactured goods and raw materials would undermine the Allied economies, clerical opinion tended nonetheless to mirror that of the wider public: Germany must pay the whole cost of the war.

As for Germany herself, it was not merely a matter of dismissing her with costs and damages, however extravagant. The Allies were morally obliged to make her an example of the fate awaiting future aggressors. Let history record that, when the opportunity presented itself, the united nations of Christendom "diagnosed not for the poltice, but for the knife; and rightly so. The world must never forget the justice wrought in full severity on those who created this terrible war, and waged it so brutally."[50] Yet punishment alone would never suffice to bring a bully nation, any more than a schoolyard bully, to

his senses. Germany needed to be humiliated before the world, and
the symbols of her pride, the Brandenburg Gate and the Niederwald
Monument, smashed to pieces and cast into the Rhine.[51]

A crucial aspect of Germany's penitence revolved around the fate
of the "war criminals." For the first time a nation's civilian and military leaders were to be held accountable and brought to justice for
their misdeeds, a radical departure from tradition and fraught with
hidden difficulties.[52] The definition of what exactly constituted a war
crime remained at best vague, more a matter of individual value
judgment than law. Insofar as the Allies were fighting for righteousness' sake, investing the government and the military with virtually
unlimited powers seemed justified. Since the Germans, on the other
hand, opposed them, anyone who ordered or carried out an order to
release poison gas, drop bombs from a Zeppelin, or sink a merchant
ship was a murderer. The authority of the state stopped short at matters of conscience; therefore even a warrior was bound to disobey in
something universally deemed wrong by rational men.[53] The first
order of business, then, should be to round up the war criminals, try
them, and punish them according to the law—whose law is unclear.

Punishing individual war criminals was to be the prelude to the
supreme task: "We must," wrote a lay correspondent to the *Challenge*, "render [Germany's] foul soul powerless for mischief."[54]
Above all, this meant uprooting the institutions and discrediting the
ideology of militarism, easy enough if undertaken sincerely. At the
apex of the civil and military establishments, the kaiser was the arch-
criminal. He had helped to plan the war; he had authorized every
enormity from the invasion of Belgium to torpedoing hospital ships;
he had allowed the Turks to slaughter the Armenians.

As was to be expected, there developed sharp differences of opinion as to his fate, exile and imprisonment being the most favored
expedients. Not that the cry of "hang the Kaiser" lacked substantial
support within the church. Maintaining that the kaiser's case was
not of a sort to be determined by "legal niceties," the largest Anglican
newspapers urged the government to threaten the Dutch with blockade or worse if they balked at extraditing him. The defenders of
Belgian neutrality had indeed travelled a long road.[55] In any case,
everyone agreed that no progress could be made in reforming Germany without first deposing William II and permanently debarring

the Hohenzollern dynasty from the imperial title. It went without saying that the mainstay of the Empire, the army, the General Staff, and the officer corps, in short the entire German war machine, would have to be dismantled and rendered incapable of functioning ever again.

Apart from the territorial adjustments that normally accompany a great war, neutralizing the threat of a resurgent Germany implied some drastic, if not altogether expropriatory, changes. Both justice and strategy decreed alterations in the boundaries of the enemy nations. Clerical commentators were usually as enthusiastic as their secular counterparts about preventing a revival of German navalism by returning Schleswig (German population and all) to Denmark and extending her southern border to the Kiel Canal; likewise, returning Alsace-Lorraine to France would rectify a historic injustice and cripple Germany's rearmament potential by withholding some of the richest mineral resources in Europe.[56] Nor were these the only territorial changes proposed. While the Allies never proclaimed openly their intention of destroying Germany as a nation, public opinion, whipped up in certain instances by ministers of religion, ignored the much-trumpeted "lessons" of the Congress of Vienna and demanded a peace of tremendous annexations and staggering indemnities. Central Europe would never know a moment's peace so long as Prussia formed the core of a united German state. An artificial entity built up through centuries of conquest, Prussia should be detached from Germany and forced to live, isolated in her old haunts east of the Elbe, as a third-rate power depending upon Allied protection.[57]

The fate of Germany's African and Oceanic colonies was of special concern to a missions-oriented church. It would be easy, and entirely wrong, to dismiss the Anglican approach to the colonial problem as merely a rationalization of imperialistic greed. If imperialism be defined in purely economic terms, whether of the Marxian variety or as expressed in J. A. Hobson's *Imperialism*, the proof-text of the prewar Left and a source of inspiration for Lenin, then the Anglican clergy were passionately anti-imperialistic. Next to the sanctity of the British constitution and the Established church, the empire held for the educated Englishman an immutable position in the scheme of things. God had created the empire to serve His Divine purpose; He had created the Englishman to administer the empire. If imperialism meant anything to the clergy, it was the sentiments expressed in Kiplings poem, "The White Man's Burden" (1899). It meant sacrificing oneself in preserving the greatest Christianizing force and civilizing influence the world had ever known, not exploiting child-peoples for the profit of the capitalist. Maintaining the empire was a religious duty.[58] Addressing his boys on the queen's first jubilee, Edward Thring, headmaster of Uppingham, proclaimed: "Woe to them who touched this inheritance with the hand of evil, and woe to them who betrayed it. Woe to all meanness of thought and aim; woe to all who forget the high duties which must be ever joined to the exercise of world-wide power and influence."[59] During the Boer War these ideals of service and stewardship became tainted with a degree of racism. Many clergymen, particularly those residing in the colonies or active in missionary work, claimed that theirs was the imperial race par excellence. Above all others, the English had taken up the white man's burden of governing the backward races for their own benefit.[60]

Ideas of this sort were still very much in evidence at the time of the Great War; only now all the arguments employed to justify the conquest of the Boer republics were brought up to date and applied in exaggerated form to Germany. Unlike the English, who always strove to establish an "ethical kinship" between themselves and the natives, the Germans knew only how to rule by brute force. Indeed, G. H. Frodsham, a former bishop of North Queensland and canon residentiary of Gloucester Cathedral, thought they were incapable of winning the love of their subjects or governing them justly because they could not "think imperially."[61]

In an emotionally charged campaign reminiscent of the Congo agitation, Germany was presented as the supreme example of the capitalist exploiter. Missionaries reported that the methods employed by German businessmen and colonial officials to extract profits surpassed the worst features of Leopold's regime in the Congo. "German rule is impossible. The German does not understand the elementary principles of humane government. He is efficient, he is polite, he is correct in his behaviour and attitude, but he is German. And being a German he sees the native as a tool; he is cruel and inhuman, and under him the African must become a slave or die."[62] Church and state supposedly worked hand-in-hand. If the Lutheran missionary failed to indoctrinate or browbeat the native into submitting to his master's every command, the police would step in to administer special treatment. They would stop at nothing to squeeze out just that last bit of work. Exterminating entire tribes; flogging with the Sjambok, a whip made of braided strips of rhinoceros hide; torturing with the "iron hat"; tossing babies into the bush to starve; and debauching African women was permissible if it increased production or satisfied the perverted tastes of the German colonists.[63]

Added to the atrocities, the other actions of Germany in Africa furnished convincing evidence that her colonial policy had been formulated with an eye to cutting Britain's imperial lifeline. Operating from a chain of strongly fortified coastal positions, a small, well-trained army supported by swarms of native troops could overwhelm South Africa. Submarines and surface raiders could then paralyze shipping in the South Atlantic, the Suez Canal, and the Indian Ocean.[64] Even more ominous than this, the militarization of the black man was bound to undermine the status of all Europeans in Africa. By systematically disparaging other white men, instructing native troops in the methods of modern warfare—charges, incidentally, levelled also by the Germans against the British—they had shattered the belief in European omnipotence. Given time, this would destroy respect for the white man in Africa and throughout the world.[65] The white man's weapons might one day be turned against himself.

Humanitarian considerations aside, the recitation of German crimes (actual and anticipated) was intended to serve a practical purpose, that of building a case against returning her colonies, all of which had fallen to the Allies by 1918. To that end, the missionary societies and organizations interested in the welfare of natives—the S.P.G., the Universities Mission to Central Africa, and the Anti-Slavery and Aborigines Protection Society—began mobilizing Anglican opinion. They were assisted in this by two influential works published and widely circulated in the last months of the conflict. The government of the Union of South Africa, eager to keep German Southwest Africa, captured by its forces in the first year of the war, published its *Report on Natives of Southwest Africa and their Treatment by Germany* (Capetown, 1918), a mine of detailed information on how the Hereros and Hottentots had been massacred for refusing to cooperate with the plantation owners. This was followed shortly by *The Black Slaves of Prussia*, an open letter in pamphlet form. The work of Bishop Frank Weston, who had raised and commanded a force of native porters in the East African campaign, it begged General Smuts to help prevent the Germans from ever returning to Africa.

Unlike the South African *Report*, which presented the awful facts and then allowed the reader to draw his own conclusions, Weston's pamphlet was an impassioned plea for the lives of his people. England had promised never to sheathe the sword until righteousness triumphed. She had encouraged thousands of Africans to flee their masters and serve against them; this was treason by anyone's definition. To return East Africa to such masters, as pacifists and certain Labour Party politicians advocated, would mean sending these trusting people to certain death. "Is it conceivable that we British should do that? and just because the people are not white? . . . God forbid!" Weston, it should be noted, though a patriotic Englishman, was first and foremost a Christian missionary; as such, he never hesitated about castigating his country where the rights of the African were concerned. *The Black Slaves of Prussia* was followed in two years by *The Serfs of Great Britain*, an impassioned protest against forced labor in the East African Protectorate (afterwards Kenya), the area he had helped conquer.

Germany, while the chief villain, had by no means been alone in disturbing the peace of the world. Yet the settlement proposed in the religious press for her accomplices rested on entirely different principles. Whereas the German problem seemed primarily one of punishment for past wrongs and preventing future aggression through destroying the economic and territorial bases of her power, the Austro-Hungarian and Turkish empires were so backward and corrupt that their very weakness invited war. To make matters worse, each ruled minorities whose struggles for nationhood threatened to tear them apart, endangering in the process the entire European community.

Publications that had stressed the importance of Austria to the European order when the war began eventually adopted the contrary view. The plan most favored contained many of the features, though not necessarily for the same reasons, of the settlement finally worked out by the peacemakers. Unlike the statesmen, who early became preoccupied with the Bolshevik threat, thoughtful Anglicans, hating Bolshevism as an ideal and because Lenin had concluded a separate peace, were evidently not yet greatly concerned about its expansive capabilities; nor were they seized with a panic-fear of "atheistical communism" until the early 'twenties, when the persecution of the Orthodox church began in earnest. They tended to see peace in Central Europe more in terms of satisfying the national aspirations of the subject peoples than of surrounding the Soviet Union with a *cordon sanitaire.* A restored Poland, a Hungary separated from Austria (which might for its safety be united with a Prussia-less Germany), and a series of buffer states between Russia and the Teutonic powers would calm a troubled area. The stability of southeastern Europe and the Balkans depended likewise on territorial adjustments: Bosnia and Herzegovina should be added to Serbia, and Italy guaranteed at least partial control over Albania and the Trentino.[66]

Whereas Germany and Austria would eventually have to be brought back into the mainstream of European life, Turkey was a tribe of bandits.[67] There had been an undercurrent of anti-Turkish sentiment going back at least to Gladstone's famous pamphlet on *The Bulgarian Horrors and the Question of the East* (1876); and ever since the first Armenian massacres in Constantinople and Anatolia in 1895, Anglican opinion had been definitely hostile to England's former ally. During the First Balkan War in 1912, the ecclesiastical authorities called openly for a victory by the Balkan states, some going so far as to collect money and offer public prayers to aid their Christian brethren.[68] No reasonable man, affirmed the Rev. W. L. Grane, could help but support a people resisting "the immoral system of unmitigated force applied by the Turks in their travesty of government to all the common relationships of life."[69]

Turkey's entry into the struggle on the wrong side strengthened the feeling that England was in a crusade. Here as elsewhere, there were those who had a field day with apocalyptic speculations. To them, the little horn of the third beast in Daniel 8:9 represented Turkey; the drying up of the River Euphrates in Revelation 12:12 meant Turkey would lose its provinces; as foretold in prophecy, the return of the Jews to the Holy Land, already begun by Zionism and the capture of Jerusalem, would usher in the millennium.[70] In any case, the "sick man of Europe," always a prominent candidate for euthanasia, would be disposed of at last. All his possessions—Palestine, Armenia, Syria, Arabia, Mesopotamia—would be taken away and governed until that indeterminate date when they would be fit to govern themselves.[71] Besides losing her possessions in the Middle East, Turkey would have to be deprived of sovereignty over certain portions of her national territory. Constantinople, defiled for nearly five centuries by "that horrible Turkish government with its harems and eunuchs and its hateful Eastern associations," must be administered either by the Allies themselves or by a powerful neutral like the United States, and the Dardanelles internationalized.[72]

The issue of the *Challenge* for the New Year, 1919, contains a full page reproduction of a pastel drawing by one F. D. Bedford. In the foreground, there is a deep crevice brimming with the discarded and broken paraphernalia of war; beyond, children of every nation and race march joyfully around a mound on top of which the crucified Christ is shown illuminated by rays symbolizing universal peace. Just below Him, amid a kneeling throng, a man and a woman stand gazing up into His face. In their hands they hold a tall staff with a banner attached: emblazoned on it are the words "LEAGUE OF NATIONS."[73]

Regardless of the title given to the organization itself—International Peace League, League to Enforce Peace, and League of Free Peoples were among those suggested—the idea of a supranational agency empowered to keep the peace took an early hold on the clerical imagination; indeed, in certain instances men were moved as if by a vision of the Beyond. Understandably so. To the older clergymen, whose placid, orderly lives had been shattered by the war, as well as to the younger generation whose lives it had changed forever, the League of Nations represented a break in the historical continuum comparable only to the event on Calvary. Alliances, *ententes*, armaments, and secret diplomacy had all failed to prevent the near-suicide of Western Civilization. Now, with the old world rapidly going to pieces and the new world still pliable enough to receive lasting impressions, the human race had the opportunity to reshape its destiny. "Our age is comparable to that which witnessed the break-up of the Roman Empire," observed the editor of the *Challenge*, "and we have a chance of rebuilding such as no previous generation in the world's history has had."[74]

Despite the skeptics, who belittled the League idea as Utopian because the Great Powers would never surrender part of their sovereignty to an international body, or because it might be a capitalist conspiracy to enslave the workers further, the vast majority of clergymen came early to its support. As early as August, 1914, at the height of the patriotic hysteria, a handful of Anglican leaders began thinking about ending permanently the "international anarchy," as G. Lowes Dickinson later called it. For want of an alternative, the present war had to be fought to a conclusion; but a better way must be made available for the future. Said B. H. Streeter:

In international affairs there is no impartial authority to enforce the law. In international affairs Judge Lynch is the only judge, and his justice is, at best, a rough justice, at the worst, no justice at all. What then? Because no ideal tribunal is forthcoming, is the offender to go unchecked, to the detriment alike of his own and his victim's moral sense? Surely not. The Christian may hope that in the future, somehow or other, whether by some future development of 'Holy Alliances' or of Hague Tribunals and the like, some means will be found of securing a relatively impartial tribunal with coercive powers to enforce its verdict. But until that is done he must recognize that Lynch law is better than no law. . . .[75]

Civilization had evolved ("progressed," in its optimistic nineteenth century meaning, was a word seldom heard at this time) to the point where existing ideas, laws, and institutions were no longer capable of coping with the problems created by science and technology. To this intellectual awareness was added a growing sense of urgency. The conduct of the war gave thoughtful people every reason to fear that the horrors they were witnessing would be as child's play compared with the way the next war would *start*. It is here, in the closing days of the Great War, that so much of the fear-psychology of the interwar period originated. Expressed in political oratory, imaginative literature and the film,[76] the belief (unfounded) that "the bomber will always get through" persisted until superseded by an equally strong faith in the omnipotency of ballistic missiles: the line leading from *The Shape of Things to Come* to *Doctor Strangelove* and *On the Beach* is a straight one.

It was widely assumed that the belligerents, carrying to its logical conclusion the principle that every citizen is a combatant, would as a matter of course prosecute the next war with methods now deemed extraordinary, albeit sometimes necessary violations of the laws of civilized warfare. Sixteen years before the splitting of the uranium atom into lighter elements, the Rev. E. W. Barnes, a noted scientist and mathematician as well as the bête noire of orthodox theologians, predicted that "the dissociation of the atom which recent science has achieved points the way to obtaining explosives of tremendous power. If ever a method is discovered of liberating the electrical energy of matter, a small bomb will destroy not a house but a city."[77] War had lost its spectacular and sporting sides, nor was it as remote as it used to be. Humanity stood at the crossroads. Either it accepted the idea of the League of Nations and moved forward into an era of peace, or ignited the kindling for the global Gehenna.

With this in mind, Bishop Gore, an indefatigable speaker and writer on behalf of the League, affirmed that everyone had in some broad and vague sense become a socialist.[78] Not that the League idea owed anything to socialistic thought, but rather that a strong affinity existed between the principles of mutuality underlying the League and the ethical teachings of Christianity. The League of Nations, he wrote in a pamphlet sent by William Howard Taft's committee for the League to every minister in the United States, had come from the spirit of God, for "it will rest upon the idea of fellowship and humanity, supreme in its interests over all separate national claims, a fellowship based on justice and the rights of the weaker as well as the stronger nations—an idea which has mainly had its origin in Christian thought and imagination. . . ."[79]

In addition to abolishing war, bound up with the League idea was the awareness that organized religion had failed to take advantage of its opportunities. When the war began, optimists had expected a great religious revival that would spark in turn a movement to reunite the churches of Christendom. Their hopes notwithstanding, the results of the National Mission of Repentance and Hope and other, less ambitious, undertakings like the Woolwich Crusade were disappointing. By the end of 1918, it had become clear that there would be no revival, and that the success of ecumenism was problematical. But man's necessity is God's opportunity. The League of Nations promised to furnish a "League of Churches" with the framework wherein they could learn to work out their differences. Each possessed what the other required for success: the churches had idealism and the accumulated wisdom of centuries, the statesmen had technical knowledge and organizational skills. The League would go the way of previous plans unless there was a basis of spiritual unity behind it, unless a closer intercourse of nations was strengthened by a closer intercourse of churches.[80] "A League of Nations based on the Sermon on the Mount is the only practical method of ensuring peace."[81]

Several of the most active propagandists for the League came from the upper ranges of the ecclesiastical establishment. Always busy with their regular duties, bishops cut corners wherever possible to enable them to participate in League-furthering activities; so much so, that the archbishop of Canterbury had to caution against diffusing their energies too widely.[82] As president of the World Alliance for Promoting the Fellowship of Nations through the Churches, Bishop Talbot pressed his clergy to mobilize opinion in their parishes; the bishop of Southwark followed the lecture circuit, speaking to gatherings on the history of the League idea; and Lord Parmoor, vicar-general of the Province of Canterbury, moved a resolution in the House of Laymen stating that "Christianity requires the recognition of the principle of the League of Nations as a safeguard against aggressive wars"[83]—the death of Bishop Percival and Henry Scott Holland that year deprived the movement of two stentorian voices. Clergymen were naturally attracted to the League of Nations Society, an organization which, in the weight it placed on recruiting an upper-class and academic membership, resembled the great Victorian ad hoc organizations for social reform. Composed of members from the principal churches in the United Kingdom, the Clergy Auxiliary Committee invited prominent divines to work for the Society. The archbishop of York, Bishops Talbot and Gore, Dean Inge, William Temple, and Paul Bull (as avid a crusader for the League as against Germany) preached and wrote on its behalf.[84]

As proposed by its clerical supporters, the organization and powers of the League of Nations differed only in minor details from the plan ultimately adopted. Its membership was to be made up of every civilized nation including Germany, provided it was a disarmed Germany showing a willingness to cooperate with her sister states. Russia, however, was another matter; she would have to be excluded, as "the other nations cannot make a league with chaos."[85] When a dispute arose, each party would submit its case as a matter of course to an agency qualified to rule on its merits or act as arbitrator. In the event that the dispute developed into a threat to the peace, or if hostilities actually began, the Council of the League would be empowered to label the aggressor and take such action as it deemed necessary to restore peace.[86]

It would be useless, if not positively dangerous, to create an impressive looking organization without the power to perform its stated function. An attack on one member of the League must be interpreted as an attack on the entire international community. Consequently, there would be two methods of dealing with aggression. First, all members and their dependencies would impose an economic boycott on the offending state. If that failed, stronger measures would be in order. While the idea of a permanent international army had numerous supporters, clerical opinion in general seems to have wanted the League to make do with a temporary force contributed by the member nations. In any case, everyone agreed that the only way to avoid a second world war was for every peace-loving state to declare its readiness to go to war under the auspices of an international organization. *Si vis pacem, para bellum.*

VIII. CONCLUSION

The experiences of the Church of England during the world crisis of 1914–1918 may be considered on two levels. They were, first, sui generis, the expression of an institution functioning within a particular social milieu and historical context; they can also be considered as a heuristic device prompting inquiry into issues of universal concern: human nature and society, war and religion.

Apart from its divine mission, the church resembles the other major institutions of society—political parties, organized labor, business, the press, and "established" intellectuals such as university professors—in that it is imbedded in, and derives sustenance from, the social matrix and its association with the state. Like these, it has the need for what sociologists term "centricity."[1] The power and prestige these institutions enjoy are conditional, being conferred with the tacit understanding that they will never stray too far from society's prevailing values and interests. As Herbert Butterfield has said: "By its alliance with power for fifteen hundred years . . . the Church committed itself to being on the whole the cement of society, the buttress of whatever was the existing order, and the defender of the *status quo*."[2]

This is not a situation congenial to ideological purists, for it implies that "principles" must be modified in accordance with objective reality. To the doctrinaire Marxist, "revisionism" is heresy; to the sectarian Christian, the gradual accommodation of the church to society, beginning in the reign of the Emperor Constantine, is a sin tantamount to a "fall" of Christianity. Yet in most societies, even in those wed to certain of their guiding principles, purists are either persecuted as menaces to public order or they become peripheral and irrelevant, idiosyncratic and "eccentric" in the true meaning of the term. The price of power, it seems, is avoidance of extremes.

The phenomenon of centricity assumes still greater importance when viewed in conjunction with the ways society molds the outlook of the individual. As members of a society we each acquire a set of common symbols, beliefs, and categories enabling us to interpret our experiences. Even that which we accept as "knowledge" and take for "reality" is in large measure a function of social learning. What is "real" to the Papuan headhunter is not necessarily real to the Oxford don; each "knows" entirely different things. Thus it may be said that "reality" is itself relative, differing as social contexts differ.[3]

These principles are readily applicable to the church in the early years of the twentieth century. By its very nature Anglicanism represents a compromise between its purpose as a religious society devoted to serving God and saving souls, and its position as the legally established faith of a powerful state. Like its progenitor, the Roman Catholic church, it is "in the world." While striving to leaven the world by its teaching, constant exposure to the varied aspects of the human condition has imparted to it a certain hard, practical quality. Unlike extreme sectarians, whose ideology and exclusiveness prevent them from participating fully, and thereby wielding power, in national life, Anglicanism recognizes and functions within the limitations imposed by the secular order. Normally tolerant of a wide range of opinions, the need to set limits to opposing factions within the church, its antifundamentalistic approach to Scripture, its history and traditions have made it wary of enthusiasts, hot gospellers whose "conscience" bids them defy time-honored norms in church and society.

In the early part of this century, as now, churchmen exemplified the prevailing social norms in their own lives. Next to the family itself, the central institutions for shaping the attitudes of the upper- and middle-class youngster destined for an ecclesiastical career were the public school and the university. First at places like Eton, Harrow, and their imitators, then at Cambridge and Oxford ("Eton over again, on a different stretch of the same river," as Henry Scott Holland put it) he underwent a course of formal instruction and informal indoctrination intended less to prepare him for a career than to fashion his character so that he would always think, speak, and carry himself as a gentleman. Through the games he played, the rules he lived by, and the friendships he made, he slowly, almost unconsciously, assimilated a code of honor and a system of values based on the "manly" virtues of bravery, sincerity, duty, and service.

Upon taking Holy Orders, he quickly discovered, if he did not already know, that the church also prized and strove to cultivate these qualities, and that with slight modification the language of the playing field, or, for that matter of the battlefield, was interchangeable with that of the religious sphere. The church, too, had its temperance "campaigns" and priests on "active duty" in the slums, its "flying squads" of evangelists, "bombing schools" for chaplains, and "front line troops."

The ability of certain institutions to "fit" so well into the social matrix largely explains their perception of threats to the established order. Groups whose power depends on their centricity are bound to fall into step with official policy, however belatedly and halfheartedly. They may loathe war. They may think *this* particular war imprudent. They may be opposed to the policy of the government of the day and favor large concessions to bring the war to an end. Yet they are ambivalent, for they have their own interests to preserve as well as a material and emotional investment in their society. Opposition to a war deemed just and necessary—or just *because* necessary—by the majority of the nation and its political leaders would be visited with punishment in the form of diminished power and prestige. National defeat would have the same effect, threatening their position and undermining their ability to pursue objectives they may consider of transcendent importance.

When institutions of this sort have opposed war, the war in question has not been perceived by the society as a menace to its existence; at the very minimum there has been disagreement about the intensity of the threat. In total war, national life becomes partially militarized, binding the individual closer to the group and groups closer to one another. In "small" wars, however, or in "policy" wars where the nation is clearly not fighting for its life, militarization is less intense and the individual less likely to be bound so closely. He becomes a spectator, viewing the struggle from the outside—an effect heightened immeasurably by modern communications media. All the personal aches, frustrations, and bitternesses that in a big war become sublimated into hatred for the enemy now have wide latitude for expression. Individuals can support the war or violently oppose it. The significant factor to note here is that dissent is being expressed among the public at large, to which ecclesiastical or other disgruntled elements from the "establishment" can adhere. It is noteworthy, however, that even when dissent is relatively acceptable, it invariably emanates from a minority, which may have to pay for its moral witness after the issue of the war has been laid to rest. For example, Bishop George Bell of Chichester, an outspoken critic of the obliteration bombing of German cities in the Second World War, was passed over when the see of Canterbury fell vacant, although he was reputedly the best qualified for the position. How many other personal defeats and blighted lives has war-opposition involved?

The moment a war policy has been approved and the conflict declared just, other agencies come into play to enable the society to close ranks. Squabbles within and between groups are resolved or shelved "for the duration," and for a time society enjoys a rare degree of tranquility. Within most individuals certain mechanisms become operative, enabling them to suppress any lingering doubts, the better to fit themselves for the common undertaking. Social reality is too complex for the nonspecialist to comprehend in any but the barest essentials, certainly too complicated when the motivations, belief-systems, and actions of other societies are to be interpreted. The simplest way to comprehend the situation is to present it to oneself in absolutist terms: "our" motives are good; "their" motives are evil. Forced or accidental exposure to new information may, however, introduce elements dissonant with the accepted theory. A person with normal intelligence is bound to note, perhaps, that a given policy of his government is not altogether just or disinterested; he may even catch his government in a lie. To prevent such doubts from incapacitating him for group action, there is an unconscious tendency for the individual to undervalue or ignore completely whatever information is inconsistent with official policy, while simultaneously giving undue weight to whatever lends it support.

The so-called "Asch phenomenon" is scientific confirmation of the phenomenon Hans Christian Anderson portrayed so charmingly in his story about "The Emperor's New Clothes." In experiments conducted by the American psychologist Solomon E. Asch, the subject is placed in a group whose members are supposed to evaluate various forms shown to them, such as determining the longer of two lines. At the start, the judgments of subject and group are consistent. But the experiment is rigged, and gradually the judgments of the subject conflict with those of the group, whose members have been instructed to give false answers. Eventually the subject, who is naturally confused and upset, will begin to "see" the forms exactly as described by his peers.[4] Whether it be called, in the special terminology of the psychologist, "spontaneous rationalization," "the strain toward consistency," or "the reduction of cognitive dissonance,"[5] the result is the same: the impetus to suppress doubt and to suspend the critical faculties comes from within the individual, although the specific rationalizations are provided by society.

These tendencies are pronounced among intellectuals. Writing in a series of articles published in 1915 as *Above the Battle*, the French pacifist Romain Rolland was astonished at the ease with which "all the forces of the spirit, of reason, of faith, of poetry and of science, all have placed themselves at the disposal of the armies in every state" for the purpose of waging "zoological wars, wars of extermination." Yet what Rolland noted and his countryman Julien Benda condemned as *La Trahison des Clercs* (1927) was no treason at all, no conscious betrayal of a belief or cause. The locus of centricity is constantly shifting. It is a sad paradox that, as society becomes increasingly radicalized, groups whose authority depends on their centricity must become radicalized in turn; to remain stationary is to allow the course of events to pass them by, rendering them eccentric.

Once again, the activities of the Church of England may be related to generalized social phenomena. England in the summer of 1914 was a troubled land. Large segments of the population had embarked upon a series of agitations the likes of which had not been seen since the "hungry 'forties." Brewing for several years, the fact that the acute stages of three major crises coincide gave the impression that society was on the verge of anarchy. Workers, women, and Irishmen were all apparently intent upon dragging society down if their demands were not satisfied immediately and completely.

As disruptive as they were, the conflicts in church and society never really constituted, nor were they intended to constitute, an assault on the body politic or its value system. Far from repudiating the Victorian thought-world, the aims of the parties to the triple rebellion were essentially conservative. Like the Ulstermen, they were concerned either with maintaining their traditional status *within* the United Kingdom, or, like the suffragettes and trade unionists, striving to remove the political and economic barriers to first-class citizenship; loyalty to England was never a matter for discussion. The forces making for disunity within the Church of England were likewise not directed toward its disruption, but to placing it in an impregnable position. Evangelicals and Anglo-Catholics, each in their own way, fought to safeguard their church from false and dangerous teachings; the modernists hoped to make its message more appealing to doubters and nonbelievers by bringing its theology into line with the best in contemporary thought.

The Great War came at a moment when intra- and intergroup strife had reached menacing proportions, a factor acting as a safety valve mechanism to ease the emotional transition from peace to war. One cannot always say with certainty whether the jubilant crowds that greeted the war were motivated more by a feeling of relief that a domestic catastrophe had been avoided than by patriotism and confidence in the righteousness of their country's cause. Whatever the motivation, confronted as they were by a powerful foreign adversary, Englishmen could safely and without loss of self-esteem break off the domestic conflict and redirect their hostilities toward the Central Powers. For the time being, people forgot their personal problems and "gave" themselves to a cause transcending all narrow sectional interests.

If this holocaust proved anything, it was that, for the overwhelming majority of people in the West, and eventually for people throughout the world, national loyalty transcended allegiance to any supernational institution or cosmopolitan ideology. To the dismay of men like Norman Angell and James Keir Hardie (to *John Bull* he was "Cur Hardie, Kaiser William's pup"), no appeal to reason or to a "higher loyalty" could withstand the cry of "the nation in danger." Shortly before he died, Hardie, by then a man broken by disappointment, wrote: "Ten million Socialist and Labour voters in Europe, without a trace or vestige of power to prevent war! . . . Our demonstrations and speeches and resolutions are all alike futile. We have no means of hitting the warmongers. We simply do not count."[6] The international peace movement did not count precisely because it *was* international. There was not then, nor is there today, an "international society" or a "world community" to encompass the life of the individual and mold him from birth. It remains to be seen whether any organization, including the United Nations, will be able to command the loyalties of men and elicit sacrifices from them as effectively as the national state.

Although the clergy as a group hated war as representing the height of folly and barbarism, and although an articulate minority opposed the South African conflict and became active in the peace movement, they recognized the necessity of force in human affairs. The proper rendering of the Sixth Commandment is "Thou shalt not murder," not "Thou shalt not kill"; and inasmuch as the motive force in international affairs was justice rather than love, killing was permissible, even praiseworthy, under the proper circumstances. This belief, of course, meant that pacifism was bound to be rejected on religious as well as patriotic grounds. In August 1914 Germany tore up a solemn agreement and invaded an innocent neighbor. Justice, honor, self-interest, and the proper relationship to God Himself demanded England's intervention.

Despite their recognition of the necessity of war, devout people still had to reckon with the ineluctable tension between Christianity's spiritual and pragmatic elements. War does, after all, involve acts contrary to the spirit of the Gospel; and there were churchmen, as there were liberals, who could not accept even a technically "just" war unless it was also waged for fundamental principles of faith and morality. When on August 6, 1914, Mr. Asquith told the House of Commons that "I do not believe any nation ever entered into a greater controversy . . . with a clearer conscience and a stronger conviction that it is fighting, not for aggression, not for the maintenance of its own selfish interest, but that it is fighting in defence of principles, the maintenance of which is vital to the civilisation of the world."[7] they could only utter a silent "amen." Sentiments that have become trite in a world ravaged by two cataclysmic wars and living under the shadow of a third, were charged then with deep emotion. All the catch phrases of the time—"war to end war," "Great War for civilization," "war to make the world safe for democracy," "sanctity of treaties"—contained just those elements they needed to reconcile themselves to their country's role in the greatest conflict in history.

Clergymen, however, might be carried several steps beyond their secular counterparts. Learned though they were in their own field, theology, their education was not designed to impart the specialized skills necessary for evaluating complex problems of politics, law, and philosophy. As a result of these deficiencies, they displayed a marked tendency to appropriate current ideas without fully testing them, to interpret them in a simplistic way—witness their treatment of Nietz-sche—and finally to "theologize," that is, to express them in purely religious terms. Ignorance and a too-willing acceptance of propagan-distic literature on the one hand, the impact of the destruction of Louvain and the early atrocity stories on the other, combined to create the picture of a thoroughly evil enemy.

The fact that organized Christianity in Germany seemed powerless to halt the carnage, indeed, its encouragement of the war lords to fight more ferociously, further deepened Anglican resentments. Whereas the various parties in the church quarrelled vehemently over the extent to which German theology was responsible for the war, they agreed in portraying the "treason" of the German clerks to the community of Christian men as the supreme crime of the war.

Ultimately, there emerged the theory that Germany had sold itself to the Devil. With certain individuals, whose number (evidently large) it is impossible to determine with precision, this idea evolved to the degree where both sides were dehumanized and treated, some-times as the incarnation, sometimes as the agents, of supernatural powers of Good and Evil. For these people the Great War became a shadow play wherein the children of light were contending against the children of darkness. We are, therefore, actually dealing with the process by which a traditional concept, the just war, with its em-phasis on legality, on proportionality, and on peace coming about through the restoration of rights, broke down under the pressure of modern machine warfare, being replaced by the crusade, an older, more dangerous, but emotionally more satisfying concept. To die for one's country, that was sweet and proper; but to fall in the assault on the citadel of Satan, that was almost Christlike.

Viewing the struggle against the background of the crusading frame of mind explains many things: why so many religious people took an uncompromising stand regarding peace; why, when the 1914 concensus began to weaken after 1917 under the pressure of the ceaseless carnage in the West and the Soviet defection, they held firm when others—the Lansdownes, elements of the trade union movement, and the socialists—wavered, redoubling their efforts to bolster efforts on the home front. Having once transformed a just war for limited ends into God's war for supernatural ends, they became immobilized emotionally and intellectually, unable to retreat from their position. The sword had been drawn; it had been blessed by the Almighty. Whatever the cost in gold and blood, there must be no sheathing it until His cause triumphed. Ignoring the pleas of the few dissenters who feared the consequences of trying to crush Germany, most churchgoing Anglicans insisted upon a hard, dictated peace. Rudyard Kipling captured their mood when he warned:

> Heavy the load we undergo,
> And our own hands prepare,
> If we parley with the foe,
> The load our souls must bear.

The date of this poem is important; it appeared in the *Times* on October 24, 1918, less than a month before the Armistice. If anything, it must be concluded that, on the whole, public opinion, and clerical opinion with it, became more intransigent as the struggle drew to a close.

The crusade, in reality an attempt on the emotional level to refurbish the nineteenth century illusion of eternal peace, progress, and prosperity by casting out the German Devil, ultimately had a chastening influence upon church and nation. The realization in later years that they had been taken in by propaganda as well as by their own predispositions induced a sense of shame and disappointment. The world had not been made safe for democracy, and England had to shoulder its share of the blame for the state of postwar Europe.

The England that faced Hitler's legions in 1939 was a more mature nation than the one that confronted the kaiser in 1914. There was no exultation or bluster in 1939. No wild sermons or fantastic claims to otherworldly objectives reverberated from the pulpits. No angels were seen over Dunkirk. The kind of talk and symbolism that went down so easily in 1914 had lost its emotive power by 1939. This change was confirmed by none other than Hensley Henson, by then bishop of Durham. When asked to preach to the troops in the first month of the war, Henson confided to his diary: "What can I say to these young soldiers which is fitting, helpful and definitely Christian? The conventional patriotic tub-thumping is out of the question. We have got past that phase. As Nurse Cavell said, 'Patriotism is not enough.' "[8]

The mood of the 'thirties partially accounts for this sobriety. A new generation had come into its own; one that had no memory of the great Queen; one for whom the prosperity, confidence, and peace of England's golden century was only something to be read about in books. The young man of the 'thirties had only the Depression and the labor exchange. By the same token, war in 1914 came when people were least prepared for it, when international tensions seemed to be abating. Mussolini's Ethiopian adventure, Franco's rape of the Spanish republic, and Hitler's antics habituated Englishmen psychologically to the idea of a Second World War years before it became an actuality.

There has been a turning away from crusading and a partial return to just war norms since the Great War. Anglican Englishmen, reflecting the national mood, entered the struggle against the Nazis, about as genuine a holy cause as it is possible to imagine, with a spirit of sadness and resignation. Church spokesmen pleaded for restraint in prosecuting the conflict. A measure of the distance they had come is revealed during that terrible winter of 1940, when the *Church Times* came forward to proclaim, softly and eloquently: "The reason why, even to win the war or win it quickly, this country cannot adopt methods of the jungle is simply that it does not wish the world to be a jungle when the war is finished. . . . The allied nations are dedicated to the cause of Christian civilization. . . . There are some steps they cannot take without abandoning the standards for which they are fighting."[9]

England has engaged in other armed conflicts since the above was written—in Palestine, Kenya, Malaya, Cyprus, Korea, Egypt, and Northern Ireland. None of these had degenerated into a holy war, probably because of circumstances peculiar to each and the fact that national survival was not at issue. Other countries have not followed this pattern, nor is there any guarantee that England will eschew crusading in the future. The United States, to cite the prime example from the contemporary world, believing its way of life menaced, has prosecuted some of its "smaller" wars as crusades. The battle against diabolical kaiserism has been superseded by the battle against atheistic communism, with all the attendant disproportionality of means and unwillingness to halt the violence short of total victory. For the English, at any rate, the Great War has been the last crusade.

The fact that ministers of religion responded to England's wars in much the same way as their fellow countrymen has led their detractors, evidently assuming that the clerical collar should confer a prescience and a high-mindedness denied to other mortals, to charge them with being better Englishmen than Christians. This interpretation will not do as it stands. It is as much a distortion to portray the whole body of the Anglican clergy as super patriots eager to bend Christian principles for sordid ends as it is to portray them as humble, self-effacing beings intent only upon preaching the Word.

Social living is riddled with dilemmas and ambiguities. It is impossible for the clergy, or for that matter *any* individual or group, to occupy an "Archimedian"[10] position outside the world of empirical social phenomena. The only fulcrum from which the world can be moved is in the world itself; men are bound up in, and shaped by, the very processes they must use. Such is the dilemma of all institutions within society, not something unique to the Church of England during the period under consideration in this study. These facts are, admittedly, hardly calculated to warm the heart, or inspire the regeneration of a materialistic age; they are, in fact, the stuff of tragedy.

The findings of modern behavioral science are supported in this conclusion by some of the oldest and most profound insights of the Christian religion. But whereas science treats such questions as the individual's susceptibility to propaganda and habituation to war as data, and hence morally neutral, Christianity probes deeper, fitting the data into a total doctrine of man.

The Christian view of human nature contains elements of high tragedy. Ever since God cast the first parents of our race out of Paradise, human nature has been flawed. The cry of Jeremiah that "The heart is deceitful above all things, and desperately wicked: who can know it?" (Jer. 17:9) is echoed by St. Paul, "For I delight in the law of God after the inward man. But I see another law in my members, warring against the law of my mind, and bringing me into captivity to the law of sin which is in my members" (Rom. 7:22–23).

Christianity holds that good and evil are inextricably mixed in man and will not be separated out in historical time, or, as St. Augustine would say, in the earthly City. Human perspectives are, therefore, inevitably limited, time-bound, relative, and marred by self-interest and pride; thus the human psyche is subject to "spontaneous rationalization" and the other phenomena we have described.

Even when man perceives the right course and consciously sets out to accomplish the works of righteousness, he is unable to translate his desires into morally unequivocal deeds and lasting structures. Man never acts from completely unmixed motives; nor is love ever unambiguous. As expounded by the American theologian and philosopher Reinhold Niebuhr, for whom William Temple had the highest regard as a man and a scholar, classic Christian philosophy holds that mutual love is "always arrested by reason of the fact that it seeks to relate life to life from the standpoint of the self and for the sake of the self's own happiness."[11] Similarly, a nation that pursues a policy of peace and is articulate in support of international law (both worthy ends in themselves), may be doing so as a means of preserving the status quo and its own position of power. "To subject human righteousness to the righteousness of God," Niebuhr believes, "is to realize the imperfection of all our perfections, the taint of interest in all our virtues, and the natural limitations of all our ideals."[12]

When taken to heart, this realization, unpleasant though it might be in light of the Renaissance tradition of man's innate goodness and potential omnipotence, is actually a resource of optimism and an antidote to fanaticism. As Bishops Gore and Temple tried to teach in the Great War, and as Bishop Bell never tired of reiterating in the Second World War, nations embark on crusades not merely because they are subject to certain specific strains, but also because, believing themselves to be in the right and intending to do good, they become drunk on their own self-serving self-righteousness. There is a tension in life. The fact that men individually and collectively become ego-involved in their undertakings, which aids them through generating the incentive and strength to persevere, means also that they can become wed to their mistakes. It is difficult to accept that a given policy is bad, because acceptance carries the admission that one's country and ultimately oneself has done wrong. People may want to liquidate a policy visibly wrong, such as a wasting military commitment. But at the same time the ego cannot face up to the shame that comes with admitting error, so continued, perhaps even stepped-up violence is called for.

Looking at the other side of the coin, a position of moral absolutism, literally a crusade for peace at all costs, can be as dangerous as a war to overthrow Satan. The placards carried by antiwar activists, ranging from the cry for workers to down tools rather than make weapons to slay their brothers in foreign lands in the Great War, to the "War is harmful to children and other living things" and the "Would Jesus Christ fight in Vietnam?" of our own day, betray a sentimentality and simple-mindedness about the realities of political life. For unilateral disarmament, or a unilateral declaration never to fight, or calling a unilateral stoppage to one's own half of a war may actually set the stage for even worse evils. To opt for the knife instead of the poltice is not always wrong; to cry out for peace is not always right.

In both of the situations described above, Christianity insists on the proper correctives: balance, prudence, humility, and an appreciation of the capabilities of man qua man. Two of the foremost political thinkers of our day have projected this insight into the sphere of the practical politician. Professor Hans J. Morgenthau of the University of Chicago struck a note worth pondering when he affirmed: "A man who was nothing but 'political man' would be a beast, for he would be completely lacking in moral restraints. A man who was nothing but 'moral man' would be a fool, for he would be completely lacking in prudence."[13] Going one step further, George F. Kennan, a former United States ambassador to the Soviet Union and author of the policy of "containment" has stated apropos to the Cold War and colonialism: "Let us, as Christians, view these resulting conflicts for what they are: tragic situations, in which the elements of right and wrong are indistinguishable to us . . . . Let us learn to view this whole subject of colonialism with humility, with detachment, with compassion for both sides. Let us not abuse the confidence of Christ by invoking his judgment one way or the other on situations that are obviously beyond the power of mortal men to prevent and are now beyond the power of mortal men to liquidate without pain and strife."[14] Here is the essence of realism, Christian as well as political.

The implications of this view of the human condition are equally valid for the life of the church. L. E. Elliott-Binns, the distinguished Anglican historian, has written that the duty of the church is to apply Christian standards as the perfect yardstick in judging human actions. But, he warned, as St. Francis in his day warned, "the Church can never raise the world by descending to the world's own level; it must

indeed stoop down to raise it, but at the same time it must not abandon its own foothold on higher ground."[14] Here, too, is tragedy; for
the church is constantly stumbling and losing its foothold. Since the
vast majority of its servants and communicants, like most human
beings, have been unable to see beyond their culture and themselves,
it has sanctioned and occasionally sanctified war, slavery, racism,
imperialism, and a host of other sins, venal and mortal.

The admonitions of Kennan and Elliott-Binns are councils of perfection, but they are good councils. Tragedy is alloyed with hope.
"We are troubled on every side," says Paul (II Cor. 4:8), "yet not
distressed; we are perplexed, but not in despair." Just as Christianity
sees human nature as disfigured by sin, it also recognizes that man
is, for all that, unique. Unlike the beast, programmed to fight or to
ruminate in the field, man's God-given intellect has endowed him
with the capacity for transcending himself, his society, and his time.
As long as there is life, nothing can be absolutely "settled."

For churchmen, as for all "intellectuals," noblesse oblige is the
watchword. To him who is given special favor, upon him are imposed special responsibilities. It is given to certain men to see more
deeply into issues than their contemporaries; courage is given to a
few of these to act on their insights. It is the duty of such men to warn
and prod their fellowmen into recognizing and striving to realize the
potentialities of their better selves. To do this, they must expose the
relative and self-interested character of the ideologies of their fellowmen, thereby neutralizing their explosive qualities. Yet, the task of
the saint, the prophet, and the hero is difficult, for he always runs the
risk of becoming eccentric. It is never enough to "know" the truth.
The vision of the prophet, however valid, is useless for good unless he
can persuade others of its truth and mobilize their energies; and he
can never do this by flaunting their "erroneous" beliefs. Likewise,
being only human, the prophet, too, is subject to the defects of his
nature. Pascal rightly observes that humility can become a source of
pride. But without those capable of seeing at least a little beyond their
own time and situation, without the Gores, the Temples, and yes,
even the Davidsons in the Great War, as well as the Bells, the Nie-
moellers, and the Bonhoeffers in a later conflict, the human tragedy
would be tragedy unmitigated.

NOTES

I. CHURCH, STATE, AND SOCIETY

1. Benjamin Disraeli, *"Church and Queen":Four Speeches* (1865), 18.
2. Chadwick, II, 241.
3. *Ch. Cong. Rpt.* (1872), 309.
4. Ibid. (1906), 21.
5. See in addition to the above: G. F. A. Best, *Temporal Pillars: Queen Anne's Bounty, The Ecclesiastical Commissioners, and the Church of England* (Cambridge, 1964), ch. IV, for the view in 1770–1840; Samuel Taylor Coleridge, *Essays on Church and State* (1838); Thomas Arnold, *Principles of Church Reform* (1833); W. E. Gladstone, *The State and its Relations to the Church*, 2 v. (1841).
6. Mandell Creighton, *The Church and the Nation: Charges and Addresses* (1901), 28, 48.
7. *Lords' Debates*, XIII (1913), 1205.
8. Cf. J. E. C. Welldon, *The Consecration of the State* (1902).
9. H. M. Burge, *A Charge Delivered to the Clergy and Workers of the Diocese of Southwark* (1916), 50–51; William Temple, *Theology, the Science of Religion* (1914), 14–15.
10. E. F. Benson, *As We Were: A Victorian Peep Show* (1930), 66.
11. W. R. Inge, *The Church in the World* (1927). The dean used this quotation in several places, without identifying the source; I have been unsuccessful in tracing it.
12. *Ch. Cong. Rpt.* (1896), 68–69. Ridding's speech, a brilliant and short exposition of the Anglican position, has much in common with the views of Matthew Arnold in the long preface to *Culture and Society* (1869).
13. Ibid., 69.
14. Stewart Headlam, quoted in Alec R. Vidler, *The Church in an Age of Revolution* (1961), 99.
15. The trials and tribulations of the church in this period are ably chronicled by P. T. Marsh in *The Victorian Church in Decline: Archbishop Tait and the Church of England, 1868–1882* (Pittsburgh, 1969).
16. *Lords' Debates*, XIII (1913), 1200.
17. *Report of the Archbishop's Committee on Church and State* (1917), 29.
18. *The Life and Correspondence of William Connor Magee*, 2 v. (1896), II, 37.
19. *K. Marx and F. Engels: On Religion* (Moscow, 1957), 125.
20. Hippolyte Taine, *Notes on England* (New York, 1876), 194.
21. Ignatius von Döllinger, *The Church and the Churches*, trans. W. B. McCabe (1862), 145.
22. W. R. Inge, *Outspoken Essays* (1920), 264. Dean Inge thought it could be verified scientifically and gave his own family as proof.
23. J. E. C. Welldon, "The Children of the Clergy," *Nineteenth Century* (Feb., 1906), passim.
24. A. M. P. Coxon, "Patterns of Occupational Recruitment: The Anglican Ministry," *Sociology* (Jan., 1967), 75; Leslie Paul, *The Deployment and Payment of the Clergy* (1964), 282.
25. By 1960, slightly better than 50 percent had landed and peerage connections. Paul, *Deployment and Payment of the Clergy*, 110, 285; R. B. McDowell, "The Anglican Episcopate," *Theology* (June, 1947), 202.
26. N. G. Annan, "The Intellectual Aristocracy," in J. H. Plumb, ed., *Studies in Social History: A Tribute to G. M. Trevelyan* (1955).
27. W. R. Inge, *Outspoken Essays: Second Series* (1925), 260–261.

28. Paul, *Deployment and Payment of the Clergy*, 283; McDowell, "Anglican Episcopate," 208; Coxon, "Patterns of Occupational Recruitment," 75.

29. J. E. C. Welldon, *Recollections and Reflections* (1915), 28.

30. Coxon, "Patterns of Occupational Recruitment," 75.

31. Paul, *Deployment and Payment of the Clergy*, 111.

32. W. J. Guttsman, *The British Political Elite* (1963), 99.

33. I.e. Eton, Harrow, Winchester, Marlborough, Shrewsbury, Rugby, Westminster, Charterhouse, Hailsbury, King Edward's (Birmingham); cf. Paul, *Deployment and Payment of the Clergy*, 283.

34. Welldon, *Recollections*, 45.

35. Charles Booth, *Life and Labour of the People of London*, third series, *Religious Influences*, 7 v. (1902), VII, 396, 419–420.

36. Randall Thomas Davidson, ed., *The Six Lambeth Conferences, 1867–1920* (1929), 358. The figures given here are slightly higher than those in *Facts and Figures about the Church of England* (1962), prepared by the Statistical Unit of the Central Board of Finance of the Church of England.

37. Davidson, *Six Lambeth Conferences*, 359.

38. *Facts and Figures*, 26. The average age in 1964 was 54; Anthony Sampson, *Anatomy of Britain Today* (New York, 1966), 182.

39. *Ch. Cong. Rpt.* (1908), 186, 176.

40. H. E. Ryle, Bishop of Exeter, ibid. (1901), 148.

41. Convocation Report No. 343 of the Committee of the Lower House of the Convocation of Canterbury on the Supply and Training of Candidates for Holy Orders, *Chron. Conv. Cant.* (1900), 15.

42. Ibid., 360–361.

43. Cf. W. J. Reader, *Professional Men: The Rise of the Professional Classes in Nineteenth-Century England* (1966).

44. *Chron. Conv. Cant.* (1901), 376. T. W. Bamford, however, points out in *The Rise of the Public Schools* (1967), 222, that, whereas the public school recruitment dwindled, given the drop in ordinands, the public school contribution to the church "remained important and dominant."

45. J. N. Figgis, *Religion and English Society* (1910), 31–32; F. J. Foakes-Jackson, *Ch. Cong. Rpt.* (1902), 387–388.

46. J. H. B. Masterman, ed., *Clerical Incomes: An Inquiry into the Cost of Living among the Parochial Clergy* (1920), 14.

47. Convocation Report No. 513 of the Committee of the Lower House of the Convocation of Canterbury on Tithe Rent-Charge, *Chron. Conv. Cant.* (1918), 3.

48. Ibid., 4, 15.

49. *Ch. Cong. Rpt.* (1896), 465–466.

50. Arthur Newsholme and H. C. Stevenson, "The Decline of Human Fertility in the United Kingdom and other Countries," *Journal of the Royal Statistical Society*, LXIX (1906), 66.

51. Ibid., 68; cf. J. A. Banks, *Prosperity and Parenthood* (1954).

52. J. W. Taylor, *The Diminishing Birth Rate* (1904), passim.; Arthur Foley Winnington-Ingram, *Fifty Years' Work in London* (1940), 48–53.

53. Banks, *Prosperity*, 142; J. A. and Olive Banks, *Feminism and Family Planning in Victorian England* (1964), 86.

54. Masterman, *Clerical Incomes*, 270.

55. *Ch. Cong. Rpt.* (1897), 416.

56. *Chron. Conv. Cant.* (1901), 132–133.

57. F. C. Arnold-Jarvis, *Ch. Cong. Rpt.* (1908), 505.

58. Chadwick, II, 212; Louis Dibdin, chancellor of the Dioceses of Durham and Rochester, *Ch. Cong. Rpt.* (1896), 181–186.

59. William Temple, *The Life of Bishop Percival* (1921), 343–344.

60. A. C. Headlam, *The Revenues of the Church of England* (1917), 10–11, 79.

61. Masterman, *Clerical Incomes*, 9–12.

62. *Chron. Conv. Cant.* (1901), 148.

63. *Ch. Cong. Rpt.* (1896), 468.

64. Masterman, *Clerical Incomes*, 6–7.

65. Richard Mudie-Smith, *The Religious Life of London* (1904), 20.

66. *Report of the Commission of Enquiry into the Property and Revenues of the Church* (1924), 15.

67. Headlam, *Revenues*, 13.

68. Ibid., 78.

69. *Ch. Cong. Rpt.* (1899), 38, 43.

70. Cf. Robert Dolling, *Ten Years in a Portsmouth Slum* (1897).

71. Booth, *Life and Labour*, VII, 80–81.

72. C. T. Fry, *Ch. Cong. Rpt.* (1908), 496; Charles Gore, ed. *Essays in Aid of the Reform of the Church* (1898), 258.

73. *Chron. Conv. Cant.* (1900), 431.

74. *Ch. Cong. Rpt.* (1908), 489.

75. Best, *Temporal Pillars*, 506.

76. Dolling, *Ten Years*, 83–86.

77. *Ch. Cong. Rpt.* (1908), 509.

78. Report No. 343, 12.

79. Ibid., 10–13.

80. *Ch. Cong. Rpt.* (1897), 400; (1902), 395.

81. Davidson, *Six Lambeth Conferences*, 350.

82. Quoted in G. L. Prestige, *The Life of Charles Gore* (1935), 218.

83. Chadwick, II, 225.

84. *Ch. Cong. Rpt.* (1904), 59–60.

85. Mudie-Smith, *Religious Life of London*, passim.

86. A. R. Buckland, secretary of the Religious Tract Society, *Ch. Cong. Rpt.* (1904), 60; Arnold Taylor, "Hodge and His Parson," *Nineteenth Century* (March, 1892), 359–362; Chadwick, ch. IV. sec. I.

87. Booth, *Life and Labour*, VII, 423.

88. C. F. G. Masterman, *In Peril of Charge* (1905), 274.

89. Prestige, *Gore*, 265–266.

90. Mudie-Smith, *Religious Life of London*, 282.

91. Masterman, *Peril*, 261.

92. Gladstone, quoted in Figgis, *Religion in English Society*, 26; Barnett in George Haw, ed., *Christianity and the Working Classes* (1906), 98.

93. G. S. Spinks, ed., *Religion in Britain since 1900* (1952), n. 16.

94. Masterman, *Peril*, 294.

95. C. F. G. Masterman, *The Condition of England* (1909), 263.

96. Booth, *Life and Labour*, VII, 428–429.

97. *Ch. Cong. Rpt.* (1898), 83.

98. Mudie-Smith, *Religious Life of London*, 98.

99. Arthur Foley Winnington-Ingram, *Work in Great Cities* (1895), 13, 16.

100. C. L. Drawbridge, *Popular Attacks on Christianity* (1913), 20.

101. A useful general account is W. S. Smith, *The London Heretics, 1870–1914* (New York, 1968); and Susan Budd, "The Loss of Faith: Reasons for Unbelief among Members of the Secular Movement in England, 1850–1950," in *Past and Present* (April, 1967).

102. Winnington-Ingram, *Work in Great Cities*, 34.

103. "Not Negotiable," *C.T.*, 3 Aug. 1914; Drawbridge, *Popular Attacks*, passim., and Clement F. Rogers, *Question Time in Hyde Park* (1918).

104. Randall Davidson, *Official Year-Book of the Church of England* (1885), 127–128; Chadwick, II, 263.

105. Haw, *Christianity and the Working Classes*, 15.

106. Masterman, *Peril*, 272.

107. Frederic Harrison, "Church and State," *Fortnightly Review*, XXVII (1877), 672.

108. H. A. James, *Ch. Cong. Rpt.* (1908), 179.

109. Mudie-Smith, *Religious Life of London*, 30–31.

110. *London Diocesan Magazine* (Aug., 1917), 198.

111. Haw, *Christianity and the Working Classes*, 54.

112. J. A. Castle, "Causes of the Church's Failure," *CH*, 1 Dec. 1917.

113. David Martin, *A Sociology of English Religion* (1967), 58.

114. H. H. Asquith, speech on "The Political Aspects of the Establishment Question" (1890).

115. McDowell, "The Anglican Episcopate"; Chadwick, II, ch. VI, pt. I.

116. *Lords' Debates*, CLXXIV (1909), 4.

117. Temple, *Percival*, 224.

118. McDowell, "The Anglican Episcopate," 206.

119. *Lords' Debates*, CLXXIV (1909), 5.

120. Cf. Roy Jenkins, *Mr. Balfour's Poodle*, (New York, 1954).

121. Quoted in Percy Dearmer, "Housing the Poor," *C.W.P.*, 12 Aug. 1902.

122. Booth, *Life and Labour, Poverty Series*, II, 21; B. Seebohm Rowntree's *Poverty: A Study of Town Life* (1899) set the figure for York at 27.84 percent, 229.

123. Canon Rawnsley of Carlisle, *C.W.P.*, 30 Aug. 1902.

124. Randall Davidson, visitation charge, *C.T.*, 16 Feb. 1912.

125. Mudie-Smith, *Religious Life of London*, 13.

126. Cf. Peter d'A. Jones, *The Christian Socialist Revival, 1877–1914* (Princeton, 1968).

127. Ibid., ch. VI.

128. M. B. Reckitt, *Faith and Society* (1932), 92; *Maurice to Temple* (1946), 138.

129. Quoted in K. S. Inglis, *Churches and the Working Classes in Victorian England* (1963), 280.

130. James Adderley quoted in Reckitt, *Faith and Society*, 106.

131. *The General Report of the Pan-Anglican Congress*, 8 v. (1908), II, 100–103.

132. Quoted in Inge, *Outspoken Essays*, I, 130.

133. Inge, *Church and the Age*, 69ff.; *Outspoken Essays*, I, 131.

134. *C.T.*, 14 Aug. 1908.

135. Inglis, *Churches and the Working Classes*, 287.

136. Ibid., 279–280; cf. Stephen Mayor, *The Churches and the Labour Movement* (1967).

137. Geoffrey Best, *Bishop Westcott and the Miners* (1967), 34.

138. Jones, *Christian Socialist Revival*, 182–183; Chadwick, II, 284–285; C. K. Francis Brown, *A History of the English Clergy, 1800–1900* (1953), 231.

139. Lansbury in Haw, *Christianity and the Working Classes*, 167–168; Bell, 488–490; Jones, *Christian Socialist Revival*, 186–187.

140. *G.*, 13 April, 1898; *C.F.N.*, 29 April 1898, Oct. 1897–Jan. 1898, 17 Aug. 1894.

141. *G.*, 11 Nov. 1901; *C.F.N.* 26 July 1901, 12 April 1908.

142. *G.*, 4 April 1906.

143. Ibid., 13 May 1908.

144. Mayor, *The Churches and the Labour Movement* contains more examples than can, or need, be cited here.

145. Cf. A. Ellegard, *Darwin and the General Reader, 1858–1872* (Götebourg, 1968).

146. *Ch. Cong. Rpt.* (1896), 132.

147. Chadwick, II, 146.

148. H. G. Wood, *Belief and Unbelief since 1850* (1955), 51.

149. Chadwick, II, 104; Dean Inge's "Bishop Gore and the Church of England"

in the first series of his *Outspoken Essays* is a just contemporary (1908) appreciation of his contribution to Anglican thought.

150. Figgis, *Religion and English Society*, 15.

151. Adolf von Harnack, *What is Christianity?* (1901), 94.

152. W. R. Inge, *The Church and the Age* (1911), 16; Percy Dearmer in Andrew Reid, ed., *The New Party* (1895), 4.

153. Winnington-Ingram, *Fifty Years*, 234; *Under the Dome* (1902), 236.

154. Albert Schweitzer, *The Quest for the Historical Jesus* (New York, 1948), 289.

155. J. K. Mozley, *Some Tendencies in English Theology from the Publication of Lux Mundi to the Present Day* (1951), 36.

156. Schweitzer, *Quest*, 354.

157. J. H. F. Peile, *The Reproach of the Gospel* (1907), 125.

158. Hastings Rashdall, *Ideas and Ideals* (1928), 112; cf. *Conscience and Christ* (1916), 274–275.

159. Cf. Alec R. Vidler, *The Modernist Movement in the Roman Church* (1934).

160. W. J. Scott, "An 'Advanced' View of the Church Crisis," *Nineteenth Century* (April, 1901), 680.

161. Temple, *Percival*, 347–348.

162. Quoted in *M.C.* (Jan., 1915), 498.

163. *G.*, 4 April 1914; *M.C.* (April, 1914), 4–5 (Nov., 1914), 441; H.M. Smith, *Frank, Bishop of Zanzibar* (1926), 177.

164. *Ch. Cong. Rpt.* (1895), 345.

165. Prestige, *Gore*, 243–246.

166. William Sanday, *Bishop Gore's Challenge to Criticism* (1914); H. M. Gwatkin, *The Bishop of Oxford's Open Letter* (1914): A. C. Headlam, "Nature, Miracles and the Virgin Birth," *C.Q.R.* (Oct., 1914).

167. *C.Q.R.* (Oct., 1914), 4; H. D. A. Major, "An Anglican Pope," *M.C.* (May, 1914).

168. Bell, 292–294; Smith, *Frank*, 186.

169. Roger Lloyd, *The Church of England, 1900–1965* (1966), 111; Smith, *Frank*, 171; H. H. Henson, "Kikuyu," *M.C.* (Oct., 1914); Bell, ch. XLII.

170. Kikuyu was settled tentatively at Easter, 1915, when Davidson issued a judgment condemning what had taken place at Kikuyu as irregular in form but meritorious in motive. Randall Davidson, *Kikuyu* (1915).

II. THE COMING OF THE GREAT WAR

1. *C.T.*, 21 Jan. 1914; *G.*, 2 Jan. 1914.

2. *G.*, 23 Dec. 1913.

3. Ian Colvin, *Carson the Statesman* (New York, 1935), 150.

4. *G.*, 27 Feb. 1914.

5. *C.T.*, 11 Oct. 1912.

6. *C.F.N.*, 30 Jan. 1914.

7. *C.T.*, 11 Oct. 1912.

8. Ibid., 8 Nov. 1912.

9. *G.*, 6 March 1914.

10. Robert Blake, *The Unknown Prime Minister: The Life and Times of Andrew Bonar Law* (1955), 194; Bell, 720–730.

11. Cf. Fred Crawford, *Guns for Ulster* (1947).

12. These events are graphically described in George Dangerfield's *The Strange Death of Liberal England, 1910–1914* (New York, 1961).

13. *C.T.*, 28 Nov. 1913.

14. Dangerfield, *Strange Death*, 307, 395, 400; cf. E. H. Phelps Brown, *The*

Growth of British Industrial Relations: A Study from the Standpoint of 1906–1914 (1959), passim.

15. *C.T.*, 11 July 1914; Egerton Swann, "The Soul of a Dean," *The Optimist*, 15 April 1914.

16. Thusfar there is no authoritative study of the status of women in Victorian and Edwardian society, or of the socio-psychological-economic factors impelling women to demand the franchise. Dangerfield's work is suggestive for the period immediately preceding the war, as are J. A. Banks, *Prosperity and Parenthood* and J. A. Banks and Olive Banks, *Feminism and Family Planning in Victorian England* (Liverpool, 1964), for the earlier period. Ray Strachey's *The Cause, A Short History of the Women's Movement* (1928) and Josephine Kamm's *Rapiers and Battleaxes: The Women's Movement and its Aftermath* (1966) say more about the movement from an organizational and political than from the psychological standpoint.

17. *Suffragette*, 22 May 1914.

18. *Lincoln Gazette*, 1 Aug. 1914.

19. *C.T.*, 15 March 1912.

20. On "The Perfect Wife" in Victorian times, see Banks, *Feminism and Family Planning*, ch. V.

21. *C.T.*, 22 March 1912.

22. "Wifely Obedience," ibid., 6 March 1914; W. E. Barnes, "Feminism," *G.*, 1 Aug. 1913.

23. Davidson to Dorothy Davis, 11 May 1908; to R. E. Purdy, 5 Jan. 1910; to unnamed correspondent, 19 June 1914, Davidson MSS.

24. Davidson to unnamed correspondent, 19 June 1914, ibid.

25. Alice M. Kidd to Davidson, n.d., ibid.

26. Annie Kenney, *Memories of a Militant* (1924), 248–249.

27. *C.T.*, 30 May 1913, 5 June 1913, 20 March 1914, 4 June 1914.

28. J. A. Hobson, *The Psychology of Jingoism* (1901), 27, 41.

29. Cf. A. J. P. Taylor, *The Troublemakers: Dissent over Foreign Policy, 1792–1939* (1957), 77–78.

30. *Ch. Cong. Rpt.* (1896), 424.

31. Quoted in ibid. (1900), 193.

32. Arthur Westcott, *The Life and Letters of Brooke Foss Westcott*, 2 v. (1903), II, 287; *C.F.N.*, 12 Jan. 1900.

33. Henry Scott Holland, "The Relief of Mafeking," *C.W.P.*, 23 May 1900.

34. I have consulted the *Peace Year Book*, reports of the various Universal Peace Congresses, the *Monthly Circular* of the National Peace Council for the years 1900–1914, the reports of the annual meetings of the Lake Mohonk conferences in New York state, and the standard history of the peace movement, A. C. F. Beales, *The History of Peace* (1931).

35. *Peace Year Book* (1910), 42.

36. Ibid. (1910–1913), passim.

37. *G.*, 10 July 1907.

38. *C.T.*, 12 July 1907; *Chron. Conv. Cant.* (1907), 75–77.

39. W. T. Stead, "Impressions from the Hague," *Contemporary Review*, CXII (1907), 722–723.

40. Cf. P. J. N. Baker, *The Life of J. Allen Baker* (1927).

41. *Peace and the Churches: Souvenier Volume of the Visit to England of Representatives of the German Christian Churches, May 26 to June 3, 1908* (1908).

42. *Chron. Conv. Cant.* (1909), 228.

43. National Council of Peace Societies, *Official Report of the Seventeenth Universal Congress of Peace* (1909), 452–457, 461. Hereafter cited as *Seventeenth Universal Congress of Peace*.

44. Ibid., 106–107; Davidson, *Six Lambeth Conferences*, 312.

45. *Seventeenth Universal Congress of Peace*, 202–212.
46. Ibid., 262–263.
47. Beales, *History of Peace*, 267.
48. J. Allen Baker, *The Churches and International Friendship: Conference at Constance, August 1st to 5th, 1914* (n.p., n.d.).
49. Davidson, *Six Lambeth Conferences*, 2–7, 312.
50. Church of England Peace League, *Annual Report* (1914), 7.
51. W. L. Grane, *The Passing of War* (2nd. ed., 1912), 166.
52. *Peace and the Churches*, 203, 240; *Ch. Cong. Rpt.* (1913), 208.
53. *Peace Year Book* (1914), 5.
54. H. N. Brailsford, *The War of Steel and Gold* (1914), 35.
55. *Seventeenth Universal Congress of Peace*, 78. For much of the same see, Lord Courtney of Penwith, ibid., 213–214; Sir Frank Lascelles, former ambassador to Berlin and uncle of William Temple, *Ch. Cong. Rpt.* (1911), 192; T. J. Lawrence, ibid., 188.
56. Charles Plater, *A Primer of Peace and War* (1915), 166–167.
57. Clive Trebilcock, "Legends of the British Armament Industry, 1890–1914," *The Journal of Contemporary History*, V, no. 4 (1970).
58. *Chron. Conv. Cant.* (1907), 79. In 1911, Davidson's wife launched the battleship *Thunderer, Times*, 2 Feb. 1911.
59. *C.T.*, 3 July 1914; *CH*, 3 July 1914.
60. *G.*, 2 July 1914; *CH*, 3 July 1914.
61. "The Perils of Kingship," *C.T.*, 3 July 1914.
62. *G.*, 28 July 1911.
63. Harnack to Pfarrer Siegmund Schultz, 17 Jan. 1912, Davidson Mss.; Bell, 656–659.
64. Bell, 661; *Nation*, 15 Dec. 1913.
65. *Times*, 18 July 1914.
66. *Commons Debates*, LXV (1914), 727–728.
67. *C.T.*, 24 July 1914; *C.F.N.*, 17 July 1914.
68. Bark Bonham Carter, ed., *The Autobiography of Margot Asquith* (Boston, 1963), 280.
69. *C.F.N.*, 31 July 1914.
70. *G.*, "The Servian Crisis," 30 July 1914.
71. Bell, 734.
72. Memory of the Dogger Bank incident endured, passing into the folklore. H. A. Vachell's 1912 novel about Harrow life, *The Hill*, has a scene where a Rugger player cuts through the opponent's center "as irresistible as a Russian battleship through a fleet of fishing smacks," p. 81.
73. *Manchester Guardian*, 1 Aug. 1914.
74. Ibid., 3 Aug. 1914.
75. Ibid., 3–4 Aug. 1914.
76. Ibid., 3 Aug. 1914.
77. Bell, 733.
78. Randall Davidson, "The Meaning of the Mission," *CH*, 6 Oct. 1916; Randall Davidson, *The Testing of a Nation* (1919), 6, 12.
79. R. H. Lightfoot, "Trust in God," *CH*, 30 Oct. 1914.
80. Henson to Worsley Borden, 17 June 1915, in E. F. Brailey, ed., *The Letters of Herbert Hensley Henson* (1950), 14.
81. *British Weekly*, 6 Aug. 1914.
82. John Clifford, *Our Fight for Belgium and What it Means* (1917), 7.
83. *The Friend*, 9 Oct. 1914.
84. Ibid., 26 March 1915.
85. Church of England Peace League, *Sermon by the Right Reverend the Lord Bishop of Lincoln* (1912).

86. *C.F.N.*, 7 Aug. 1914.

87. Ibid.; Edward Lee Hicks, "The War and the Treaty of Peace," *The Optimist*, 15 Oct. 1914; J. H. Fowler, *The Life and Letters of Edward Lee Hicks* (1922), 171–172; Edward Lee Hicks, *The Church and the War* (1914), 7; *Lincoln Gazette*, 8 Aug. 1914.

88. *Ch. Cong. Rpt.* (1896), 424.

89. *Lords Debates*, CI (1902), 938–939.

90. Temple, *Percival*, 251.

91. *Chron. Conv. Cant.* (1909), 227–228.

92. *Times*, 12 Aug. 1914; *Hereford Mercury*, 30 Sept. 1914.

93. *M.C.* (May, 1915), 122–123; Temple, *Percival*, 362–363.

94. For the resolutions of the various socialist congresses see W. E. Walling, *The Socialists and the War* (New York, 1915).

95. Ben Tillett, "Why the Workers Must Fight in this War," *John Bull*, 10 Oct. 1914.

96. *Manchester Guardian*, 4 Aug. 1914; *CWTH* (Sept., 1914), 257.

97. Holland to N. S. Talbot, 6 Sept. 1914, in Paget, *Holland*, 313.

98. Ibid., 322.

99. Henry Scott Holland, "Britain's Vision and Response," *C.W.P.*, 13 Jan. 1915.

100. Egerton Swann, "The War and Socialist Doctrine," *The Optimist*, 15 Oct. 1914; Jones, *Christian Socialist Revival*, 236.

101. *C.S.* (April, 1915), 62.

102. Egerton Swann, "Socialism and Nationalism," ibid. (Oct., 1914), 195.

103. "Murder in the Thieves' Kitchen," ibid., 197.

104. Conrad Noel, *An Autobiography* (1945), 107.

105. B. W. Randolf, former principle of Ely College, "Our Refuge and Strength," *S.F.T.* (1914), 10.

106. *The Optimist*, 15 Oct. 1914.

107. *C.F.N.*, 4 Dec. 1914; cf. David Mitchell, *Women on the Warpath: The Story of the Women of the First World War* (1966), 45–63.

108. *CWTH.* (Oct., 1914), 195.

109. J. B. Waldron, "Justice or Revenge?" *John Bull,* 7 Nov. 1914.

III. THE NATURE OF THE ENEMY

1. Arthur Foley Winnington-Ingram, *A Message for the Supreme Moment* (1916), 6; cf. Arthur Foley Winnington-Ingram, *A Charge Delivered to the Clergy and Churchwardens of London in St. Paul's Cathedral, October 19, 1905.*

2. *Church Union Gazette* (Oct., 1914).

3. B. H. Streeter, "The Church's Failure and Some Remedies," *M.C.* (Aug., 1916), 205–206.

4. Hastings Rashdall, "What is a Christian Foreign Policy?" *CH*, 20 Oct. 1916.

5. Robert Woodfield, "That Catholic Faith and Revolution," *C.S.* (Sept., 1915), 173.

6. Paul Bertie Bull, *Peace and War* (1917), 102–105.

7. *Peace and the Churches*, 130.

8. Mrs. Charles Kingsley, *Charles Kingsley: His Letters and Memories of His Life*, 2 v. (1877), II, 334–335.

9. F. W. Farrar, "Keep Innocency," *C.F.N.*, 15 Dec. 1899; J. E. C. Welldon, *Ch. Cong. Rpt.* (1913), 95.

10. *Peace and the Churches*, 137.

11. Ibid., 188–189.

12. "The Blessing of War," *C.T.*, 1 Dec. 1899; *C.F.N.*, 17 Nov. 1899.

13. *Seventeenth Universal Congress of Peace*, 80.

14. J. E. Watts-Ditchfield, *Ch. Cong. Rpt.* (1913); Dr. Alfred Caldecott, dean of the faculty of theology, King's College, London, quoted in Grane, *Passing of War*, 217; *C.T.*, 10 Oct. 1913.

15. *CWTH* (Sept., 1914).

16. "Murder in the Thieves' Kitchen," 196–197.

17. William Sanday, *The Meaning of the War for Germany and Britain* (Oxford, 1915), 101–102.

18. *CWTH* (Dec., 1914), 358, 361.

19. *CH,* 22 Jan. 1915.

20. Edward Lyttelton, *What Are We Fighting For?* (1914), 30.

21. "The War," *C.T.*, 29 April 1898.

22. H. D. Rawnsley, *The European War, 1914–1915: Poems* (1915), 50.

23. Quoted in Smith, *Frank*, 186.

24. H. J. Wotherspoon, "The War and the Sins of the World," *CWTH* (Sept., 1917), 280; J. P. Malleson, "A Day of the Lord," *Contemporary Review* (Aug., 1916), 230.

25. Arthur Foley Winnington-Ingram, *Rays of Dawn* (Milwaukee, 1918), 16.

26. G. A. Studdert- Kennedy, *Rough Talks by a Padre* (1918), 122.

27. H. D. Rawnsley, *Against a Premature and Inconclusive Peace* (Carlisle, 1917), 17–18.

28. *Manchester Guardian*, 21, 26, 27 Sept. 1914.

29. F. S. Roberts, *Lord Roberts' Message to the Nation* (1912), 4–5.

30. T. T. Norgate, "What Determined 'The Day'?" *CH,* 20 Nov. 1914. The myth that the widening of the Kiel Canal was completed in accordance with a pre-determined time-table for aggression has been perpetuated by R. C. K. Ensor in *England, 1870–1914* (Oxford, 1936), 481–482. This is not to say that Germany was totally guiltless for the war. As Fritz Fischer demonstrates in his *Germany's Aims in the First World War* (New York, 1968), perhaps the most extreme of the postwar counter-revisionist works, German world policy had precipitated the crises of 1905, 1908, and 1911. Taken together, these created an atmosphere of tension wherein any minor conflict could have touched off a world conflagration. German recklessness in egging on Austria to finish off Serbia despite the certainty of drawing in the other powers undermines the argument that the war arose from a series of incredible blunders, accidents, or the necessities imposed by railway time-tables. Yet it must be reiterated that there is nothing to confirm the propagandists' claim that Germany wanted *this* particular war at *this* particular moment in history, having prepared for "the Day" years in advance.

31. J. W. Diggle, "The Inner Meaning of the War," *Nineteenth Century* (Oct., 1917), 736; Euston Nurse, *Prophecy and the War* (1915), 20.

32. M. R. Allnutt, "The Kaiser's Model: Attila, the Hun," *C.F.N.*, 12 April 1915.

33. C. R. Ball, *The War* (1914), 25.

34. Studdert-Kennedy, *Rough Talks by a Padre*, 39–41, 195.

35. Cf. Leonard Krieger, *The German Idea of Freedom* (Boston, 1957).

36. Studdert-Kennedy, *Rough Talks by a Padre*, 42, 45.

37. William Temple, *The Holy War* (1915), 12.

38. W. M. Sinclair, *Difficulties of Our Day* (1905), 46–48.

39. William II, "The Fight Against Amalek," *C.W.P.*, 23 Jan. 1901.

40. *Peace and the Churches*, 240–241.

41. Alfred E. Fried, *The German Emperor and the Peace of the World* (1912), vi.

42. *Durham Chronicle and County Gazette*, 14 Aug. 1914.

43. "The Warning from Germany," *G.*, 4 Nov. 1908.

44. There is a literature consisting of hundreds of items dealing with prophecy and the war. Some of the more lucid pieces in the collections of most large libraries

are: R. K. Arnaud, *The New Prophecy* (1917); J. Gill Ward, *The World Drama in Revelation and History* (1917); H. G. Lancaster, *Prophecy, The War, and the Near East* (1919); Paul Tyner, *Christ or Kaiser?* (1915): Marr Murray, *Bible Prophecies and the Plain Man* (1915).

45. *The Encore*, 13 Sept. 1914, 15 Oct. 1914, 26 Nov. 1914.

46. *Lincoln Gazette*, 12 Sept. 1914; *Punch*, 5 May 1915.

47. *Yorkshire Gazette*, 28 Nov. 1914.

48. J. G. Lockhart, *Cosmo Gordon Lang* (1949), 249.

49. Quoted in Charles Smyth, *Cyril Forster Garbett* (1959), 401.

50. *R.*, 4 May 1916; Studdert-Kennedy, *Rough Talks by a Padre*, 195.

51. On the sociology of intellectuals and their use of ideological tools as weapons see: Seymour Martin Lipset, *Political Man: The Social Bases of Politics* (Garden City, 1963); H. H. Gerth and C. Wright Mills, *From Max Weber: Essays in Sociology* (New York, 1967); Roberto Michels, "Intellectuals," *The Encyclopedia of the Social Sciences* (New York, 1935); Georg Simmel, *Conflict* (Glencoe, 1964); Joseph Schumpeter, *Capitalism, Socialism and Democracy* (New York, 1942), 145–155.

52. H. G. Wells, "The War of the Mind," in *The War That Will End War* (New York, 1914), 97, 98.

53. Karl Mannheim, *Ideology and Utopia: An Introduction to the Sociology of Knowledge* (New York, 1936), 159.

54. "The War," *Church Intelligencer* (March, 1915).

55. W. H. G. Armytage, *Four Hundred Years of English Education* (1964), 185.

56. A. C. Benson, *The Upton Letters* (New York, 1906), 160–161; see also his *The Schoolmaster: A Commentary Upon the Aims and Methods of an Assistant-Master in a Public School* (New York, 1908).

57. "The Position of German in English Schools," *Modern Language Teaching* (April, 1908), 68–81; "The Study of German in Public Secondary Schools," ibid. (Nov., 1908), 195–198; *Report of the Annual Meeting . . . of the Anglo-German Friendship Society* (1911), 7–8.

58. A. C. Headlam, *The Training of Candidates for Ordination* (1913).

59. M. G. Glazebrook, et al., "The Training of Ordinands," *M.C.* (March, 1917), 583; A. C. Headlam, "The National Mission," *C.Q.R.* (Oct., 1916), 16.

60. Winnington-Ingram, *Work in Great Cities*, 46.

61. Creighton, *Church and Nation*, 230.

62. Bell, 489.

63. Quoted in Arthur Marwick, *The Deluge: British Society and the First World War* (Boston, 1965), 45.

64. A sampling of the literature, consisting of some two thousand sermons and several hundred pamphlets and articles, discloses no mention of other German intellectuals. Houston Stewart Chamberlain's *Foundations of the Nineteenth Century* 2 v. (1911),whose racist, anti-Semitic interpretation of history made him so vulnerable, was mentioned only once by a clergyman, Dean Inge. Hegel, Schopenhauer, Werner Sombart, Max Weber, Thomas Mann, Friedrich Meinecke—a bevy of intellectuals who either played a key role in shaping the German mind or used their abilities to support extreme nationalism—were not mentioned at all.

65. F. S. Roberts, "The Supreme Duty of the Citizen in the Present Crisis," *Hibbert Journal* (Oct., 1914), 5.

66. J. A. Cramb, *Germany and England* (1914), 6, 78.

67. Walter Kaufmann, *Nietzsche* (New York, 1956), 362; *Peace Year Book* (1915), 117–118.

68. Crane Brinton, *Nietzsche* (New York, 1965), 202.

69. Arthur Foley Winnington-Ingram, "The Holy War," *S.F.T.* (1914), 6.

70. Fritz Stern, *The Politics of Cultural Despair* (Garden City, 1965), 344.

71. W. R. Inge, *Faith and Knowledge* (Edinburgh, 1905), 115; "Nietzsche and the Philosophy of Violence," *R.*, 4 Dec. 1914, 11 Dec. 1914.

72. F. R. Barry, *Religion and the War* (1915), 8.

73. Figgis, *Religion and English Society*, 33; cf. his *Studies in Political Thought from Gerson to Grotius*, 1st ed. (1907), 84.

74. F. R. Barry, "Tolstoy, Nietzsche, and the Cross," *Interpreter* (April, 1915); *The War and Christian Ethics* (1914); John Neville Figgis, *The Will to Freedom, or the Gospel of Nietzsche and the Gospel of Christ* (1917).

75. Tyner, *Kaiser or Christ?* 23.

76. Brinton, *Nietzsche*, 201.

77. Bainbridge Bell, "Christ or Nietzsche?" *CH*, 9 Oct. 1914.

78. C. L. Drawbridge, *Christianity and War* (n.d.), 7, 9.

79. Friedrich Nietzsche, *The Case of Wagner*, para. 4.

80. J. P. Malleson, "A Day of the Lord," *Contemporary Review* (Aug., 1916), 231; James Plowden-Wardlaw, *The Test of the War* (1916), 45, 49.

81. Ibid., 44–45; Percy Dearmer, *Patriotism* (Oxford, 1915), 8; G. A. Studdert-Kennedy, *The Hardest Part* (1918), 37; *CWTH* (Oct., 1914), 293.

82. Sanday, *The Meaning of the War*, 56.

83. Barbara W. Tuchman, *The Proud Tower, A Portrait of the World Before the War, 1890–1914* (New York, 1966), 331; Koppel S. Pinson, *Modern Germany* (New York, 1966), 309. In his plan to dismember Germany after the Second World War, Henry Morganthau, Jr., secretary of the Treasury under Franklin Roosevelt, took note of the persistence of the ideas of General Bernhardt [sic] in German thought; he also quoted from works written by Treitschke in 1916!—such is the stuff of decisions on the highest levels of government! Henry Morganthau, Jr., *Germany is Our Problem* (New York, 1945), 109–110.

84. There was an element of rought justice in his treatment by the army. Bernhardi had some contemptible personal qualities, revealed when he challenged a brother officer, half-blind and invalided in the war of 1870, to a duel for criticizing the historical writings of the General Staff. A court of honor later upheld Bernhardi's action, depriving the officer of the right to wear the uniform. Alfred Vagts, *A History of Militarism* (New York, 1959), 26.

85. Friedrich von Bernhardi, *Denkwüdigkeiten aus meinem Leben* (Berlin, 1927), 367; *The Optimist*, 15 Oct. 1914, 188; C. E. Playne, *The Neuroses of the Nations* (New York, 1925), 141; Karl Demeter, *The German Officer Corps in State and Society* (1965), n. 391.

86. Bernhardi, *Germany and the Next War*, 19, 45, 48, 79, 85. Treitschke said much the same thing: "A state that set out to despise faith and loyalty on principle, would continually be threatened by enemies, and therefore would entirely fail to attain its purpose of being a physical power." *Politik*, II, 455.

87. *Nineteenth Century* (Oct., 1914).

88. *C.T.*, 9 Oct. 1914.

89. *Appeal to Evangelical Christians Abroad* (1914), 19–20.

90. *To the Christian Scholars of Europe and America* (Oxford, 1914).

91. *C.T.*, 2 Oct. 1914; *C.F.N.*, 2 Oct. 1914; *CH*, 19 Sept. 1914; *R.*, 27 Aug. 1914, 1 Oct. 1914.

92. *C.F.N.*, 21 Jan. 1916, published a number of excerpts from German sermons; these were taken from the *Methodist Times*, 13 Jan. 1916. Cf. A. Shadwell, "German War Sermons," *Hibbert Journal* (July, 1916).

93. Hensley Henson, to cite a notable example, believed that Lutheranism was partially responsible for preparing the way for Hitler. *The Good Fight* (1940), 14.

94. Viscount Halifax, ed., *Some Considerations Affecting Religion Arising Out of the War* (1914), 21; Plowden-Wardlaw, *The Test of the War*, 26; H. W. Hutton, "Two Ideals of Life," *G.*, 10 July 1916.

95. Golo Mann, *The History of Modern Germany since 1789* (New York, 1968), 10.

96. C. E. Osborne, *Religion in Europe and the World Crisis* (1916), 159; Herbert Bury, "Is Anything Wrong with German Protestantism?" *Nineteenth Century* (Feb., 1916), 363.

97. J. F. Foakes-Jackson, "German Theology and the War," *M.C.* (Oct., 1914), 339–340; Osborne, *Religion in Europe*, 10.

98. Dr. Arnold quoted in *C.F.N.*, 26 Oct. 1917; Bishop King, ibid., 23 June 1916.

99. *R.*, 3 June 1915; Philip Norton, *C.F.N.*, 16 Aug. 1915; cf. *R. O. P.* Taylor, *Germanism at its Great Assize* (1914), 1–8.

100. *C.T.*, 15 Jan. 1915; H. R. Baylis, *The War From a Churchman's Point of View* (1914), 18. Dean Inge ridiculed such ertremists without mercy: "It appears that the sack of Louvain and the destruction of Rheims Cathedral are the logical applications either of the Lutheran doctrine of justification or of the higher criticism. Surely, after such an object-lesson, we shall give up these errors and return to orthodox Catholicism, the creed of Alva and Torquemada, or to the simple Christianity of the gentle Cromwell." *C.W.P.*, 6 Dec. 1914.

101. Foakes-Jackson, "German Theology and the War," 340.

102. Halifax, *Some Considerations*, 21. It is perhaps ironic that during the 1913 debate on Welsh disestablishment Lord Halifax praised the kaiser for fostering in Germany a sense of the necessity of religion to character-building and as a prop to the state. *Lords' Debates*, XIII (1913), 1126.

103. W. R. Inge, *Lay Thoughts of a Dean* (1926), 311; W. Danks, "The Consecration of War," *M.C.* (Jan., 1915), 653; Bull, *Peace and War*, 50.

104. Hooker, *Laws of Ecclesiastical Polity*, Bk. I, ch. I, 70. Milton declared that "a certain immutable and internal necessity of acting rightly, independent of all extraneous influence whatever, may exist in God conjointly with the most perfect liberty. . . ." *The Prose Works of John Milton*, 5 v. (1853), IV, *A Treatise on Christian Doctrine*, 35. Both, of course, later qualify themselves by stating that God, who is always good, freely created the laws under which He operates. Hugo Grotius, in *The Rights of War and Peace* (New York, 1901), 28, said much the same thing: "For since the law of nature is perpetual and unchanging, nothing contradictory to it could be commanded by God, who is never unjust."

105. W. C. E. Newbolt, "The Meaning and Value of Suffering," *C.W.P.*, 26 April 1916.

106. Studdert-Kennedy, *Rough Talks by a Padre*, 58.

107. At least this was the motto used by the *Church Times*, 4 Sept. 1914, to summarize his philosophy.

108. Bernhardi, *Germany and the Next War*, 29.

109. A. O. Lovejoy, *The Great Chain of Being* (New York, 1965), 60.

110. Charles Kingsley, *Village Sermons and Town and Country Sermons* (1879), 215.

111. Hooker, *Ecclesiastical Polity*, Bk. I, ch. III, 73.

112. J. W. Diggle, "The Harvest of War," *C.F.N.*, 16 Oct. 1914.

113. F.W. Orde-Ward, ibid., 22 Jan. 1915. The noted American preacher Joseph Fort Newton, who later became an Anglican, phrased it differently: "if our religion is right, if God is a reality, and the order of the world is moral, our enemies are wrong! The very stars in their courses are against them." Quoted in Ray H. Abrams, *Preachers Present Arms!* (New York, 1933), 57.

114. J. P. Maude, "The Dawn of a New Era," *C.W.P.*, 10 Feb. 1915.

115. G. A. Studdert-Kennedy, *Lies!* (n.d.), 111.

116. Rawnsley, "Rheims Cathedral," *The European War*, 78.

117. Diggle, "Inner Meaning of the War," 735.

IV. FROM THE JUST WAR TO THE APOCALYPTIC CRUSADE

1. Rawnsley, *Against a Premature and Inconclusive Peace*, 6.

2. Lactantius, *Divine Institutes*, vi, 20. Cf. W. P. Patterson "War," *Encyclopedia of Religion and Ethics*, XIII (New York, 1913); James Moffatt, "War," *Dictionary of the Apostolic Church*, II (Edinburgh, 1918). For the best general account of pacifism in the early church, written by a pacifist himself, see C. J. Cadoux, *The Early Christian Attitude to War* (1919).

3. *Theodosian Code* (Princeton, 1952), 16:10:20.

4. Excerpts from the major pacifist and bellicist statements have been collected in Albert Marrin, ed., *War and the Christian Conscience, Augustine to Martin Luther King, Jr.* (Chicago, 1971).

5. Charles Kingsley, *True Words for Brave Men* (New York, 1886); Frederick Denison Maurice, "War," lecture xi of *Social Morality: Twenty-One Lectures Delivered in the University of Cambridge* (1869); Brooke Foss Westcott, "Our Attitude Towards War," in *Lessons from Work* (1901); J. M. Wilson, *The Shepherd and the Wolf: Christ's Sanction of Defensive Warfare* (1914) and *Christ's Teaching on War and Warfare: A Sermon* (Birmingham, 1917); James Martineau, "Right of War," in *National Duties and Other Sermons and Addresses* (1903); P. T. Forsyth, *The Christian Ethic of War* (1916).

6. *Ch. Cong. Rpt.* (1900), 184.

7. J. B. Mozley, "War," in *University Sermons* (New York, 1876), 104–105.

8. Quoted in Roland H. Bainton, *Christian Attitudes Toward War and Peace* (New York, 1960), 242.

9. C. E. Osborne, *Religion in Europe and the World Crisis* (1916), 198.

10. The literature devoted to rehabilitating Russia is immense, and the following are intended only to be suggestive. Percy Dearmer, "Our Great Ally," *CWTH* (March, 1915); "The Soul of Russia," *Nineteenth Century* (Jan., 1915); "The Issues of the War," *C.Q.R.* (Oct., 1915); Herbert Bury (bishop of Northern and Central Europe), "Russia's Three Leads," *Contemporary Review* (Jan., 1915).

11. Africa, No. I, 1904: Cd. 1933. Cf. E. D. Morel, *Red Rubber* (Liverpool, 1905).

12. *Lords' Debates*, CLXXIX (1907), 417.

13. *Daily Chronicle*, 30 July 1907. This and many other newspaper clippings are preserved in the Davidson papers at Lambeth.

14. Cf. Ruth Slade, "English Missionaries and the Beginning of the Anti-Congolese Campaign in England, " *Revue belge de philologie et de l'histoire*, XXXIII (1955); Neal Ascherson, *The King Incorporated: Leopold II in the Age of Trusts* (New York, 1964).

15. Elie Halévy, *History of the English People in the Nineteenth Century*, VI, *The Rule of Democracy* (1953), 42.

16. J. E. C. Welldon, "The Training of the English Gentleman in the Public Schools," *Nineteenth Century* (Sept., 1906), 406. Until his death almost thirty years later, Welldon issued a stream of books and articles expounding upon the connection between the public schools, the ruling classes, the church, and Christian ethics. Cf. *Recollections and Reflections* and *Forty Years On (A Bishop's Reflections on Life)* (1935), passim.

17. The model for Tom Brown, the Rev. Bulkeley Owen Jones, became chancellor of St. Asaph Cathedral, dying in January, 1914, at the age of ninety. The Rev. Augustus Orlebar inspired the character of Slogger Williams. *C.F.N.*, 30 Jan. 1914.

18. Studdert-Kennedy, *Rough Talks by a Padre*, 28.

19. *G.*, 14 Oct. 1915.

20. Gwendolen Stephenson, *Edward Stuart Talbot* (1936), 252; Bell, 786–787.

21. E. H. Holmes, *The Message of the Soldiers* (1917), 14; *C.T.*, 28 April 1916.

22. J. A. Palmer, *C.F.N.*, 22 Oct. 1915.

23. *Punch*, 21 Oct. 1914.

24. Herbert Hensley Henson, *War-Time Sermons* (1915).

25. Hewlett Johnson, "Our Prayers in War," *Interpreter* (Oct., 1914), 3.

26. E. Scott Moncrieff, "Are We Worthy to Win?" *S.F.T.* (1914), 9–10; cf. Walter Felce, "Germany's Attack on Christ," a sermon preached on 4 Oct. 1914, in *War and Freedom* (1914).

27. Edward Lyttelton, *What Are We Fighting For?* (1914).

28. George Bernard Shaw took the latter position in *Common Sense about the War* (1914), Gilbert Murray the former in *How Can War Ever Be Right?* (Oxford, 1914).

29. A Maude Royden, *The Great Adventure, The Way to Peace* (1915), 7.

30. Edmund Burke, *Letters On A Regicide Peace, Works* (Boston, 1866), V, 318.

31. Gilbert Murray described this commonality as a cosmos, and believed that Europe after 1914 had gone from cosmos to chaos. *The Ordeal of this Generation* (1929), ch. VI. For an Anglican opinion on this subject, differing from Murray's only in the greater emphasis placed on religious sanctions, see Henson, *War-Time Sermons*, 203–204.

32. Welldon, "Training of an English Gentleman in the Public Schools," 402, 404.

33. F. Y. Leggatt, "The War Cry," *S.F.T.*, # 18, 18.

34. Goshen to Grey, 8 August 1914, *Why We Are At War* (Oxford, 1914), 200.

35. *G.*, 12 Dec. 1918.

36. Studdert-Kennedy, *Rough Talks by a Padre*, 136.

37. Paul Bertie Bull, *Our Duty in Time of War* (1914), 5.

38. Ibid., 15.

39. Henson, *War-Time Sermons*, 48–49.

40. Cf. H. L. Goudge, *The British Israel Theory* (1922).

41. Lancaster, n. 137.

42. *R.*, 7 Aug. 1914. The next day, the French newspaper *La Croix* said essentially the same thing: "*L'histoire de France est l'histoire de Dieu. Vive le Christ que ami les Francs!*"

43. Winnington-Ingram, *Rays of Dawn*, 23; *The Church in Time of War*, 7.

44. S. C. Carpenter, "Tempore Belli," *Interpreter* (Jan., 1914), 14–15.

45. Gilbert Murray, "First Thoughts on the War (August, 1914)," in *Faith, War, and Policy* (New York, 1917), 7.

46. Henson, *War-Time Sermons*, 69.

47. *The Optimist*, 15 July 1916, 59.

48. Studdert-Kennedy, *Rough Talks by a Padre*, 130–131.

49. E. F. Benson, *Mother* (New York, 1925), 219.

50. Quoted in E. A. Payne, *The Baptist Union, A Short History* (1958), 180.

51. *C.T.*, 27 Nov. 1914; *C.F.N.*, 12 Feb. 1915.

52. Geoffrey Gorer, *Exploring English Character* (1955), 263–266. Gorer also notes that during the Second World War, one out of every three servicemen carried some form of protective magic.

53. Inge, *Lay Thoughts of a Dean*, 304; C. S. Peel, *How We Lived Then* (1929), 71.

54. W. T. Hollins, "A Vision of Angels," *R.*, 2 Sept. 1915. The whole uproar was probably traceable ultimately to Arthur Machen's *The Angels of Mons* (1915), a fictionalized representation intended as a fund raising device.

55. H. C. Beeching, *Armageddon* (1914), 14.

56. *C.F.N.*, 1 April 1915.

57. Davidson to Asquith, 13 May 1915, Davidson MSS.

58. *CH*, 21 May 1915; *G.*, 27 May 1915.

59. The love he was able to elicit from the people was proverbial. Asked Bishop Maud (whom he called "Jack Kensington") on his deathbed: "It must be terrible to be loved as you are loved." S. C. Carpenter, *Winnington-Ingram* (1949), 333–335.

60. *G.*, 10 June, 24 June, 1 July 1915; *C.T.*, 1 Oct. 1915.

61. The bishops of Liverpool, Sodor and Man, Buckingham, Pretoria, and Carlisle are all good candidates, all having proclaimed the Holy War at about the same time. *R.*, 10 June 1915; *CH*, 21 May 1915; *G.*, 1 July 1915; *Carlisle Diocesan Magazine* (July, 1915), 100.

62. F. H. Keeling wrote shortly before his death to Canon William Danks of Canterbury: "Few Englishmen out here hate their enemies—I feel as sorry for the Germans as for our own men in the bombardments. . . . The 'Holy War' is Christian cant of the worst kind. It is all rot to suppose we are white and the Germans black." *Keeling Letters and Recollections* (New York, 1918), 260.

63. Basil Bourchier, *"For All We Have and Are"* (1915), 2–3. The title of this book was taken from a poem by Kipling, published when the war began.

64. *C.T.*, 30 July 1915.

65. "The Bishop's Address on the War," *Carlisle Diocesan Magazine* (July, 1915), 100, 105.

66. *R.*, 13 May 1915; Bull, *Peace and War*, 50.

67. *Oxford Diocesan Magazine*, quoted in *CH*, 9 July 1915; *G.*, 17 June 1915; W. Lockton [Walter Lock?], "A Holy War," *CWTH* (April, 1916).

68. "A Holy War," *G.*, 1 July 1915; cf. *R.*, 10 June 1915.

V. THE CHRISTIAN AND THE SWORD

1. On the pacifism of the historic peace churches see: Franklin H. Littel, *The Origins of Sectarian Protestantism* (New York, 1964); Harold S. Bender, "The Pacifism of the Sixteenth Century Anabaptists," *Mennonite Quarterly Review* (Jan., 1956); G. H. Williams, *The Radical Reformation* (Philadelphia, 1962).

2. R. Tudur Jones, *Congregationalism in England, 1662–1962* (1962), 359–360.

3. See Vera Brittain, *The Rebel Passion* (Nyack, New York, 1964).

4. A. Maude Royden, *The Great Adventure: The Way to Peace* (1915); cf. Joan M. Fry, ed., *Christ and Peace* (1915). Dr. Royden was no "Sermon on the Mount pacifist," abandoning pacifism in the face of Nazi aggression and advising those who could not help England in the struggle to please keep quiet and not hinder her with words. *Christian Century*, 16 April 1941.

5. *British Weekly*, 2 Nov. 1916.

6. *A Challenge to Militarism* (1918); Mrs. Henry Hobhouse, *I Appeal Unto Caesar* (1917), 16–17.

7. E. W. Barnes, "The Treatment of the C.O.," *CH.*, 7 Sept. 1917; "Reprisals," ibid., 28 July 1918.

8. Hewlett Johnson, "Our Prayers in War," *Interpreter* (Oct., 1914); *Searching for Light: An Autobiography* (1968), 57.

9. R. Ellis, *H. R. L. Sheppard* (1942); H. R. L. Sheppard, *We Say 'No': A Plain Man's Guide to Pacifism* (1935) 1. C. E. Raven, *War and the Christian* (1938), 160; Brittain, *Rebel Passion*, 90.

10. There is little available on this subject. A. P. Thornton's *The Habit of Authority* (1966) is of uneven value.

11. According to *A Challenge to Militarism*, 20 percent of the conscientious objectors in prison were clerks, 10 percent in the building trades, 7.25 percent merchants, and 21.25 percent tailors, chemists, and carmen; only 5.75 percent were professional men.

12. Prestige, *Gore*, 389; R. J. Campbell, *The War and the Soul* (1916), 18.

13. J. N. Figgis, "The Sword and the Cross," *CH*, 18 Sept. 1914.

14. Studdert-Kennedy, *Rough Talks by a Padre*, 61.

15. Hooker, *Ecclesiastical Polity*, Bk. II, ch. I.

16. Bull, *Peace and War*, 21.

17. Ibid., 19.

18. *London Diocesan Magazine* (Feb., 1914), 34.

19. David Newsome touches on this question in his important work, *Godliness and Good Learning* (1961).

20. Bishop Moule, "The Soldier and His Lord," *R.*, 22 Feb. 1917; "In Touch with the Unseen," ibid., 9 Sept. 1915; *London Diocesan Magazine* (Feb., 1916), 35; *C.F.N.*, 29 Dec. 1899. Even Dick Sheppard addressed boys as members of "the great army of the Church, the army of Jesus Christ, our Master." *Ch. Cong. Rpt.* (1913), 287, 288.

21. Quoted by R. L. Outhwaite, *Commons' Debates*, LXXVIII (1916), 703.

22. See J. E. C. Welldon, *The Consecration of the State* (1902) and Herbert Hensley Henson, "Good Citizenship," *S.F.T.* (1914).

23. *C.T.*, 16 April 1915.

24. William Lowndes, *The God that Answereth by Fire* (1917), 28.

25. St. Ambrose, *Duties of the Clergy*, in *The Nicene and Post-Nicene Christian Library*, I, 27, 129.

26. Letter to Ernest Howard Crosby in *Tolstoy on Civil Disobedience and Non-Violence* (New York, 1967), 186–187.

27. M. G. Glazebrook, "Christian Nations and War," *C.F.N.*, 4 Sept. 1914.

28. St. Augustine, *Epistles*, 189; Frederick Maurice, *The Life and Letters of Frederick Denison Maurice* 2 v. (1884), II, 418.

29. Herbert Hensley Henson, "The Paradox of Christianity," *CH*, 12 Feb. 1915.

30. Duty, said Hensley Henson, is for the Anglican "the stern daughter of the voice of God." *C.W.P.*, 13 Jan. 1915. On the whole question of the obligations of the citizen to the state see, Henson, "Good Citizenship," *C.W.P.*, 23 April 1902, also Hastings Rashdall, "The Ethics of Conscientious Objection," *M.C.* (May, 1916).

31. W. C. E. Newbolt, "God's Register," *C.T.*, 20 Aug. 1915; Goudge, "Christianity and War," 39.

32. Cf. *Homily against Disobedience and Wilful Rebellion* (1571).

33. Temple to Davidson, 28 Feb. 1915, Davidson MSS.

34. F. A. Iremonger, *William Temple, Archbishop of Canterbury* (1950), 544–545. In a *York Diocesan Leaflet* of 1935, Temple branded pacifism as a recrudescence of three ancient heresies: Manichaeism, because the pacifist "makes a sharp contrast between spiritual and material forces, and holds that the material cannot be completely subordinated to the spiritual"; Marcionism, because he maintains a "view of the New Testament as so superseding the Old Testament as to abolish it"; and Pelagianism because he believes in "man's capacity apart from conversion and sanctification to obey the Counsels of Perfection . . . a view which regards man as capable by the action of his own will of living by love only."

35. J. W. Graham, *Conscription and Conscience* (1922); Stephen Hobhouse, *Autobiography* (Boston, 1952), passim.

36. Graham, 351; Hobhouse, 171.

37. *G.*, 27 March 1918.

38. Graham, *Conscription and Conscience*, 268, 271; Hobhouse, *Autobiography*, 164.

39. "Anarchic Dartmoor," *R.*, 11 Oct. 1917; *G.*, 11 Oct. 1917.

40. Gore, *Lords' Debates*, XXI (1916), 907; Hobhouse, *Autobiography*, 157; A. J. K. Martyn, *CH* 20 Aug. 1915.

41. *CWTH* (Aug., 1916), 229.

42. *CH*, 16 May 1915, 26 Oct. 1916, 9 Nov. 1917, 23 Nov. 1917.

43. *CWTH* (May, 1916), 132.

44. Gore, *Lords' Debates*, XXI (1916), 908; XXVI (1917), 1001.

45. 623 were court-martialled twice, 491 three times, 202 four times, and 18 five times. *CH*, 9 Aug. 1918.

46. Boothby to Davidson, 26 May 1917; Salter to Davidson, 27 Nov. 1916. Davidson MSS.

47. Davidson to Lord Hugh Cecil, 1 Dec. 1916, ibid.

48. Holmes, *Colours of the King*, 33; S. A. Alexander, "Peace and War," *G.*, 11 Feb. 1915.

49. Immanuel Kant, *Perpetual Peace* (New York, 1948), 6.

50. Robert Fulton, *Torpedo War and Submarine Explosives* (New York, 1801), 6.

51. Quoted in W. R. Inge, *The Fall of the Idols* (1940), 187.

52. Cf. Lewis Coser, *The Functions of Social Conflict* (Glencoe, 1964), 124.

53. *Lords' Debates*, XXV (1917), 633–634.

54. "Memorandum on the Military Use of Poisonous Gases (n.d.) Davidson MSS.

55. Royden, *Great Adventure*, 10.

56. *CWTH* (April, 1915), 104.

57. *C.F.N.*, 1 April 1915.

58. H. M. Gwatkin, *Britain's Case Against Germany* (1917), 10.

59. *C.T.*, 3 Dec. 1915, 12 May 1916.

60. *G.*, 18 July 1918.

61. B. H. Liddell Hart, *The Remaking of Modern Armies* (1927), 83.

62. *CH*, 21 May 1915, 6 June 1915.

63. *John Bull*, 10 July 1915.

64. Bell, 759.

65. A. Sheppard to Guy Vernon Smith, 22 Oct. 1915, Davidson MSS.

66. Davidson to Maurice Bonham Carter, 19 May, 1915, ibid.

67. Talbot, *Lords' Debates*, XXIV (1917), 1030; *G.* 20 May 1915; *R.*, 20 May 1915.

68. 162 were killed and 432 injured in the raid of June 13; a total of 1,570 civilians were killed and 5,611 injured by enemy action. Marwick, *Deluge*, 197–198.

69. *Globe*, 20 Oct. 1915, 266 June 1917; *Daily Express*, 27 June 1916, 6 July 1917; *Clarion*, 22 June 1917; *Times*, 5, Oct. 1915; *R.*, 10 Feb. 1916.

70. Pemberton Billing, "Six Bombs for One," *John Bull*, 23 June 1917.

71. Sir Arthur Conan Doyle, "The Uses of Hatred," *Times*, 26 Dec. 1917.

72. Bell, 777.

73. *CH*, 22 June 1917.

74. Herbert Nalder to Davidson, 17 June 1917, 23 June 1917, Davidson MSS.

75. J. J. Compton to Davidson, 18 Feb. 1916, ibid.

76. H. D. A. Major, "Sentimentalists and Casuists," *M.C.* (Aug., 1917), 212, 213.

77. *C.T.*, 15 Dec. 1916.

78. "A Proposal," ibid., 24 April 1917.

79. Ibid., 2 Aug. 1918.

80. Ibid., 25 Oct. 1918.

81. *C.Q.R.* (Oct., 1918), 144.

82. Bainton, *Christian Attitudes Toward War and Peace*, 207. I have quoted more of this sermon than Bainton. The complete text is in *C.W.P.*, 8 Dec. 1915.

83. Winnington-Ingram, *Under the Dome* (1902), 246; *The Church in Time of War*, 33.

VI. THE CHURCH IN THE WAR

1. Elie Halévy, *The Era of Tyrannies* (New York, 1965), 266.
2. *CH*, 21 July 1916; *The Official Year-Book of the Church of England* (1916), 190; (1917), 169; S.P.C.K., *Annual Report* (1917), 21.
3. W. T. Elliott, "Pouring in Oil and Wine," *S.F.T. # 11* (1914), 22.
4. Roger Lloyd, *The Church of England, 1900–1965* (1966), 222.
5. Bell, 764; Lloyd, *Church of England*, 222.
6. *Summa Theologica*, II, q. 40, art. 2.
7. Derby to Davidson, 16 Nov. 1915; Davidson to Derby, 18 Nov. 1915, Davidson MSS.
8. *C.T.*, 1 Jan. 1915.
9. Harford, *Moule*, 237.
10. *Durham Chronicle and County Gazette*, 14 Aug., 18 Sept., 25 Sept. 1914.
11. *C.F.N.*, 8 Jan. 1915.
12. Stewart Headlam, *Some Old Words about the War* (1915), 6.
13. Winnington-Ingram, *Fifty Years*, 119; "A Call to Arms," in *The Church in Time of War*; Carpenter, *Winnington-Ingram*, 282.
14. *C.F.N.*, 16 April 1915.
15. W. C. E. Newbolt, "The Right," *C.T.*, 13 Aug. 1915.
16. Canon Holmes, quoted in G. Bedborough, ed., *Arms and the Clergy* (1934), 21.
17. A. W. Gough, *Repentance and Strength* (1916), 72.
18. *G.*, 15 April 1915.
19. C. H. W. Johns, "Who is on the Lord's Side?" *S.F.T. #9* (1914), 14.
20. *CH*, 13 Nov. 1914.
21. Leggatt, "The War Cry," 16.
22. *The Encore*, 22 Oct., 26 Nov. 1914; 21 Jan. 1915.
23. *Ch. Cong. Rpt.* (1913).
24. Johns, "Who is on the Lord's Side?" 16.
25. *C.T.*, 29 Jan. 1915, 5 Feb. 1915; *London Diocesan Magazine* (June, 1915), 168.
26. Bull, *Peace and War*, 64.
27. Winnington-Ingram, *The Church in Time of War*, 56; Campbell, *With Our Troops in France*, 36.
28. James Bent, *From Training Camp to Fighting Line* (1915), 33.
29. W. W. Holdsworth, "Impressions of a Field Hospital," *Contemporary Review* (May, 1916), 637–638.
30. C. F. G. Masterman, "*The Temper of the People*," ibid. (July, 1915), 7.
31. T. G. Clarke, *R.*, 6 Jan. 1916.
32. *G.*, 3 Feb. 1916; J. B. Lancelot, *Francis James Chavasse, Bishop of Liverpool* (1928), 199.
33. *Times*, 24 Sept. 1914.
34. *CH*, 5 Nov. 1915, 14 Dec. 1915.
35. Murray, *Faith, War, and Policy*, 232; T. B. Strong to Davidson, 18 Sept. 1914, Davidson MSS.
36. Quoted in E. C. Mack, *Public Schools and British Opinion since 1860* (New York, 1941), 130.
37. *Official Year-Book of the Church of England* (1916), 7.
38. R. W. F. Singers-Davies, *Times*, 22 Feb. 1915. The German figures were as depressing, Professor Diessmann reporting that out of the 511 men enrolled in the Department of Theology at the University of Berlin, 60 percent were serving in the trenches. *C.F.N.*, 1 Oct. 1915.
39. *Facts and Figures*, 38.

40. J. R. H. Moorman, *B. K. Cunningham* (1947), 69.
41. *Chron. Conv. Cant.* (1915), 478.
42. *G.*, 20 Aug. 1914.
43. *Chron. Conv. Cant.* (1915), 475.
44. *C.T.*, 11 Sept. 1914.
45. Ibid., 4 June, 1915.
46. *M.C.* (May, 1916), 47; *G.*, 4 May 1916, 18 June 1916.
47. *M.C.* (May, 1916), 47.
48. Circular Letter, 2 Sept. 1914, Davidson MSS.
49. Davidson to bishop of Salisbury, c. Sept., 1914, ibid.
50. *Commons' Debates*, LXXVI (1915), 490.
51. Ibid., LXXVIII (1916), 393.
52. Ibid., 698.
53. Ibid., 696.
54. *G.*, 14 Sept. 1916.
55. Davidson to Chaplain-General, ibid., 27 Sept. 1917.
56. E. A. Lea, *C.T.*, 17 Dec. 1917.
57. H. T. Walters, *G.*, 11 Jan. 1917.
58. Iremonger, *Temple*, 193.
59. *C.W.P.*, 27 Sept. 1916.
60. *R.*, 28 Sept. 1916.
61. *C.T.*, 21 Dec. 1915.
62. *Lords' Debates*, XXIX (1918), 725–730.
63. *Times*, 24 April 1918. Cf. "The Clergy on a War Footing," *C.T.*, 26 April 1918.
64. Gore to Davidson, 20 May 1918, Davidson MSS; bishop of Birmingham to Davidson, 16 July 1918, ibid.; *London Diocesan Magazine* (June, 1918), 113.
65. *G.*, 27 May 1915; *CH*, 28 May 1915.
66. J. A. Legh, "The Vicar as Shellmaker," *C.F.N.*, 25 June 1915.
67. Christopher Cheshire, "National Service," *CWTH* (June, 1917), 168.
68. "The Parson and the Plow," *CH*, 20 April 1917; "National Service—the Peril of Delay," ibid., 23 March 1917.
69. 10 Jan. 1917, Davidson MSS.
70. *G.*, 18 March 1917.
71. Ibid., 17 May 1917.
72. Wakefield to Davidson, 17 July 1918, Davidson MSS.
73. *M.C.* (June, 1917), 101; P. R. Matheson, *The Life of Hastings Rashdall* (Oxford, 1928), 152, 167.
74. Bell, 823.
75. *G.*, 15 March 1917; *C.F.N.*, 25 Feb. 1916.
76. *G.*, 1 July 1915.
77. *CH*, 9 July 1915.
78. *C.T.*, 23 July 1915; Winnington-Ingram, *The Church in Time of War*, 317.
79. *G.*, 22 Feb. 1917; *C.T.*, 16 Feb. 1917.
80. *G.*, 17 Feb. 1916, 8 Feb. 1917, 2 March 1916.
81. Ibid., 8 July 1915, Feb.-March, 1917, passim.
82. The index of real wages in 1914 was 174, 142 in 1917. S. B. Clough and C. W. Cole, *Economic History of Europe* (Boston, 1952), 712, 720, 721.
83. Gough, *Repentance and Strength*, 51.
84. Studdert-Kennedy, *Rough Talks by a Padre*, 87.
85. William Temple, *Go Forward: Thoughts on the National Crisis* (1915), 8–9, 12–13.
86. Herbert Hensley Henson, "The Church of England after the War," in F. J. Foakes-Jackson, ed., *The Faith and the War* (1915), 248.

87. Cf. Winnington-Ingram, *The Church in Time of War*, 244.

88. *The Army and Religion: An Enquiry and its Bearing upon the Religious Life of the Nation* (1919), 189.

89. *Chron. Conv. Cant.* (1900), 92–101.

90. Winnington-Ingram, "The National Mission of Repentance and Hope," in Basil Bourchier, ed., *What is Wrong? Nine Addresses of the National Mission of Repentance and Hope* (1916), 15. The denominational disposition of the British Army in 1916 was: Church of England, 70 percent; Roman Catholic 14 percent, Presbyterian 7 percent, Wesleyan 4 percent, Baptist and Congregationalist 1.2 percent, other Protestants 0.6 percent. *Official Year-Book of the Church of England* (1916), 93.

91. Stephenson, *Talbot*, 223–225.

92. Ibid., 228.

93. Prestige, *Gore*, 372.

94. *The Army and Religion*, 448.

95. Ibid., 447–449.

96. Donald Hankey, *A Student in Arms* (1917), 108–109. Hankey was borne out in precisely the same terms by two of the keenest clerical observers of religion in the army: Neville Talbot in *Thoughts on Religion at the Front* (1917), and in *As Tommy Sees Us* (1917) by the Presbyterian A. Herbert Gray.

97. Quoted in William Purcell, *Woodbine Willie* (1962), 133–134.

98. Bell, 850.

99. Lockhart, *Halifax*, II, 247–248.

100. Bell, 761.

101. *G.*, 13 June 1918.

102. J. E. Adams, *The Chaplain and the War* (1915), 31.

103. C. E. Playne, *Society at War* (Boston, 1931), 210.

104. *G. A. Studdert-Kennedy, by His Friends* (New York, 1929), 129.

105. C. E. Montague, *Disenchantment* (1922), 70.

106. G. A. Studdert-Kennedy, *The Sorrows of God and other Poems* (New York, 1924), 52.

107. See H. E. Oliver, ed., *"When the Men Come Home": Some Objectives of the National Mission* (1916).

108. Bell, 768–769.

109. Iremonger, *Temple*, 214.

110. Bishop Ridgeway of Salisbury, address of diocesan synod, *C.T.*, 16 April 1915; Iremonger, *Temple*, 206.

111. *Facts and Figures, #3* (1966), 54–55; *Official Year-Book of the Church of England* (1916), 428; (1919), 412; (1968), 176.

112. Carpenter, *War and the Soul*, 22; Dudden, *Problem of Suffering*, 124; Holmes, *Message*, 53.

113. Basil Wilberforce, *The Battle of the Lord* (1915), 165.

114. Dudden, *Problem of Suffering*, 20–22; archbishop of Armagh, "To the Nation's Manhood and Chivalry," *C.W.P.*, 16 Sept. 1914.

115. J. R. Diggle, "The Ethics of War," *Hibbert Journal* (Oct., 1914), 27.

116. Bull, *Peace and War*, 55–56.

117. Bourchier, *For All We Have and Are*, 48–49.

118. Plowden-Wardlaw, *The Test of War*, 118; Smith, *The Bishop of London's Visit to the Front*, 77; Dudden, *Heroic Dead*, 2–12; *C.T.*, 28 May 1915.

119. Lord William Gascoyne Cecil, "The Ministry of Sorrow," *C.W.P.*, 21 April 1915.

120. Basil Wilberforce, *Why Does not God Stop the War?* (1919), 15–16.

121. *CH*, 7 Jan. 1916.

122. Winnington-Ingram, *Rays of Dawn*, 12.

123. *C.F.N.*, 23 Oct. 1914.

124. J. Duncan, ibid., 27 Nov. 1914.
125. Ibid., 26 Feb. 1915.

VII. FOR A JUST AND LASTING PEACE

1. Temple, *Christianity and War*, 16.
2. Augustine, *Quaestionum in Heptateuchum Libri VII*, vi, 10; Epistles, CLXXXIX, 6.
3. F. T. Woods, "The Church's Part in the Preparation for the New Age," H. H. Henson, ed., *The Church of England* (1919), 218, 220; J. W. Diggle, Pastoral Letter, *Carlisle Diocesan Magazine* (Jan., 1918), 5.
4. Hicks, *The Church and the War*, 15–17.
5. *Bristol Times and Mirror*, 4 Sept. 1915.
6. A. E. M., "To England," *R.*, 4 Sept. 1914, italics added.
7. Bull, *Peace and War*, 123.
8. See Herbert Butterfield's *Christianity, Deplomacy and War* (1953) for a penetrating discussion of the consequences of war for otherworldly ends.
9. J. W. Diggle, "Is it Peace, Jehu? Some Perils of Peace," *Nineteenth Century* (Feb., 1917), 222.
10. *C.T.*, 30 June 1916.
11. S. A. Alexander, "The Religion of Valour," *G.*, 2 March 1916.
12. *C.T.*, 16 Oct. 1914.
13. T. T. Norgate, "Three Months and their Meaning," *CH*, 13 Nov. 1914.
14. *Goodwill*, 29 March 1915, 65, 66.
15. Davidson to A. J. Mason, 10 Oct. 1914; to Söderblom, 9 Oct. 1914, Davidson MSS.
16. Davidson to C. C. Cotterill, 16 March 1915, ibid.
17. W. R. Inge, *More Lay Thoughts of a Dean* (1931), 223. For the Roman Catholic interpretation see Anthony Benson, C.S.F.C., *Pope Benedict XV and the War* (1915) and Denis Gwynn, *The Vatican and War in Europe* (1941).
18. Inge, "Hope, Temporal and Eternal," 115–116.
19. Osborne, *Religion in Europe*, 163.
20. Quoted in E. J. Dillon, "The Pope and the Belligerents," *Contemporary Review* (May, 1915), 163.
21. The long introduction to E. R. Norman's *Anti-Catholicism in Victorian England* (1968) and Geoffrey Best's article on popular Protestantism in R. Robson, ed., *Ideas and Institutions in Victorian England* (1967) are valuable introductions to this subject.
22. *R.*, 18 Nov. 1915.
23. There is a vast literature dealing with prophecy, the war, and the pope, most of it unreadable. The following are perhaps the best introduction to the subject: Augusta Cook, *The Present War in the Light of Divine Prophecy* (1914); E. P. Cachemaille, *The Prophetic Outlook To-Day* (1917). The Protestant Truth Society, of which J. A. Kensit was head, published its anti-Catholic works, among them *Rome Behind the Great War* (1919) and *What I Saw in Ireland* (1919). During the Second World War he maintained that Pius XII favored the Nazis.
24. Murray, *Bible Prophecies*, 275.
25. Catholic Association for International Peace, *Appeals for Peace of Pope Benedict XV and Pope Pius XII* (Washington, n.d.), 3–6.
26. The Stockholm Conference, summoned in May by a group of Dutch and Scandinavian socialists seconded by their brethren in the Petrograd Soviet, aimed at determining the articles of a democratic peace which the various workers' organizations would later urge their governments to accept. Denounced as a German

hoax even by Christian Socialists, it ended a dismal failure when the Allied governments refused passports to the would-be delegates.

27. "The Vatican and the Germanic Powers," *Contemporary Review* (Oct., 1917), 411.

28. *C.Q.R.* (Oct. 1917), 138, 140; *G.*, 16 Aug. 1916.

29. *Daily Mail*, 13 Dec. 1916.

30. *CWTH* (Jan., 1917), 7.

31. *C.F.N.*, 15 Dec. 1916.

32. A. H. T. Clarke, *R.*, 7 Aug. 1914.

33. William T. Manning, *Our Present Duty as Americans and Christians* (New York, 1917); *Great Britain's Part in the World War* (1917). For a general, if biased, view of the American churches see Ray H. Abrams, *Preachers Present Arms*.

34. Winnington-Ingram, *Rays of Dawn*, 193.

35. Albert Bushnell Hart, ed., *Selected Addresses and Public Papers of Woodrow Wilson* (New York, 1918), 167–170.

36. Burton J. Hendrick, *The Life and Letters of Walter H. Page*, 2 v. (1924), II, 205–207.

37. Sir C. E. Callwell, *Field Marshal Sir Henry Wilson, His Life and Diaries* (New York, 1927), I, 306.

38. *R.*, 28 Dec. 1916.

39. G. Lowes Dickinson, *The Choice Before Us* (1917), 264.

40. Hart, *Addresses and Public Papers of Woodrow Wilson*, 175.

41. Hendrick, *Page*, II, 213.

42. *CH*, 7 Dec. 1917.

43. *Daily Telegraph*, 29 Nov. 1917.

44. *CH*, 7 Dec. 1917; *CWTH* (Jan., 1918), 5.

45. *CH*, 1 Feb. 1917.

46. *G.*, 29 Aug. 1918.

47. *C.T.*, 7 Dec. 1917; *G.*, 6 Dec. 1917.

48. Prestige, *Gore*, 389.

49. Lyttelton to Davidson, 14 Jan. 1915, Davidson MSS.

50. G. F. Browne, bishop of Bristol, "Peace by the Sword," *Times*, 2 Nov. 1918.

51. H. R. Wakefield, *A Fortnight at the Front* (1915), 34.

52. Actually, nothing like the later Nuremberg trials took place. A handful of minor war criminals were tried by German courts, receiving light sentences. Punishing men for acting under orders was a new concept in 1918, and cooler heads realized that the Germans could have faulted the Allies with the same crimes or worse, as they were to do at Nuremberg. The *Challenge* emphasized that the "war criminals" would in effect be tried by the victors, not for their crimes but for being so unfortunate as to be defeated. *CH*, 6 Oct. 1916, 18 Oct. 1918.

53. T. S. Horsfall, ibid., 6 Dec. 1918.

54. Bishop Watts-Ditchfield of Chelmsford, *G.*, 7 Nov. 1918.

55. *C.T.*, 22 Nov. 1918, 29 Nov. 1918.

56. "War and Peace," *C.Q.R.* (July, 1917), 339; "Seeking Peace," *G.*, 10 Jan. 1918.

57. *CH*, 9 April 1915.

58. The literature by clergymen exalting Britain's civilizing mission is very large. Hensley Henson's sermon during the Boer War, "The Peacemakers," *C.W.P.*, 11 June 1902, deserves recognition as a classic in imperialistic oratory. See also: A. C. Headlam, *Universities and the Empire* (1907); John Ellison and G. H. S. Walpole, *Church and Empire* (1907).

59. Quoted in *C.F.N.*, 12 Jan. 1900.

60. A. T. Wirgman, "The Boers and the Native Question," *Nineteenth Century* (April, 1900), 597.

61. G. H. Frodsham, "Is England Worth it All?" *G.*, 10 June 1915; cf. A. H. Cruickshank, "The Time for War," *S.F.T.* #9 (1914), 27.

62. Frank Weston, *The Black Slaves of Prussia* (New York, 1918), 17.

63. Ibid., passim.

64. General Smuts, *CH*, 8 Jan. 1918; "War and Peace," *C.Q.R.* (July, 1917), 341.

65. G. H. Frodsham, "The British Empire after the War," *G.*, 23 May 1918; Weston, *Black Slaves of Prussia*, 19.

66. "A Plea for Austria," *G.*, 7 Sept. 1916; *C.Q.R.* (July, 1917), 339–340.

67. "The Unchanging East," *C.T.*, 18 Oct. 1912; "The Turkish Problem," ibid., 27 April 1917.

68. Ibid., 25 Oct. 1912.

69. W. L. Grane, "The Passing of the Turk," *Peace Year Book* (1913), 31–32.

70. E. P. Cachemaille, *Turkey: Past, Present and Future in Prophecy* (1916); see also the works of Lancaster and Murray, passim.

71. "The Turkish Problem," *C.T.*, 27 April 1917; *C.Q.R.* (July, 1918), 337.

72. "The War, Peace and After," *C.Q.R.* (Jan., 1919), 341.

73. *CH.*, 3 Jan. 1919.

74. Ibid., 11 Jan. 1918.

75. Streeter, *War, this War, and the Sermon on the Mount*, 10.

76. I. F. Clarke's *Voices Prophesying War, 1763–1984* (1966) is a fascinating study of changing styles in the fiction of warfare.

77. E. W. Barnes, "A League of Nations," *CH*, 26 July 1918.

78. Church of England Peace League, *The League of Nations: Addresses by the Lord Bishop of Lincoln, the Lord Bishop of Oxford, and Canon Masterman* (1919), 6.

79. Charles Gore, *The League of Nations: the Opportunity of the Church* (New York, 1918), 18; *CH*, 6 Aug. 1918.

80. *C.Q.R.* (Jan., 1919), 344.

81. W. J. Chamberlain, *CH*, 24 Jan. 1919.

82. Davidson to F. H. Stead, 5 Aug. 1918, Davidson MSS.

83. *CH*, 1 Nov. 1918; bishop of Southwark to G. K. A. Bell, 3 Oct. 1918, Davidson MSS; *C.T.*, 1 March 1918.

84. League of Nations Society, leaflet, *Clergy Auxiliary Committee* (1917); cf. Henry R. Winkler, *The League of Nations Movement in Great Britain, 1914–1919* (New Brunswick, 1952).

85. Gore, *League*, 22.

86. Lang, *Lords' Debates*, XXX (1918), 425–426; *CWTH* (Sept., 1918), 244–245; Bull, *Peace and War*, 123; *C.Q.R.* (Jan., 1919), 342.

VIII. CONCLUSION

1. D. W. Harding, *The Impulse to Dominate* (1941), 74. I have leaned heavily on this book here and elsewhere in this chapter.

2. Herbert Butterfield, *Christianity and History* (New York, 1950), 135.

3. See P. L. Berger and T. Luckman, *The Social Construction of Reality* (New York, 1967), "Introduction: The Problem of the Sociology of Knowledge."

4. Solomon E. Asch, "Studies of Independence and Conformity: A Minority of One Against a Unanimous Majority," *Psychological Monographs*, LXX (1956).

5. C. E. Osgood and P. Tannenbaum, "The Principle of Congruity and the Principle of Attitude Change," *Psychological Review*, (1955); Leon Festinger, *A Theory of Cognitive Dissonance* (Stanford, 1957); Bruno Bettelheim, "Individual and Mass Behavior in Extreme Situations," *Journal of Abnormal Psychology*, XXXVIII (1943).

6. Quoted in Peter Brock, *Twentieth-Century Pacifism* (New York, 1970), 12.

7. H. H. Asquith, *The War: Its Causes and Its Message* (1914), 7.

8. Henson, *Retrospect*, III, 47.

9. *C.T.*, 4 Oct. 1940.

10. I owe this allusion to Florian Znaniecki's *The Social Role of the Man of Knowledge* (New York, 1968), xv.

11. Reinhold Niebuhr, *The Nature and Destiny of Man*, 2 v. (New York, 1964), II, 82.

12. Reinhold Niebuhr, *Beyond Tragedy: Essays on the Christian Interpretation of History* (New York, 1937), 246.

13. Hans J. Morgenthau, *Politics Among Nations: The Struggle for Power and Peace*, 4th ed. (New York, 1967), 13.

14. George F. Kennan, "Foreign Policy and Christian Conscience," *Atlantic Monthly* (May, 1959).

15. L. E. Elliott-Binns, *Reconstruction: The Church's Part* (1943), 91.

SELECT BIBLIOGRAPHY

BIOGRAPHIES, MEMOIRS, LETTERS

Baker, P. J. N., *The Life of J. Allen Baker*, 1927.
Benson, A. C., *The Upton Letters*, New York, 1906.
Bernhardi, Friedrich von, *Denkwürdigkeiten aus meinem Leben*, Berlin, 1927.
Brabant, F. H., *Neville S. Talbot, 1879–1943: A Memoir*, 1949.
Carpenter, S. C., *Winnington-Ingram*, 1949.
Colson, Percy, *Life of the Bishop of London* [Winnington-Ingram], 1935.
Fowler, J. H., ed., *The Life and Letters of Edward Lee Hicks*, 1922.
Fox, Adam, *Dean Inge*, 1960.
G. A. Studdert-Kennedy, by His Friends, New York, 1929.
Harford, J. B. and Macdonald, F. C., *Handley Carr Glynn Moule, Bishop of Durham*, 1922.
Henson, Herbert Hensley, *Retrospect of an Unimportant Life*, 3 v., 1942.
Hobhouse, Stephen, *Autobiography*, Boston, 1952.
Housman, Laurence, *War Letters of Fallen Englishmen*, 1930.
Iremonger, F. A., *William Temple: His Life and Letters*, Oxford, 1948.
Johnson, Hewlett, *Searching for Light: An Autobiography*, 1968.
Kennie, Annie, *Memories of a Militant*, 1924.
Kingsley, Mrs. Charles, *Charles Kingsley: His Letters and Memories of His Life*, 2 v., 1877.
Knox, E. A., *Reminiscences of an Octogenarian, 1847–1934*, 1934.
Lancelot, J. B., *Francis James Chavasse, Bishop of Liverpool*, 1928.
Lockhart, J. G., *Charles Lindley, Viscount Halifax*, 2 v., 1936.
————, *Recollections and Reflections*, 1915.
Lyttelton, Edward, *Memories and Hopes*, 1925.
Major, H. D. A., *The Life and Letters of William Boyd Carpenter*, 1925.
Matheson, P. E., *The Life of Hastings Rashdall*, Oxford, 1928.
Moorman, J. R. H., *B. K. Cunningham*, 1947.
Newbolt, W. C. E., *Years that are Past*, n.d.
Noel, Conrad, *An Autobiography*, 1945.
Paget, Stephen, ed., *Henry Scott Holland: Memoir and Letters*, 1921.
Prestige, G. L., *The Life of Charles Gore*, 1935.
Purcell, William, *Woodbine Willie (G. A. Studdert-Kennedy)*, 1962.
Raven, C. E., *A Wanderer's Way*, New York, 1929.
Roberts, R. Ellis, *H. R. L. Sheppard*, 1942.
Smith, H. Maynard, *Frank, Bishop of Zanzibar*, 1926.
Smyth, Charles, *Cyril Forster Garbett*, 1959.
Stephenson, Gwendolen, *Edward Stuart Talbot*, 1936.

The place of publication is London unless otherwise indicated.

Temple, William, *The Life of Bishop Percival*, 1921.
Welldon, J. E. C., *Forty Years On*, 1925.
————, *Recollection and Reflections*, 1915.
Wells, H. G., ed., *Keeling Letters and Recollections*, New York, n.d.
Wilcox, J. C., *Contending for the Faith: John Kensit, Reformer and Martyr*, 1902.
Winnington-Ingram, Arthur Foley, *Fifty Years' Work in London, 1889–1939*, 1940.
Woods, C. E., *Archdeacon Wilberforce*, 1917.

SERMONS, SPEECHES, AND PAMPHLETS

A Soldier, *Listen—and Think, A Sermon on the War*, 1914.
Adams, J. E., *The Chaplain and the War*, 1915.
Asquith, H. H., *The War, Its Causes and its Message*, 1914.
Ball, C. R., *The War*, 1914.
Barker, Ernest, *Neitzsche and Treitschke: The Worship of Power in Modern Germany*, Oxford, 1914.
Barry, Frank Russell, *The War and Christian Ethics*, 1914.
————, *Religion and the War*, 1915.
Baylis, H. R., *The War from a Churchman's Point of View*, 1914.
Beeching, H. C., *Armageddon*, 1914.
Bell, C. C., *God's Peace*, 1918.
Bell, G. K. A., *The War and the Kingdom of God*, 1916.
————, *The Church and Humanity*, 1946.
Benedict XV, *His Holiness Benedict XV on the Great War*, 1916.
Bent, James, *From Training Camp to Fighting Line*, 1915.
Boddy, A. A., *The Real Angels of Mons*, 1915.
Bourchier, Basil G., *"For All We Have and Are,"* 1915.
————, ed., *What is Wrong? Nine Addresses for the National Mission of Repentance and Hope*, 1916.
Box, G. H., "Christian Citizenship," *S.F.T., #3*, 1914.
Bull, Paul Bertie, *Christianity and War, An Appeal to Conscientious Objectors*, 1918.
————, *God and Our Soldiers*, 1904.
————, *Our Duty at Home in Time of War*, 1914.
————, *Peace and War*, 1917.
————, *Sermon on the 'League of Nations' Preached at Holy Trinity, Sloane Street, on July 27, 1918*, 1918.
Burroughs, E. A., *A Faith for the Firing Line*, 1915.
————, *The Eternal Goal*, 1915.
————, *Faith and Power*, 1914.
Campbell, R. J., *A Letter to an American Friend*, New York, 1918.
————, *The War and the Soul*, 1916.
————, *With Our Troops in France*, 1916.

Carr, J. A., "The Christian's Citizenship," *S.F.T., #3*, 1914.

Catholic Association for International Peace, *Appeals for Peace of Pope Benedict XV and Pope Pius XII*, Washington, D.C., n.d.

Chadwick, W. Edward, *German Christianity (?) and the Great War*, n.d.

Church of England Peace League, *Addresses on the League of Nations by the Lord Bishop of Lincoln, the Lord Bishop of Oxford, and Canon Masterman*, 1919.

————, *Three Sermons on the Promotion of Permanent Peace*, 1916.

————, *Three Sermons on Things Which Make for Peace*, 1916.

————, *Three Sermons on War*, 1914.

Clifford, John, *The War and the Churches*, 1914.

Clutton-Brock, A., *Are We to Punish Germany, if We Can? Papers for War-Time*, Oxford, 1915.

————, *Bernhardism in England, Papers for War-Time*, Oxford, 1915.

————, *The Cure for War, Papers for War-Time*, Oxford, 1915.

Cook, Vallance, *Our Brave Dead: What Becomes of Them?* 1916.

Crum, J. M., "Christians and Reprisals," *CH*, 18 Feb., 1916.

Cunningham, William, *British Citizens and their Responsibility to God*, 1916.

Davidson, Randall Thomas, *Kikuyu*, 1915.

————, *The Testing of a Nation*, 1919.

————, "War and Christianity," *C.T.*, 9 April, 1915.

Dearmer, Percy, *Patriotism, Papers for War-Time*, Oxford, 1915.

Drawbridge, C. L., *Christianity and War*, n.d.

————, *Popular Attacks on Christianity*, 1913.

Dudden, F. Holmes, *The Delayed Victory and other Sermons*, 1918.

————, *The Future Life*, 1915.

————, *The Heroic Dead and other Sermons*, 1917.

————, *The Problem of Human Suffering and the War*, 1916.

Felce, Walter, *The War of Freedom and the Unity of Christendom*, 1915.

Figgis, John Neville, "The Sword and the Cross," *CH*, 18 Sept. 1914.

Foakes-Jackson, F. J., "A Spiritual Contest," *S.F.T. #4*, 1914.

————, "Chivalry," *S.F.T., #18*, 1915.

————, "The Great War Explained to Soldiers," *S.F.T., # 14*, 1914.

————, "Vengeance is Mine," *S.F.T., #15*, 1914.

Formby, C. W., *Why Did God Allow the War?* 1914.

Garbett, Cyril Forster, *The Challenge of the King*, 1915.

————, *The Christian and the Sword, War-Time Tracts for the Workers, #2*, 1916.

Gore, Charles, *Crisis in Church and Nation*, 1915.

————, *The Basis of Anglican Fellowship*, 1914.

————, *The League of Nations: The Opportunity of the Church*, New York, 1918.

————, *War and Christianity*, 1914.

————, *The War and the Church*, 1914.

Gough, A. W., *God's Strong People*, 1915.
———, *Repentance and Strength*, 1916.
Gwatkin, H. M., *Britain's Case Against Germany*, 1917.
Halifax, Lord, ed., *Some Considerations Affecting Religion Arising out of the War*, 1914.
Headlam, Stuart D., *Some Old Words about the War*, 1915.
Henson, Herbert Hensley, *Christian Liberty and other Sermons*, 1918.
———, "Good Citizenship," *S.F.T.*, #3, 1914.
———, *War-Time Sermons*, 1915.
Hicks, Edward Lee, *The Church and the War*, Oxford, 1914.
Hillis, N. D., *Murders Most Foul*, 1917.
Hogg, A. G. *Christianity and Force*, Oxford, 1914.
Holmes, E. E., *The Colours of the King*, 1914.
———, *The Message of the Soldiers*, 1917.
Horsley, J. W., *Retaliation in Kind*, 1916.
Ivens, C. L., *Six Sermons on the War*, 1914.
———, *Sermons for Empire Day*, n.d.
———, *Through Clouds of Darkness*, 1918.
———, *Victory, Peace, Remembrance*, 1918.
Kingsley, Charles, *True Words for Brave Men*, New York, 1886.
———, *Village Sermons and Town and Country Sermons*, 1879.
Knapp, Charles, *The War and Religious Education (Forewarned, Forearmed)*, 1915.
Lancastrian, *The War and Our Social Problems*, 1914.
Lang, Cosmo Gordon, *The Church and the Clergy at this Time of War*, 1916.
———, *The Inspiration of Victory*, Washington, D.C., 1918.
———, *The Source of Power*, Washington, D.C., 1918.
———, *The Testing of the Nations*, Washington, D.C., 1918.
League of Nations Society, *The Demand of the Church for a League of Nations*, 1918.
Leggatt, F. Y., "The War Cry," *S.F.T.*, #18, 1915.
Lock, Walter, *The Church's Duty in Influencing Belligerents With Regard to a Lasting Peace*, 1918.
Lyttelton, Edward, *Britain's Duty To-Day*, 1915.
———, *What Are We Fighting For?* 1914.
McClure, E., *Germany's War Inspirers*, 1915.
Martineau, James, *National Duties and other Sermons and Addresses*, 1903.
Maud, J. P., *Our Comradeship with the Blessed Dead*, 1915.
Moberly, W. H., *Christian Conduct in War Time*, Oxford, 1914.
Moule, H. C. G., "The Nation and the War," *G.*, 1 July 1915.
———, "The Strong Christian Man," *CH*, 12 Nov., 1915.
Moulton, J. H., *British and German Scholarship*, Oxford, 1915.
Mozley, J. B., *University Sermons*, New York, 1876.

Muir, John, *War and Christian Duty*, Paisley, 1916.

Murray, Gilbert, *How Can War Ever be Right?* Oxford, 1914.

———, *Thoughts on the War*, Oxford, 1915.

Paget, Henry L., *In the Day of Battle*, 1915.

———, *Records of the Raids*, 1918.

Plowden-Wardlaw, James, *The Test of the War*, 1916.

Potter, J. Hasloch, *The Judgment of War*, 1915.

Rashdall, Hastings, "The War and German Theology," *CH*, 17 Sept. 1915.

Rawlinson, A. E. J., "War and Peace: A Sermon to Schoolboys," *CH*, 29 Nov. 1918.

Rawnsley, H. D., *Against a Premature and Inconclusive Peace*, Carlisle, 1917.

———, *The European War: Poems*, 1915.

———, *Three Sermons*, Carlisle, 1915.

Robinson, Armitage, *Holy Ground*, 1914.

Royden, A. Maude, *The Great Adventure: The Way to Peace*, 1915.

———, *The Hour and the Church: An Appeal to the Church of England*, 1918.

Ryle, Herbert E., *The Attitude of the Church towards War*, 1915.

Sanday, Dr. William, *Bishop Gore's Challenge to Criticism*, 1914.

———, *In View of the End*, Oxford, 1916.

———, *The Deeper Causes of the War*, Oxford, 1914.

———, *The Meaning of the War for Germany and Great Britain*, Oxford, 1915.

Shaw, George Bernard, *Commonsense About the War*, 1915.

Sheppard, H. R. L., *We Say 'No': The Plain Man's Guide to Pacifism*, 1935.

Smith, A. L., *The Christian Attitude toward War*, Oxford, 1915.

Streeter, B. H., *War, This War and the Sermon on the Mount*, Oxford, 1915.

Talbot, Edward Stuart, *The War and Conscience*, 1914.

———, *The Visions of Youth*, Oxford, 1915.

Taylor, R. O. P., "Germanism at its Great Assize," *S.F.T.*, #8, 1914.

Temple, William, *Christianity and War*, Oxford, 1914.

———, *Go Forward: Thoughts on the National Crisis*, 1915.

———, *The Holy War*, 1915.

———, *Our Need of a Catholic Church*, Oxford, 1915.

Thomas, J. M. Lloyd, *The Immorality on Non-Resistance*, Birmingham, 1915.

Titterton, C. H., *Armageddon, or the Last War*, 1916.

To the Christian Scholars of Europe and America: A Reply from Oxford to the German 'Address to Evangelical Christians,' Oxford, 1914.

Tuting, W. C., *The War and Our Religion*, 1914.

Tyner, Paul, *Christ or Kaiser? The Great War's Main Issue*, 1915.

Wace, Henry, *The Christian Sanction of War*, 1914.
————, *Religion and the War*, 1918.
————, *The War and the Gospel*, 1917.
Wakefield, H. R., *Life Won Through Death*, 1917.
War-Time Tracts for the Workers, 1916.
Westcott, Brooke Foss, *Lessons from Work*, 1901.
Weston, Frank, *The Black Slaves of Prussia*, New York, 1918.
————, *The Case Against Kikuyu*, 1914.
————, *Ecclesia Anglicana: For What does She Stand?* 1914.
Wilberforce, Basil, *The Battle of the Lord*, 1915.
————, *Why Does Not God Stop the War?* 1919.
Winnington-Ingram, Arthur Foley, *A Message for the Supreme Moment*,
    1916.
————, "Christ or Odin?" *C.T.*, 16 Oct. 1914.
————, *The Church in Time of War*, Milwaukee, n.d.
————, *The Eyes of Flame*, 1914.
————, *Good Friday and Easter Day*, 1915.
————, "The Holy War," *S.F.T., #4*, 1914.
————, *Into the Fighting Line*, 1910.
————, *Life for Ever and Ever*, 1915.
————, *Rays of Dawn*, Milwaukee, 1918.
————, *The Soul of a Nation*, 1915.
————, *Victory and After*, Milwaukee, 1920.
————, *The War and Religion*, Birmingham, 1916.
Woods, H. G., *Christianity and War*, 1916.
Worsey, F. W., *Under the War Cloud: Nine Sermons on the War*, 1915.

PERIODICAL ARTICLES OF SPECIAL IMPORTANCE

Anson, Harold, "The Training of the Clergy," *CH*, 22 March 1918.
Barnes, E. W., "Reprisals," *CH*, 22 June 1917.
————, "The Treatment of the C.O.," *CH*, 7 Sept. 1917.
Barry, F. R., "Tolstoy, Nietzsche and the Cross," *Interpreter* (April,
    1915).
Bury, Herbert, "Is Anything Wrong with German Protestantism," *Nine-
    teenth Century* (Feb., 1916).
Cecil, Lord William Gascoyne, "German Patriotism," *Hibbert Journal*
    (April, 1916).
Coxon, A. P. M., "Patterns of Occupational Recruitment: The Anglican
    Clergy," *Sociology* (Jan., 1967).
Dearmer, Percy, "The Soul of Russia," *Nineteenth Century* (Jan., 1915).
Diggle, J. W., "The Deceitfulness of War," *Contemporary Review* (Oct.,
    1914).
————, "The Ethics of War," *Hibbert Journal* (Oct., 1914).

———, "The Inner Meaning of the War," *Nineteenth Century* (Oct., 1914).
Dorrity, David, "God and the War," *M.C.* (April, 1917).
Foakes-Jackson, F. J., "German Theology and the War," *M.C.* (Oct., 1914).
Hardwick, J. C., "The German Anti-Christ," *M.C.* (Oct., 1914).
Headlam, A. C., "On Episcopal Incomes and Palaces," *CH*, 4 Feb. 1916.
Henson, Herbert Hensley, "Christianity and War," *C.Q.R.* (Oct., 1914).
Kelly, Herbert, "German Idealism," *C.Q.R.* (April, 1916).
———, "Eschatological Interpretations and War," *C.Q.R.* (Jan., 1915).
Major, H. D. A., "An Anglican Pope," *M.C.* (May, 1914).
———, "Clerical Peace-Mongers," *M.C.* (April, 1915).
———, "Reprisals," *M.C.* (July, 1915).
———, "Sentimentalists and Casuists," *M.C.*, (Aug., 1917).
McDowell, R. B., "The Anglican Episcopate," *Theology* (June, 1947).
Masterman, C. F. G., "The Temper of the People," *Contemporary Review* (July, 1915).
Newsholme, Arthur, and Stevenson, T. H. C., "The Decline of Human Fertility in the United Kingdom and other Countries," *Journal of the Royal Statistical Society*, LXIX (1906).
Rashdall, Hastings, "The Ethics of Conscientious Objection," *M.C.* (May, 1916).
Robertson, F. A. de. V., "An Indictment of the Clergy," *CH*, 2 Nov. 1917.
Shadwell, A., "German War Sermons," *Hibbert Journal* (July, 1916).
Talbot, Edward Stuart, "The Clergy and Military Service," *Contemporary Review* (Feb., 1916).
Welldon, J. E. C., "Conscience and the Conscientious Objector," *Nineteenth Century* (May, 1916).
———, "The Training of the English Gentleman in the Public Schools," *Nineteenth Century* (Sept., 1906).

GENERAL WORKS

Abrams, Ray H., *Preachers Present Arms*, New York, 1933.
Angell, Norman, *The Great Illusion*, New York, 1912.
Armytage, W. H. G., *Four Hundred Years of English Education* Cambridge, 1964.
Ascherson, Neal, *The King Incorporated: Leopold II in the Age of Trusts*, New York, 1964.
Ausubel, Herman, *In Hard Times: Reformers among the Late Victorians*, New York, 1960.
Bainton, Roland H., *Christian Attidudes toward War and Peace*, New York, 1960.
Bamford, T. D., *The Rise of the Public Schools*, 1967.

Banks, J. A., *Prosperity and Parenthood*, 1954.

———, and Olive Banks, *Feminism and Family Planning in Victorian England*, Liverpool, 1964.

Beales, A. C. F., *The History of Peace*, 1931.

Bernhardi, General Friedrich von, *Germany and the Next War*, trans. Allen H. Powles, 1914.

Best, G. F. A., *Temporal Pillars: Queen Anne's Bounty, the Ecclesiastical Commissioners and the Church of England*, Cambridge, 1964.

Booth, Charles, *Life and Labour of the People of London*, 3rd ser., *Religious Influences*, 1903.

Brittain, Vera, *The Rebel Passion*, Nyack, N.Y., 1964.

Brock, Peter, *Twentieth Century Pacifism*, New York, 1970.

Brown, C. K. Francis, *A History of the English Clergy, 1800–1900*, 1953.

Bryce, James, *Essays and Addresses in War-Time*, New York, 1918.

———, ed., *Report of the Committee on Alleged German Outrages*, 1915.

Burroughs, E. A., *The Christian Church and War*, 1931.

Butterfield, Herbert, *Christianity and History*, New York, 1950.

Cadoux, C. J., *The Early Christian Attitude to War*, 1919.

Carpenter, J. Estlin, ed., *Ethical and Religious Problems of the War*, 1916.

Chadwick, Owen, *The Victorian Church*, 1966.

Chambers, Frank P., *The War Behind the War: A History of the Political and Civilian Fronts*, 1939.

Church of England, *Church Congress Reports*, 1899–1920.

———, *The Chronicle of the Convocation of Canterbury*, 1914–1918.

———, *The York Journal of Convocation*, 1914–1918.

———, *The Official Year-Book of the Church of England*, 1914–1918.

Churchill, Winston S., *The World Crisis*, New York, 1923.

Clarke, I. F., *Voices Prophesying War, 1763–1984*, 1966.

C.O.P.E.C., *Christianity and War*, 1925.

Coser, Lewis, *The Functions of Social Conflict*, Glencoe, 1964.

Cramb, J. A., *Germany and England*, 1914.

Creighton, Mandell, *The Church and the Nation: Addresses and Charges*, 1901.

Crockford's Clerical Directory, 1914–1919.

Cruttwell, C. R. M. F., *A History of the Great War*, Oxford, 1964.

Dangerfield, George, *The Strange Death of Liberal England*, New York, 1961.

Davidson, Randall Thomas, *Six Lambeth Conferences, 1867–1920*, 1929.

Demeter, Karl, *The German Officer Corps in State and Society*, 1965.

Dickinson, G. Lowes, *The Choice Before Us*, New York, 1917.

———, *Religion: A Criticism and a Forecast*, New York, 1905.

Dolling, Robert, *Six Years in a Portsmouth Slum*, 1897.

Elliott-Binns, L. E., *Religion in the Victorian Era*, 1964.

Ellul, Jacques, *Propaganda*, New York, 1962.

Facts and Figures about the Church of England, 1962.

Figgis, John Neville, *The Will to Freedom: Or, the Gospel of Nietzsche and the Gospel of Christ*, 1917.

——, *Religion and English Society*, 1910.

Foakes-Jackson, F. J., ed., *The Faith and the War*, 1915.

Garbett, Cyril Forster, *In an Age of Revolution*, 1952.

Gore, Charles, ed., *Essays in Aid of the Reform of the Church*, 1898.

Gorer, Geoffrey, *Exploring English Character*, 1955.

Goudge, H. L., *The British Israel Theory*, 1922.

Graham, John W., *Conscription and Conscience*, 1922.

Grane, W. L., *The Passing of War*, 1912.

Gray, A. Herbert, *As Tommy Sees Us*, 1917.

Guttsman, W. J., *The British Political Elite*, 1963.

Halévy, Elie, *The Era of Tyrannies*, trans. R. K. Webb, New York, 1965.

Handley, Hubert, *The Fatal Opulence of Bishops*, 1901.

Hankey, Donald. *A Student in Arms*, New York, 1917.

Harding, D.W., *The Impulse to Dominate*, 1941.

Hart, A. Tindall, *The Country Priest in English History*, 1959.

Hart, B. H. Liddell, *The Remaking of Modern Armies*, 1927.

Haw, George, ed., *Christianity and the Working Classes*, 1906.

Headlam, A. C., *The Training of Candidates for Orders*, 1913.

——, *The Revenues of the Church of England*, 1917.

Henson, Herbert Hensley, ed., *The Church of England: Its Nature and Its Future*, 1919.

——, *Church Problems, A View of Modern Anglicanism*, 1900.

Hobhouse, Mrs. Henry, *I Appeal Unto Caesar*, 1917.

Hügel, Baron Friedrich von, *The German Soul*, 1916.

Inge, W. R., *A Pacifist in Trouble*, 1939.

——, *The Church and the Age*, 1912.

——, *The Church in the World*, 1927.

——, *The End of an Age*, 1948.

——, *The Fall of the Idols*, 1940.

——, *Lay Thoughts of a Dean*, New York, 1926.

——, *More Lay Thoughts of a Dean*, 1931.

——, *Outspoken Essays*, 1920.

——, *Outspoken Essays*, 2nd ser., 1925.

——, *Vale*, 1934.

Inglis, K. S., *Churches and the Working Classes in Victorian England*, 1963.

Jones, Peter d'A., *The Christian Socialist Revival, 1877–1914*, Princeton, 1968.

Kohn, Hans, *The Mind of Germany*, New York, 1965.

Krieger, Leonard, *The German Idea of Freedom*, Boston, 1957.

Lasswell, Harold D., *Propaganda Technique in the Great War*, 1927.

Lovejoy, A. O., *The Great Chain of Being*, New York, 1965.

Mack, E. C., *Public Schools and British Opinion since 1860*, New York, 1941.

Macnutt, F. B., ed., *The Church in the Furnace*, 1918.

Malim, F. B. *Alma Matres*, Cambridge, 1948.

Marsh, P. T., *The Victorian Church in Decline: Archbishop Tait and the Church of England, 1868-1882*, Pittsburgh, 1969.

Martin, David A., *Pacifism: An Historical and Sociological Study*, 1965.

———, *A Sociology of English Religion*, 1967.

Marwick, Arthur, *The Deluge: British Society and the First World War*, Boston, 1965.

———, *Britain in the Century of Total War*, 1968.

Mayor, Stephen, *The Churches and the Labour Movement*, 1967.

Masterman, C. F. G., *The Condition of England*, 1909.

———, *England after War*, 1923.

———, *In Peril of Change*, 1905.

Masterman, J. H. B., ed., *Clerical Incomes: An Inquiry into the Cost of Living among the Parochial Clergy*, 1920.

Mathews, Basil, ed., *Christ and the World at War*, 1917.

Mitchell, David, *Women on the Warpath*, 1966.

Montague, C. E., *Disenchantment*, 1922.

Mozley, J. K., *Some Tendencies in English Theology from the Publication of Lux Mundi to the Present Day*, 1951.

Mudie-Smith, Richard, *The Religious Life of London*, 1909.

Murray, Gilbert, *Faith, War, and Policy*, New York, 1917.

National Council of Peace Societies, *Official Report of the Seventeenth Universal Congress of Peace*, 1909.

Newsome, David, *Godliness and Good Learning: Four Studies on a Victorian Ideal*, 1961.

Norman, E. R., *Anti-Catholicism in Victorian England*, 1968.

Oliver, H. A., ed., *"When the Men Come Home": Some Objectives of the National Mission*, 1916.

Osborne, Charles E., *Religion in Europe and the World Crisis*, 1916.

Paul, Leslie, *The Deployment and Payment of the Clergy*, 1961.

Peace and the Churches. Souvenier Volume of the Visit to England of Representatives of the German Christian Churches, 1908.

Playne, Caroline E., *Britain Holds On, 1917-1918*, 1933.

———, *The Neuroses of the Nations: The Neuroses of Germany and France before the War*, 1925.

———, *The Pre-War Mind in Britain*, 1928.

———, *Society at War, 1914-1916*, Boston, 1931.

Ponsonby, Arthur, *Falsehood in War Time*, 1928.

Rashdall, Hastings, *Conscience and Christ*, 1916.

Raven, Charles E., *Is War Obsolete?* 1934.

Raymond, John, ed., *The Baldwin Age*, 1960.

Read, J. M., *Atrocity Propaganda, 1914-1919*, New Haven, 1941.

Reader, W. J., *Professional Men: The Rise of the Professional Classes in Nineteenth Century England*, 1966.
Reckitt, M. B., *The Church and the World*, 3 v., 1940.
———, *Faith and Society*, 1932.
———, *For Christ and the People*, 1968.
———, *Maurice to Temple*, 1946.
Shotwell, J. T., *War as an Instrument of National Policy*, New York, 1929.
Simmel, Georg, *Conflict*, Glencoe, 1967.
Smith, W. S., *The London Heretics, 1870–1914*, New York, 1968.
Spinks, G. S., ed., *Religion in Britain since 1900*, 1952.
Squires, J. D., *British Propaganda at Home and in the United States from 1914–1917*, Cambridge, Mass., 1935.
Studdert-Kennedy, G. A., *The Hardest Part*, 1918.
———, *Lies!* n.d.
———, *Rough Rhymes of a Padre*, New York, 1918.
———, *Rough Talks of a Padre*, New York, n.d.
———, *The Sorrows of God and other Poems*, New York, 1924.
The Army and Religion: An Enquiry and its Bearing upon the Religious Life of the Nation, 1919.
Thornton, A. P., *The Habit of Authority*, 1966.
Tooke, Joan D., *The Just War in Aquinas and Grotius*, 1965.
Ward, Mrs. Humphrey, *England's Effort*, New York, 1919.
Wells, H. G., *The War that Will End War*, New York, 1914.
Why We are at War, Oxford, 1914.
Wilkinson, Rupert, *The Prefects: British Leadership and the Public School Tradition*, 1964.
Winkler, Henry R., *The League of Nations Movement in Great Britain, 1914–1919*, New Brunswick, N.J., 1952.
Winnington-Ingram, Arthur Foley, *Work in Great Cities*, 1896.
Willis, Irene Cooper, *England's Holy War: A Study of English Liberal Idealism during the Great War*, New York, 1928.
Wright, Quincy, *A Study of War*, Chicago, 1965.
Yule, G. U., "On the Changes in the Marriage and Death-Rates in England and Wales during the Past Half-Century," *Journal of the Royal Statistical Society*, LXIX (1906).

INDEX